A
C *in* Practice
T

Case Conceptualization in Acceptance & Commitment Therapy

PATRICIA A. BACH, PH.D.
DANIEL J. MORAN, PH.D., BCBA

New Harbinger Publications, Inc.

Publisher's Note

This publication is designed to provide accurate and authoritative information in regard to the subject matter covered. It is sold with the understanding that the publisher is not engaged in rendering psychological, financial, legal, or other professional services. If expert assistance or counseling is needed, the services of a competent professional should be sought.

Distributed in Canada by Raincoast Books

Copyright © 2008 by Patricia Bach and Daniel J. Moran
New Harbinger Publications, Inc.
5674 Shattuck Avenue
Oakland, CA 94609
www.newharbinger.com

Cover design by Amy Shoup
Text design by Michele Waters
Acquired by Catharine Sutker
Edited by Jean Blomquist

Library of Congress Cataloging-in-Publication Data

Bach, Patricia A.
 ACT in practice : case conceptualization in acceptance and commitment therapy / Patricia A. Bach and Daniel J. Moran.
   p. ; cm.
 Includes bibliographical references and index.
 ISBN-13: 978-1-57224-478-8 (hardback : alk. paper)
 ISBN-10: 1-57224-478-X (hardback : alk. paper)
 1. Acceptance and commitment therapy. I. Moran, Daniel J. II. Title. III. Title: Acceptance and commitment therapy in practice.
 [DNLM: 1. Cognitive Therapy--methods. 2. Adaptation, Psychological. 3. Mental Disorders--therapy. 4. Patient Participation. 5. Self Concept. 6. Treatment Outcome. WM 425.5.C6 B118a 2008]
 RC489.C62B37 2008
 616.89'1425--dc22
                                    2008002065

10   09   08

10   9   8   7   6   5   4   3   2   1

First printing

To Hannelore Bach—my mother, teacher, cheerleader, friend.
—PAB

"You should dedicate the book to me, and Louden, and Mommy. And Grandma B too, 'cuz she's your ma. Okay?" —Harmony Moran, seven years old (August 20, 2006)
She was right!
—DJM

.

Contents

Dear Reader:

Welcome to New Harbinger Publications. New Harbinger is dedicated to publishing books based on acceptance and commitment therapy (ACT) and its application to specific areas. New Harbinger has a long-standing reputation as a publisher of quality, well-researched books for general and professional audiences.

Case conceptualization in mental health care can be thought of as a process of framing psychological problems with at least two sets of eyes focused on finding durable solutions. It functions like a lighthouse beacon, illuminating what is known about a client, pointing therapists and clients alike in a direction, and suggesting what to do to get there. How such problems are framed makes a huge difference in what happens, or fails to happen, next. When case conceptualization is off the mark, it can have disastrous consequences for the client and weaken your ability to help as a therapist. This is why case conceptualization is so important in therapy. ACT is no different in this regard.

ACT is a newer third generation behavior therapy that has the look and feel of Eastern and more experiential psychotherapies, and is built on a technical account, evidentiary principles, and theory that share a close affinity with the cognitive behavioral tradition. In a way, ACT is all of these and none of them, which is why folks wishing to learn ACT can find it challenging to learn and hard to apply. Inevitably, therapists interested in learning ACT ask: How do I apply ACT to my clients? This book will help you find the answer.

ACT in Practice is a great resource for readers who wish to learn how to conceptualize a wide range of problems from an ACT perspective. Without going into too much detail about the scientific and conceptual underpinnings of ACT, this intensely practical book provides brief and concise explanations of the six core ACT processes that feed many forms of human suffering and then teaches therapists how to link each of them to specific ACT intervention strategies and treatment targets. The choreography of ACT case conceptualization is well illustrated in this book, and as you will see, the dance is fluid, shifting, recursive, process focused, and nonlinear. *ACT in Practice* is a way of thinking that includes knowing what to look for, and when, and for what purpose. This book will help you learn to put this know-how into practical ACT*ion*.

A unique focus of the book is on ways to integrate ACT case conceptualization and individualized treatment. Throughout the book, you will find client-therapist transcripts drawn from the authors' clinical work, along with occasional commentary about the therapist's thinking processes and strategy. You will also find several user-friendly forms and exercises; all with the intent of helping you learn to apply ACT in assessing and treating the people that seek you out because they are suffering. In short, this book offers technical and conceptual knowledge, general tools and strategies, and practical skills that will nurture your ability to adopt an ACT therapeutic stance in your clinical practice.

Putting ACT into practice can appear seductively simple and experientially hard. The authors will walk you through why this is so, but for now, much of it has to do with what the work entails. ACT is an approach that is built on a model of human suffering that is counterintuitive: one where therapists are susceptible to the same forces that create vitality and those that trap and ensnare their clients and lead them to suffer.

ACT also challenges some deeply entrenched, Westernized ideas about health and wellness: that pain is bad and must be gotten rid of, that feeling good is more important than just about anything else in life, and that feeling and thinking well is necessary in order to live well. For these and other reasons, Section III of the book includes opportunities for you to practice recognizing and experiencing how ACT-relevant processes play out in your own life, for good and for ill. You get to practice ACT in practice for yourself. These exercises will help you more fully describe and model an ACT-consistent stance in your clinical work.

Other workbooks and therapist guides in the New Harbinger ACT Book Series are more problem-specific and provide detailed descriptions of specific ACT techniques. They describe how to implement value-guided behavioral activation generally, and for specific types of problems. *ACT in Practice* offers some of that too, and will help you develop a solid framework so that you may avoid misapplying ACT techniques in a rigid and inflexible way. A solid ACT case conceptualization framework is necessary for effective ACT practice. Studies suggest that what you learn in this book will help you be a more effective therapist too.

As part of New Harbinger's commitment to publishing sound, scientific, clinically based research, John Forsyth, Ph.D., Steven C. Hayes, Ph.D., and Georg Eifert, Ph.D., oversee all prospective ACT books for the Acceptance and Commitment Therapy Series. As ACT Series editors, we review all ACT books published by New Harbinger, comment on proposals and offer guidance as needed, and use a gentle hand in making suggestions regarding content, depth, and scope of each book. We strive to ensure that any unsubstantiated claim or claims that are clearly ACT inconsistent are flagged for the authors so they can revise these sections to ensure that the work meets our criteria (see below) and that all of the material presented is true to ACT's roots (not passing off other models and methods as ACT).

Books in the *Acceptance and Commitment Therapy Series*:

- Have an adequate database, appropriate to the strength of the claims being made

- Are theoretically coherent—they will fit with the ACT model and underlying behavioral principles as they have evolved at the time of writing

- Orient the reader toward unresolved empirical issues

- Do not overlap needlessly with existing volumes

- Avoid jargon and unnecessary entanglement with proprietary methods, leaving ACT work open and available

- Keep the focus always on what is good for the reader

- Support the further development of the field

- Provide information in a way that is of practical use to readers

These guidelines reflect the values of the broader ACT community. You'll see all of them packed into this book. They are meant to ensure that professionals get information that can truly be helpful, and that can further our ability to alleviate human suffering by inviting creative practitioners into the process of developing, applying, and refining a more adequate approach. Consider this book such an invitation.

Sincerely,
John Forsyth, Ph.D., Steven C. Hayes, Ph.D., and Georg H. Eifert, Ph.D.

Preface

A client recently said, "I'm not getting where I want to be in life because I am afraid of being afraid." Such paradoxes are common among therapy clients, and indeed among all of us. A paradox commonly encountered by therapists is that putting ACT into clinical practice is both easier and harder than it looks. Sometimes ACT looks like common sense and it's easy to say, "It's nothing new" or "I'm already doing that," while missing the importance of function and context during treatment. At other times, ACT and the underlying theory look impossibly difficult, while careful consideration reveals the simple elegance of many ACT tenets. *ACT in Practice* is our approach to ACT case conceptualization, and we hope you find it works for you and moves you in many valued directions with respect to working with your clients.

Acceptance and commitment therapy is growing in empirical support and clinical utility, and is also becoming more prominent in mainstream awareness. Peer-reviewed journals are publishing more accounts of the usefulness of ACT as a therapeutic approach, and a recent meta-analysis (Hayes, Luoma, Bond, Masuda, & Lillis, 2006) supports its effectiveness. Publications and workshops about third-wave behavior therapy and mindfulness are available for a wide variety of clinical concerns, from anxiety to anger, smoking to seizure disorders, and borderline personality disorder to parent coaching. ACT has generated increasing attention from the popular press, and the number of involved practitioners and investigators from the international behavioral science community is steadily growing. Interest in ACT is emerging among seasoned therapists, trainees, and students, and this is likely due to evidence of its effectiveness, its focus on existential as well as behavioral issues, the tight link between theory and practice, and its incorporation of philosophy and mindfulness traditions.

The growing body of ACT literature developed in the same science tradition that established the importance of empirically supported therapies (ESTs). ACT imbues these therapy methods with a stance that includes a focus on life values, mindfulness, and the influence of language on human suffering. ACT investigators also maintain values of not only developing the applied interventions that constitute ACT, but also describing basic principles of human behavior and cognition, and the theoretical and philosophical underpinnings of the endeavor. The aim is a comprehensive psychology more adequate to address human suffering with precision, scope, and depth (cf. Hayes & Berens, 2004).

As an increasing number of therapists contact acceptance and commitment therapy, the question each will inevitably ask is "How do I apply this to my clients?" The answer will only be partially answered with treatment manuals. Practitioners often criticize treatment manuals as being too general and targeting only very circumscribed diagnostic criteria. While these treatment-manual approaches are essential to doing clinical research, the hortative "do it this way" approach to therapy does not gel with the flexibility therapy often requires and the fluid manner in which each therapeutic relationship unfolds.

This introduction to case conceptualization in ACT will help the therapist apply the ACT framework and clinical behavior analysis concepts to different clients. You will learn to recognize six behavioral processes that influence problematic behavioral repertoires: fusion, experiential avoidance, weak self-knowledge, attachment to the conceptualized self, persistent inaction or impulsivity, and poorly clarified values. You will also learn how to utilize the six core processes of acceptance and commitment therapy—defusion, acceptance, contacting the present moment, self as perspective, committed action, and values—in order to formulate a treatment approach to address those behavioral repertoires. Case conceptualization takes individualized assessment data regarding the historical and current environment that influence a person's clinically relevant behaviors, and facilitates development of treatment goals and the planning of the therapeutic processes aiming toward those goals. Each person's behavioral concerns need to be observed and a plan drawn out to ameliorate those concerns, and progress toward meeting clinical goals should be regularly reassessed. This book will support you in discovering which elements of the person's struggle require acceptance and which require change, and how to collaborate with the client on setting and meeting those goals.

This book will explore and illustrate ways to incorporate the successful methods of acceptance and commitment therapy into individual treatment via detailed case illustrations and transcriptions on how to conceptualize cases and conduct ACT for the variety of clinical concerns characterized by experiential avoidance. This book will also introduce you to a fresh way of looking at behavior.

ACT is regarded by some as difficult to understand due its focus on undermining the destructive, unhelpful, dysfunctional effects of language and, in part, because of ACT's use of unfamiliar concepts, such as cognitive defusion and deliteralization. Through case examples, user-friendly exercises, and a pragmatic style, we plan to help "frontline" therapists learn to properly apply an ACT framework in assessing and intervening with clients. In other words, while it is an ACT truism that "language leads to suffering," our aim is to discuss ACT with accessible language and examples to minimize the suffering of the reader. ACT comes from the rigorous science of behavior analysis and the philosophy of functional contextualism, and our aim is to make such topics palatable and digestible for beginning consumers of this literature so that ACT can be more accessible to therapists who are new to this work.

Section 1, An Introduction to ACT Principles, provides a brief overview of ACT and includes basic material on case conceptualization, applied behavior analysis, and relational frame theory, the theory of language and cognition on which ACT is based. It also includes clinical cases that will be revisited throughout the book. Transcripts and case examples will lace through every chapter, and our clinical examples will function as multiple exemplars for the new ACT therapist. All clients in this book are fictional clients, and yet they are composites of real clients and typical of clients seen in our practice.

Section 2, The Fundamentals of ACT Case Conceptualization, provides an introduction to performing ACT case conceptualization, and then a deeper description of the six core processes and their relationship to clinically relevant behavior, as well as assessment considerations in ACT.

Section 3, Putting ACT into Practice, emphasizes how to apply ACT in practice. The clinically directed chapters of the book will have two noteworthy sections: "Stance of the Therapist" and "Checking In." "Stance of the Therapist" sections are an adjunct to learning ACT by allowing you to grasp ACT principles through applying them to your own life. These personal explorations can be important in order for you as therapist to fully describe and model ACT work. Using boxes for this information allows the book to flow naturally as an instructive case-conceptualization manual and allows you to do the personal work at your own pace. ACT therapists take an approach of radical acceptance, recognizing that we therapists also move in the same language environment as our clients and as such are subject to the same struggles with avoidance and fusion. We address this by providing examples of how you might apply ACT principles to yourself while doing ACT with your clients. The "Checking In" sections will give you opportunities to test your own learning, including the chance to apply the new knowledge to case vignettes and compare responses to the authors' suggestions for best practices.

No single book or workshop will provide enough information for one to become an ACT therapist. This book will both broaden the appeal of and support the practical applications from the original ACT text (Hayes, Strosahl, & Wilson, 1999) and other newer texts. The original ACT book is full of philosophical and basic science material that helped lay the foundation for this therapeutic endeavor. *Act in Practice* complements that book with a practical orientation aimed to present ACT principles in a manner friendly to individuals with or without prior ACT knowledge or behavior analytic training. Sometimes we'll be writing the way a coach would explain things: in a directive and motivational style. At other times, we'll write like a reporter: in a style focusing on objective data and principles. Through this combined approach, the reader will learn the hows and the whys of case conceptualization in acceptance and commitment therapy.

Acknowledgments

We are very fortunate to have had the opportunity to write this book and to contribute to developing a psychology more adequate to the human condition. Though only one of us can be listed as first author, this work is an outcome of equal effort. Five years ago there was one book on acceptance and commitment therapy, and as the only two ACT therapists in the Chicago area, we began regular lunch meetings to discuss ACT. Those conversations led us to team up for ACT practice, peer supervision, and training, and then to write this book together. Today there is a vibrant and growing local and world-wide ACT community, and more than a twenty ACT books for professionals and for self-help. Acceptance and commitment therapy is growing because of the dedication of many professionals to the communitarian approach that is so critical to science. There are many people who influenced our work with ACT case conceptualization and many more who helped us see this project to the very end. We appreciate all of the assistance from the researchers and practitioners who clarified our understanding of this material and helped us make it digestible for a broader audience.

We would especially like to thank Steven Hayes, Kelly Wilson, John Forsyth, Kurt Salzinger, Richard O'Brien, Albert Ellis, Hank Robb, Robyn Walser, Thane Dykstra, Mohammed Al-Attrash, and Joann Wright for their commitment to helping us as scientist-practitioner-authors. Many colleagues and friends—too many to name—served as peer consultants and trainers, and offered ongoing support and input: you know who you are! We would also like to thank our families for their support and willingness to put up with our frequent absence while working on this project. Our students and trainees deserve our thanks for their ongoing feedback on how to most effectively communicate ACT case conceptualization and treatment. Great gratitude goes to the people at New Harbinger Publications who recognized the vision of this book. Finally, we would like to reiterate our thanks to the behavior therapy community for providing a context for us to live out value-directed behavior.

SECTION 1

An Introduction to ACT Principles

CHAPTER 1

An Orientation to ACT

The clinicians in our world aim to reduce human suffering and are all working very hard. Clinical social workers, pastoral counselors, marriage and family therapists, and life coaches are all "in the trenches" working to help people through direct services. Behavioral scientists are looking for the things and events that cause, exacerbate, and maintain human suffering, as well as those that promote positive behavioral health or alleviate human suffering. The continued collaboration between "front liners" and the research community is yielding important discoveries about what undergirds human suffering and how to most effectively deliver direct services. The practitioners and investigators in the ACT community believe they have begun to tap a bit further into what makes human life so difficult at times and also what can be done to help.

The largest boost in mainstream awareness of ACT to date occurred in 2005 when Steven Hayes published *Get Out of Your Mind and Into Your Life*, the first ACT book written for a lay audience (Hayes & Smith, 2005), and *Time* magazine (Cloud, 2006) featured a story about ACT. Although ACT is a relative newcomer to the mainstream press, it has been around since the early 1980s, with discussion taking place primarily among academics, and the preliminary research being reported in academic journals and professional meetings. However, by 2007, more than ten thousand mental health professionals had received ACT training and more than one hundred empirical studies had been published. These studies examined the impact of ACT processes and the utility of ACT in the treatment of specific mental health problems, and explored relational frame theory, the basic model of language and cognition underlying ACT (Hayes et al., 2006). Research continues and early outcome investigations support the utility of ACT in the treatment of a wide variety of clinical concerns.

ACT research has been conducted with subjects presenting with many common mental disorders and clinical concerns that bring individuals to psychotherapy. While not an exhaustive list, a few of the areas of clinical interest in which there have been published ACT outcome studies conducted include social anxiety disorder, depression, polysubstance abuse, agoraphobia, psychosis, work stress, chronic pain, smoking, trichotillomania, and self-harm (Hayes et al., 2006). In addition to these, many more basic research studies examine specific ACT processes. We find it interesting that ACT outcomes often differ in surprising ways from outcomes seen in research on other treatment approaches.

Differences Between Outcomes with ACT vs. Other Treatment Approaches

An immediately apparent difference between ACT and most other treatment approaches is the treatment of human suffering. Many treatment approaches begin with an assumption that negatively evaluated thoughts and feelings—for example, anxiety, depression, obsessions, or delusions—are problems to be gotten rid of. In contrast, in ACT these unwanted thoughts and feelings are not regarded as primary treatment targets. Rather, attempts to avoid these unwanted private events are seen as dysfunctional in that avoidance behaviors are often dysfunctional and can prevent the client from experiencing desired life consequences. The ACT model of suffering suggests that difficult thoughts and feelings are an inevitable aspect of human existence rather than problems to be gotten rid of. Life includes painful events. Attempts to avoid pain tend to magnify the pain rather than eliminate it (Hayes et al., 1999, pp. 60–62).

ACT focuses on the individual's behavior and the context in which it occurs. Therefore assessment is focused on the presenting problems of the client while considering that person's past and current environment. The outcome criterion of ACT is "successful working." This means that the goal of ACT work is to get the person's behavior to work successfully, according to that person's values and desired ends and in that person's current context, given all the experiences that person had before then. This is in contrast to the more mechanistic medical model, in which assessment emphasizes assigning diagnostic labels and has symptom reduction as the primary outcome criterion. For example, assessment and treatment for anxiety under the medical model might emphasize exploring contexts in which anxiety occurs for the purpose of assigning a diagnosis, for example, social anxiety disorder versus generalized anxiety disorder. After the diagnosis is decided, the practitioner then prescribes medication to reduce anxiety or uses cognitive restructuring (that is, replacing irrational beliefs with more rational ones) with the goal of decreasing anxiety. In contrast, an ACT therapist might assess contexts in which anxiety occurs and what the client does when feeling anxious. For example, does the client avoid or escape anxiety? The functions of anxious behaviors, for example, avoiding certain situations or performing rituals to minimize or avoid anxiety, take center stage in ACT clinical work. (For now, think of the function of behavior broadly as its purpose; for more on a functional account of behavior, see chapters 2 and 3.) The centrality of these functions in ACT renders the *Diagnostic and Statistical Manual of Mental Disorders* (DSM) diagnostic categorization relatively unimportant. (Of course, the *DSM* remains a practical tool for communication with other professionals and in working with third-party payers.) Instead of regarding decreased anxiety as the only desirable outcome, ACT treatment emphasizes the client changing her relationship to anxiety in order to function more effectively in contexts where avoiding or escaping anxiety leads to undesirable life outcomes (Hayes et al., 1999, pp. 151–152). In the case of Shandra, a mother who wants to stop giving her adult son money that he uses to buy heroin, which do you suppose might be the more effective approach: helping her get rid of the guilt she feels when she says no to her son, or helping her say no to her son while simply noticing the natural feelings she labels "guilt"? For Rick, a socially anxious client, does the clinician need to target reduction of his flushed face and feelings of nervousness, or increase his social behavior regardless of the associated physiological changes and feelings? (You'll learn more about Shandra and Rick later in this chapter.)

The lack of emphasis on symptom reduction in ACT has led to some counterintuitive ACT research findings. For example, people being treated for chronic pain might report little decrease in pain during ACT treatment, and yet report increased activity and quality of life and decreased pain behaviors (Dahl, Wilson, & Nilsson, 2004). Depressed clients treated with ACT showed no change in a measure of depression even while reporting increased activity and willingness to engage in activities they had previously avoided due to associated pain. However, they then showed decreases on depression measures several months after treatment ended (Zettle & Rains, 1989). Psychotic clients treated with ACT actually showed an increase in reported delusional beliefs and hallucinations, even while staying out of the hospital longer than subjects not treated with ACT (Bach & Hayes, 2000). Of course, these findings are only counterintuitive when considered from non-ACT perspectives, and these outcomes make perfect sense in the context of the aims of acceptance and commitment therapy. ACT outcomes emphasize changes in overt behavior, for example, going to work *while* feeling depressed, or saying yes to going on a social outing that is sure to be anxiety provoking, rather than taking the position that depression or anxiety or any other symptom must decrease in order for the client to change her behavior. Desirable changes following ACT treatment occur at the level of changing how the individual relates to the symptoms rather than in changing the symptoms per se. (If this point is not yet clear, stick with us and it will become clearer as you read through the book.)

This is not to say that ACT does not lead to symptom relief. Several ACT clinical trials have shown decreases in symptom severity, often beginning relatively later during the course of treatment or even weeks after treatment ends. That is, subjects receiving ACT treatment show earlier behavior change that is often followed by decreases in symptom severity, while subjects in other treatment conditions often show less behavior change while showing greater early decreases in symptom severity (Hayes, 2007). Further, behavior change is observed during ACT treatment even in cases where there is little or no change in symptoms, such as self-reported anxiety or hallucinations. ACT therapists and researchers are aware of the long history of research on other cognitive behavioral therapies and understand that certain other treatment approaches can work. That said, ACT therapists and researchers do believe that ACT also works, and works by a different mechanism than other cognitive and behavioral treatment approaches. Unfortunately clinical research has not yet answered the question "What treatment is most effective for which type of individual, and under which set of circumstances?" (Paul, 1969, p. 44). The continued collaboration between the frontline treatment providers and the investigators is essential to answer this question.

The Essential Components of ACT

As we turn to the essential components of ACT, we'd like to begin with a very comprehensive definition of ACT. For those new to ACT, the definition may seem a bit dense, but please stay with us. After reading this book, we trust that you'll return to this definition and find it a succinct summary of all that ACT is. (You may also find it helpful now to read the last sentence of the definition first.) Hayes (2006b) defines ACT as

> a functional contextual therapy approach based on Relational Frame Theory which views human psychological problems dominantly as problems of psychological inflexibility fostered by cognitive fusion and experiential avoidance. In the context of a therapeutic relationship, ACT brings direct contingencies and indirect verbal processes to bear on the experiential establishment of greater psychological flexibility primarily through acceptance, defusion, establishment of a transcendent sense of self, contact with the present moment, values, and building larger and larger patterns of committed action linked to those values. Said more simply, ACT uses acceptance and mindfulness processes, and commitment and behavior change processes, to produce greater psychological flexibility.

Note that the desired outcome in ACT is not symptom reduction (though symptoms may and often do decrease). The desired outcome is increased psychological flexibility, that is, the opportunity for the client to persevere or change her behavior in the service of attaining valued goals and outcomes.

ACT is based on the assumption that the core problem most clients face is *experiential avoidance*, which is the avoidance of one's own unwanted thoughts, feelings, sensations, and other private events. Avoidance may have its uses with respect to the tangible world, as when one avoids driving on a road where the bridge is out or avoids touching a hot stove. However, in the realm of thoughts and feelings, attempts to avoid unwanted private experience can paradoxically increase unpleasant private experience and lead to forms of avoidance—such as substance abuse, agoraphobia, compulsive behavior, and aggressive acting out—that cause even more problems. ACT turns conventional wisdom on its head. In ACT, attempting to control private experience is seen as the problem rather than the solution. That is, strategies used to control private experience create more problems than they solve. Throughout the book, we will discuss how ACT therapists use metaphor, paradox, experiential exercises, values clarification, and mindfulness techniques, as well as more traditional behavior therapy interventions, to help clients experience the futility of their control strategies and to foster greater flexibility in the presence of those experiences that they have been trying to control.

The Core ACT Processes

ACT in practice can be understood in terms of six interrelated processes—acceptance, defusion, contact with the present moment, committed action, self as context, and values (Hayes, Strosahl, Bunting, Twohig, & Wilson, 2004)—and core intervention strategies for tackling psychopathology in terms of these processes. The core processes are related to each other in many important ways, and none of the six should be considered completely discrete. It should come as no surprise that the contextual approach of ACT would have interrelated processes that cannot be defined without the other principles.

The following model of the six core processes in ACT work has been humorously named the "hexaflex" model. The term was meant to be a clever shorthand term for discussing a hexagon-shaped model used to illustrate the processes influencing flexibility. Although the term was meant to be amusing, it has stuck among those using ACT. Our case-conceptualization model will use this term, as well as derivations of it, throughout this book.

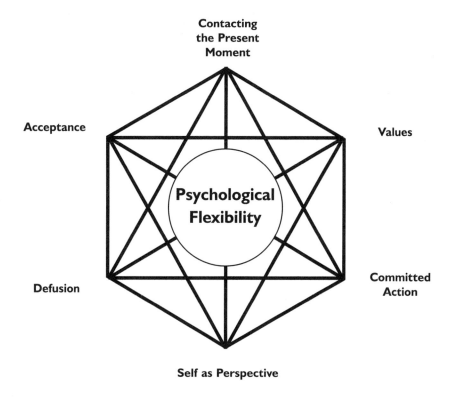

Six Core Processes: The ACT Hexaflex Model

Acceptance

Acceptance is an often misunderstood concept. Acceptance does not mean liking or wanting one's experience and current conditions. Instead, *acceptance* means willingness to experience what one is experiencing "fully and without defense" (Hayes, 1994, p. 30). Given the client's history and the road she has chosen to walk, certain events (such as anxiety and anger) are likely. The ACT therapist gives the client opportunities to be willing to have the inevitable feelings that arise during that stroll down life's road, and to experience the feelings as they are (just feelings) and not as something to be avoided. Acceptance interventions are synonymous with willingness, and the client learns not to blame herself for her problems, does not strive to change private experience, and is willing to face fear and other unwanted psychological events when doing so accompanies moving in a valued direction on that chosen road.

Defusion

Defusion strategies are therapy techniques that aim to decrease unhelpful effects of language and cognition. *Cognitive fusion* occurs when thoughts are taken literally, as if thoughts are not merely thoughts but rather are what they say they are. This may influence the person to respond to verbal rules and evaluations rather than the events of the present moment. For instance, clients who are fused with the thought "No one likes me" do not see it as merely a thought, but instead takes it as a literal truth. Because of this, they approach people they meet through the lens of "No one likes me." This may lead to avoiding social interaction even when social interaction is available from people who might actually like them. Fusion is a by-product of language, and it is easy to fall into self-defeating behavior when thoughts are taken literally (Hayes et al., 1999, pp. 72–74). Consider the person who experiences obsessions about germs or paranoid delusions that a simple action, such as going out of doors, will result in death. Defusion allows the individual to see thoughts as thoughts rather than regarding thoughts as literal truths about the world. The thoughts of germs and the danger of the outside world are seen as "chatter" and cognitive by-products of one's history. Defusion frees the client to act on the basis of values and the current environmental contingencies rather than on the basis of fused verbal content.

Contacting the Present Moment

Contact with the present moment is best defined experientially. Right now as you read these words, can you be fully aware and attend to what you are reading? Notice that you are reading this book right now and right where you are. Try to take a moment and notice your experience right now, and notice "now" over and over again. Notice also that "now" instantaneously becomes "then" and slips out of reach. Be present with the sights, smells, and sounds in the environment. Become aware of the contact your body is making with other things around you, such as the floor or your chair. Notice your feelings and body sensations. As you notice, you are aware of your experience in that moment. Words tend to pull us out of the present moment. Have you ever noticed that the words you use while thinking are usually reminiscing about the past or planning the future? Even when you say to someone, "Come here right now," by the time they hear and respond to their perception of "now," your "now" is already in the past. When we learn to contact the present moment, we learn to embrace all that the moment affords, (for example, depressive or joyous thoughts, anxiety-provoking or laugh-inducing images, and so on), and notice that thoughts, feelings, and sensations come and go in an endless stream and are no more or less than private events. From this stance of contact with the present moment, we can act mindfully and on the basis of chosen values—even while experiencing unwanted private events. Willingness exercises and mindfulness exercises, such as meditation, are two types of interventions used to increase contact with the present moment.

Committed Action

Committed action is behaving in the service of chosen values. In many conceptualizations, committed action is where the "rubber meets the road" in therapy. It happens when clients actually engage in important, clinically relevant, overt responses that put their lives back on track. These may be behaviors that clients previously avoided, or they may be newly learned skills. In the service of life-affirming goals, clients execute behavior they have been too inflexible to execute until now. Committed action interventions are often drawn from traditional behavior therapy rather than being unique to ACT.

At this point in our discussion of core ACT strategies, notice the overlap among the components of ACT. Notice that committed action involves acceptance, values, and contact with the present moment. Notice that acceptance involves defusion, and defusion involves acceptance, and so on. This overlap will begin to make more sense as you learn about ACT's functional contextual approach in chapter 2, and you will also see domain overlap in the model of psychopathology. Put another way, the core strategies are not separate strategies in an absolute sense, yet it is useful to discuss them as distinct strategies. Note also that it is even difficult to describe them as only interventions; each one of the core strategies may also be described as outcomes of other interventions. For instance, a defusion exercise might increase acceptance, or an acceptance exercise might increase committed action, and so forth. This may seem confusing at the moment, but as you become familiar with ACT, you will begin to notice the flexibility of the core strategies; you may apply them differently in different contexts as each unique client presents with unique complaints and goals and values.

Self as Perspective

Self as perspective requires consideration of different senses of self and self-knowledge. According to the ACT literature, there are three ways of looking at the self: self as content, self as process, and self as context. *Self as content* includes one's personal verbal descriptions and evaluations. For example, one client may describe himself as a man who is thirty-five years old, is an accountant, likes dogs, has a social phobia, is bad at relationships, and so on. *Self as process* is the ongoing self-awareness or the sense of self where one notices ongoing processes, such as thoughts, feelings, and bodily sensations, such as "Now I am feeling anxious" or "Now I have a headache." *Self as perspective*, which is also called self as context or the observing self, is a transcendent sense of self. (We will use the terms "self as perspective" and "self as context" interchangeably.) Self as perspective is not an object of verbal evaluations; instead it is the locus from which a person's experience unfolds. Self as perspective is transcendent in that it has no form or verbal content. Instead, it can be thought of as the place from which observations are made. As such, it is the least talked about sense of self, and it is a sense of self that has no boundaries (Barnes-Holmes, Hayes, & Dymond, 2001). The felt experience of self as perspective can be a boon to increasing willingness and acceptance as well as a positively evaluated experience in its own right. ACT provides experiential opportunities to become present with the self as perspective (see chapters 7 and 11).

Values

Values are verbally construed global outcomes or chosen life directions (Hayes et al., 1999). An ACT therapist may often ask questions like "What do you want your life to be about? In what direction do you want to move?" The metaphor of "moving in a direction" or toward a compass point is used to characterize values. Values are distinct from goals, though goal attainment can be in the service of values. In contrast to goals, which by definition are not here and now but are to be attained in the future, values are always lived in the present moment. Valuing happens here and now. Also, goals are often articulated in terms of what is missing from our lives, while values are articulated based on how we want to live our lives with reference to global rather than discrete outcomes—for example, the value of having loving relationships rather than discrete goals such as having more friends, getting married, or having a child. The metaphor of values as moving in a direction is apt because if, for example, we say we want to direct our life toward "heading west," we can go endlessly in the direction west without ever having to stop. We might attain certain goals along the way while we travel west, just as one might pass through Budapest or Chicago while traveling west, but we never "arrive at" west! More practically, we might say that we value lifelong learning. We might put it, "Hey, I like the idea of spending my life learning new things." We might attain the goals of earning a college degree or reading a really difficult science text (like Newton's *Principia* or Hayes et al.'s *Relational Frame Theory*), which are in the service of our value of lifelong learning. At the same time, however, our value is never attained because we always have more to learn and further to go in the direction of lifelong learning. Likewise, the ACT therapist can point out that, whether verbalized or not, the client is always moving in a direction, perhaps even a direction that leads to unwanted outcomes from an ACT perspective, such as living a restricted life in the service of avoiding anxiety.

Values increase willingness to have unwanted thoughts and feelings and dignify the pain that often accompanies them. A common misconception about ACT is that the therapist doesn't care about client distress associated with unwanted thoughts and feelings, and that a therapist should be concerned with helping the client eliminate unwanted thoughts and feelings. In contrast, the ACT position is that unpleasant thoughts, feelings, and sensations often accompany moving in valued directions. For instance, the person asking someone on a date might be rejected; the person in a committed relationship may lose her beloved to separation or death; the person beginning a new venture might experience doubt and anxiety. Avoiding these inevitable painful thoughts and feelings leads to a restricted and often joyless life, while a focus on values brings vitality and willingness to experience whatever pain might be experienced in a life well lived.

Values are chosen, and they are always "perfect" in that they are not right or wrong. That is, only we can choose our values. A therapist might be tempted to criticize the values of a client, and if this happens, the therapist criticizes the client's values from the perspective of her own chosen values. For instance, a therapist might be tempted to criticize a client who chooses to drop out of school based on the therapist's own value of education as a desirable outcome. So what is a therapist to do? Practice acceptance, defusion, and committed action! Practice ACT in practice.

We will elaborate on this orientation to ACT throughout the book, and it can be used while you formulate case conceptualizations. The six core processes—acceptance, defusion, contact with the present moment, committed action, self as perspective, and values—only hint at the richness of ACT, and this outline does not adequately suggest how to fully practice ACT. We will stroll through the next few chapters to discuss case conceptualization and the fundamentals of clinical behavior analysis, and then return to the refrain of the acceptance and commitment strategies.

Case Presentations

We'll discuss several different clients and clinical presentations throughout the book as a way of showing how case conceptualization works in concrete, therapeutic situations. Transcripts and case examples will lace through all of the chapters. We will also follow the journey of two clients—Shandra and Rick, who were introduced briefly earlier in the chapter—with a bit more detail. While Shandra and Rick are fictional, they are composites of real clients and typical of clients seen in our practice.

Meet Shandra

Shandra decided to see an ACT therapist after reading a magazine article about ACT. Shandra reports that she has struggled with depression for most of her adult life.

She is forty-eight years old, divorced, and currently living with a man she has been seeing on and off for twelve years. She has two adult children, a son and a daughter. She is employed as an assistant manager of a department store where she has held various positions for twenty-two years. Her boyfriend, Charles, is unemployed. He does seasonal construction work and rarely works during winter months. Shandra complains that finances are tight while he is not working, and that he drinks to the point of intoxication three or four times a week, verbally abuses her while drinking, and is inattentive and uncommunicative when recovering from an evening of drinking.

Shandra says that she wants treatment so that "I can be happy like other people. I cry all the time and that isn't normal." Shandra describes many treatment goals. "I want to leave Charles. I know he's bad for me, but when I kick him out, then I miss him too much and I just can't stand being alone." She also wants to improve her relationships with her children. "I want to figure out how to help them. I don't know how to make them listen to me, and they just keep messing up. The only time they seem to talk to me is when they want money. I can't afford to keep helping them, and I feel guilty when I say no. I know that I wasn't a very good mother, so it's kind of my fault that they are in trouble." Shandra also wants to make peace with her past. "I want to forgive my stepfather and my ex-husband for what they did to me and my daughter, but I get so angry when I think about what they did to us. It's not very Christian of me, and sometimes I think I hate them, and it makes me want to cry. I just think I am a bad person. Just bad."

Shandra reports that "when I look at my life, it's nothing like I imagined it would be. There's nothing to be happy about and nothing to look forward to. I cry a lot, and I don't really have any friends because I don't want anyone to know about my business and how depressing my life is. I've tried therapy and it helps some but not all that much. I've been taking Prozac for years and it doesn't seem to be helping me anymore. I sleep a lot when I'm not at work—there's nothing else to do. I've gained thirty pounds in the last two years, so I don't even look good anymore. I used to feel like no matter how bad I felt, at least I looked good and now that's not even true anymore. I feel like I'm just old and washed out. I try to be happy and to ask God to help me, but I don't think he is listening because everything just keeps getting worse. And my kids … I know it's partly my fault, but they make me so mad and so sad. My son, Jim, just got out of jail again, and I almost wish he was back in again because at least when he's in jail, he's not always bothering me for money. And my daughter, Karen … well, she lost her job again, so now she's coming to me for more money too. How can I say no when it's my fault that they're in so much trouble? If it weren't for me, they would be better off."

Shandra says that she first became depressed after the birth of her first child. She dropped out of high school at age seventeen when she became pregnant. She and her boyfriend, Louis, got married just after she turned eighteen and a month before their son, Jim, was born. Sixteen months later, they had their daughter, Karen. "I never wanted to go to college, and I didn't want to get married so young either. I wanted to enjoy being young, dating, partying, having fun, and instead I was home with babies.

I was depressed for years and I never got any mental help, and I started feeling better after I started working. It felt good to be making money and getting out of the house and talking to adults."

Shandra reports, "I felt better for a while and then my world fell apart. I found out that Louis was molesting Karen—I came home early from working a night shift and caught him in bed with her. I couldn't believe it. My stepfather did the same thing to me, and I vowed I would never let it happen to my daughter. I divorced Louis and that's the first time I went into therapy. It helped some, but Karen blamed me and Jim blamed me too, and everyone blamed me that we were poor and living on our own. No one knew what really happened. How could I tell them what Louis did? And I know they were all judging me for leaving my husband because they didn't know what he had done, so I just kind of shut down and stopped seeing my friends and talking to the other girls at work. I didn't talk about my stepfather with that therapist because I felt like it was history and done and over with, but maybe I should have."

Shandra sought psychotherapy a second time after a difficult six-month period when her son had his first legal troubles, and her daughter, then nineteen, learned she was pregnant and moved in with her boyfriend. This was also the same time when Shandra and her current boyfriend, Charles, broke up for the first time. "I started taking Prozac then, and I didn't stay in therapy very long. It didn't seem like talking did much good. I didn't want to talk about the past. I wanted to feel happy right away and help my kids get their acts together. I still felt like everything that happened was my fault even though my therapist said that it wasn't my fault."

Shandra saw a therapist for the third time five years ago and continued therapy for four years. During that time, she and Charles broke up and reunited several times and, according to Shandra, her depression worsened. "I know he's bad for me and I try to date other men, but there just don't seem to be any good ones out there, and then I get so lonely that I go back to Charles and we start all over again. I want my kids to do better so I can stop feeling guilty and worrying all the time. But how can I help them if I can't even help myself? I don't know if therapy really helped, but it felt good to talk to someone every week since I don't have any girlfriends to talk to. I quit because I couldn't afford it after Charles was unemployed for a while and Jim needed money for a lawyer. And then I read this article about ACT and it sounded different from everything else I've tried. Maybe this will help me get rid of my depression once and for all."

Meet Rick

After months of deliberation, Rick called the local community mental health center and said, "I need some counseling." The intake coordinator assessed Rick's concerns as centering around anxiety issues, so she made an appointment for Rick to meet with a counselor familiar with evidence-based treatments for anxiety and also the ACT approach.

Rick is in his late twenties and lives alone in a two-bedroom condo in a downtown metropolis. He works as an electronics engineer and is dissatisfied with his career path. He complains that his feelings of anxiety prevent him from interacting with coworkers, and he feels isolated from his peers. He occasionally plans to speak up during staff meetings or "at the watercooler" but feels his cheeks flush so much that they become very warm. He says, "I tell myself all the time, 'Don't do anything embarrassing' and I just like … don't do anything at all." When he knows he will have to talk about the work going on in his department, he feels a looming dread for a few days prior to the meeting. He reports "a kind of sick twittery feeling in my stomach before talking to some people." He has not dated in almost ten years, since his girlfriend left him while they were both in college. He reported that his breakup was very difficult for him and was a surprise. Instead of becoming more socially active with peers after she left him, he threw himself into his studies. He occasionally smoked marijuana with acquaintances and since leaving college has continued smoking marijuana regularly and by himself, especially when feeling bored or frustrated.

"The reason I need counseling is pretty obvious. I hate my job, get paid squat, but at the same time, I won't quit, ask for a raise, or a transfer. Same with getting high. I don't even enjoy it. I just do it to take the edge off. I don't have any friends. I see everyone else getting married and whatnot. I haven't been with a girl in years, man. The future is bleak. I'm a fucking loser with no end in sight."

After some probing, it turns out that Rick is a well-schooled engineer with creative abilities. He spends much of his spare time using computers, mostly playing video games, surfing the Web, and chatting online with, as he puts it, "computer geeks." He has written one piece of shareware that has been fairly well distributed among the computer community, and he occasionally works on the second version of that program.

Rick was adopted by his parents when they were in their mid-forties. He was their only child, and he was reared in a loving home with traditional Judeo-Christian, mid-American values. His father died while Rick was in college, and Rick recalls him as "just this accountant guy who came home for dinner, which we ate in silence, and then he read the paper. I didn't get much from him. But he was okay to me, though. Nothing bad … nothing great, though." His mother currently resides in a nursing home where he visits two times a month. He said, "I love my ma. She's been there for me … someone I could talk to. I was such a nebbish when it came to talking to other kids my age, especially in high school, but she always tried to relate to me. She was cool. Not now though … she's just … senile. Going to visit her is a real drag. She doesn't talk much. I feel like crap that I have to go to the nursing home and visit her, and I feel like crap that I feel like crap. Ya know? What's worse is sometimes I just get high when I should be going to see her. I just can't take how weird it is to go see her, and I can't take how guilty I am for not going to see her. It's just easier to sit home and 'get baked.'"

Rick suggested that his therapy goals were "to give up smoking so much friggin' pot. I'm almost thirty years old for crying out loud." He also wants to "stop feeling so nervous and freaked out about talking to people. I'm smarter than most of my coworkers, but I never speak up, even when I know better than them. I just hate that sick feeling in my gut ... and the way my face gets all red and stuff." In addition, Rick intimated, "I'd like to stop feeling so crummy about my mom, and just go visit her without the guilt. It'd be nice to get some friends too."

We will revisit Shandra and Rick throughout the book, and you will get to know them well as they begin acceptance and commitment therapy.

CHAPTER 2

Clinical Behavior Analysis and the Three Waves of Behavior Therapy

When a therapeutic relationship begins, both client and therapist bring their hopes and expectations for how the treatment will unfold. Some clinical dyads may agree to discuss the quality of the client's interpersonal history, and others may collectively interpret dreams and fantasies. Some clients find value in having someone to talk to, and others want advice. There are plenty of clinicians to provide these types of interactions, and in the appropriate situations, ACT therapists may provide these types of interactions too.

And quite often people enter into a therapy relationship in order to change the way they approach life. Their hopes and expectations are to think, feel, and act differently. The person wants relief from the suffering that robs his life of vitality. Maybe he wants to change his dangerous habits, feel less depressed or anxious, or stop sabotaging his social relationships. For some clients, just having the right relationship with a therapist can alleviate suffering. And at the same time, there is a substantial literature on evidence-based treatments which goes beyond just the therapeutic relationship that can assist with these clinical problems. Exposure exercises, social skills training, and behavioral activation techniques are just a few interventions that have been shown to be useful with important clinical concerns (see Nathan & Gorman, 2002) and go beyond just having the requisite therapeutic relationship. Prior to jumping into ACT case conceptualization, it is important to understand the applications and theories of behavior therapy, functional analysis and assessment procedures, and the basic principles of behavior and language, from a clinical behavior analysis point of view. Having such a background will assist you in performing ACT more thoroughly and appropriately.

An Introduction to Clinical Behavior Analysis

Clinicians who assess what types of events in the client's life trigger the clinical problem and then attempt to alter client behavior through empirically supported interventions or principles are acting in accordance with a basic tenet of clinical behavior analysis. Behavior analysis postulates that the "primary purpose of psychological science is prediction and control" (Smith, 2001, p. 189). This tenet, offered by B. F. Skinner (1953), runs through the behavior analytic literature, and also through much of clinical psychology. Most therapists assess the variables that "predict" the client's symptoms and then try to control their occurrence or impact. (Incidentally, many modern behavior analysts have replaced "prediction and control" with the expression "prediction and influence," which is not only more palatable but also a more realistic description.) So if you are interested in predicting what triggers your client's problems and then having some influence on those problems, you have therapeutic hopes and expectations similar to clinical behavior analysts. ACT and functional analytic psychotherapy (FAP; Kohlenberg, R. J., & Tsai, 1991) are two of the major approaches to clinical behavior analysis.

Clinical behavior analysis has its roots in Skinner's (1953) theoretical work. Over fifty years ago, Skinner described fundamental behavior analytic principles related to treating drug abuse, anger problems, anxiety, and depression. Skinner can be considered a polarizing figure in psychology, and behavior analysis is often given poor press by other therapeutic traditions for being too sterile or rigidly scientific (perhaps due to behavior analysts' own history of public relations mishaps). However, we hope you will choose to hold (and just notice) any reservations or negative perceptions you might have about applying behavior analysis to interpersonal clinical psychotherapy while reading this book. Not only is the post-Skinnerian behavior analysis fostering interesting, interpersonal, and clinically rich psychotherapy exchanges, but Skinner (1953) himself has also suggested that "[t]herapy consists, not in getting the patient to discover the solution to his problem, but in changing him in such a way that he is able to discover it" (p. 382).

Clinical behavior analysts do understand that therapy is a journey of discovery, and the approach of the current ACT community includes exploring and utilizing effective techniques from the existential, humanistic, and dynamic camps, as well as other approaches, as long as they are based on a functional analysis of behavior and have treatment utility. If it appeared to be useful in promoting acceptance, a Gestalt "empty chair" technique or dream interpretation might be incorporated into ACT work. In addition, looking at the latent content of a client's verbal behavior, which is typically the fodder for psychodynamic work, is suggested as a possible area for relational frame theory analyses (Hayes, Barnes-Holmes, & Roche, 2001) and a potential area for ACT exploration. You will see throughout the book that the clinical behavior analyst wholly embraces the person, individualizes each assessment, and then treats that person's clinical concern with principles and interventions that have been shown to work with others.

These principles and interventions have a legacy in behavioral sciences, and the remainder of this chapter will discuss the waves of development that preceded modern clinical behavior analysis. As such, we will cover the details of classical conditioning and operant conditioning as they are relevant to applied behavioral interventions. ACT therapists draw from this tool chest of concepts and interventions. The exposure-based therapies, skills training, and contingency management programs that come from over a century of experimentation are critical to behavior therapy as conceptualized by the ACT approach, and it appears prudent to understand behavioral principles and methods during an ACT case conceptualization. So before looking at where we are, let's look at where we came from.

ACT and the Waves of Behavior Therapy

In 1964, Eysenck defined behavior therapy as "the attempt to alter human behavior and emotion in a beneficial manner according to the laws of modern learning theory" (p. 1). Over forty years have passed since Eysenck's conceptualization of "modern learning theory," and as long as modern learning theory continues to be what is current at the time (such as relational frame theory), then ACT is certainly a part of the long-standing behavior therapy approach. Even as long ago as 1970, Yates offered the following:

> Behavior therapy is the attempt to utilize systematically that body of empirical and theoretical knowledge which has resulted from the application of the experimental method in psychology and its closely related disciplines (physiology and neurophysiology) in order to explain the genesis and maintenance of those abnormalities by means of controlled experimental studies of the single case, both descriptive and remedial. (p. 18)

Given this definition, ACT is firmly ensconced in the behavior therapy community—that is, as long as you replace the antiquated term "abnormalities" with "dysfunctional behavior." While no single definition of "behavior therapy" has garnered consensus from the behavioral community (Kazdin & Wilson, 1978), Spiegler and Guevremont (2003) suggest that behavior therapy is scientific and active, has a present focus, and uses learning theory, which does indeed describe ACT.

ACT has grown out of the behavioral tradition and is considered to be part of the third wave of behavior therapy. Before looking at the third wave, let us briefly look at the first two waves while being cautioned that "the demarcation lines which are so clear in some scientific situations have become blurred in the case of psychology" (Kantor, 1963, p. 29). It is important to note that these three waves are arbitrary distinctions that facilitate discussion about the development of modern psychotherapy. Like the life of a person being divided into childhood, adolescence, and adulthood, there are distinctive events and transitional periods that lead to substantive change, but the entity is still the same and continually growing incrementally, and sometimes imperceptibly. In other words, "Hold it lightly."

The First Wave of Behavior Therapy

The first wave of behavior therapy grew out of a desire to link theory and behavior change techniques to scientifically sound principles. Unlike psychoanalysis, the dominant school of therapy at the time, early behavior therapists rigorously tested their theories and interventions. The first wave is linked to traditional clinical applications, such as systematic desensitization and counterconditioning models. Pavlov's basic experimental research in the early 1900s (1927) set the stage for John B. Watson's experiment with Little Albert (Watson & Rayner, 1920).

Both Pavlov and Watson demonstrated that an otherwise innocuous environmental event, such as the presentation of a bell (in Pavlov's experiment with dogs) or a white rat (in Watson's experiment with Little Albert), was a neutral stimulus (NS) because it did not elicit certain target reflexive responses. However, they observed that other environmental events, such as meat powder or a loud noise, respectively, functioned as an unconditioned stimulus (UCS) that did elicit reflexive salivation or a startle-and-cry response, which are unconditioned responses (UCR). When the NS of a bell or a white rat are paired with a UCS in a temporally contiguous fashion (close in time), the NS can become a conditioned stimulus (CS) as its presentation will elicit the conditioned response (CR). In other words, experiencing the NS (bell/white rat) paired with the UCS (meat powder/loud noise), can eventually lead to the bell or white rat having conditioned stimulus (CS) properties, and the CR (salivation/crying) will occur in the presence of the CS (bell/white rat), even if the UCS (meat powder/loud noise) is absent.

This classical conditioning model imparted a naturalistic approach describing the acquisition of conditioned emotional responses and how certain life experience could directly condition physiological responses related to anxiety, depression, anger, and sexual dysfunction. This progression from basic to applied investigations led to interventions with in vivo exposure and modeling work by Mary Cover Jones (1924), the application of progressive muscle relaxation by Edmund Jacobson (1929), and other clinical applications by pioneers such as O. Hobart Mowrer (1950), Joseph Wolpe (1958), and Arnold Lazarus (1973). The general idea in counterconditioning and exposure treatments was for the clinician to repeatedly present the CS either in the absence of the UCS or while eliciting competing reflex responses, so that the CS-CR relationship would diminish and eventually extinguish. The first wave was successful in forwarding scientifically based clinical psychotherapy techniques, and also in challenging the unsubstantiated mentalistic theories dominating that era. The success of first-wave behavior therapy was impressive as evidence-based behavioral theory led to testable hypotheses and to technologies useful for treating many behavior problems.

Classical conditioning work continues to be expanded by third-wave behavioral scientists (for example, Forsyth, Palav, & Duff, 1999), and the effective first-wave techniques unquestionably hold their importance in modern behavior therapy. These concepts may prove critical to appropriate treatment for clients, and nicely dovetail into an ACT intervention. In fact, Twohig, Hayes, and Masuda (2006) show how exposure treatments play an important role in second-wave and third-wave approaches. Since unobservable phenomena such as thoughts and feelings are central to many clinical problems that bring individuals into treatment, the first-wave focus on observable and operationally defined target behaviors, and the lack of an adequate account of human language and cognition, resulted in a relatively narrow focus unappealing to many interested in broader concepts (Hayes, 2004).

Challenges to the First Wave

Early behavior therapy linked basic research to applied endeavors. However, much of the demonstrated success was limited to work with children, people with developmental disabilities, or those with clinical concerns from direct conditioning, such as specific phobias (Yates, 1970). Hayes and Hayes (1989) suggest these early successes may be because it "is only with these populations that the thorny issues of verbal behavior can be minimised [sic]. Not so with 'neurotics'" (p. 292). These "neurotics" also experience conditioned emotional responses related to anxiety, depression, anger, and sexual dysfunction, but these concerns become thorny because there may not be a direct learning history to point to regarding the CSs and CRs, and stimulus generalization may be inadequate to explain why the person has acquired these clinical concerns. Acquisition of these clinical problems may have been modeled or learned verbally without direct conditioning. In other words, verbally able adults without a specific and circumscribed conditioning experience presented a different challenge to first-wave clinicians.

In addition, people who suffer the clinical problems often seen in therapy don't just complain about their physiological responses, but also complain that they are avoiding situations that provoke these responses, and that just thinking or talking about the problem is aversive. Human language makes the direct aversive conditioning more complex. As mentioned regularly in the ACT literature, a rat will not avoid reporting an aversive event. Human beings, however, will sometimes not only avoid reporting it, but can reexperience the emotional responses during reporting (see "Mutual Entailment," in chapter 4).

Beyond that, the first-wave behavior therapy approaches did not directly deal with other thorny issues, such as a person's lack of a functional repertoire of overt behaviors important in social contexts, such as social and assertiveness skills. Our clients' goals in therapy are rarely to merely address the aversive physiological experience; they also want to learn new ways to relate to environmental events. Direct conditioning interventions by early behavior therapists were incomplete for addressing these broader clinical concerns.

Another shortcoming of the first wave was that questions about language and cognition were left unanswered, or were answered unsatisfactorily. It lacked an integrated understanding of the "mind," and there were philosophical problems encountered with metaphysical and methodological behaviorism (for further discussion, see Hayes, 1988). There was a trough after the crest, if you will, which set the second wave in motion.

The Second Wave of Behavior Therapy

The second wave of behavior therapy brought two distinct advancements: operant psychology and cognitive therapies. Incidentally, Hayes (1988) suggests that the first and second waves of behavior therapy are divided by classical conditioning and operant conditioning application respectively, but Eifert and Forsyth (2005) suggest that the first wave was about conditioning per se, and the second wave was about the cognitive revolution. It was the inadequacies of the classical conditioning paradigm that paved the way for both operant psychology endeavors and the inclusion of cognitive methods, so both are placed here in the same second wave.

Operant Psychology: A Primer in Principles and Applications

ACT was developed within the behavior analysis tradition. Because complete and sophisticated case conceptualization will require an understanding of how the consequences of our clients' behavior influence their ongoing clinically relevant repertoire, we offer the following review of operant psychology basics.

Operant psychology grew from Skinner's basic work on principles of reinforcement. Operant psychology's three-term contingency has often been described as an A-B-C model of antecedent, behavior, and consequence. This A-B-C is markedly different from the A-B-C model that describes the cognitive model and which will be seen later in this chapter. In fact, the antecedent, behavior, and consequence model is a bit oversimplified. A more thoroughgoing behavioral analysis includes a four-term contingency model: motivational operations, discriminative stimuli, response, and consequential stimulus event. This model posits that given certain *motivational operations* (MO), which are briefly described as "states" of deprivation or satiation of the individual, and in the presence of certain *discriminative stimuli* (S^D) in the environment (see "Stimulus Control," in chapter 3 for a further explication), an individual will engage in a certain response (R) that is followed by an environmental stimulus (S**) event. (We will explain the superscripts for the abbreviations shortly.) The consequences of the response can increase the likelihood of that behavior, and this is called reinforcement (^{R}). The consequence of a response can decrease the likelihood of that behavior, and this is called punishment (^{P}). The consequence of the behavior can be the addition of certain stimuli, which is called a positive consequence ($^+$), or the removal of stimuli, which is called a negative consequence ($^-$).

Positive reinforcement. For example, when a boy is food deprived (MO) and is in the presence of a caregiver (S^D), there is a probability that he will engage in the response (R) of saying, "I want food." If food is then presented, and that consequence increases the probability of the same response given the presence of the caregiver and in the food-deprived state in the future, then the behavior o f saying, "I want food," was positively reinforced. There was an addition of certain stimuli (the food), which makes it a positive consequence, and the food increased the probability of that behavior in that particular context, which is considered a reinforcing consequence. In behavior analytic shorthand, the response was followed by stimuli that were positively reinforcing (S^{R+}). The MO and the S^D occur simultaneously prior to the response. The dot in the shorthand diagram below speaks to a probability function; discriminative stimuli do not always lead to certain responses, thus there is no direct arrow. In contrast, responses always have a consequence of one type or another, so there is a direct arrow between the symbols for response and consequence.

$$\boxed{\begin{array}{l} \text{MO} \\ S^D \quad \bullet \quad R \quad \rightarrow \quad S^{R+} \end{array}}$$

Negative reinforcement. Negative reinforcement occurs when a stimulus is taken away from the person, and that removal increases the likelihood of the behavior that preceded it. A typical example would be a woman scratching an itch. In the presence of a skin irritation (S^D), the response of scratching that area of her skin with her fingernails (R), can lead to the removal of that stimulus. In other words, the itching stops, which negatively reinforces (S^{R-}) that response when there is a skin irritation again.

Positive punishment. Positive punishment and negative punishment are also terms for behavioral consequences. Positive punishment is the presentation of environmental stimuli that decrease the likelihood of the response that preceded the consequence. In the presence of an electrical outlet (S^D), a girl sticks her finger in the socket (R). The girl receives a shock. If the shock reduces the probability that she will stick her finger in a wall outlet in the future, the behavior was positively punished (S^{P+}).

Negative punishment. Negative punishment is the removal of environmental stimuli after a response that reduces the probability of that response occurring again. A typical example is when a teenager is grounded. In the presence of his parents (S^D), the son makes an obscene finger gesture (R), which is followed by the removal of his car keys and driving privileges. If he doesn't make those finger gestures again in their presence, his behavior was negatively punished (S^{P-}).

Extinction. Additionally, it is important for clinicians to note that even when some responses have reliably led to reinforcers, sometimes the reinforcers are no longer available. When this occurs, we cannot say that the behavior is being reinforced or punished. In this case, the discontinuation of reinforcement is called *extinction* and influences a special behavioral phenomenon. At first, when the previously reinforced response is no longer reinforced, there is often an increase in the response frequency, followed by a decrease in response frequency. For example, imagine you are "soda-pop deprived" (MO) at lunchtime. You go to a soda machine (S^D), put in your money, and then press the button (R) that gets you your soda (S^{R+}). That entire stream of behaving is reinforced by the presentation of the soda can. What happens when the machine malfunctions and when you press the button, the reinforcer doesn't come? Most people will press the button again, and again, and maybe even increase the intensity of the response. This is called the "extinction burst." It might even be correlated with some conditioned emotional responses (such as anger or increased adrenal gland responses). But if the soda machine does not yield the reinforcer, eventually the responding stops and the individual walks away from the machine sans soda. This is an example of what happens when the response is "on extinction." In the nomenclature, this is often written as (S^{EXT}).

It is important for clinicians to also consider what happens if the reinforcer is presented during the extinction burst. Suppose while you are pounding very forcefully on the machine on the fifth strike, the soda can rolls out. Consider what you might do next time. The more intense "extinction burst" responding has been reinforced, and the next time this environmental event occurs, your first response may be to pound forcefully on the soda machine a few times. In more clinically relevant contexts, reinforced extinction bursts can be seen with children's temper tantrums, and also with escalating parasuicidal behaviors of a multiproblem client. In both examples, the individuals received attention as a reinforcer for certain behaviors (tantrum/ threatening self-harm), and when they no longer got the attention they "wanted," there was an increase in the frequency and intensity of the behavior. The caregiver sometimes wants to stop this extinction burst before it gets "out of control," and gives the child just what he wanted during the more intense responding. How intense will the tantrum or parasuicidal gestures be next time the person "wants" (is deprived of) attention?

Considerations about behavioral terminology. It is important for readers who are new to operant terminology to consider two things. First, the science of behavior might have made an unfortunate choice in terminology: reinforcement, punishment, negative, and positive all have other connotations in the English language. In behavioral terminology, "positive" does not mean good or warm and fuzzy, and "negative" does not mean bad or describe the valence of the consequence. For instance, suppose a boy is deprived of his dad's attention (MO), and then the boy sees his dad is watching TV and also sees the remote control on the table (S^D). He takes the remote and changes the channel (R). The result is a serious smack in the face from his dad. For many people, the smack in the face seems like a punisher, and it was probably intended to be such by the dad. But this interaction can, for some attention-deprived children, actually increase the recalcitrant behavior. In effect, if the boy continues to engage in changing the channel and other defiant behaviors for his dad's attention, then those smacks are actually positively reinforcing. When using these behavior analytic terms, we are describing the *function* of the behavior—that is, the behavior effectively functions to get dad's attention even if that attention consists of a smack in the face—not the value or slang emotional terms that are associated with the events. From a colloquial standpoint, there really isn't anything positive or reinforcing about a child who annoys his dad who in turn hits the child. But using behavioral terminology, since the response frequency has been increased in probability as a result of the presentation of the smack, it is correctly labeled an instance of positive reinforcement.

Recall too that in behavioral terminology "punishment" describes the reduction of the probability of a response following a consequence. For instance, being incarcerated in prison might not be punishment if it does not affect the probability of the behavior that was functionally related to the incarceration. Given the high recidivism rates of some crimes and for some people, prison time is not a punisher according to behavioral terminology. Spanking also may or may not be a punisher. For some people, a spanking may decrease the frequency of the behavior that preceded it (for example, a child telling Mom a fib). However, a spanking may, for some people at some times, increase the frequency of the behavior that preceded it (for example, a lonely man paying a dominatrix and saying, "One more time, please.") In this man's case, his behavior of returning to the dominatrix and saying, "One more time, please," is actually increased by the spanking!

The second thing to consider is the expansive literature about basic behavioral principles. Beyond these simple descriptions of consequences, the analysis of behavior includes discussion about reinforcement schedules, details about the lawfulness of behavior (matching law, law of effect), the effects of deprivation, rule-governed behavior, and different ways to measure responses, to name just a few of the complex influences on human behavior. This primer is just to help you understand these terms as you stroll through this book, and ACT therapists are encouraged to become familiar with the basic behavioral principles describing human action so they can be applied to help the client.

Operant psychology in clinical work. The significant amount of research on these basic operant principles eventually led to ecologically useful second-wave applications. Ogden Lindsley, the person known to have coined the phrase "behavior therapy" in 1954 (see Calkin, 2005), demonstrated that individuals with psychiatric diagnoses could acquire functional repertoires through proper contingency management (Lindsley, 1956, 1963; Skinner, Solomon, & Lindsley, 1954). Teodoro Ayllon and Nathan Azrin forwarded operant psychology's agenda with clinical research on token economies and contingency management (Ayllon, 1963; Ayllon & Azrin, 1964, 1968; Azrin & Nunn, 1973). The applied behavior analysis movement stemmed from works from these early investigators, who showed that operant psychology's four-term contingency could be applied to many overt behavior problems (see Cooper, Heron, & Heward, 1987). These methods can be applicable to an ACT case conceptualization, especially in the area of committed action, which we will discuss in chapters 8 and 15.

The Cognitive Revolution: Primer in Principles and Applications

The more popular part of the second wave was the advancement of cognitive therapies. In 1958, Albert Ellis proposed the first cognitive psychotherapy methods, suggesting that clinicians help their clients by teaching them to alter their thinking. Ellis's theory, currently called rational emotive behavior therapy (REBT), suggests that when a client holds an irrational belief about things that happen in his life, he is more likely to feel negative emotions and to act dysfunctionally. And if he can replace the irrational beliefs with more rational beliefs, then he might behave more appropriately toward desires and experience less negative feelings when presented with adversity. This type of clinical intervention was similarly suggested in the early 1960s by Aaron Beck, who proposed that individuals are often emotionally affected by the way they cognitively distort interpretations of their world, their future, and their self (Beck, 1963; Beck, Rush, Shaw, & Emery, 1979).

The cognitive model. Coincidentally, this part of the second wave can also be talked about with an A-B-C model. Although the different brands of cognitive therapies sometimes use different terminology, the general consensus in cognitive therapy is that there are activating events (A; Ellis, 1975) or actual events (A; Beck et al., 1979) that occur in the environment. These events can be public or private. When an A occurs, individuals then hold certain interpretations or beliefs (B) about the A. When these beliefs (B) about the A are irrational or faulty, this leads to negative and unhealthy consequences (C). Cognitive therapy pioneers suggest that the therapy is founded on rational philosophies, and both Beck and Ellis quote Epictetus (AD 55–138) to demonstrate the legacy of the rational approach: "Man is disturbed not by things, but by the views he takes of them." The philosophical legacy of this approach is also seen in the following quotes that are often used in discussing cognitive therapy:

> The universe is transformation; our life is what our thoughts make it.
>
> —Marcus Aurelius (AD 121–180)

> There is nothing either good or bad but thinking makes it so.
>
> —Shakespeare (1564–1616)

The "correction of misconceptions." Arnold Lazarus (1972), whose work is also found in the first wave, suggested during the cognitive revolution that "the bulk of psychotherapeutic endeavors may be said to center around the correction of misconceptions" (p. 165). This "correction of misconceptions" makes up the bulk of the interventions from the cognitive revolution. Whether the client's negative thoughts are verbally disputed or reality tested experientially, the main idea is to replace the faulty or irrational cognition with an alternate cognition that works better.

In the cognitive therapy approach of Beck and others, the therapist describes how thinking influences feeling, and holds that if a person has certain *cognitive distortions* (such as inaccurate beliefs about the self, others, or the world), he is quite likely to feel negative emotions. This cognitive therapy approach contends that correcting these cognitive distortions through reality testing or reattribution techniques will lead to improved clinical outcomes. For instance, in *Cognitive Therapy of Depression* (Beck et al., 1979), the authors use an example (p. 165) of a clerical worker who has a brief interaction with a nurse where the female nurse says, "I hate medical records," and treats the clerical worker curtly. According to the vignette, the clerical worker reports feeling sadness, slight anger, and loneliness. When the clerical worker is asked to write down the cognitions associated with this experience, the worker writes, "She doesn't like me." The cognitive therapist takes this cognition and shows the client that he is personalizing and making an arbitrary inference about the interaction. The cognitive therapist then attempts to correct these cognitive distortions through reality testing and reattribution. When therapist and client consider other interpretations, the clerical worker may realize that the nurse is just generally unhappy, or that her hatred of medical records is not equivalent to hating medical record clerks. The clerical worker may correct the distortion by recognizing that the nurse is under a lot of pressure or by considering that the nurse is silly for having that attitude because medical records are important to hospital work. Cognitive therapy supposes that changing these types of distorted thoughts by testing their reasonableness or by replacing them with new and more "accurate" (that is, "nondistorted") thoughts will lead to improved clinical outcomes. And this therapeutic endeavor is a powerful intervention, as cognitive therapy has been shown in double-blind placebo research to be as effective as psychiatric medication in improving outcomes for individuals with depression (Casacalenda, Perry, & Looper, 2002), as well as showing positive clinical outcomes for several other clinical concerns (see Nathan & Gorman, 2002).

In Ellis's rational emotive behavior therapy approach, the therapist also describes how thinking influences feelings, and that if a person holds certain *irrational beliefs* (such as rigid, illogical, unhelpful, or inaccurate beliefs about the self, others, or the world), he is quite likely to feel negative emotions. This cognitive therapy approach contends that replacing these irrational beliefs or cognitive distortions through disputation or experiential techniques will lead to improved clinical outcomes. In *A Practitioner's Guide to Rational Emotive Therapy* (Walen, DiGiuseppe, & Dryden, 1992), the authors use an example (p. 146) of a man who is feeling guilty for having yelled at his daughter in the middle of the night because she woke up and was calling for her mother. The dialogue between the client and the therapist shows the client saying, "I went in there and started shaking her, and yelled, 'Stop it, stop it, stop it ... I can't stand it'" [ellipses original]. The REBT clinician notices that the client said that he "can't stand" his daughter's crying and suggests that this is an irrational statement by asking a question.

T[herapist]:   Did you stand it?

C[lient]:   I got through it. I didn't like it.

T[herapist]:   That's right, you didn't like it. But you didn't die, though, right?

C[lient]:   (inaudible murmur)

T[herapist]:	Alright. See, you made an irrational statement to yourself. *I Can't Stand It.* In other words, she must not do this to me. That's what gave you irrational anger…
C[lient]:	…I'm telling myself that I can't stand something. I guess what you're saying is that when I say that, I make myself more angry?
T[herapist]:	Absolutely. You got it! You're the one … you're the author of your own feelings. (p. 148)

The REBT therapist goes on to teach the client that the client's thinking is making him irritate himself about the crying in the middle of the night. The REBT approach would suggest disputing the thought "I can't stand it," and then observing and verbalizing instances where the client "can stand it," and replacing the irrational belief with "I may not like this, but I can stand it." According to REBT, this new, more rational cognition would lead to more functional responses.

Both of the aforementioned cognitive approaches also include the first-wave interventions of exposure and skills training, thus the name: *cognitive behavioral* therapy (CBT). The second-wave pioneers encouraged therapists to maintain structure and have a directive approach to clinical sessions, and also to include doing homework during the week to maintain clinical gains from each session. CBT practitioners also influenced clients to keep daily diaries or thought records to help with reattribution and disputation throughout the 167 hours per week the client wasn't with the therapist. These therapeutic conventions also have a place in third-wave therapies.

These basic tenets of the cognitive therapies dovetailed nicely with traditional office-based psychotherapy because it could remain a talk therapy. And the second-wave pioneers saw the importance of integrating the first-wave approaches and operant psychology with these cognitive therapy methods, and cognitive behavioral therapies began to progress with research that demonstrated their efficacy as treatments for a myriad of clinical concerns. Garnering the empirical support from scholarly investigations and the financial support of managed care, CBT has been established as a powerfully effective force in clinical psychology.

Challenges to the Second Wave

The second wave was certainly robust with important findings and forward movement in establishing evidence-based psychotherapy methods in the health care system. And even though CBT is powerful, there are some theoretical and practical concerns to contend with.

Theory and practice: Ships passing in the night? Despite positive outcome studies, the development of CBT interventions did not come from basic research or established scientific principles, and the treatment continues to rely on hypothetical constructs from cognitive mediational theories. This is a significant departure from the first-wave approach to behavior therapy and impedes the growth of psychology as a natural science. We must carefully consider that CBT has made positive strides in the treatment of many disorders by conceptualizations about altering cognitive schema and disputing irrational beliefs, yet we must also recognize that "schema" and "beliefs" have not been satisfactorily defined or measured. There are numerous outcome studies promoting CBT's efficacy and effectiveness, but there is still cause for concern because the basic theoretical principles that are supposed to underlie the therapy have not been satisfactorily described in ways that are measurable and readily tested through research.

Cognitive therapy is in many ways divorced from cognitive science. At best, the two cross paths every once in a while. Terms like "irrational thoughts," "overgeneralization," and "black-and-white thinking" are standard fare during a CBT discussion, but they are not found readily in the cognitive science literature. These CBT interventions are cognitive insofar as they are about thinking, but the interventions do not have roots in the basic cognitive sciences (Hayes et al., 2006). The interventions were devised from a top-down approach rather than a bottom-up approach. One may ask, "Why is that a problem?" The problem is that research has not shown that the main CBT strategies aimed at changing a person's cognitions have actually been an important component in the CBT protocol. In Dobson and Khatri's (2000) article "Cognitive Therapy: Looking Forward, Looking Backward," the authors review the CBT tenets dating back to the late 1950s. Given almost fifty years of development, when the authors ask, "What are the effective ingredients of cognitive therapy?" they are forced to reply, "[T]his question has no answer at present" (p. 912). They continue to review the literature on depression treatments and admit that "behavioral interventions were as powerful in treating depression as adding any other cognitive dimensions; there was not additive benefit to providing cognitive interventions in cognitive therapy" (p. 913; see Jacobson, N. S., et al., 1996, for the article they were reviewing). Longmore and Worrell's (2007) meta-analysis reviewed cognitive therapy research and suggests "there is little empirical support for the role of cognitive change as causal in the symptomatic improvements achieved in CBT" (p. 173).

In some ways, cognitive behavioral therapy can be looked at much like the work of phlogiston theorists from the eighteenth century. Phlogiston theory was used to explain how fire worked and what it was made of. Essentially these theorists were discussing the essence of fire, and they hypothesized that the structure of all matter contained elements, such as phlogiston, that were activated in order to produce fire. Unfortunately for the model, further research was completed and we now know that fire is a result of oxygen, heat, and fuel. For the sake of brevity, suffice it to say, "phlogiston" is not a part of the chemical makeup of wood or gasoline but was just used as an explanatory fiction. But it is important to consider that even the most fervent advocate of this erroneous phlogiston theory was successful in setting fires. These theorists were capable of lighting their pipes, boiling water in a kettle, and even starting a bonfire, and it all occurred in spite of the absence of phlogiston. A theory can be built around entirely incorrect and hypothetical principles, and the result of the theorist's behavior governed by the theory can still be successful. The CBT literature shows important effects with some populations, but the conscription of hypothetical constructs to describe what is happening in therapy remains a concern.

Nonresponders may require a different approach. Even though the CBT literature shows important effects with some populations, there remain treatment nonresponders who may be helped with different approaches. The National Institute of Mental Health (NIMH) Treatment of Depression Collaborative Research Program (Elkin et al., 1989) took on the Herculean task of comparing cognitive therapy to psychopharmacology and placebo in a large multisite study. After sixteen weeks of treatment, both the cognitive therapy and pharmacological treatment had a positive response rate of approximately 58 percent of the subjects. While this is truly edifying and important to us as clinicians, it is also important to notice that approximately 42 percent of the subjects did not improve significantly. CBT for depression is helpful, and yet CBT clinicians are challenged by the fact that they are not always going to be successful using this approach.

Alternative views about the second-wave change agenda. Another significant challenge to the second wave is that the empirical literature doesn't predict some of what is supposed to be happening with cognitions. For instance, "thought stopping" has been suggested as a treatment in some earlier cognitive psychotherapy approaches (Foa, Davidson, & Frances, 1999; Hackman & McLean, 1975), and also in popular self-help resources (Davis, Eshelman, & McKay, 2000; www.WebMD.com; www.coping.com). The thought-stopping technique appears to be built from the mechanistic principle of removing problematic parts of the system. (See "Mechanism," below, for more on mechanism and psychology.) *Thought-stopping techniques* are used to distract the client from an unwanted, intrusive thought by privately shouting "*stop*" and/or snapping a rubber band around the wrist. Ostensibly this approach will punish the intrusive thinking; however, thought stopping has come to be regarded as a weak intervention in some of the CBT literature (for example, Steketee, 1993). In addition, the empirical literature suggests that thought suppression is not only ineffective but may actually influence a rebound effect, meaning that the unwanted thoughts actually increase in frequency. Wegner, Schnieder, Carter, and White (1987) showed that "thought suppression has paradoxical effects as a self-control strategy, perhaps even producing the very obsession … it is directed against" (p. 5). Research has shown that it is not only ineffective in the long run (Beevers, Wenzlaff, Hayes, & Scott, 1999), but also that if someone tries to suppress a given thought while in a certain mood, that thought is highly likely to return when that mood returns (Wenzlaff, Wegner, & Klein, 1991). So if trying to eliminate thoughts doesn't work very well, what might happen when trying to restructure a thought?

Take for example the phrase "The apple doesn't fall far from the tree." Go ahead and fill in the blank at the end of the next seven words: The apple doesn't fall far from the _____. It is quite likely you said tree. This time, don't say tree. Restructure part of this phrase, which you've heard over and over again. Don't say tree this time: The apple doesn't fall far from the _____. Were you successful?

What did you say, and why did you say it? Many people still hear themselves think the word "tree." But even if you were successful and said something else entirely (like bushel, cart, or phone booth), you chose that other word because it wasn't tree. Methods of restructuring thoughts can still evoke the thought that you are trying to get rid of.

A concern with cognitive restructuring approaches is that the client still contacts the problematic stimuli while emitting the restructured thought. When treating an overly competitive anger client, an REBT therapist may find the client saying something like "I must win" and call that phrase irrational. It is irrational because the thought is not only untrue, but can, for some clients, lead to negative behaviors and emotions. In brief, REBT suggests replacing that "must" with something more rational, such as "would like to." The person may even be cajoled by the therapist that they are "musterbating," which might have a slight punishing effect on those particular "must" responses. But recall the aforementioned thought suppression literature, and consider whether altering one part of the private thought could actually act alone in changing the behavior. Given what we know about rebounding, could "musterbation" truly be stopped in the heat of the mood? Might using the phrase "would like to" as a rational replacement still beget "must" for some folks? This is certainly not to say that REBT interventions do not work, but perhaps the effectiveness comes more from other parts of the REBT package, such as exposure or behavioral homework. The emergence of third-wave behavior therapy was partially influenced by this debate about the effectiveness of cognitive restructuring, and paved the way for "noticing" and "having" thoughts in therapy rather than changing their content.

The Third Wave of Behavior Therapy

Recent research in language and cognition (Hayes, Barnes-Holmes, et al., 2001) and integrative work with other approaches were greatly influential to ushering in the third wave of behavior therapy. Therapy applications such as functional analytic psychotherapy (FAP; Kohlenberg, R. J., & Tsai, 1991), dialectical behavior therapy (DBT; Linehan, 1993), mindfulness-based cognitive therapy (MBCT; Segal, Williams, & Teasdale, 2002), functionally enhanced cognitive therapy (FECT; Kohlenberg, R. J., Kanter, Bolling, Parker, & Tsai, 2002), and behavioral activation therapy (Martell, Addis, & Jacobson, 2001), among others (Borkovec & Roemer, 1994; Jacobson, N. S., & Christensen, 1996; Marlatt, 2002) have moved behavior therapy into a new era. Mindfulness, acceptance, dialectics, spirituality, and the contingent use of the therapeutic relationship are increasingly becoming a part of behavior therapists' clinical approaches.

The third wave of behavior therapy remains a behavior therapy. Recalling Eysenck and Yates's definitions earlier in the chapter, behavior therapy is still rooted in science and is developed through empirical testing. This is not to suggest that ACT and its fellow travelers in the third wave are better than or more effective than therapies from the first two waves, but it should belie criticism that the third-wave therapies aren't behavior therapies or do not have an eye on basing treatment on evidence.

The third wave of behavior therapy and clinical behavior analysis is moving closer to the vision of development of a psychology more adequate in addressing clinical concerns by taking a dimensional rather than categorical/syndromal medical model approach to understanding and treating problems of living. The dimensional approach looks at the spectrum of how a client is functioning in different areas of living rather than pigeonholing symptoms into diagnostic categories (see Hayes, Wilson, Gifford, Follette, & Strosahl, 1996). These third-wave approaches endeavor to treat behavioral problems with behavioral interventions without longing for turnkey cures from pills or using convenient explanatory fictions in case conceptualization. Thus, this approach will have different measures and goals for success. Third-wave approaches reconsider the etiological and diagnostic approach taken by mainstream psychology, which places them in a different position when developing treatment plans. In many ways, psychopathology, treatment, and even the definition of "mental illness" are reconsidered and redefined in the third wave. To date, the third-wave approach shows early promise in dealing with clinical concerns (Hayes et al., 2006).

A Pivotal Philosophical Point

The limited success in the earlier waves' development of an adequate account of cognition set the stage for a fresh philosophical approach to science and an alternate way of thinking about thinking. Some third-wave approaches are founded on functional contextual philosophical assumptions rather than on mechanistic assumptions.

Mechanism

Both the first and second waves can be described as mechanistic in their philosophy. A *mechanistic* model of human behavior can most adequately be described as if the behaving person were a sort of machine that can be understood by describing the discrete parts, workings, interconnections, and forces that act on the machine. For instance, the metaphors of the heart as a pump or of the brain as a computer are mechanistic models for explaining human behavior. Mechanists look at their subject matter as if it naturally has a categorical order; as if, in a psychological event, an antecedent event (A) occurs, turns the cog of the irrational belief (B), which flips the switch of the emotional consequence (C). They then apply this model to other similar psychological events. The statements made in mechanism are evaluated as "true" when those statements correspond to the model. When a scientist has a hypothesis about something and then does an experiment using the more mainstream hypothetico-deductive research methodology (for example, t-tests, ANOVA), the scientist is basically checking if the data correspond with the hypotheses or model of the world. This is what is meant by a correspondence-based "truth criterion." Those fancy words basically say that, in mechanistic views of the world, something is said to be true when it corresponds to a model (Hayes, Hayes, & Reese, 1988; Pepper, 1942).

Mechanism proposes that when a machine isn't working correctly, parts can be swapped out and replaced. Mechanistic psychology approaches suggest that when a faulty cognition, such as "I must win," leads to dysfunctional outcomes for the machine, replacing the "must" with "would like to" can lead to symptom reduction. The aim is to have the client's thinking and behaving correspond to the model way of thinking and behaving (without faulty cognitions). ACT, in contrast, is based on a functional contextual rather than mechanistic philosophical foundation (Hayes et al., 1988; Pepper, 1942).

Functional Contextualism

Now let's just take a moment before charging any further into the philosophy of science. If you promise not to let your eyes glaze over, we'll promise to do what we can to make this useful. These truly are important points for the clinical work. ACT is not offering just techniques to string together in therapy, but rather a new stance and perspective to use while conceptualizing and treating behavioral concerns.

The unit of analysis. *Functional contextualism* focuses on the ongoing act-in-context as the subject matter (as opposed to looking at the subject matter as if it were a machine with parts). The thing being analyzed is an interrelated unit. Functional contextual analyzing focuses on the ongoing behaving of a client and also the environment in which the behaving is occurring. When we talk about the four-term contingency of the motivational operation, the discriminative stimuli, the response, and the consequential stimuli, we are actually talking about a single unit. It is not four different pieces that we are analyzing but rather the unitary event.

- Motivational operation

- Discriminative stimuli

- Response

- Consequential stimuli

} The Unit of Analysis

Truth criteria. In functional contextualism, statements are "true" when they lead to "successful working." The functional contextual scientists are less prone to see if their statements correspond to a model but rather more interested to see if their statements will lead to a desired end. This is why single-subject designs are more attractive to behavior analytic scientists: a baseline is measured, then a variable is altered to see what happens, and then the variable is reversed back to see if the measure of interest returns to baseline. The question "Do my interventions succeed in changing the measure in the desired manner?" is better answered by inductive (single-subject A-B-A designs) rather than deductive (hypothesis-testing) research.

Clinical behavior analysis and functional contextualism. Okay, the phrase "functional contextualism" is just a pair of words ACT therapists use to describe their way of thinking about behavior, and functional contextualism truly is a different way of thinking about the world (and about behavior) as compared to mechanism. It is culturally deviant to look at human behavior this way because many popular views of behavior look at human beings mechanistically. Functional contextualists don't. To reiterate, what we look at is the *ongoing act-in-context. Ongoing* relates that we investigate our subject matter of behavior over a period of time. (Frankly, it's a bit redundant because behaviors must happen over time; behavior is understood as an event unfolding over some period of time rather than at a single point in time.) The *act-in-context* piece is a single phrase. The object of assessment is the pairing of the person's action with a particular environment. We examine the behavior-environment relationship as a whole, not as separate from each other—as in a distinct behavior and detached environment. In functional contextualism, an analysis of behavior is meaningless without a context, just as an environment is meaningless without an organism.

In functional contextualism, psychological events are viewed as interactions between an organism and its environment, which is understood as historically and situationally defined contexts (Hayes, 2004). This means that the current environment and past consequences for behavior have an impact on the person. With an eye on past contingencies and current environmental influences, the functional contextualist aims for successful working as the truth criterion. The aim is to succeed in increasing our ability to describe, predict, and influence behavior. Clinical behavior analysis embraces the goals of description, prediction, and influence of behavior, and clinical behavior analysis is broadly "defined as the application of the assumptions, principles and methods of modern functional contextual behavior analysis to 'traditional clinical issues'" (Dougher & Hayes, 2000, p. 11). Clinical behavior analysis aims to approach those goals with precision, scope, and depth.

Relational frame theory (RFT) is a functional contextual account of human language and cognition, and might be well applied to clinical concerns because basic RFT research suggests how language and cognition, while contributing to human evolutionary survival and success, also lead to much human suffering. RFT will be described more thoroughly in chapter 4. Language and cognition become problematic when individuals become fused with their thoughts in ways that increase experiential avoidance, lead them to follow futile change agendas, and sap vitality. ACT, a clinical application built on basic RFT research, assumes that clinical change occurs when the context of behavior changes toward successful working rather than when the form of behavior changes toward an established model. Thus, rather than emphasizing the form of behavior, the functions and contexts of psychological events are explored. This means that even a client's presenting problem needs to be addressed with a change in the context of the behavior and not necessarily addressed in changing the form of the behavior. ACT therapists might not try to change the frequency, intensity, or duration of certain forms of problems but rather change the context of the so-called problems. For example, for the socially anxious person, anxiety is a context for avoiding social situations. Instead of assuming he must decrease his anxious thoughts and feelings before he can have a social life, he might instead begin to engage with others socially even while having anxious thoughts and feelings. When the aim of therapy is psychological flexibility, perhaps living a life worth living is the clinical target, and not the reduction of certain symptoms.

Valued Living vs. Symptom Reduction

Throughout this chapter, we've looked at the technical and philosophical differences between the three waves of behavior therapy. Another perspective in the ACT approach that separates it from first- and second-wave therapies is the applied goal of increasing psychological flexibility and valued living rather than the mainstream clinical psychology goal of symptom reduction. This is not to say that CBT and other mainstream clinical approaches aren't implicitly aimed at clients' living lives of value, but rather that ACT makes it a main point in the approach.

The empirically supported treatment (EST) literature is clearly important in shaping clinicians' understanding of what works for clients and what doesn't. The purpose of the EST movement is to promote the interventions that have been rigorously investigated and demonstrated to have efficacy with clinical populations. Applied scientists aim to show that certain interventions yield quicker and/or more lasting clinical change, and do so in the hope that research consumers and frontline therapists will adopt these substantiated approaches to affect better change with their clients. The dependent variables in these investigations are usually about symptom reduction. Nathan and Gorman (2002) summarize the research for "treatments that work," and it appears that a main goal of the investigations is to show how ESTs reduce, eliminate, or decrease symptoms better than a control group. This is not to criticize the research but rather to illuminate the fact that much of the randomized control trial (RCT) research aims at decreasing symptoms as the goal. Not surprisingly, this aim at reducing dysfunctional parts of a person's repertoire is mechanistic, and so is the hypothetico-deductive research methodology for most of the RCTs.

Again, the EST literature is particularly rigorous, edifying, and also quite validating to clinical psychology, and we're not planning on criticizing the work. There isn't much bathwater—it's mostly baby. And note that the ACT approach suggests that the *change agenda*—that is, the aim to reduce or eliminate private events—might be problematic too. In the cases where ESTs aren't working for clients, could it be that the clients' unwillingness to have their private events and experiences is the very reason for those experiences occurring? When clients are invited to have their private experiences as they are, fully and without defense, in the service of living their lives the ways they most desire, might following through on that invitation be the real clinical change that we all are aiming for? ACT asks clients, "Can you have the symptom *and* follow your values?" Honestly, which would you rather choose: to never have negative private experiences and also not follow through on your greatest aspirations, or to accept that negative experiences occur while following through on your deepest desires? This is not to say that the ACT therapist relishes unpleasant experiences such as anxiety and depression, and symptoms often do decrease in severity and frequency following an ACT intervention;

however, that's not the primary aim, and ACT interventions aimed solely at reduction of symptoms are likely to be drastically misguided. Instead, the ACT client is challenged to follow through on her greatest aspirations even when doing so might be accompanied by unwanted thoughts, feelings, and sensations (see chapter 14 for more on willingness).

ACT's approach to symptoms, philosophy, cognition, and applied endeavors may make it seem different from traditional and cognitive behavioral therapies, but it was born from the same tradition. Clinical behavior analysis and its fellow third-wave surfers maintain the time-honored commitment to science and evidence-based treatment. In the context of behavior therapy, new data and intractable old problems have set up an opportunity for something new, and ACT may be one of the new mutations to be selected to fit these challenges.

Checking In

Take this opportunity to conceptualize how the first and second waves would have treated Shandra and Rick.

How might the third wave of behavior therapy conceptualize their cases?

Now you have a basic understanding of behavior therapy. Next we will turn to learning the rudiments of ACT, starting with the functional analysis of clinically relevant behavior and other assessment issues.

CHAPTER 3

Functional Analysis and ACT Assessment

Behavioral assessment has a deep and broad history in psychology. Assessment can take many forms, given the client's presentation and the practitioner's goals and assumptions. While certain assessment procedures have their place in clinical work (for example, intellectual evaluation and genograms), this chapter will focus on assessment in the pursuit of ACT case conceptualization. Before learning ACT case conceptualization, the therapist must be familiar with the elements of behavioral assessment. Assessment by clinicians should aim toward having high treatment utility (Hayes, Nelson, & Jarrett, 1987), which is "the degree to which assessment is shown to contribute to beneficial treatment outcome" (p. 963). For therapists using a functional contextual approach, the central point of clinical assessment is to help the client reach relevant goals. Assessment helps the clinician to select target behaviors to be addressed and also to determine if a treatment strategy is working. In this chapter, we will discuss how ACT-based functional assessment differs from mainstream assessment, and how behavior analysis and functional contextualism inform assessment in order to aid in case conceptualization. If you are not familiar with functional assessment, there are undoubtedly some terms in this chapter that will be unfamiliar to you, and we have kept it as uncomplicated as possible. Understanding the basics of functional assessment will surely facilitate understanding the remainder of this volume.

Structural vs. Functional Approaches to Assessment

ACT aims to expand behavioral repertoires and foster greater psychological flexibility. This approach is relevant for individuals exhibiting experiential avoidance and clinical concerns that diminish the ability to live a vital and values-driven life. We will narrow our focus here to clinical assessment directly related to these aims. The traditional use of interviews and questionnaires is important in ACT assessment. However, ACT assessment departs from the mainstream in its aim of understanding the function of an individual's behavior in her own environment rather than comparing that behavior to group norms or a standardized checklist of "symptoms."

The Structural Approach

Structuralism basically states that when there is a malformation in the structure or the makeup of an organism, then problems will manifest because of the flawed formation of the foundation. This approach is characteristic of the medical model, and in biomedical pursuits, structuralist thinking can certainly produce successful outcomes.

Structural Approaches to Medicine

If a patient has certain malformed structures, an operation, medication, or other treatments to repair the structure can be health restoring or lifesaving. For example, if a child is born with a congenital heart defect that obstructs blood flow, then this malformation can lead to dizziness, fainting, headaches, chest pain, or other health disorders. There is a problem with the structure, and corrective surgery such as balloon angioplasty or other surgical methods can be used to repair the physical structure. Other examples of health problems arising from problems in the biological structure include the presence of microorganisms, high cholesterol and plaque buildup, and broken bones. These are all problems that can be discussed as structural problems, and they can sometimes be repaired by addressing the form of the problem.

In behavioral health, it still is possible that certain structural treatments can influence better behavioral health. When a person is acting irritable and has poor concentration, proper medical assessment may reveal that the person has obstructive sleep apnea, which influences problematic behaviors during the day. These behavioral concerns stemming from sleep apnea can be reduced by surgically changing the structure of the person's airways. In this case, structural change can lead to improved behavioral functioning.

Psychopharmacological interventions can also be used to address structural change during treatment of psychological problems. Medication that helps reduce, increase, or alter the production and reuptake of certain neurotransmitters can be seen as changing the structural makeup of the client's biochemistry in the service of influencing behavior. Depending on the treatment question and context, structuralism can be an effective approach.

Structural Approaches to Psychology

Much of early psychology and the current mainstream approaches assessment and treatment from a structuralist point of view. Freud's theory of the id, ego, and superego promotes structuralism because it implies that the formation of these structures of the psyche can cause psychological disorders. Psychoanalytic techniques aimed at altering the structures, by reducing psychic energy cathected or blocked in one of these three structures, were hypothesized to lead to better psychological health. Personality theories focusing on different parts of the person or entities that influence behavior and psychological well-being are very likely structural theories.

The *Diagnostic and Statistical Manual of Mental Disorders,* especially the earlier editions, appear to endorse a structuralist approach. In the *DSM's* effort to avoid allegiance to any particular theoretical orientation, it has become slightly less structural over time. Yet practitioners use the *DSM* to diagnose clients as if they have a particular disorder, as if it were a formal, internal, or inherent quality of the person, that is, a form of pathology rather than a pattern of behavior.

In those cases, the clinician is using the *DSM* in a structural manner, and that can lead to problematic case conceptualization. For instance, a teenager doesn't have a conduct disorder in the same way that he might have a broken clavicle or a streptococcal infection. Let's say Johnny exhibits aggressive and antisocial behavior in the context of established rules, with a comparatively high degree of frequency and duration, and this situation results in his not contacting typical, long-term academic, social, or vocational reinforcers. He does not have a structure per se to be repaired in this situation. It is unlikely that a surgical or chemical intervention to his makeup will ethically and appropriately address his behavior.

Clinicians will find it more useful to talk about Johnny's ongoing behaving in the context of his life. However, thanks to the limitations of language and our tendency to use descriptive terms as if they were causal events, clinicians are often stuck talking about the "thingness" of his ongoing stream of acting. Johnny's ongoing responding gets boiled down to a label that may be reified or treated as though it had a material, concrete existence. Diagnostic labels such as "conduct disorder" can be used in an unhelpful manner, especially when they become reified or defined circularly: "How do we know Johnny has conduct disorder? Because he vandalizes the community, sets fires, and uses weapons." "Why does he vandalize, set fires, and use weapons? Because he has conduct disorder." In Johnny's case, a structural view of the problem misses the other very powerful influences on his behavior: the antecedents and consequences of his behavior. A functional view specifically focuses on these causes of behavior. Johnny's aggressive and socially inappropriate behaviors are a function of how his environment is set up and then consequates his responses. Let's take a look at the functional approach and then return to Johnny.

The Functional Approach

According to *Merriam-Webster's Collegiate Dictionary* (11th ed.), one definition of *function* is "the action for which a … thing is specially fitted or used or for which a thing exists: purpose (p. 507)." The law of effect says that behavior is a function of its consequences. When clinical behavior analysts talk about the function of behavior, they are speaking about the antecedent and consequential stimulus events that increase the likelihood of that class of behavior. Using the definition of function given above, they are talking about what selects the behavior's likelihood to be fitted in that situation, or less technically, how that behavior is used, and why it exists. In other words, what is the purpose of the behavior?

Purpose

The dictionary definition given above suggests that function is similar to *purpose*. Skinner (1953) says, "purpose is not a property of the behavior itself; it is a way of referring to the controlling variables" (p. 88). For behavior analysts, those controlling variables are considered the consequences of the behavior, and the antecedents that are correlated with consequences. According to Skinner, "Instead of saying that a man behaves because of consequences which *are* to follow his behavior, we simply say that he behaves because of the consequences which *have* followed similar behavior in the past" (p. 87, Skinner's emphasis). Colloquially we say that people do things for a future goal, but the future cannot control the present. It is because of an established learning history that responding in the present functions appropriately in the ongoing "now." If the organism is reliably contacting reinforcers in the now, then over many observations it may appear that the responses are under the control of reinforcers in the future, but it is actually the past conditioning history that is happening in the present observation. Put another way, the future is the past brought to bear on the present (Hayes, 1992).

Functional Considerations

To contrast the functional approach with the structural approach, consider that "[f]unctionalist approaches to behavior de-emphasize the form that the problem takes and shift attention to the purposes that the behavior might serve for the individual" (Sturmey, 1996, p. 5). Looking at the purpose of behavior is at the heart of operant psychology (Skinner, 1974). "[U]nderstanding behavior as being a sample of the problem rather than a sign of some other underlying condition, is an important characteristic of functional assessment" (Follette, Naugle, & Linnerooth, 2000, p. 102). When one espouses that "biting your nails means you are nervous" or "chewing ice is a sign of sexual frustration," the person is conjecturing rather that looking at the behavior. A relaxed and sexually satisfied person can calmly bite her nails in order to trim them or chew ice because she hasn't had a drink of water for some time.

Let's go back to the example of Johnny's hostile behaving, and look at it with a functional behavior analytic approach. The way he is acting may be negatively reinforced by a reduction in or removal of task demands from authority figures, and a reduction in aversive interactions with his parents. In other words, these adults find his behavior so egregious that they don't ask him to do mature tasks because it will rile him up. The results of his vandalizing and bullying may be so aversive to his authority figures that they actually just leave him alone. In this way, for Johnny, the consequence of his actions lead to a less pressured lifestyle, so when a task demand is put on him, he will more likely respond with destructive behavior, such as fire setting or truancy. In a way, the probability of his behavior is reinforced (made more likely) because it helps him avoid these task demands and avoid talking to his parents.

His antisocial behaviors may also be positively reinforced. Such "conduct-disordered" behaving might be consequated by access to stolen goods, verbal kudos from his peers, and more opportunities to contact other reinforcers (sleeping in, watching more TV). His problem behavior is maintained as long as it has "purpose."

There is an alternate possibility that in the past his appropriate behaviors were put on extinction or punishment schedules. Perhaps his history of appropriate conduct was ignored by his parents, or his attempts at affection and achievement were rebuked and ridiculed. His socially appropriate conduct was not maintained by the consequences, and because a person's life is a continuous series of behaving, there is time and opportunity for a new repertoire to slowly emerge and develop as an operant. Ironically, his "conduct-disorder" repertoire is also probably reinforced by the negative attention that he gets from family and teachers who are trying to stop the behavior. For the functional contextualist, these ongoing acts-in-context are important to the analysis.

Understand that functional contextualists and ACT therapists do use diagnostic terms like conduct disorder. Given certain contexts (like working with Johnny), it is important to use the acknowledged terminology. Using the structurally based terms also gives the therapist a chance to practice behavioral flexibility. Using *DSM* terms isn't anathema in clinical behavior analysis. After all, it can lead to successful working if success is defined by writing understandable interdisciplinary team notes, billing insurance companies, and communicating to caregivers.

Functional Analysis in Clinical Work

Functional analysis is an investigation of the environmental causes of behavior. Clinical behavior analysis has attempted to examine the environmental causes of psychopathology for some time. Skinner (1953) proposed that ineffective and dangerous human behavior can be a result of environmental influences. Salzinger (1975) maintained that "abnormal behavior is no more unlawful than so-called 'normal behavior,'" (p. 215), and Lewinsohn and his colleagues (Lewinsohn, Youngren, & Grosscup, 1979; Lewinsohn, Hoberman, Teri, & Hautzinger, 1985) developed a functional model of depression as well as a functionally based approach to the treatment of depression (Lewinsohn, Munoz, Youngren, & Zeiss, 1986; Brown, R. A., & Lewinsohn, 1984).

Although behavior analysis as a field is attempting to develop more incisive procedures for exploring the causes of behavior, no unified method of functional analysis has been widely accepted. Kanfer and Grimm (1977) and Carr (1977) made pioneering contributions to this endeavor, and both contributions suggest that clinically relevant responses are plainly a function of problematic consequences and antecedents. Approaches for performing functional analyses have been described by many authors (see Carr, Landon, & Yarbrough, 1999; Iwata, Dorsey, Slifer, Bauman, & Richman, 1994; Miltenberger, 2001; Paclawskyj, Matson, Rush, Smalls, & Vollmer, 2000). Here we will take a look at a number of important functional analysis principles as they apply to ACT.

Analyzing Consequences

The ACT therapist should be continually wondering about the function of the client's target behavior during initial case conceptualization and throughout treatment, asking, "What is the 'purpose' of the target behavior?" The major focus is on the positively or negatively reinforcing consequences of the client's behavior. Responses can be classified as any of four types of consequential control: tangible reinforcement, social attention, physical/automatic reinforcement, and task avoidance/escape functions. Complex human behavior is multiply caused, and therefore the contingencies can include a combination of these four categories. An in-depth look at functional analysis concepts and methods is beyond the scope of this book, and there is still value in taking a closer look at each of these functions for the purposes of applying ACT in practice. For further material on adding methods of functional analysis to case conceptualization, see Cooper, Heron, and Heward (1987) and Catania (1992).

Tangible Reinforcement

Behavior governed by the consequential presentation of physical items is said to have "tangible functions." For example, searching the beach with a metal detector may be said to be governed by the tangible items found during this activity. For some, the sandy treasures found can have reinforcing properties. If the person continues beachcombing as a result of finding of coins and jewelry, the behavior has tangible functions. Can you think of other types of contingencies that might maintain beachcombing even if the person never finds any treasures? (See next section for answers.)

For a more clinically relevant example, let's look at young Johnny again. One of the reasons he may be called conduct disordered is because he frequently robs people at knifepoint and steals old ladies' purses. These responses may be maintained by the acquisition of goods and money, both of which are tangible, concrete items that can have reinforcing properties. Consider that Johnny is deprived of certain items like dollar bills and the things they buy (MO) and he sees a woman with a fancy purse (S^D). He runs up and steals the purse from the lady (R). As a result, there is a consequential change in his environment, namely, the acquisition of dollar bills (S^{R+}). (These abbreviations and symbols were introduced in chapter 2 and will be discussed further in the next few sections.)

MO
(Deprived of money)

S^D •   **R**   → S^{R+}
(Woman with fancy purse)   •   Steals purse →   Acquires money

---

If there is an increased probability that he will steal in the presence of ladies with purses during his state of financial deprivation (and deprivation of things money buys), we can say that the acquisition of money was a tangible reinforcer. He could, of course, be purse snatching for other reasons (to impress his peers, to escape boredom, or a combination of these) and that is why we analyze the functions. If there were only one function of behavior, analysis would not be needed.

Social Attention Functions

Frequently people will engage in behavior just to gain the attention of other people. Actors in a community drama club, for example, may volunteer to put on Shakespeare's plays simply to gain the approval and admiration of people in their town. We asked you in the previous section what might keep a beachcomber combing even if nothing were found. The answer? Social attention functions. Suppose a young man meets a woman while using his metal detector by the shoreline. The conversation and attention from the woman (as a consequence for his going to the beach with his interesting metal detector) may reinforce his beach-visitation responses. He continues to go to the beach despite not finding coins and jewelry, because of the social attention from his new girlfriend. So even if he didn't find any valuable tangible treasures, he might continue beachcombing for the treasured social attention.

In the example of Johnny, we discussed the social reinforcement of his destructive behaviors. It is possible that his illegal behavior is reinforced by the respect and admiration of his fellow delinquents. Esteem and appreciation are not the only types of attention that can serve as a reinforcing consequence. Even disrespectful attention filled with contempt can maintain a person's behavior. (This is sometimes called negative attention, which colloquially refers to attention that is critical or punitive, and is not a technical term in behavior analysis.) Johnny might continue his antisocial behavior just to get attention from his dad, who has stopped talking to him otherwise, even if the only attention he receives from his father is insults.

A functional analysis can also help us understand the self-injurious behavior of an individual with a developmental disability. If head banging is frequently followed by attention from a caretaker who runs over asking him to stop (and not followed by any other measurable stimulus changes), we can say attention maintains the response.

Reflect on the behavior of some of your own clients or acquaintances. Do you know people who are overdramatic or flamboyant? Could it be that their ostentatious behavior is governed more by the leers, jeers, and sneers of other people rather than by their "personality" or because they have a histrionic personality disorder? Are there people you know who work very hard at an underpaid job and stay committed to their vocation because of the love and appreciation they receive? (Do you know any homemakers?) Consider that individuals in given contexts will engage in responses just because, in the past, those responses led to behavioral changes on the part of other people. Their behavior is governed by social attention functions.

Physical and Automatic Functions

Not surprisingly, there are sensory reinforcers for some responses. Behaviors generate tactile, visual, gustatory, and auditory stimulation that can maintain the frequency of responses (Rincover & Devany, 1982). Olfactory, kinesthetic, and proprioceptive stimulation can also influence responding. Actions influenced by the sensory stimulation from the environment are said to have physical functions. For example, after dining alone, it is probable that eating a cheesecake dessert is governed by the sensory event of tasting the pastry. As another example, drinking beer can have pleasant sensory consequences too (not that your abstemious authors would know this firsthand!). Although you might guess that for some people, beer drinking has social functions—and, as we will soon discuss, beer drinking can have escape functions, too—for some folks, drinking can have a combination of physical, social, and escape/avoidance functions: the taste of the beer, the company of friends, and the opportunity to forget about workday stress can all cohere as the purpose of their drinking.

Some actions, such as whistling a tune while walking alone or rubbing your own temples during a headache, can be said to have automatic functions. Responses that directly produce their own reinforcers not mediated by other people or external events can be said to be *automatic reinforcers*. Skinner (1953) did say that "part of the universe is enclosed within the organism's own skin" (p. 257), and that consequences can occur as "private events" and can be part of natural science endeavors, such as functional analyses. The individual banging his head mentioned in the previous section might be banging his head simply for the consequential change in stimulation he feels on his forehead. Do you crack your knuckles while alone in the car or clear your throat when you wake up in the morning? Can you think of anything else you do for the solitary virtue that it just feels good? (And if you can't think of anything, ask your significant other; these behaviors may be so automatic that you don't notice them. It's a good bet that your significant other notices you scratch your rear end, clear your throat, twirl your hair, and so on.) Those behaviors have automatic functions.

If you are trying to tease out physical functions from automatic functions with your ACT client, we suggest reconsidering the purpose of your analysis. Remember that your aim is toward successful working. Functional analysis was forged in the realm of applied behavior analysis for individuals with developmental disabilities. Because of this, the client's verbal behavior might not have engendered any clinical concerns. Sensory reinforcers do influence our clients' relevant responses, so they should be part of our analysis. Physical/automatic functions may be involved with our talk therapy clients in cases like inappropriate masturbation, overeating, or substance abuse. It is also quite probable that the language-able clients are evaluating their physical/automatic consequences as aversive and engaging in problem solving in order to get rid of these difficulties. Let's discuss how such avoidance and escape functions are important to ACT.

Avoidance or Escape Functions

As discussed earlier, negative reinforcement describes an environment-behavior relationship when there is an increased probability of a given behavior that contingently removes or diminishes relevant aversive environmental stimuli.

Escape. Catania (1992) defined *escape* as "the termination of an aversive stimulus by a response" (p. 374). If Johnny is at his high school and then cuts class after third period because he is fed up after negative interactions with his teachers, his behavior has an escape function.

Avoidance. In contrast, *avoidance* is "the prevention of an aversive stimulus by a response" (Catania, 1992, p. 364). When Johnny stays home altogether the next day and doesn't come into contact with teachers at all and therefore has no negative interactions with them, we can suppose that his behavior has avoidance functions.

Experiential avoidance. For ACT work, we will focus a great deal on the avoidance piece, especially because experiential avoidance is the target of interventions aimed at increasing psychological flexibility. "*Experiential avoidance* is the phenomenon that occurs when a person is unwilling to remain in contact with particular private experiences (for example, bodily sensations, emotions, thoughts, memories, behavioral predisposition) and takes steps to alter the form or frequency of these events and the contexts that occasion them" (Hayes et al., 1996, p. 1154, emphasis added). The coiners of the phrase "experiential avoidance" include escape as part of the definition, and give examples of how substance abuse, obsessive-compulsive disorder (OCD), panic disorder with agoraphobia, and borderline personality disorder can be conceptualized as experiential avoidance. We invite you to consider the following case examples of clinical problems maintained by experiential avoidance functions.

■ Case Study: Roberta

Roberta is a decorated employee at a Veterans Administration hospital. Her skills as a data technician are unparalleled, and she is able to perform her job well even though her social skills are impaired. She reports that she is "painfully shy" and resists making presentations to coworkers. In fact, she turned down a promotion as a Web-based information technology trainer for the VA because she would be asked to monitor and make public responses to a Listserv. She said she is afraid of meeting new people, won't go to the grocery store because she fears that "everyone is staring" at her, and is reluctant to make phone calls, even to service representatives at utility companies. She does have a close network of social contacts, primarily family (similar-aged siblings and cousins).

Roberta exhibits a persistent and marked fear of interpersonal contexts and performance evaluations, which causes her significant social and occupational impairment. Given her presentation, a clinician could diagnose her with social anxiety disorder. Note that a criterion for this disorder is that "feared social or performance situations are *avoided* or else are endured with intense anxiety or distress" (American Psychiatric Association [APA], 2000, p. 417, emphasis added). Recall that a functional contextualist would not say she has this disorder, but rather that she exhibits this collection of responses within given important contexts. This is not just splitting hairs or abuse of jargon, but a useful way of considering her behavior as governed by environmental events that may be altered by a therapist.

Before going further, please recognize that we wouldn't diagnose someone with this disorder if they chose to avoid meeting a known sociopath, refused to be physically leered at by a group of strangers, or habitually hung up on rude telemarketers. Although the latter three avoidance responses are formally similar to Roberta's behaviors, we are not concerned with acts alone but acts-in-context. The relevant environmental stimuli speak to whether or not avoidance is clinically relevant.

In her social history assessment, Roberta reports having always been a wallflower and mostly being happy socializing with her extended family. She also reports no recollection of ever experiencing anything severely embarrassing and doesn't recall any public humiliation in her life. This lack of direct traumatic experiences is a fairly regular clinical observation, and "across most of the anxiety disorders, finding a traumatic event to account for etiology—with the exception of … PTSD …—is unusual" (Forsyth, 2000, p. 158; see also Lazarus, 1984; Menzies & Clarke, 1995; Mineka & Zinbarg, 1996). To put a finer behavior analytic point on it, "[T]he life of a clinically anxious person may thus be influenced by iterations and reiterations of public and private events with reactive properties traceable to initiating conditions only through an almost fractal pathway involving the processes of stimulus generalization, derived relational responding, and transformation of stimulus functions" (Friman, Hayes, & Wilson, 1998, p. 143). To summarize, trauma isn't the only way to develop an anxiety disorder. A history of multiple social interactions along with verbal evaluations of antecedents and outcomes (for example, "I felt anxious and that's bad" or "I was rejected and I am afraid to be rejected again") can also influence anxiety responses in the absence of a traumatic event.

The careful assessor might probe for a behavioral deficit in social skills and prescribe training to remediate this concern. But recall that Roberta does have interpersonal relationships with her family. Training in initiating social contact is still certainly a treatment option, but there is also more to consider in this case because she isn't saying she can't engage with others; she is saying she won't engage others because she is afraid. In addition to a potentially underdeveloped social repertoire, she also has a firmly developed avoidance repertoire. Note that even though she is a computer whiz, she won't even proctor an online course for work, which her boss said could be done from the solitary comfort of her own office. To reiterate, she is avoiding a pay raise even though she's only asked to continue working in an environment with a computer; no face-to-face contact is involved. Where might the direct, historical, aversive experience be with that? After all, she already works with computers all day.

Her resistance to the promotion and to other people is very likely a result of her avoiding the private experiences, such as thoughts and feelings, that come along with interacting with others. She might say, "I'm too much of a pinhead to run a Listserv" or "People are just out to screw me. I'm better off staying away from them." She might also feel her heart rate rise and feel nauseated when deciding about going out in public. These are aversive experiences, and staying home, being a wallflower, and rejecting career opportunities are all in the service of avoiding the private events.

And aren't her "solutions" part of her problem? When her coworker takes the promotion that she turned down, isn't she more prone to interpret that as evidence that people are out to screw her? After years of sitting alone in the VA cafeteria because she is guided by these verbal rules, isn't she just that much more likely to be treated poorly by office mates, which in turn perpetuates her verbal evaluation of others as aversive? What if she could recognize that these are merely thoughts and temporary physiological events? What if she could accept the feelings, defuse from the thoughts, and commit to the values that helped her develop her current and otherwise fulfilling lifestyle as a competent data tech and integrated member of her family instead of following this verbally mediated avoidance repertoire?

■ Case Study: Anton

Consider a case different in topography but similar in function. Anton was a victim of clergy molestation as a young boy. He is plagued by thoughts of guilt, such as "I should have told my dad" and "I could have stopped this bastard from hurting all the others," and also self-denigration: "I deserved it" and "I am nothing." He also gets psychogenic throat and stomach pains that occasion vivid flashbacks of the abuse events. Anton says there are days when he tries to convince himself that he is okay despite it all by telling himself, "I was just a little boy," "It can't be my fault," and "I didn't deserve this." Those days are the most troublesome because "it's like a constant war inside my head."

As an adult, he has been through a series of jobs, usually quitting or getting fired because of his alternating hyperactive and lethargic behavior. He supports himself by selling methamphetamine. He says, "Not only do I rake in the cash, but the lifestyle is a rush. Keeps my mind off shit, ya know?" When the flashbacks become intense, he drinks large amounts of vodka to help him forget. While intoxicated, he and his female "customers" engage in weekend-long binges of substance abuse and unconventional sex practices. When he sobers up, he is faced with more guilt and self-denigration, perpetuating his "solution."

His substance abuse and high-risk behavior are in the service of avoiding private events. Anton is obviously unwilling to remain in contact with his bodily sensations, emotions, thoughts, and memories, and takes extreme steps to alter the form, frequency, and situations that occasion these events. What if Anton's therapist could show him that his solution is just more of the problem? From there, perhaps he could learn that he is separate from his verbal content, and his therapist could gently and compassionately help him notice that thoughts could be just experienced or had, and feelings noticed, and this could be done in the service of living a vital life by executing response-ability right now. Anton is not responsible for his problems in the sense of causing them, and he can take "response-ability" for the direction of his life by changing his responses to difficult thoughts and feelings in this sense he is response-able.

■ Case Study: Blake

Blake exhibits behavior related to schizophrenia, paranoid-type criteria. He is twenty-four years old and was diagnosed with schizophrenia during his freshman year of college. He believed his roommates were reading his e-mail, and soon he believed his e-mail was available to everyone on campus. He was kicked out of the dormitory after he destroyed his roommates' computers. He was hospitalized and, after his release, had assault charges filed against him after he threw a toxic substance at his chemistry professor during a laboratory class. (Blake believed that the professor was trying to poison him with toxic fumes.) The charges were later dropped. Then he was expelled.

Since being expelled from school, Blake has been hospitalized eight times. He lived with his parents for a while, and they kicked him out of their home three years ago because they feared for the safety of their other children after Blake threatened them while acutely psychotic and delusional. Today Blake lives in a hotel room rented by the month. This is his fifth housing placement in three years. He receives disability income. He has held a series of jobs and reports that he would like to be employed full-time.

Each time he is hospitalized, the cyclical pattern is similar: He leaves the hospital with antipsychotic medication and a plan for outpatient treatment. He has a housing placement and sometimes gets a part-time job. He stops taking his medication, then misses appointments with his treatment providers. He becomes delusional and sometimes he experiences command hallucinations where voices order him to harm others. He drinks to lessen the intensity of the voices. He quits his job or leaves his home or threatens people he lives or works with. He is hospitalized again.

The criteria for Blake's type of schizophrenia are that a person experiences perse-cutory delusions, auditory hallucinations, and, unlike other subtypes of schizophrenia, negative symptoms are absent (APA, 2000). The primary intervention for treatment of schizophrenia is pharmacotherapy. There is much research on biological causes of schizophrenia and biological causes dictate a biological cure. Some clients also receive psychosocial interventions including skills training, cognitive therapy, and assertive community treatment.

Considered functionally, "schizophrenia" is not a useful descriptor. If we consider Blake's delusional beliefs and hallucinations as target clinical concerns, first-wave behav-ioral approaches might aim to instruct him not to talk about delusional thought content. If this were successful, he would experience fewer negative social consequences. Skills training might be used to teach him "symptom management skills" such as distraction and self-soothing for coping with auditory hallucinations.

Cognitive theories of delusional beliefs posit that delusional beliefs function to maintain self-esteem (Bentall, 2001); that is, the individual's self-esteem is preserved if he believes that he has failed because others wish to harm him rather than because he is a failure. Cognitive interventions for delusional beliefs emphasize verbal challenges to beliefs and behavioral tests of delusional beliefs (Kingdon & Turkington, 1994). In Blake's case, a therapist might challenge a delusional belief—such as a belief that his landlord is stealing from him—by asking him to provide evidence for that belief and disputing the evidence Blake provides. As a test, he may be asked to leave money out on a day the landlord is scheduled to visit to see if the landlord steals it. The goal is to change the content of Blake's beliefs.

Considered in terms of emotional avoidance, a functional assessment suggested that Blake was engaging in several forms of emotional avoidance. First, he stopped taking his medication because he did not want to be mentally ill and taking his medication was related to mental illness and reminded him of his mental illness. When he stopped taking medication, he had fewer thoughts about himself as a mentally ill person. Unfortunately he also had more delusional thoughts.

Blake also appeared to engage in avoidant behavior around auditory hallucinations. He drank or followed command hallucinations "to make them stop talking." Considered functionally, the hallucinations are not seen as the problem. Instead the relationship between the hallucinations and overt behavior is considered problematic. Hallucinations can be treated as similar to any thoughts Blake might have, and defusion and acceptance strategies can be used by the clinician (Bach & Hayes, 2002).

With respect to delusional beliefs, one fruitful approach can be to explore the rela-tionships among Blake's symptoms, his overt behavior, and his desired life outcomes. He would like to be employed and he acknowledges that when he stops taking his medi-cation, his symptoms interfere with his functioning. He avoids thinking of himself as "crazy" by not taking medication, and then he actually behaves in a "crazy" manner and loses jobs, friends, and apartment leases. Defusion can also be used to target responses to delusional beliefs. Considered functionally, instead of seeing a delusional belief as a problem to be eliminated, the clinician can explore Blake's behavior in relation to his symptoms. Defusion can be used to change Blake's relationship to his symptoms so he relates to the process rather than content of his symptoms. He also avoids paranoid beliefs by acting in accordance with the content. He can get rid of the thought that "they're trying to harm me" if he quits his job or attacks the threatening other "harmer." In contrast, defusion can also be useful for distancing him from the content of delusions. His thought content does not have to change if he can relate to it differently.

What if Blake could see schizophrenia as a problem that affects cognitive processes and learn to relate to verbal content differently? What if he were willing to be present with avoided content and no longer needed to avoid the thought "I'm crazy?" What if he accepted rather than avoided or tried to change content?

Checking In

Consider your own experience: are there ways in which you behave primarily to avoid unwanted thoughts or feelings?

- For instance, do you say yes when you want to say no or quickly avert your eyes from the charity worker soliciting your donation so you won't feel guilty?

- Do you avoid disagreeing with others because you will feel anxious if you do?

- Do you turn down a party invitation because you don't know many people attending and that would be uncomfortable?

- How do you engage in experiential avoidance?

- We will revisit experiential avoidance problems throughout the book.

Analyzing Antecedents

It's fairly obvious that events that happen before a response can have influence on people's behavior. Very simply, things happen and we react to them. You encounter a stop sign before applying your brakes at an intersection. But most people think that what is happening in the environment is the direct cause of the subsequent behavior, as if a person were a billiard ball: when the cue ball hits him, he moves. We hope that our discussion of consequences from the behavior analytic point of view illustrated an additional view that a history of consequences has strong influences on the probability of responses. Stopping at the stop sign isn't caused by the stop sign; it is governed by a history of consequential kudos from our driving instructors and the avoidance of traffic violation fines. However, this knowledge of consequential control does not relegate antecedents as unimportant, for they are critical variables to functional analyses. In behavior analysis, there are different categories for defining environmental events as antecedents, and we'll discuss setting events, motivational operations, and stimulus control as they relate to ACT work.

Setting Events

In an analysis of behavior, the stimuli that occur just before and just after the response (that is, temporally contiguous stimuli) are critical to the analysis. The overarching, broader contingencies also belong in a thorough functional analysis. Kantor (1959) posited that "setting factors" were the circumstances, such as stimulus and response functions, that had been developed through past environment-behavior interaction that had a more global effect on behavior. *Setting events* are historically established and progressing environmental stimuli arranging the relevant contingencies that impact behavior. Bijou and Baer (1961) maintain that "a setting event is a stimulus-response interaction, which simply because it has occurred will affect other stimulus-response relationships which follow it" (p. 21).

Suppose your thirty-year-old client received a large inheritance when he was twenty-five years old. His five-year history of stimulus-response relationships with respect to this windfall has likely set the stage for his current behavioral repertoire. There are broad and long-standing implications involved with his financial situation. He has greater access to material reinforcers, he might have experienced interpersonal difficulties because of his change in financial standing, and what used to be reinforcing (a simple dinner at home) might not have the same kind of sway over his behavior as what he currently has access to (a gourmet meal at a fancy restaurant). His socioeconomic status is a setting event.

Therapists can arrange setting factors to evoke trust with the client by maintaining a relaxing waiting room, keeping appointments, and setting boundaries. Establishing a steadfast stimulus-response history of interpersonal interactions and providing a safe environment is a way to utilize setting factors in therapy.

Expanded contextual factors, such as a history of abuse, becoming a parent, getting a certain kind of education, or living in a particular village, all have antecedent impact on a person's response probabilities and should be contemplated in a functional analysis.

Motivational Operations

Motivational operations (MO)—also known as establishing operations (EO)—are setting events that can be defined with greater precision and specificity. Keller and Schoenfield (1950) coined the term *establishing operation*, and according to Michael (1993) it is defined as "an environmental event, operation, or stimulus condition that affects an organism by momentarily altering (a) the reinforcing effectiveness of other events, and (b) the frequency of occurrence of the type of behavior that had been consequated by those other events" (p. 58). In other words, antecedent variables temporarily modify how effective a consequence will be on behavior, and they actually impact the probability of emitting a response. Setting events are capable of the same results, and they are typically considered less measurable or manipulable than MOs.

The oft-used example of a motivational operation is food deprivation. Lab rats are often kept at below 80 percent of their free-feeding weight before being put in the operant chamber for a good reason: when food deprived, they are motivated to respond. The food deprivation alters the effectiveness of the food pellets, and thereby assists in evoking the operantly shaped lever-pressing responses. Imagine what would happen if behavior analysts were doing experiments with rats and pigeons that were satiated prior to the investigation. By withholding food from the animal, the experimenter contrives an EO that ensures that the animal will respond at a high rate. The same can be done with water, shelter, ambient temperature, and social contact.

States of intoxication can also serve as a motivational operation. Think about how someone can be at a dance club for hours without dancing while they are slowly consuming alcohol. The alcohol consumption can have reinforcer establishing and evocative effects for the dancing behavior. The dance floor was available for a while, but it's not until the establishing operation of intoxication is in place that the person starts to do the hustle.

Emotions and mood states of a client can be motivational operations if they alter the effectiveness of typical reinforcers and influence the frequency of a response class. A depressed mood potentially participates in the anhedonic behavior of the client. The depressed person experiences previously interesting events (such as socializing) as neutral or aversive. Not only does the depressed mood reduce the effectiveness of social interactions as a reinforcer, it also changes the probability of leaving the apartment or picking up the phone.

Further, including motivational operations in the functional analysis swings the gate open for a proper analysis of what is happening with concomitant classically conditioned responses (CRs; see chapter 2). A thorough functional analysis must investigate conditioned stimulus/conditioned response relationships, and whether conditioned emotional responses are participating in the clinical presentation. For example, the sweating, heart palpitations, and increased breathing rate involved in physiological anxiety can operate as an antecedent to other operant behaviors. A comprehensive analysis will keep an eye on these CRs when formulating and implementing treatment.

Stimulus Control

Responses are reinforced in some situations, but not all. This is a simple fact of life learned quickly by the baby who gets lots of hugs and praise for playing with her stuffed animals, sippy cup, and other innocuous items around the house. But when she attempts to touch one little electrical socket, all hell breaks loose. It's the same topographical response (playing as touching, fingering, and exploring), but a whole new result. She has just experienced *differential reinforcement*, which "refers to reinforcing a response in the presence of one stimulus or situation and not reinforcing the same response in the presence of another stimulus or situation" (Kazdin, 2001, p. 41). When a behavior is continually consequated in the presence of one contextual variable, and the same behavior is not similarly consequated in the presence of a different contextual variable, then the presence of each variable signals that the correlated consequences will probably follow the response.

As noted in chapter 2, discriminative stimuli (S^D) are the contextual variables that are correlated with reinforcers. They occasion the opportunity for reinforced behavior, and this is acquired by experience with these differential consequences. The converse is a *nondiscriminative stimulus* ($S^\triangle$; pronounced "S delta"), which is correlated with the absence of reinforcers for that response. S^Ds and $S^\triangle$s are antecedent stimuli, and after contacting the contingencies involved with these stimuli, the reinforced behavior is more likely to occur in the presence of the S^D and less likely in the presence of the $S^\triangle$. Responses differentially influenced by these stimuli are said to be under *stimulus control*. The baby girl's avoidance of wall outlets but continued approach to toys is an exhibition of stimulus control.

Stimulus control pervades daily life. A man doesn't write an e-mail unless the computer monitor is on, doesn't answer a phone unless it rings, and doesn't ask his wife for sex if she's got an icepack on her head and there's an aspirin bottle on the nightstand.

Inappropriate stimulus control can participate in the acquisition and maintenance of clinically relevant repertoires. Twelve-step programs tell recovering addicts to avoid their old "places and faces" because their same old friends in the same old environments will likely occasion a relapse. This advice from "Bill W." and clinical researchers in relapse prevention (Marlatt & Gordon, 1985) is about using stimulus control to the client's advantage. Stimulus-control problems are also evident in a person exhibiting borderline personality disorder. It would be reasonable for a young woman to become enamored with a man who is attractive, well-employed, and charming, but not so reasonable if he were all those things, and married. Flirting, sending notes, and frequent phone calling might actually be functional behavior if a woman wants a date, but that same behavior exhibited to a man in a committed relationship becomes aversive to him and likely to others. Not being able to discriminate who to direct these advances toward is a case of the environment exhibiting poor stimulus control over her behavior. Not being able to notice that the man does not appreciate her advances is a case of really poor stimulus control. This type of situation can contribute to the relationship instability of many multiproblem clients.

"Inappropriate behavior" of all kinds is often a problem of defective stimulus control. Telling off-color jokes may be positively reinforced around the office, but not when the boss is around. Telling someone that you are deeply in love with her is a great display of intimacy, but not on the first date! Similarly, giving cash as a Christmas present is great for your mail carrier but probably not for your significant other. Avoiding a snarling dog foaming at the mouth is a good idea, but avoiding Grandma's house because she has a toy poodle suggests problematic stimulus control.

Antecedents play a role in influencing behavior, and during a functional analysis it is important to investigate if there is a significant lack of discriminative control or if it has been inappropriately developed (Follette et al., 2000). A thorough functional analysis may also uncover that appropriate antecedents are absent. If a person seeks counseling for depression, a functional analysis may find that the major contributor to his mood disorder is that he has been unemployed for several months. Further analysis may also show that he is a highly educated computer graphic imager with great leadership skills. But then the therapist also realizes that the therapy is going on in a suburb of Helena, Montana, where there are extremely limited available jobs in graphic imaging. Reinforcers for his job-seeking behaviors are on a very lean schedule. In this case, the antecedents for effective behavior are downright absent. The ACT therapist is watchful for absent and inappropriate stimulus control.

The Process of Functional Analyses

The purpose of executing a good functional analysis is to execute good treatment. Follette et al. (2000) explain that if a functional analysis is to have treatment utility, the process must be iterative and self-correcting. This suggests that functional analysis is ongoing with the client, session after session, and that the clinician should always be working on some part of the cycle of assessment.

The Six-Step Cycle to Functional Analysis

The classic functional analysis cycle has six steps (Follette et al., 2000).

Step 1: Identify the clinically relevant behaviors and the contextual variables that support the problems. Prioritizing which clinical concern should be the first or primary target for therapy, and uncovering the client's strengths and weaknesses are also part of the assessment at this step.

Step 2: Determine the consequences (tangible, social, physical, or avoidance) most influential on the maintenance of the response class. Also, determine how the prevailing setting events, MOs, CS-CR relationships, and S^Ds impact the problem. Using the ABC Functional Analysis Sheet (see appendix A for complete sheet) can assist in performing a simple functional analysis determining the relationships between antecedents, behaviors, and consequences.

ABC Functional Analysis Sheet

ANTECEDENT What happened *before?*	BEHAVIOR What did you *do?*	CONSEQUENCE What happened *after?*
Day & Time:		

Step 3: Construct an intervention plan based on these functional analyses. Linking functional assessment to effective intervention is the central theme of applied behavior analysis. Treatments for clinically relevant responses maintained by tangible reinforcers might most effectively include an aim to reduce access to those tangible items, or to make those tangibles contingent on more psychologically healthy behavior. If problematic behavior is maintained by the inappropriate social attention of a spouse, for example, perhaps family counseling regarding the spouse's participation in the problem might be therapeutic. The alteration of the negative and positive reinforcement contingencies is crucial to treatment. When possible, altering MOs and contact with S^Ds can also play an important role in therapy.

With ACT, the therapist will be vigilant about experiential avoidance, and then approach the clinically relevant environment-behavior relations with interventions aimed to diminish the impact of the verbal stimuli that support the avoidance and motivate the client to commit to a behavioral repertoire that is more likely to contact important reinforcers.

Step 4: Implement the functionally based treatment.

Step 5: Assess the outcome of the previous steps, reappraising whether there was a change in the target behavior. This type of appraisal occurs throughout the functional assessment, and it is especially important to ask assessment questions once an intervention is in place. For example, the therapist might need to assess if experiential avoidance is continuing despite attempts to develop acceptance strategies. If so, perhaps acceptance is misunderstood, or the client hasn't clarified her values so that clinical improvement can be maintained.

Step 6: Evaluate the assessment outcomes by asking if the intervention led to successful working. If it did, the treatment for that problem can move into maintenance and relapse prevention. If it did not, then the clinician returns to step 1 to identify any relevant characteristics of the client and environment that would contribute to the intervention. As mentioned, a functional analysis is iterative and self-correcting (Follette et al., 2000). Behavior analysts do not expect to run through the six steps just once from beginning to end. Clinical work cycles between assessment and intervention, mostly doing both at the same time, and improving the intervention incrementally as new data arise.

Checking In

Briefly return to chapter 1 to review the cases of Shandra and Rick, and then consider these questions:

What are the functions involved with Shandra being so socially isolative?

What functions maintain Rick's pot smoking?

Functionally Analyzing the Functional Analysis

Remember, the radical behavioral approach incorporates the assumption that even the scientist-practitioner is influenced by environmental contingencies. Be mindful that your own treatment behavior and functional analyzing responses are ongoing acts-in-context. As such, they are susceptible to social, tangible, and avoidance-based contingencies that can pull the clinical work off track. When possible and appropriate, clinicians are strongly urged to measure the progress of their clients' behavior objectively and mechanically to avoid clinical biases (Moran & Tai, 2001). Continual data collection also helps contend with unreliable self-reports by clients saying they are or are not seeing clinical improvement. Another word of caution regarding functional analysis: Be watchful for the client's problematic change agenda coming through. During the interview process in step 1 and throughout the cycle, see if you can detect your client's desire to be rid of private events or certain experiences. Make sure that you don't get sidetracked into using your functionally based treatment skills to support your client's or your own problematic eliminative agenda.

Assessment in ACT

ACT work is dedicated to the scientific pursuit of understanding and positively influencing human behavior. As such, functional contextualists have committed to developing measures involved with the acceptance and commitment domains so that these factors are more readily understood and can be assessed for change. Many of the assessment tools discussed below are in development or have not had their psychometric properties completely evaluated. However, this is the beginning of a good list of tools and methods. To the extent possible, consider incorporating some of them into your practice.

Committed Action

Third-wave behavior therapy shares the same respect for ongoing measurement in a therapeutic endeavor as the first two waves. In fact, this particular section will describe methods very similar to the way first- and second-wave behavior therapists approach clinical measurement. *Committed action* is about executing behaviors in the direction of important life goals. The steps in this direction can be measured by the response dimensions. Human behavior can be assessed by its frequency, intensity, duration, latency, and perseverance. These measures belong in ACT.

Frequency is the measure of the number of times a behavior occurs in a given period. For example, the obese individual can be asked to keep a weekly chart of how often he eats per day, how frequently he goes to the gym in a week, or how frequently he binges per month. Rate of response has always been a critical measure to behavior analysis, and Skinner even boasted that his most important scientific contributions were rate of response and the cumulative response recorder. Looking at how many times a response occurs over a period of time is an elegant measure of how much influence the environment has on the operant. The method of assessment is amenable to checklists, wrist counters, and hash marks on calendars.

Intensity is a measure of the magnitude of force or energy of a behavior. This is clearly a response dimension when talking about overt behavior. We might be interested in not only how many times a person lifts a barbell but also the weight of the barbell in kilograms. From a clinical point of view, we might assess how many drinks a person has (frequency) and also whether those are drinks of light beer with a low alcohol content or homemade gin with a high alcohol content (intensity). If we are interested in emotional variables, intensity may have to be self-reported on a subjective units of distress scale (SUDS). This is commonly heard when the therapist asks, "How angry/anxious/depressed were you on a scale of 1 to 10?"

Duration is a measure of the continuance of a particular response class: once the response starts, how long does it continue before it ceases? A person may be interested in measuring how long he meditates once he sits down to do so because he wants to work up from three minutes of meditation to fifteen minutes. More clinically, we may want to know how long a person can be exposed to aversive stimuli before making an incompatible experiential avoidance move. For instance, how long can your client maintain eye contact before looking away or talk about an uncomfortable issue before changing the subject? Duration of sobriety is significant to substance abuse treatment. Timing how long a man with a history of clergy abuse can be inside a church or how long a person with OCD and contamination fears can hold a doorknob are measures of duration. The ACT approach isn't necessarily going to aim at reducing the duration of private events—they are to be experienced, not eliminated. But timing how long a person can engage in a life experience event (exposure exercises) can be key treatment data. It provides insight into how flexible client behavior is and can be a measure of commitment in the moment.

Much the same can be said for *latency measures*, which are assessments of how long it takes for a person to engage in a response once the response opportunity arises. A man with social phobia can self-monitor how long it takes him to leave the comfort of his car and go into his workplace. It is a measure of delay prior to an important response. It is also a matter of perspective. He may be in the car ruminating for a long time (a duration measure) or not at work when he could be (a latency measure).

Perseverance is slightly different from these dimensions in that the assessor is looking for different environments or stimulus events that occasion certain responses. Clinicians interested in the contextual variables of a response class are looking for its perseverance. Asking a client with anger problems about what sets him off during the day is an assessment of perseverance: "Tell me what gets you angry in the morning/during your work commute/at work/at lunch/at home" and so on. Knowing what environments evoke the clinical problem can assist in developing better scenarios for exposure exercises and also help plan times to work on coping skills.

Values

In endeavoring to assist clients with values clarification, the ACT client may be asked to write down her summary of what personal value-directed living might look like. Hayes, Strosahl, and Wilson (1999) provided the Values Narrative Form, Values Assessment Rating Form, and the Goals, Actions, Barriers Form to assist clients in articulating what was personally important and vital to them.

The Valued Living Questionnaire (VLQ; Wilson & Groom, 2002) addresses the relative importance a person would place on each of ten personal life areas, and then asks how consistent the person's recent behavior has been with respect to their values imbued in each life area. The *Valued Living Questionnaire Working Manual* (Wilson, 2006a) has a great deal of information for the use of the VLQ and values-based work in general for therapy.

Ciarrochi and Blackledge (in Ciarrochi & Bilich, 2006) forwarded the Personal Values Questionnaire (PVQ) targeting values clarification. The authors "wanted to describe each value's domain in a way likely to influence subjects to write relatively ACT-consistent values—even if these subjects had not been exposed to ACT therapy" (Ciarrochi & Blackledge, 2005). The tool assesses nine areas of a person's life (family, friends, work, and so on) in a qualitative fashion, and then attempts to quantify the motivations for each value. The Social Values Survey (Ciarrochi & Blackledge, 2005) is an abbreviated version usable with adolescents.

Targeting values during assessment is made very practical using Dahl and Lundgren's (2006) Values Bull's-Eye. Using the figure of an archery bull's-eye target, clients are asked to rate how closely their recent behavior "hit the mark" with respect to valued living. The tool was used in Dahl and Lundgren's clinical research program with individuals with seizure disorders and is available in their book. It is also available at www .contextualpsychology.org, the website of the Association of Contextual Behavioral Science in Ciarrochi and Bilich's (2006) collection of ACT related assessment instruments.

Acceptance

A linchpin assessment tool in ACT work has been the Acceptance and Action Questionnaire (AAQ; Bond, 2006). The first AAQ emerged from collaborative efforts (Hayes, Strosahl, Wilson, et al., 2004) aimed at developing a brief general measure of experiential avoidance applicable to population research. This seven-point Likert scale self-report questionnaire aims to appraise a person's need to avoid negative private content, to have cognitive and emotional control, and to be able to take important action in the face of these private events. There are several versions of the AAQ, varied slightly in the number of questions (AAQ-9, AAQ-16, and AAQ-22), and some of the overlapping questions on each have been slightly altered on the other assessments. A revised version, the AAQ-II, has also been published (Hayes, 2007) and continues to be developed and put through validation studies.

Greco, Murrell, and Coyne (2005) developed a related measure for youngsters. The Avoidance and Fusion Questionnaire for Youth (AFQ-Y) includes seventeen Likert scale items aimed at fusion and experiential avoidance. According to the authors, the "research suggests that the AFQ-Y may be a useful and child-friendly measure of core ACT processes" (Greco, 2006). Sandoz and Wilson (2006) have also constructed the Body Image Acceptance Questionnaire (BIAQ), which is a twenty-nine-item, seven-point Likert scale to assess the extent to which an individual shows acceptance toward negative feelings and thoughts about body shape and/or weight.

The Chronic Pain Acceptance Questionnaire (CPAQ; Geiser, 1992) is a staple assessment in ACT-based treatment research with individuals dealing with pain problems (McCracken, 1998; McCracken, Vowles, & Eccleston, 2004). The latest version of the CPAQ is a twenty-item Likert scale yielding scores for two subscales: activity engagement and pain willingness. The idea behind the assessment is to see if clients can move forward in their important life goals in the presence of their pain, so it lends itself well to ACT work (McCracken & Eccleston, 2006). By the time you read this book, there may be still newer measures. One source for ACT-related measures, including reliability and validation data, is www.contextualpsychology.org.

Defusion

Properly measuring the extent to which a client is disentangled from her private verbal behavior would be a boon to an ACT therapist's work. Of course, given the privacy of these events, clinicians must rely on self-report to get close to this kind of information. The White Bear Suppression Inventory (WBSI; Wegner & Zanakos, 1994) attempts to take a crack at this bear of a task. The WBSI assesses an individual's inclination to squelch aversive cognitive content. The ten-item Likert scale can be interpreted with norms, and has been correlated with treatment effects for folks with anxiety concerns (Smari & Holmsteinssen, 2001). Keep in mind that the aforementioned AFQ-Y also has a component of defusion measurement.

Defusion measures can be developed idiographically. While symptom- or disorder-specific measures are still in their infancy (and depending on the disorder, perhaps have not been developed yet), general assessment procedures, such as self-report measures of relative influence of thoughts and feelings, will serve to assess how much impact they are having. Subjective units of distress scales and individualized Likert scales may be practical tools. Bach and Hayes (2002) demonstrate the use of idiosyncratic measures for the frequency, distress, and believability of psychosis symptoms, and provide a good model for your own development of clinical measures. Eifert and Forsyth (2005) propose using established measures, such as the Automatic Thoughts Questionnaire-B (ATQ-B; Hollon & Kendall, 1980) and the Thought-Action Fusion Scale (TAF; Shafran, Thordarson, & Rachman, 1996), and enhancing the queries with a simple believability scale (for example, 0 = completely unbelievable to 6 = completely believable) in order to assess defusion.

Contacting the Present Moment and Perspective Taking

The combination of these two domains—contacting the present moment and perspective taking—can be measured with mindfulness assessments. There is an irony to measuring mindfulness because mindfulness is a pursuit of nonevaluation. Remember that context is critical to understanding function, so when we have our scientist-practitioner hats on, there is nothing wrong with (unworkable about) appraising the process and products of mindfulness. However, from the meditator's point of view, evaluation can be had but not held, and a continued striving for measuring one's own mindfulness during a mindfulness exercise would very likely be unworkable.

The Mindfulness and Attention Awareness Scale (MAAS; Brown, K. W., & Ryan, 2003) is a fifteen-item, six-point Likert scale that has been relatively well validated with convergent and divergent scales. The established psychometric properties of the MAAS make it a popular research tool, and it is important to consider that the focus of the MAAS is on attending and being aware, and it does not focus on other mindfulness elements, such as a reduced posture of striving and acceptance of private events. This is not to say that the tool has no clinical utility. It can be used to differentiate between people who practice mindfulness and people who do not, and it did well in "examining the role of mindfulness in the psychological well-being of cancer patients" (Carlson & Brown, 2005, p. 29). The MAAS was also significantly correlated in the positive direction with emotional intelligence, openness to experience, and well-being, while being negatively correlated with social anxiety and ruminating measures.

The Kentucky Inventory of Mindfulness Skills (KIMS; Baer, R. A., Smith, & Allen, 2004) is a thirty-nine-item, five-point Likert scale, and is divided into four different factors: observing, describing, acting with awareness, and accepting without judgment. "Exploratory and confirmatory factor analyses clearly support the proposed four-factor structure, and expected correlations with a variety of other constructs were obtained" (Baer, R. A., Smith, Hopkins, Krietemeyer, & Toney, 2006, p. 29). The scale content was inspired by the dialectical behavior therapy approach to mindfulness, and Baer, Smith, and Allen (2004) show that scores from a sample of people with borderline personality disorder were significantly lower than a sample of students on three of the four scales.

The Mindfulness Questionnaire (MQ; Chadwick, Hember, Mead, Lilley, & Dagnan, 2005) is a clinically relevant measure of mindfulness with a sixteen-item, seven-point Likert scale. The items query distressfulness of private events and also how the client deals with the stress. Although the instrument measures four areas of mindfulness—observation, letting go, nonaversion, and nonjudgment—the psychometric research suggests using a unitary score for the MQ. Along with good internal consistency, the MQ also significantly correlates with the MAAS, showing significant positive correlations with mood scales and significant differences between people who meditate and people who do not. Participants in a mindfulness-based stress reduction program also showed a significant increase in MQ scores.

The Cognitive Affective Mindfulness Scale (CAMS; Feldman, Hayes, Kumar, & Greeson, 2004; Hayes & Feldman, 2004) is a twelve-item, four-point Likert scale aimed a measuring attention, awareness, present focus, and acceptance/nonjudgment of thoughts and feelings in everyday life. It yields a single score; is reported to have good internal consistency; is negatively correlated with experiential avoidance, worry, rumination, depression, and anxiety; and is positively correlated with ability to repair one's mood, cognitive flexibility, clarity of feelings, and well-being (Baer, R. A., et al., 2004; Feldman et al., 2004; Hayes & Feldman, 2004). A. M. Hayes and Harris (2000) report an increase in the CAMS score in individuals being treated for depression using a mindfulness-based approach.

Other Measures

The nonspecific assessment methods typically used in therapy to track progress over time and to get insight on how the person in doing between sessions are very welcome in the ACT work. Use of diary cards, checklists, event logs (see chapter 6), and other self-monitoring worksheets pointed toward the therapeutic endeavor can add important data to the treatment as well.

A final word about assessment results: ACT does not share the same eliminative agenda of many other approaches to psychotherapy, and outcomes may be perplexing or surprising at first. In Bach and Hayes (2002), the psychotic individuals receiving ACT treatment reported more hallucinations and delusions but a decrease in believability, and they also spent a significantly longer period of time than control subjects staying out of the hospital. In Dahl, Wilson, and Nilsson (2004), people with chronic pain reported no change in levels of pain when compared to controls, but showed less sick days and accessed fewer medical resources than controls. When considering measures of change in ACT, a therapist must be mindful that the widely accepted measures of symptom reduction may not be appropriate in an ACT context. At the fifth week of ACT treatment, during the administration of the Beck Depression Inventory–II (Beck, Steer, & Brown, 1996), a client said aloud, "I don't criticize or blame myself more than usual. Why does that get zero points? I still do, but I thought we were working on it not mattering anymore, not that I keep doing it." In saying so, he was knocking on the door of a welcomed treatment termination.

CHAPTER 4

Relational Frame Theory

Relational frame theory (RFT) is a functional contextual theory of human language and cognition with a basic science research approach aimed at understanding these human processes. Relational frame theory is much broader than ACT since only some RFT research is aimed at applying RFT to psychotherapy. ACT is one application of RFT. A single chapter cannot do a comprehensive theory justice. Our aim is more modest: to provide a basic introduction to relational frame theory and relational framing and to suggest how RFT might be useful in carrying out ACT in practice. For a more comprehensive account, see Hayes, Barnes-Holmes, and Roche (2001).

The ACT Therapist and RFT

Do ACT therapists need to know RFT in order to be effective clinicians? The answer is no. Clearly there are effective ACT clinicians who know little about RFT. Does knowing something about RFT enhance one's effectiveness as an ACT therapist? Anecdotal evidence says yes. To date, there is no research on this topic, and many ACT therapists who have become familiar with relational frame theory report that understanding RFT has been useful for guiding their case conceptualization, and for selecting and developing interventions. Therefore we believe it is worthwhile to include a chapter about RFT in this volume. Consider this analogy: a therapist could do good behavior therapy without being able to technically describe the principle of negative reinforcement, but if she could, it would likely add a great degree of sophistication to her therapy.

What's Different About RFT?

If the goal of applied psychologists is to predict and influence behavior, Skinner and his predecessors and contemporaries provided an account of behavior adequate to describe animal behavior and much of human behavior. However, their account did not go far enough in describing advanced human cognitive and language behavior. A post-Skinnerian account of behavior is needed to describe human language and cognition in a manner useful for predicting and influencing human verbal behavior and overt behavior influenced by verbal contingencies.

The behavioral principles described in chapter 3 are adequate for understanding, describing, predicting, and influencing animal and human behavior, but some human behavior is qualitatively different from animal behavior. An operant account of behavior is sufficient to unpack the contingencies involved in a rat pressing a lever to get food; it is insufficient to account for a person following a recipe to prepare a meal. Members of some species are clearly able to recognize individual members of their group, and no animal could describe the relationship between himself and his mother's sister's children's children. Animals can learn information about the location of food or predators from their peers, and only from other animals they observe or smell or hear. In contrast, humans alive today can read words penned by Aristotle more than two thousand years ago or use the Rosetta stone to decipher hieroglyphics. Humans can use architect's drawings in order to construct a variety of homes, while beavers and birds and bugs typically construct a single type of abode, the design of which is apparently genetically encoded. In sum, there are certain human behaviors that cannot be explained adequately by the scientific principles used to describe animal behavior.

Some have suggested that animals can engage in behavior similar to human language (Kastak, D., & Schusterman, 1994; Kastak, C. R., & Schusterman, 2002). Critics argue that such repertoires are extremely rare in animals, have only been developed in laboratory settings after laborious training regimens with limited species, and when the limited repertoire is developed, it is still learned in a manner consistent with RFT's predictions about the need for multiple exemplar training (Hayes & Berens, 2004), though not showing all the features that define human-derived relational responding. Frankly, even if animals could readily engage in relational framing, that wouldn't change the relevance of RFT as a way of discussing the principles of relational conditioning.

Demystifying Relational Frame Theory

RFT is often scary to the uninitiated. "Relational framing is operant behavior that affects the process of operant learning itself" (Hayes, Fox, et al., 2001, p. 45). So far so good—and then the innocent therapist wanting to learn more might peruse an article or book chapter hoping to learn something about relational framing when suddenly he is confronted with something like this:

Crel {A rx B and B rx C ||| A rp C and C rq A}

He glances at this string of symbols and is reminded of calculus, computer programming, foreign languages, or any other subjects he found difficult to comprehend, and he relegates the RFT article to the pile of garbage and old newspapers.

We want to assure you that RFT is not as incomprehensible as it may seem at first glance. In fact, you have been framing relationally for as long as you can remember. RFT is complicated in part because we have to use verbal behavior in order to talk about verbal behavior. In reading this far, you have certainly been framing relationally, and even understanding that you don't understand the preceding string of letters and symbols is evidence that you may be proficient at framing relationally. It may seem ironic that you have been framing relationally as you learn about relational frame theory. On the other hand, you have been digesting food for as long as you can remember even if you don't know how to describe the process of digestion.

"Relational Frame Theory embraces the simple idea that deriving stimulus relations is learned behavior" (Hayes, Fox, et al., 2001, p. 21). The things we deal with on a daily basis might be related in any number of ways and in terms of formal or abstract properties. That is, stimuli might be related to one another on the basis of their size, color, shape, sound, texture, toxicity, utility, class membership, value, attractiveness, and so on. One stimulus may be related to another based on size: this is bigger than that. When such a statement is made, the person is engaging in relational responding. Relational responding is not unique to humans; however, arbitrarily applicable derived relational responding appears to be unique to humans. Let us unpack some of those terms and break them down into simpler components.

Relational Responding

Relational responding is operant behavior. It is something organisms do, and it is shaped by environmental contingencies. From a functional contextual point of view, relationships don't exist as corporeal things; two things are related as evidenced by an organism's behavior. Remember that we are interested in looking at the act-in-context. Relational responding occurs when the behavior of a person or animal is influenced by features or properties of two or more stimuli. Animals exhibit relational responding through conditioned discrimination, and humans engage in derived relating as well as conditioned discrimination.

Conditioned Discrimination

Conditioned discrimination, also known as transposition in the behavioral literature, is demonstrated when an organism can make a response based on a relationship between two physical stimuli. For example, a colleague of ours trained his dog to always select the larger among a group of specific stimuli, namely sticks. The dog (we'll call him Sydney) liked chasing sticks thrown by his owner (we'll call him Bob). Bob used *conditioned discrimination trials* to train Sydney to always select the larger of any pair or groups of sticks available. Specifically, when there were two or more sticks available, Bob trained Sydney to selectively choose sticks on the basis of their size by only throwing the stick for Sydney to chase when Sydney chose the largest of available sticks. So if there were three sticks and Sydney picked up the smallest or intermediate-size stick and dropped it at Bob's feet, Bob would ignore Sydney. When Sydney brought the largest of the two or three or more sticks, Bob would throw the stick for Sydney to chase. After many trials with many sticks of many sizes or, put another way, through *multiple exemplar training*, Sydney learned to always bring the largest stick for Bob to throw. Sydney related sticks, or stimuli, on the feature of size. There are other features he might have related sticks on; Bob could have trained Sydney to select the lighter-colored stick, or to select sticks from softwood trees rather than hardwood trees. And since Bob used multiple exemplar training, that provided Sydney with many opportunities to compare different kinds of sticks. After many weeks of training and exposure to hundreds of sticks, and no matter how many stick features were available for comparison, Sydney reliably chose the largest of the available sticks. Sydney became so adept at relating stimuli that when Bob threw a two-foot stick for Sydney to chase, Sydney would often return with a four-foot stick— perhaps expecting that the game would continue in the presence of this new and very big stick. Sydney had become an expert in making conditioned discriminations between stimuli on the basis of a physical property. This is one type of relational responding.

Derived Relational Responding

Derived means "inferred from facts or premises" as opposed to from direct experience. Therefore, *derived relational responding* is based on verbal descriptions of (that is, indirect experience with) events rather than on direct contact with events. For instance, one can directly experience what sweet potato pie tastes like only by actually eating sweet potato pie. In contrast, if one has tasted pumpkin pie, one could derive what sweet potato pie tastes like through learning that "sweet potato pie tastes similar to pumpkin pie." (If you thought "tastes similar to" was a relational response, you are on the right track.) Another example: After a history of learning that "big" is the opposite of "little" and being told that John is bigger than Mary, one could derive that Mary is littler than John even without ever directly seeing John and Mary.

While animals can make conditional discrimination responses, they do not appear able to make derived relational responses. While there are some similarities between the two types of responding, there are also some important differences between Sydney learning to select the larger of two stick options and a human learning to select the larger of two stock options; of a pigeon learning to select the brighter of two lights and a teacher learning to select the brighter of two students; and of a rat learning to select the warmer of two water samples and a parent learning to select the warmer of two babysitters.

The primary difference between conditioned discrimination and derived relational responding is that conditioned discriminations are based on nonarbitrary features of the stimuli. Here, by "nonarbitrary" we mean that one can distinguish the stimuli on the basis of physical properties or features of stimuli that are selected in the context of the animal's behavioral repertoire and that can be apprehended through the senses. The dog can see the relative size of the sticks, the pigeon can see the brighter of two lights, and the rat can feel the difference between the temperatures of available water samples. Size, brightness, and temperature are apprehended through the senses—they are nonarbitrary.

In contrast, a human can learn arbitrary relations. A person doing derived relational responding does not relate the word "nectarine" to an actual nectarine in the same manner as an animal relates the size of one stick to another or the brightness of one light to another. The word and the object do not share physical properties. The actual nectarine does not resemble the word "nectarine" in any way. One cannot taste or smell or touch or eat the word, and yet a person can learn to relate the word stimulus and the fruit stimulus such that they are readily related as being equivalent. The stimuli are related according to contingencies of reinforcement established by the verbal community one participates in. In a verbal community, saying "nectarine" is reinforced when the person is in the presence of that red- and orange-colored, round fruit with a distinctive odor and taste. Humans can relate stimuli on the basis of arbitrary features while animals relate stimuli on nonarbitrary physical features only.

Arbitrary and Arbitrarily Applicable

Arbitrary means "discretionary" or "depending on choice or social whim." Arbitrary is different from "determined, fixed, and decided." Nonarbitrary features of the environment are those features that can be apprehended through the senses: seen, touched, smelled, and so on. Arbitrary features of the environment vary according to social whim. For example, bats, black widow spiders, Newfoundland dogs, and black panthers are black. That is not arbitrary, they are born that way—the outward appearance of their fur, skin, or shell is black in color. On the other hand, it is arbitrary that English-speaking humans call their color "black." The German-speaking social group reliably reinforces calling the color of bats and Newfoundland dogs "schwartz," the Spanish-speaking group reinforces "negro," French-speaking societies use "noir," and so on.

When two children, Mary and John, are born, their sex is determined by their nonarbitrary, obvious, primary external sex characteristics. However, it is arbitrary that we call people with a penis "boys" and people with a vulva "girls." And it is arbitrary that Mary is more often the name of a girl, while the name John is more often assigned to a boy.

Arbitrarily applicable means that the relationships among stimuli are established by social convention. For instance, the relationship between a name for something and the thing named is completely arbitrary; one choice for a word or name could be made as opposed to another. As the English language was developing, the people could have described the color of bats and Newfoundland dogs as "nildy." We could have nildy widow spiders and nildy panthers. After rugby games, kids would come home all nildy-and-blue. We'd say that the stock market crash in 1929 happened on Nildy Thursday. Nildy would be the opposite of white. The color of the ink on this page is nildy, and so on. So, if it is arbitrary, why is "black" rather than "nildy" or any other word used to describe the color?

Sticks and stones can break our bones, and we are free to call them sticks and stones or gjzds and wpyfs. Parents can choose any name for their children; the choice is arbitrarily applicable. On the other hand, although language is arbitrarily applicable, it is usually not arbitrarily applied. In England, your behavior will be reinforced for saying, "Bats are black," and in Austria it will be reinforced for describing their color as "schwartz." In England, you could decide that since words are arbitrarily applicable, you will just go ahead an arbitrarily apply words. But if you said to someone, "Bats are nildy," how successful would you be in a conversation?

You could call a stick a "gjzd" and a stone a "wpyf," but you probably would not—not because you couldn't, but instead because it probably wouldn't work for you. Your behavior would most likely not be reinforced by other speakers in your verbal community for doing so. As the RFT axiom goes, language is arbitrarily applicable but not usually arbitrarily applied. So to answer the question why a bat's color is called "black" rather than "nildy," it is because the local verbal community reinforces that particular response. Even if it is arbitrary, it's just not arbitrarily applied. Bottom line: You can call something whatever you choose to, but you probably won't. You'll call it what the community, by social convention and whim, calls it.

This arbitrariness is not only a feature of words or names. People will readily answer questions such as "What is the opposite of cat?" by saying, "dog." Or when asked, "What is a cat like?" a person might reply, "a chair," "a friend," or "a sunset." Some of these relations are based on personal history with the stimuli (for example, my cat was my friend), some appeal to nonarbitrary features as verbally contacted (for example, a cat and a chair both have four legs), and some are related through complex individual and unique verbal networks (for example, cats and sunsets are both members of the class "beautiful things").

Now we're ready to take relational responding a step further. *Relational framing* (or framing relationally) "is a specific class of responding that shows the contextually controlled qualities of mutual entailment, combinatorial entailment, and transformation of stimulus functions" (Hayes, Barnes-Holmes, et al., 2001, p. 33). Let's take a closer look at each of those contextually controlled qualities.

Mutual Entailment

Language-able people who can learn to relate the sound "nectarine" with a red- and orange-colored, round fruit with a distinctive odor and taste can also coordinate the red- and orange-colored, round fruit to the sound "nectarine." This may seem obvious, and that is because you have been doing it for a long time. Animals have not demonstrated the ability to relate two stimuli bidirectionally like that. "Arbitrary stimulus relations are always mutual: If A is related to B, then B is related to A" (Hayes, Fox, et al., 2001, p. 29). This is the definition of *mutual entailment*: when two stimuli are related, the relation between stimuli A and B can also be described in terms of a relationship between B and A. If A is larger than B, then B is smaller than A. If A is equal to B, then B is equal to A. If A is a member of the class B, then B is a class that has A as a member. If A is west of B, then B is east of A.

To make it less abstract, if an elephant is larger than an ant, then an ant is smaller than an elephant. If 4 is equal to 2 + 2, then 2 + 2 is equal to 4. If dogs are members of the class "canine," then canine is a class that has dogs as members. If Chicago is west of New York, then New York is east of Chicago. If a red- and orange-colored, round fruit is a nectarine then a nectarine is a red- and orange-colored, round fruit.

Please consider how remarkable this skill is. You have probably never ever considered the two small U.S. towns of Bay Park, New York, and Mokena, Illinois. And if we told you one thing—that Bay Park is east of Mokena—you could derive that Mokena is west of Bay Park even though you were not told that additional relationship specifically. You are capable of doing that because of a skill, an operant behavior, called derived relational responding. What is fascinating about this skill is that it can be applied to a vast number of stimuli, creating innumerous potential relationships. There have been serious attempts to show mutual entailment in animals, including rats, sea lions, and chimpanzees (Kastak, C. R., & Schusterman, 2002), and so far only humans have been shown to be capable of robust mutual entailment.

Combinatorial Entailment

A person can be taught that a red- and orange-colored, round fruit is called a "nectarine." The same person can be taught to read the letters N-E-C-T-A-R-I-N-E as corresponding to the spoken word "nectarine." With the skill of mutual entailment, the person will also say "nectarine" in the presence of the fruit or the letters N-E-C-T-A-R-I-N-E. Now, when the person can choose a red- and orange-colored round fruit in the presence of the written word N-E-C-T-A-R-I-N-E, even if that person has never been trained to do so before, we are seeing more derived relating. "*Combinatorial entailment* applies when, in a given context, if A is related to B, and B is related to C, then as a result A and C are mutually related in that context" (Hayes, Fox, et al., 2001, p. 30, emphasis added). This means that when one stimulus is related to two or more stimuli, the relation between any pair of stimuli can be described in terms of any other pair of stimuli. For example, if A is larger than B and B is larger than C, then B is smaller than A and C is smaller than A. If A is equal to B and B is equal to C, then A is equal to C. If A is a member of the class B and B is a member of class C, then B is a class that has A as a member and C is a class that has A and B as members. If A is west of B and B is west of C, then B is east of A and C is east of A and B.

For concrete examples, if houses are more expensive than cars and cars are more expensive than shoes, then cars are less expensive than houses and shoes are less expensive than houses. If Yorkshire terriers are dogs and dogs are canines, then Yorkshire terriers are canines. If Chicago is west of New York and New York is west of London, then New York is east of Chicago and London is east of Chicago and New York. Combining this ability with mutual entailment demonstrates just how generative language can be. These abilities are learned behaviors.

Transformation of Stimulus Functions

Transformation of stimulus functions is at once more and less comprehensible to clinicians, and is described as "[w]hen a given stimulus in a relational network has certain psychological functions, the functions of other events in that network may be modified in accordance with the underlying derived relation" (Hayes, Fox, et al., 2001, p. 31). If stimulus A has a particular psychological function in contexts where stimulus A is equivalent to stimulus B, then stimulus B will acquire a similar particular psychological function. For example, if stimulus A elicits anxiety and one learns that stimulus B is equivalent to stimulus A, then the functions of stimulus A will be transformed such that stimulus B also elicits anxiety. Further, in contexts where stimulus A has a particular psychological function and A is smaller than stimulus B, then stimulus B will acquire greater psychological functions. If stimuli A and B are money denominations, and stimulus A is framed as smaller than B, then stimulus B will be more valuable than A. If stimulus A, a poodle puppy, elicits anxiety in the dog-phobic girl, greater anxiety elicitation may occur when told she is visiting the neighbor's house where a bigger, St. Bernard dog (stimulus B) lives.

Transformation of Stimulus Functions and Clinical Work

Suppose that someone, through a history of direct conditioning, is frightened of snakes. If he is naive about the names of specific snakes, he may feel nothing when someone shouts, "Look, it's an asp!" On the other hand, suppose he reads a magazine article about asps being a type of snake. He's never encountered an asp in real life and the magazine doesn't even have a picture of an asp. Further, he has never been bitten by an asp, and has never been negatively reinforced for running away from an asp. And then he sees someone point and say, "Look, it's an asp!" He may feel fear even though he cannot see what his companion is pointing at and even though has never encountered an asp. The stimulus functions of asp have been transformed by the participation of "asp" in a hierarchical frame with "snake," as learned from the magazine article. The previously neutral functions of "asp" will be transformed by the functions of "snake," which will transfer through the hierarchical relationship between "asp" and "snake." And remember, the person is engaging in the response of relational framing; the asp-snake relationship is an arbitrarily applicable relational response. And continue to remember that ACT attempts to undermine these types of challenging relations. There are critical ACT interventions that utilize the arbitrariness of language to undermine this type of relational responding that leads to unhelpful behaviors.

For a more clinically relevant example, consider a client with body dysmorphic disorder who believes that he is unusually thin and that it is bad to be too skinny and it would be good to gain weight. He may have already heard time and again that "steroids are bad" during his preteen years. Suppose that someone he respects says that "steroids help you bulk up." Since "steroids" is now in a frame of coordination with "bulk up" and "bulk up" is in a frame of coordination with "gain weight" and "gain weight" is in an evaluative frame with "good," the functions of "steroids" may be transformed from "bad" to "good," and the young man who avoided steroids because he thought them bad may now abuse steroids because the functions of steroids, as verbally construed, have been transformed from bad to good through arbitrarily applicable derived relational responding. He may suffer the direct contingencies of an enlarged heart, sterility, premature hair loss, and other consequences of steroid abuse, and the verbally derived functions of steroids ("good") may dominate over the nonverbal and life-threatening consequences of steroid abuse. Remember this RFT concept when we talk about asking our clients, "What does your experience tell you?" This man's steroid taking is governed by abstract verbal relations as much as by his own experience, and defusion and values work may help reorient him to a healthier lifestyle.

Transformation of stimulus functions may also play a role in problematic avoidance and negative self-evaluation. Suppose someone learns that garbage and feces and maggots are dirty. And she learns that dirty things are disgusting, gross, bad, and so on. Her behavior is also reinforced for avoiding the aversive properties of these stimuli (that is, she moves away from the smelly garbage), and her compliance responses when told to avoid those stimuli are also reinforced. Now suppose her parents tell her that "sex is dirty." One possible outcome is that since "dirty" and "sex" are being framed together, the functions of "dirty" will transfer to "sex," so now "sex" will have similar functions to "dirty." In other words, the combinatorial entailment and transformation of stimulus functions will lead "disgusting," "gross," and "bad" to be related to "sex," and as an outcome she will avoid sex. However, another possible outcome is that she will engage in sexual activity, and through more transformation of stimulus functions, the functions of "dirty" will transfer to her. She may begin to regard herself as dirty, disgusting, gross, and bad when she thinks about sex, or desires sex, or engages in sexual activity. Of course, it is also possible that she will have a healthy and satisfying sexual life, and that she will evaluate that "sex is good" and notice the thought that "my parents say that sex is dirty," and through a conditional relational frame relate that if "I think that sex is good" and "my parents think that sex is dirty," then "Mom and Dad are wrong" or "I disagree with my parents."

For an even more abstract example, consider a client with claustrophobia who feels anxious in confined spaces. Suppose that the same client is told that "relationships are confining." Now he feels more and more anxious in the context of the growing closeness between him and his sweetheart as the functions of "close relationship" have been transformed from "good/positive/life enhancing" to "confining" through the equivalence relation established between "relationship" and "confining." Now his claustrophobia may expand from fear of closets and elevators to closets, elevators, and close relationships.

Arbitrarily applicable derived relational responding is defined as behavior that has the properties of mutual entailment, combinatorial entailment, and transformation of stimulus functions. Animals cannot do this, and human arbitrarily applicable derived relational responding seems to contribute to uniquely human achievements as well as uniquely human challenges. It is incumbent on the ACT therapist to functionally analyze these clinically relevant challenges to see how they can be addressed with classical, operant, and relational conditioning interventions.

RFT Lingo: Talking the Talk

Part of what sometimes makes RFT difficult to grasp is the language used to describe the theory. Terms like "relational framing," "hierarchical," and "relata" may be unfamiliar or used in unfamiliar ways. Some of the terms that show up frequently in the RFT literature are briefly described below.

Relational Frames and Relata

Relational frames aren't things somewhere in the brain, nor are they mentalistic terms, like "schema" or "memories." The term *relational frames*, although grammatically used as a noun, is a way of talking about human responses. (Making actions into nouns is extremely common: people sign up for a five-kilometer run, and also dive in the pool for a swim.) It is becoming more common to say that people are "engaged in relational framing" or "framing relationally." Keep in mind that we are talking about something people do.

We relate stimuli in many different ways. It is useful to name these relations—for example, correspondence, comparison, difference, and so on. "Relational frame" is the general term; in specific contexts, the term "comparative frame," "hierarchical frame," or other specific frames might be used. Or the response may be described as "a frame of comparison" or "a frame of correspondence." "Relata" are the stimuli related. For instance, in "white is the opposite of black," white and black are the relata, and opposition is the relation. One might say that white and black are in a frame or relation of opposition. Names and examples of several types of relations are listed below.

Common Relations Between Stimuli

Correspondence: Grandpa is old. The audible stimulus "old" is the same as the textual stimulus = O-L-D.

Similarity: "Young" is similar to "youthful.'"

Comparison: In the context of experience, old people are wiser than young people.
In the context of health, young people are more robust than old people.

Difference:	Old is different from black.
Hierarchy:	Black and white are both members of the class "color."
	Color is a class that contains black, white, blue, and red as members of that class.
Opposition:	Young is the opposite of old and white is the opposite of black.
Temporal:	Old people were born before young people.
Conditional:	If you are older than sixty, then you get a senior citizen's discount.
	If you are younger than eighteen, then you cannot vote.
Causal:	Oxidation causes silver to turn black.
Deictic:	She is old here/now and she was young there/then.

There are many more relations (for example, homophonic, isomorphic, orthogonal, and so on), but the list above provides exemplars of more commonly encountered varieties of relations.

Relational and Functional Contexts

A *relational context* refers to contextual stimuli in which "a history of a particular kind of relational responding is brought to bear on the current situation" (Hayes, Fox, et al., 2001, p. 30). (In some RFT literature, a relational context is indicated as C_{rel} pronounced "C real." We will use the term "relational context" rather than the abbreviated form.) The relational context can include the words spoken, the tone and manner with which the words are said, if the speaker is pointing at something, and other cues that facilitate mutual entailment and combinatorial entailment. This is sometimes referred to as the "context of literality."

A simple way to discuss relational contexts is by discussing a common parlor game. In Twenty Questions, a person tries to guess which object in a room someone else is thinking of by posing questions that narrow the objects so an accurate guess might be made. For example, the guesser might ask, "Is it bigger than a bread box?" which establishes a frame of comparison between the selected object and a bread box. The person selecting the object compares the selected object with a bread box in terms of size and answers yes or no, which is a cue for the guesser to scan the room for only those objects that are smaller or larger than a bread box. Then the guesser might ask, "Is it living?" which is a stimulus for hierarchical relating, and the answer to the question will tell the guesser whether or not the object is a member of the class "living things." The next question might be "Was it here yesterday?" which is a stimulus for before-after relating, and so on ("Is it higher than four feet off of the ground?" "Is it red?"). The guesser is ultimately trying to name an object in a frame of coordination with what the other person is thinking of. After asking twenty questions that evoke various kinds of relational responding, the guesser may correctly (or incorrectly!) guess that "you are thinking of the pretty blue vase on the coffee table."

In contrast, a *functional context* refers to the "contextual stimuli that select particular psychologically relevant, non-relational stimulus functions in a given situation" (Hayes, Fox, et al., 2001, p. 33). (In RFT literature, a functional context is often indicated as C_{func} pronounced "C funk.") The functional context is relevant to the transformation of psychological aspects with respect to the relational framing. Suppose the guesser above is told, "You are correct! You win the game! By the way, that blue vase was a birthday gift from Uncle Bob." And suppose the guesser dislikes Uncle Bob intensely. She might now feel a surge of disgust, frown, and then say, "What an ugly vase!" even when a moment ago she called it pretty. In a context where Uncle Bob is related to the vase, the vase acquires some of the stimulus functions of Uncle Bob. Those stimulus functions are based on our guesser's history with Uncle Bob—on her actual experience with him. The link between responding and actual experience, rather than purely relating stimuli, is what distinguishes functional contextual from relational contextual stimuli. Notice that not all functions of Uncle Bob will transfer to the vase; the guesser will not say, "The vase is my mother's brother" or "The vase has a beard." Only psychologically relevant functions will be transformed.

Rules and Rule-Governed Behavior

Behavior analysis treats rule-governed behavior as different from contingency-shaped behavior (Skinner, 1969). In brief, *contingency-shaped behavior* is influenced by direct contact with the environment, and *rule-governed behavior* comes from verbal behavior about the environment. There is an obvious difference between learning to snowboard by riding down a mountain (being shaped by the environmental contingencies of gravity and momentum, and so on) and by reading about how to snowboard (trying to learn through verbal stimuli only). Of course, with snowboarding, contingency shaping is critical to becoming better at it. Now what if that snowboard was kept in a locker with a combination lock; would you rather try to open that lock with verbal rules—turn the knob left three times to 24, right once to 17, left once to 45, then pull—or through contingency shaping of trying every combination? Complex human behavior is influenced toward effective functioning by both verbal rules and direct natural contingencies.

Skinner suggested that verbal rules function as discriminative stimuli that are contingency specifying, and are considered antecedents correlated with the availability of reinforcement. Behavior analysts (Barnes-Holmes, O'Hora, et al., 2001; Hayes & Hayes, 1989) suggest that the definition is problematic because the term "specifying" was not thoroughly explained by Skinner. These authors also argue that new knowledge about derived relational responding facilitates our understanding of "specifying" and therefore helps behavior analysts to understand rule-governed behavior. Very briefly, the mutual and combinatorial entailment in a verbal rule helps transform stimulus functions in the environment-behavior relationship. Take the rule "When asked for a password to see your e-mail, type 'htapinos2.'" This rule is an antecedent that specifies the response (typing "htapinos2") and the reinforcer (seeing e-mail). The "specify" part calls for relational framing: the person must have a history of framing stimuli in a mutual and combinatorial way leading to transformation of stimulus functions so that a stimulus such as "type" relates to direct experience with the behavior of pressing keys on a keyboard in that context. Following verbal rules requires relational framing.

Not all rules are helpful, such as "Take steroids to bulk up" or "I need to help my kids by giving them money" or "Anxiety is terrible and I can smoke pot to get rid of it." Rules have also been shown to lead to insensitivity to direct contingencies (Baron & Galizio, 1983; Hayes, Brownstein, Haas, & Greenway, 1986; Shimoff, Catania, & Matthews, 1981). For instance, a person following the rule "the expressway is the fastest route to work" may continue driving on it while the expressway is under construction and traffic is moving slowly, failing to consider alternate routes to work by rigidly following the rule.

Types of Rule-Governed Behavior: Tracking, Pliance, and Augmenting

Tracking, pliance, and augmenting are classifications for rule-governed behavior and are related to case conceptualization in ACT (see Hayes & Hayes, 1989, and Barnes-Holmes, O'Hora, et al., 2001, for an extended analysis). These terms classify rule-governed behavior in terms of how a particular rule affects the behavior of the person following the rule.

Tracking. *Tracking* is a type of "rule-governed behavior under the control of the apparent correspondence between the rule and the way the world is arranged" (Hayes, Zettle, & Rosenfarb, 1989, p. 206). For instance, a new driver is given the rule "Press your foot on the break pedal to stop the car." If, when driving, she presses the brake when she wants to stop and finds that the car indeed stops moving, she is tracking. As another example, if a child is told, "If you wear your mittens when it is cold outside, your hands will stay warm," then she is tracking the rule when she puts on her mittens and notices that her hands stay warm.

Pliance. This is a type of "rule-governed behavior under the control of apparent socially mediated consequences for a correspondence between the rule and relevant behavior" (Hayes et al., 1989, p. 203). Notice this technical term is the root of the word "compliance." An instance of pliance is called a ply. *Pliance* is rule-governed behavior like tracking; however, the role of socially mediated consequences makes it distinct from tracking. Let's say a new driver is told by her instructor to "hit the brakes!" If the reason why is unknown to the driver and she brakes anyway, her behavior is governed by the social contingencies of being compliant to her instructor's wishes. If a child wears mittens because "Mommy told me to put on the mittens she knitted for me," she is engaging in pliance.

To see how there can be conflict between these two forms of rule-governed behavior in context, imagine that a child who is told by her mother to wear her mittens is also told by a bigger kid, "If you wear your mittens when it is cold outside, then everyone will think you're a baby." This child might forgo mittens in order to avoid ridicule; she will also have cold hands. Her behavior is under the control of socially mediated consequences rather than under the control of other relevant nonsocial consequences (having warm hands). In this instance, she may track that wearing mittens will lead to warm hands, and her behavior is under the control of pliance in that it is governed by the socially mediated consequence of "wearing mittens is ridiculed."

Augmenting. This is a type of rule-governed behavior "under the control of apparent changes in the capacity of events to function as reinforcers or punishers" (Hayes et al., 1989, p. 206). The word "augment" suggests enhancing or heightening a state of affairs. Augmenting is more subtle than pliance and tracking, but no less important. Put more simply, *augmenting* occurs when certain things in the environment have their functions changed because of what was said about them. Advertisers rely on augmenting to sell their products; for example, "Wouldn't you look good driving a Toyota?" or "An ice-cold Budweiser would hit the spot." Toyotas and Budweisers are in the person's environment, but their ability to reinforce the person's responses is likely increased after hearing these types of commercials.

Augmenting is clinically relevant in relation to both values and avoidance. For instance, when a person makes a values statement such as "I value staying physically fit," this statement may function as an augmental by increasing the probability that the speaker will go on that morning jog rather than sleep an extra thirty minutes. That values statement increases the reinforcing functions of jogging. Alternately, problematic augmenting may increase avoidance when an individual follows a rule such as "this anxiety is unbearable." This type of verbal behavior may function as an augmental and thus increase the aversive functions of anxiety. As you may notice in the above examples, augmenting is often combined with pliance and tracking.

Importance of Rule-Governed Behavior

Overall, the rule-governed behavior literature (Barnes-Holmes, O'Hora, et al., 2001; Hayes & Hayes, 1989) in behavior analysis clearly suggests that rules are often adaptive in complex human functioning. The literature also suggests that some rules lead to missing out on valued reinforcers, can conflict with other rules, and can influence a poorly adapted repertoire of responding. Whether the person is influenced by effective rules or poorly working rules, both require relational framing. And when rules lead to ineffective and pathological rules, those influences can be subjugated by certain ACT interventions that undermine problematic verbal behavior. Helping a client to clarify his values and to just notice that he is telling himself to follow certain unhelpful rules rather than buying into those rules can assist in making clinical gains.

Applying RFT to ACT

ACT in practice is always RFT in practice. Thinking about the client's presenting complaints and in-session verbal behavior in terms of relational frames adds an additional dimension to case conceptualization, functional assessment, and treatment planning. Thinking about interventions in terms of relational framing adds yet another dimension to treatment planning.

For example, let's return to Shandra, whom we first met in chapter 1. Early on Shandra describes how she gives her children money to alleviate unwanted feelings. She complains, "I want my kids to do better so I can stop feeling guilty and worrying all the time." We might view this as negative thinking, as a symptom of depression, or as an irrational belief. Considered in RFT terms, we might note that she is relating guilt and worry to her children's success or failure in a causal sense: that her children's behavior is the cause of her guilt and worry. Or conversely, she might be relating "giving money" to "helping" and relating "helping" to her "success as a parent." She may be relating treatment success to "not feeling guilty or worrying." She is relating her children's behavior and the consequences of their behavior to her success as a parent. These possibilities suggest fusion with a conceptualized self, emotional avoidance, and action in the service of reducing guilt and worry. We could explore these ACT concepts and other possibilities in our assessment of her behavior, and our assessment might suggest ACT interventions that might be useful. Those interventions would target Shandra's relational responding.

Examples of the Differences Between ACT and Cognitive Restructuring Interventions

We can also consider ACT interventions in terms of RFT. Let's look at the situation of Rick, whom we also met in chapter 1. Rick reports that prior to business meetings when he knows he will have to talk about the work going on in his department, he feels a looming dread for a few days prior to the meeting. What might be a treatment goal with respect to his anxiety? A therapist might teach him relaxation skills so his anxiety will be reduced. This sort of intervention, while perhaps useful, is not an RFT intervention (although the process of teaching relaxation skills involves relational responding). And relaxation training is consistent with his goal of decreasing anxiety. So far, so good. However, if we would like to use defusion, we will have to be careful that we don't undermine an ACT rationale. In other words, if the clinician decided to use relaxation training as well as defusion and willingness, she would have to be very careful in presenting her treatment rationale for both intervention approaches. Rick might relate relaxation training with "getting rid of anxiety is good" with "anxiety is bad." This relating might inadvertently weaken defusion and willingness interventions aimed at accepting anxiety or increasing contact with the present moment.

Alternately, we might explore the content of Rick's thoughts about going to meetings and look for irrational beliefs. For example, perhaps he has the thought "it would be terrible to make a fool out of myself at work." We could use cognitive restructuring to change these beliefs to more rational ones. We would have to be very careful in combining this approach with defusion, because cognitive restructuring presumes that thought content is problematic and tries to change responding within the relational context. Disputing "it would be terrible to make a fool out of myself" in order to make it sound more like "it is undesirable to look foolish, but I can take it" is changing the verbal responding in the relational context. Defusion, on the other hand, is based on the premise that fusion with thoughts is problematic. The ACT intervention would be less about changing the form of the thought in the relational context and more about the context of function. The intervention would illuminate the context of function, showing how the thought can be simply experienced or "had." Thoughts like "it would be terrible if …" can be accepted as verbal events and do not have to transform the stimulus functions toward the clinically relevant behaviors leading to Rick avoiding work or avoiding the thought. The clinician would want to avoid sending a mixed message of disputing and defusing. The disputing tries to knock out the power of the words on words' own terms: by altering what is said and what is meant. Defusion reduces the influence of the words by drawing out the contextual variables that support the meaning of words. And remember Einstein's pithy quote: "We can't solve problems by using the same kind of thinking we used when we created them." So to help Rick, we'd pick a functional intervention that might involve having him experience his thoughts differently. For instance, we might have Rick say, "I can't pick up the pen," while picking up a pen with the aim of changing the functional relationship between his thought content and his behavior.

Let's revisit Shandra. Suppose the clinician uses a "normalizing" intervention, where the clinician might say to Shandra, "Of course you feel guilty! Who wouldn't, given your history of everyone telling you that you are responsible for other people's behavior?" Is this a functional or relational intervention? The clinician is not trying to change her guilt. Normalizing her guilt may not make her feel less guilty, and there are two ways the clinician might go with this. The clinician might be creating a relational context where "guilt" is related to "normal" and thus weaken Shandra's relational network where "guilt" was in a frame of correspondence with "bad." Shandra may still feel guilty, and, at the same time, she may feel less bad about feeling guilty.

Alternately, the clinician may elaborate on the normalizing statement by asking for examples of situations where Shandra feels guilty. In doing so, the clinician may establish that Shandra believes that if she feels guilty, then she has done something wrong, and that if her children feel bad, then she has done something wrong. Through combinatorial entailment and through transformation of stimulus functions, when her children feel bad, Shandra will feel guilty. If her goal is to avoid feeling guilty, and feeling guilty follows "when others feel bad, then I must have done something bad," then the only way to avoid guilt is to avoid others or to make certain that others never feel bad. Some therapeutic approaches might try to convince her that she should not feel guilty or might suggest that other people's bad feelings are not sufficient evidence that she had done something bad. However, given her years of experience and the persistence of her relational responses, she is unlikely to stop feeling guilty or stop thinking that she has done something bad because a therapist suggests that she is thinking in a distorted or irrational manner. An ACT approach might suggest that she act on the basis of values while accepting and noticing the feelings rather than by trying to avoid guilt. The success of this type of intervention might be evidenced by Shandra saying no to her children while feeling guilty.

It is not that an ACT therapist desires Shandra to continue feeling guilty. Rather, the ACT therapist recognizes that relational networks are difficult to dismantle. Once a verbal relation has been established, it is a part of one's history. Relational networks work by addition rather than by subtraction. Trying to change one's verbal relations by adding new relations does not eliminate the first relation—it elaborates the verbal network (Wilson, Hayes, Gregg, & Zettle, 2001). There are many contexts that support making sense of the world, and sense making tends to elaborate rather than shrink relational networks. If someone tells Shandra that she should feel good about herself rather than bad, it is not as if the relationship between herself and "bad" is eliminated. (In this regard, human behavior is not mechanistic; one faulty thought can't be replaced by a new and improved thought.) With the sense-making agenda, in contexts where "I am bad" shows up, she may at best have the additional thought "and I should think that I am good." Worst case is that now feeling bad about herself becomes something to feel bad about; for example, "Oh no! I shouldn't be thinking that." Then Shandra will have one more thing to feel bad about.

Thinking about cases in RFT terms is more than just an academic exercise. Thinking about what you're doing in RFT terms can increase your own flexibility and aid in creating your own novel metaphors and exercises, and in tailoring interventions to specific clients. You are strongly encouraged to learn more about RFT through the contextualpsychology.org website, which is the home of the RFT tutorial by Eric Fox, or to read Hayes, Barnes-Holmes, and Roche (2001) for a more thorough analysis.

CHAPTER 5

What Is Case Conceptualization?

Case conceptualization is an integration of assessment data focused on the client's clinically relevant behaviors, the information regarding the historical and current environment that influences those behaviors, the mutually developed treatment goals, and the planned therapeutic process used to approach those goals. Case conceptualization is in part a creative process of the clinician, and it is also guided by evidence-based principles.

Case conceptualization includes:

■ Information regarding the client's problem

■ The past situations that shaped the person's problem

■ The current situations that maintain this problem

■ The short- and long-term goals for therapy

■ Developing an evidence-based treatment plan

Case conceptualization has also been called case formulation and working hypothesis in the literature. Throughout this book, these terms may be used interchangeably for style purposes, but we will primarily use "case conceptualization" for consistency. In ACT case conceptualization, the assessment tracks the six processes of the ACT approach—defusion, acceptance, self as context, values, contact with the present moment, and committed action—and assists the therapist in facilitating greater psychologically flexibility. Luoma, Hayes, and Walser (2007) suggest that ACT case conceptualization "leads to a more focused, consistent, and thorough intervention" (p. 227).

In general terms, case conceptualization elucidates "*what the client is like* as well as theoretical hypotheses for *why the client is like this*" (Berman, 1997, p. xi, emphasis in original). Beyond the hypothesizing of the clinically relevant what and why, the clinician needs to conceptualize treatment goals, such as where the client is going and how to best get there. For a brief example, when beginning to make an ACT case conceptualization about how to work with Rick, a therapist might look at what his problems are (avoiding visiting his mother and smoking marijuana); why those problems came to exist and why they are maintained (to avoid anxiety and guilt); and how to address these avoidance responses (assist him in becoming more mindful and accepting of his guilt, defusing from verbal rules for getting rid of his unwanted feelings, and engaging in committed, valued behavior through empirically supported methods of treatment).

In her edited volume encompassing several different case conceptualization methods, Eells (1997) attempts to define case conceptualization in a manner that would be acceptable to various theoretical approaches by saying that "psychotherapy case formulation is essentially a hypothesis about the causes, precipitants, and maintaining influences of a person's psychological, interpersonal, and behavioral problems.... [It] should serve as a blueprint guiding treatment, as a marker for change, and as a structure enabling the therapist to understand the patient better" (pp. 1–2).

Persons (1991) suggests case conceptualization is used "as a basis for choosing among the treatment interventions described by the [clinician's] therapeutic model" (p. 102), and also says that "case formulation is the therapist's compass [because] it guides the treatment" (Persons, 1989, p. 37). The blueprint and compass assist the client and clinician in deciding which clinical concerns are most important, which variables influence the problems and treatment outcome, and which treatments are most appropriate for the case (Haynes & O'Brien, 2000; Haynes & Williams, 2003).

A useful case conceptualization, whether it is in ACT or another approach, consists of descriptive information about the client gathered through a thorough diagnostic evaluation and intake interview (including family and social history, medications, presenting problem, and so on) and leads to prescriptive recommendations for therapy (Sperry, Gudeman, Blackwell, & Faulkner, 1992). In addition, the process may also facilitate the formation of a therapeutic alliance, influence therapist empathy, and improve the quality of supervision for student-therapists (Kuyken, 2006). Further research regarding these potential benefits is necessary, yet intervention research is far outpacing the conceptualization research. In fact, conceptualization has received scant attention from the early psychotherapy literature (Porzelius, 2002); we will briefly summarize what has been written in the major psychotherapy traditions so that we can compare and contrast with ACT case conceptualization. Surveying the case conceptualization literature shows that Freud's classical psychoanalysis may be the strongest and earliest proponent of case conceptualization.

Case Conceptualization in Psychoanalysis

Freud's principal contribution to modern case conceptualization is simply his development of a model for explaining human behavior and psychopathology. Even his most vehement detractors must credit him for this historical contribution of conceptualizing the major influences on a person's life as explanations for psychopathology, as he is argu-ably the first clinician to discuss the influence of early childhood learning experiences and interpersonal factors on clinical concerns. Freud and his colleagues also emphasized using a detailed interview process while developing a treatment plan. Modern therapists continue to focus the first few psychotherapy sessions on gathering assessment data.

Freud relayed his theory through several complex case presentations (for example, "Dora," 1905/1953; "the Wolf Man," 1918/1963), clearly favoring an idiographic approach to psychopathology. Freud's case study approach is shared among groups who initially opposed psychoanalysis, most notably in the behavior therapy and the applied behavior analysis fields, where single-subject designs are paramount. Additionally, psychodynamic therapists continue to maintain that people show their pathology in their interaction with the therapist. This fundamental idea continues in the practice of behavior therapy and especially in the functional analytic psychotherapy model (FAP; Kohlenberg, R. J., & Tsai, 1991). Looking for experiential avoidance and psychological inflexibility "in the room" is part of the ACT therapist's job, and in this regard ACT overlaps with FAP and psychoanalysis. While ACT may differ in several important ways from psycho-analysis, Freud's seminal work regarding an individualized focus on each case is ACT consistent.

Case Conceptualization in Client-Centered Therapy

The ACT therapist would also do well to consider the humanistic approach to case con-ceptualization and evaluation. Rogers (1951) warns that there can be "a degree of loss of personhood as the individual acquires the belief that only an expert can accurately evaluate him, and that therefore the measure of his personal worth lies in the hands of another" (p. 224). The ACT approach acknowledges the ubiquity of suffering and the vulnerability of all people—including so-called experts—to problems in living. Seeing the pervasiveness of human suffering and that all people can fall into language traps, the ACT therapist radically accepts the client's clinical concerns and also attempts to reduce the imbalance of power between the two people in the therapy room by making sure the treatment plan and therapy unfold as a collaborative process.

The human relationship between the therapist and client is ever present in ACT. As noted throughout the ACT literature, we are all "swimming in the same soup." We all benefit from our shared language, and also collectively and individually feel its bite. Oftentimes the ACT therapist will dispense with the clipboard and pen during the first meeting and sit next to, rather than across from, the client in an effort to level the playing field. This of course is a matter of style and must be used judiciously with each therapist-client dyad. The drawback of such an approach is that the interview data are not recorded immediately, and yet one might ask if, on balance, the presession assess-ments and questionnaires might do the job of that first question-and-answer session and allow the therapist-client interaction to unfold more naturally during the first session. In addition, the postsession notes for the first few sessions might also require more diligence and time if the intake is done with a more humanistic approach. We might also consider that a collaborative therapeutic relationship is given a better chance to thrive when the clinician joins the client in such a way. And from a functional contextual point of view, we can consider that in the context of therapy, we are going to begin to tear down some walls and unwrite some of the "rules of engagement" (see chapter 2 for more on functional contextualism).

The humanistic tradition rejects diagnoses outside of their utility as descriptions, and Rogers (1951) explains that "psychological diagnosis as usually understood is unnecessary for psychotherapy and may actually be detrimental to the therapeutic process" (p. 220). Functional contextualism also rejects categorical diagnosis with additional reasons. Categorizing or pigeonholing a collection of "symptoms" based on the topography or obvious form of the behavior does very little to address why the person exhibits those behavioral symptoms. In other words, the categorical approach ignores the function of "symptoms."

Hayes, Wilson, Gifford, Follette, and Strosahl (1996) suggest that the categorical nosology used by the DSM is inadequate. In addition, the currently popular DSM diagnoses lack treatment utility (Kupfer, First, & Reiger, 2002; Hayes et al., 1987; Persons, 1989). These authors instead suggest a dimensional approach to clinically relevant behavior. In other words, just because a therapist properly assesses a group of symptoms that cohere under a DSM category, that diagnosis does not necessarily lead to appropriate treatment unless a functional analysis of the signs and symptoms is conducted (see chapter 3 for an explanation of functional analysis). In many ways, the atheoretical approach of the DSM creates a theoretical and etiological vacuum that case conceptualization aims to fill.

The typical client-centered therapist's attitude toward case conceptualization appears quite similar to the functional contextual approach: hold it lightly. Humanistic authors Goldman and Greenberg (1992) agree that "knowledge of certain nosological categories or syndromes can be helpful to experiential therapists but that they are best conceived of as descriptions of patterns of functioning rather than of types of people" (p. 404). ACT practitioners would agree for similar humanistic and additional, scientific reasons.

A humanistic therapy approach, with its emphasis on empathy, can also imbue the case-conceptualization process with value. Some authors (Kuyken, 2006; Eells, 1997) suggest that the process of case conceptualization "normalizes" the clinical concern and may lead to greater empathy from the clinician. The ACT stance fosters greater empathy because the therapist does not entertain the assumption that people can achieve an ongoing state of complete "healthy normality." In fact, the ACT/RFT literature (Hayes, Barnes-Holmes, et al., 2001; Hayes et al., 1999) suggests that normal language processes have important useful effects and also have detrimental effects on valued living. Discussing the myth of "healthy normality" during the development of the relationship and the development of the case conceptualization may help the clinician embrace the client and the "problem" with greater empathy. Normalizing symptoms is not only a part of case conceptualization. It can also serve as a psychoeducational intervention on its own because it often decreases client distress (which is more of an unintended effect in

ACT, but likely welcomed by the client this early in therapy). The client's concerns are seen as a natural outcome of historical and external events rather than as something inherently "wrong with" her. An empathic orientation can foster the client-therapist relationship, and the quality of the relationship has been linked to positive outcomes in therapy (Wright & Davis, 1994). In addition, a focus on the relationship as an important therapeutic factor has a firm place in clinical behavior analysis (Callaghan, Naugle, & Follette, 1996; Kohlenberg, B. S., 2000; Kohlenberg, R. J., & Tsai, 1991).

Case Conceptualization in Cognitive and Behavioral Therapies

Integrating assessment data, assessing environmental influences, developing treatment goals, and making a treatment plan are the primary goals of behavioral and cognitive therapies during the early stages of the intervention. In that way, case conceptualization is observed in the works of seminal behavior therapists (Lazarus, 1972, 1973; Wolpe, 1958). Behavior therapists have continued to embrace case conceptualization (Hersen & Porzelius, 2002; Koerner & Linehan, 1997; Persons, 1989; Turkat, 1985), and mostly employ the functional analysis of antecedents and consequences in their work.

Meyer and Turkat (1979) relate a simple three-phase progression for behavior therapy that includes interviewing the client, experimenting with intervention methods to investigate how the behavior changes and is maintained, and then modifying the intervention so the treatment gains are maintained. This assess-intervene-modify treatment approach is valued by most behavior therapists (Spiegler & Guevremont, 2003; Cooper et al., 1987), and informs the behavior analytic approach of ACT.

There are several approaches to cognitive behavioral therapy (CBT), and while each has unique features, they also offer variations on a main theme. The different waves of cognitive behavioral therapy were discussed thoroughly in chapter 2, and we will broadly summarize their case conceptualization approaches here for comparison purposes. Most CBT models take an A-B-C, or alternately named S-O-R, approach. Concisely, the basic premise of CBT models is that an event occurs (an activating event or stimulus [S]), and the person has a private reaction (a belief about the event or an organismic [O] response) that leads to important clinically relevant actions (emotional consequences or responses [R]). Briefly, the mechanistic worldview (see chapter 2) of most CBT conceptualizations would suggest that certain events beyond the person's control will always occur (that is, the activating event or stimulus), and if the person changes the details of what they think about or how they interpret that event (with a new belief or organismic response), then they would feel or act differently—that is, with more functional consequences or responses—in the face of that uncontrollable event.

CBT case conceptualizations typically focus on assessing and then changing what the person believes (the B) by showing that her core beliefs, schema, or fluent thinking patterns might be irrational (Ellis, 1962) or distorted (Beck et al., 1979). The therapist can use disputation of irrational thoughts or behavioral experiments to both test and alter dysfunctional interpretations, and also to capitalize on the effects of exposure. Additional functional interventions such as exposure, contingency management, and social skills training are also included in therapy. Persons (1989) and Haynes and O'Brien (2000) detail how therapists can prioritize which clinical concerns to target first and how to best link the intervention with the problem. While the literature supporting the cognitive behavioral therapy case conceptualization is sparse, it appears to be growing (Haynes & Williams, 2003).

Empirically Supported Treatments (ESTs) and Case Conceptualization

Clinicians are increasingly pressed to use interventions that are empirically supported or evidenced based. While empirical evidence generally supports clinicians in their practice, it can also have the unintended effect of promoting attention to general findings rather than to the specific concerns of the individual client.

ESTs Pose a Challenge to Case Conceptualization

Ironically, an apparent obstacle for widespread case conceptualization in behavior therapy comes from behavior therapy's greatest strength: empirically supported treatments. ESTs are practices developed from the best-known empirical evidence for clinical decision making while caring for a client. ESTs are established through psychotherapy outcome research, and this scientific support has helped cognitive behavioral therapy grow in effectiveness and popularity, as well as garner favor from third-party payers. While these outcome studies are heuristic for effectively applying behavioral principles and for pointing toward future research directions, the controlled outcome studies require standardization of treatment rather than individualization of treatment. This state of affairs poses a dilemma for the clinician doing individualized case conceptualization: our best therapies suggest doing the work one particular way for all clients presenting with a particular problem. This may lead clinicians to ask, "Do I follow the very general treatment guideline or tailor the therapy to this particular client?"

Case Conceptualization Poses a Challenge to ESTs

A major clinical concern with the EST research is that the methods used to control for confounds in the research are not usually found in the real world of actual individual therapy in most client-therapist relationships. For instance, clients with dual diagnoses or those taking medication may be excluded from research and bear little resemblance to clients encountered in the real world. Hence, EST research can lack utility in everyday clinical work (that is, ecological validity). For many practitioners, individualization of assessment and treatment may suggest or require departure from standardized empirically supported treatment protocols, and outcome studies generally lack this important individualized connection in several important domains. Assessment, treatment, and the link between assessment and treatment are all typically performed uniformly across the participants in clinical research.

In outcome research, the assessment is often diagnostic and used for selection criteria. It may also be performed by an intake specialist rather than the clinician. In individualized therapy, the client does not get "deselected" from treatment for having comorbid conditions or assessment scores that are not up (or down) to par, but this might happen in research. In the community outside of academe, the assessment is often performed by the frontline clinician and aimed toward treatment. And in behavior therapy, there can be less emphasis on diagnosis and more on other dimensions of the problem (Hayes et al., 1996).

The treatment methods in EST research are explicitly standardized in order to investigate the efficacy of the particular treatment. Individualized treatment allows greater flexibility and appeals to the individual's strengths and weaknesses. This is not an indictment of standardized research. The concern is that the successful practices developed from group design research may be rigidly adhered to when applying these principles to an individual client who may or may not resemble the average research subject. It remains to be seen if a flexile approach to certain practices can improve clinical psychology's effectiveness, but years of successful individualization in applied behavior analysis treatments (Cooper et al., 1987) suggest that such flexibility may be worthwhile. Following rules for behavior can lead to insensitivity to contingency changes (for example, Shimoff et al., 1981), and that also goes for the behavior of making clinical decisions. In other words, rigidly following a pattern of rules about how to diagnose and treat problems may lead the clinician to miss subtle changes in the client's behavior. A total obedience to manualized EST procedures is also somewhat unlikely given that the ethical code in the behavior analytic tradition strongly promotes individualized treatment (Baer, D. M., Wolf, & Risley, 1968). In addition, it is also quite possible to research the efficacy and effectiveness of individualized case conceptualization (Persons, 1991).

Cautions Regarding Case-Conceptualization Usage

Individualized case conceptualization has both advantages and limitations. The following caveats are designed to aid the clinician during early assessment and case conceptualization and while selecting appropriate interventions.

Conflicting Views About the Usefulness of Case Conceptualization

There are two important cautions for clinicians applying case formulation. First, there is a paucity of evidence that case conceptualization is an important contributor to treatment outcomes. It is our hope that this ACT case-conceptualization model will stand up to rigorous testing. It is built upon the behavior analytic tradition, which clearly demonstrates effectiveness with functional analyses of single cases. Luborsky and Crits-Christoph (1998) provide support for the treatment utility of their psychodynamic case-conceptualization model, suggesting that case-conceptualization research can be a fruitful clinical endeavor. However, some research suggests case conceptualization may not always be important. Schulte, Kunzel, Pepping, and Schulte-Bahrenberg (1992) demonstrated in one study with phobic clients that manualized treatment surpassed the two individualized treatment groups. Emmelkamp, Bouman, and Blaauw (1994) replicated this finding with individuals diagnosed with obsessive-compulsive disorder. These investigations imply that manualized, rather than case-specific approaches, can lead to superior outcomes.

Concerns with Clinical Bias in Case Conceptualization

The second consideration is that case conceptualization may lead to unreliable decision making and clinical bias. Tversky and Kahneman (1974) demonstrate that when people are presented with ambiguous and incomplete information, they will use a decision-making heuristic, or rule of thumb, to make inferences about the missing data. Often these "cognitive shortcuts" are adaptive and are "good enough" as solutions, even if they are suboptimal. In other words, the added costs of optimal solutions do not always outweigh the benefits of "good enough" options. Occasionally part of the data plus a good educated guess is more helpful than waiting for all the data or not guessing at all.

The problem with decision heuristics is that important clinical decisions may be made without all of the data. According to Kuyken (2006), "[T]he decision making and clinical judgment literature suggest that heuristics are likely to play a role in CBT formulation processes, and that these are problematic in circumstances of high uncertainty, time pressure, and other forms of stressors" (p. 13). In other words, some situations might influence a therapist to rigidly buy into their case conceptualization, and thus they might exhibit the same problem as their client: they might believe their words too much and not be psychologically flexible enough to appropriately help the client. The therapist will be generating several hypotheses for the case conceptualization, and needs to hold them lightly and be flexible when the client's behavior doesn't conform to the hypothesis. In order to engender flexibility, the therapist must exhibit flexibility.

However, the case-conceptualization baby does not have to go out with the biased bathwater. In order to combat the effects of these potential biases, Moran and Tai (2001) say that "it is prudent for therapists to use the single subject treatment design because this mechanical prediction technology reduces the deleterious biases involved in using clinical judgment" by tracking the client's ongoing progress with objective measures (p. 196). In other words, graphing or tabulating objective data can give a less biased perspective about the client's progress.

Of course, sometimes a "good enough" explanation is the best a clinician can do, even in the face of terrible human suffering. Optimal solutions may have costs that the client-therapist team cannot afford. An ACT theme that will be reiterated throughout this book is that if you value something, you need to value it with your behavior. In other words, when a clinician values helping a client improve his life situation, something needs to be done, even if it is suboptimal, especially given the enormous complexity of our subject matter.

It is important to recognize that a case conceptualization is a creative product of the clinician and that it is also based on empirically derived constructs. Much like the development of a scientific theory, observations are made about a subject and then related to other observed data. The synthesis of a theory, whether simple or complex, applied or basic, is still a product of the theorist's historical and current background. It is presumable that more incisive theories and conceptualizations will come from scientists possessing sophisticated assessment tools and a thorough understanding of the literature regarding their subject matter. That is why it is incumbent on you, the ACT therapist, to stay apprised of the current state of the assessment and intervention literature. It may also be helpful to understand that case conceptualization is an ongoing process and the initial conceptualization is but a starting point subject to revision at any moment as treatment unfolds.

Acceptance and Commitment Therapy and Case Conceptualization

The burgeoning ACT literature shows great promise (Hayes et al., 2006) and an ACT case-conceptualization model may provide all the aforementioned benefits, such as assisting with the synthesis of data, aiding the development of treatment goals, establishing the relationship, providing a context for worthwhile supervision, and facilitating an improved stance of empathy.

Because ACT is a functional contextual approach (see chapter 2), the case conceptualization may diverge somewhat from traditional conceptualization. As mentioned earlier, case-conceptualization methods often use a categorical and topographical approach (Hersen & Porzelius, 2002; Luborsky & Crits-Christoph, 1998; Persons, 1989; Weerasekera, 1996). These approaches categorize problems based on the collection of observed and reported symptoms and look to treat all people with the same category of psychological problem similarly. Through an interview, a clinician may gain enough topographical information about the client's problem to arrive at a categorical diagnosis from the *Diagnostic and Statistical Manual of Mental Disorders*; however, this category diagnosis based on the collection of symptoms is inadequate for devising a treatment plan and quite often ignores the function of the presenting "symptoms."

The ACT case-conceptualization model promotes a dimensional and functional approach. We do not look at problematic feelings and symptom reduction per se, but rather investigate how a particular behavioral repertoire can interfere with valued life goals and how a person can become more psychologically flexible with what life presents her. When ACT is used with individuals with chronic pain (Dahl & Lundgren, 2006; Dahl et al., 2004), the primary aim is not to reduce the actual experience of the physical pain (though it might decrease), but to move the person in valued, interpersonal, rich, life-affirming directions even while in the presence of the pain. Clients are asked to experience what life presents them as they move forward and toward their desired ends: "Can you feel pain, or depressed, anxious, angry, and/ or guilty, and still do what is really important to you?"

During ACT conferences and on the ACT-related Listservs, people often talk about doing the "ACT dance," as if the client and therapist are waltzing together step-by-step through the main tenets of the approach delineated in the hexaflex model. A case conceptualization helps the dyad choose what dance to do together and sets the rhythm and the tempo. Our aim is to step with you through the ACT approach and see how one move leads to another.

The Fundamentals of ACT Case Conceptualization

CHAPTER 6

Conceptualizing Functionally

How does a therapist conceptualize a case in ACT terms? In this chapter, we will consider the ACT model of psychopathology as one framework for case conceptualization. We will work through examples of case conceptualization as it occurs at the broad level of the client's presenting complaints and as it occurs dynamically in session in the context of the therapeutic relationship.

Conceptualizing a Case

As defined earlier, case conceptualization is a synthesis of assessment data, the information regarding how the past and current environment influences clinically relevant behaviors (including the in-session environment), the mutually developed treatment goals, and the planned processes to approach those goals. In addition to utilizing the behavioral measures and assessment tools mentioned in chapter 3, the ACT therapist uses interviewing skills and dialogue to gather information critical to planning effective treatment. Questionnaires about the presenting problems and social history intakes are used to help the therapist understand the clinical concern as it is experienced by the client. The therapist attends to the content of what the client says and does during their interpersonal process, and queries both about behavior occurring in session and client descriptions of behavior occurring outside of the session. The challenge to the therapist is to observe the client's behavior through the lens of functional analysis as described in chapter 3 and also through the six core components of ACT. Ideally the therapist will be conceptualizing the case by considering the functional relationships observed between the client's behavior and the environmental variables that support problems or influence clinical gains.

Conceptualization Using the ACT Model of Psychopathology

ACT case conceptualization deviates from traditional linear and mechanistic models. It is not simply that A leads to B leads to C in a linear fashion. The hexaflex diagram aptly demonstrates the mutual and facilitative relationships among all of the psychologically important domains of behavioral flexibility. All six domains can relate to any and all of the other domains. The ACT therapist doesn't simply observe a problem and prescribe an intervention to lead to a singular outcome at the end. ACT is a nonlinear process with the aim of increasing psychological flexibility through interventions from each of the six interrelated domains. While the hexaflex model described in chapter 1 contains only desirable processes, the ACT model of psychopathology is a view of processes that lead to unworkable solutions to client problems and tend to narrow behavior repertoires. These six domains can be characterized as processes consistent with psychological inflexibility—thus we call it the "inflexahex" model (diagram from Hayes et al., 2006).

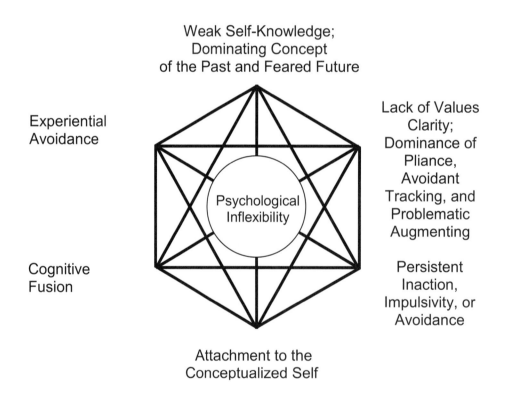

The Inflexahex Model of Psychopathology

According to an ACT model of psychopathology, clinically relevant behavior can be described in terms of the processes on the inflexahex diagram. The ACT therapist's task is to formulate functional explanations for client behavior in terms of these processes. We'll begin with a brief description of the processes and follow this with a few case examples.

Experiential Avoidance

As mentioned in chapter 1, experiential avoidance is attempting to eradicate or resist contact with one's own unwanted thoughts, feelings, sensations, and other private events. When people attempt to rid themselves of unwanted private experience, the strategies not only often fail but can actually increase the unpleasant event. Perhaps even more importantly, when people attempt to avoid private events with clinically relevant behaviors, the relatively more "successful" methods of avoiding thoughts and feelings tend to lead to greater life problems. Consider problematic avoidance in the following scenarios:

- If a man doesn't want to think about his shame for a past crime, he can score some heroin and nod off for a few hours, and develop habit of doing so.

- A woman who doesn't like the feelings of nervousness when she goes outside can elect to stay inside her home for weeks or years on end.

- A teenager hates having private images that she is contaminated, and she can rid herself of those private events (for a few minutes) by washing with bleach … again and again.

- A man who thinks he has been disrespected and feels less macho on the highway when he gets cut off by another motorist can rid himself of these private events by acting very aggressively (or even violently) toward the so-called offender.

Many people behave as if the private experiences of shame, nervousness, contamination, and dejection (as well as other so-called negative events) are problems that should be eliminated. People are often given the message from society to pursue happiness and relaxation and avoid unpleasant emotions and thoughts (Hayes et al., 1999, p. 75) above all else. This experiential avoidance agenda has two drawbacks. The first is that a vital life is bound to include experiences of sadness, anger, and other feelings that we label "uncomfortable." Anyone dedicated to a meaningful mission in life knows that there is bound to also be difficulty and disappointment at times. Avoiding emotional struggle and practical difficulties is impossible when one has become committed to personally worthwhile long-term goals.

The second drawback of experiential avoidance is that it usually doesn't work. As discussed in our review of cognitive behavioral therapy in chapter 2, thought suppression is not effective, as it often increases the frequency of unwanted thoughts in the long run (Beevers et al., 1999; Wegner et al., 1987). Further, such avoidance seems to be the problematic process that transforms ordinary feelings, urges, sensations, and thoughts into clinical issues (Eifert & Forsyth, 2005; Kashdan, Barrios, Forsyth, & Steger, 2006; Kashdan & Breen, 2007).

Attempts to avoid private experience often lead to more problems than they solve. During case conceptualization, tune in to how the client engages in experiential avoidance:

- What is the client unwilling to contact in life and how much vitality is he sacrificing to that end?

- Does the client frequently change the subject, zone out for an extended duration, or lose eye contact with you?

- Does the client primarily say, "I don't know," when you ask an emotionally laden, interpersonally important question?

- Does the client make throwaway comments, such as "I really like my new job and stuff ... I don't know."

- Does the client answer a question in a manner that avoids the import of that question?

Summarize your client's avoidance moves in the experiential avoidance area on the Inflexahex Case-Conceptualization Worksheet (see appendix B; also see "Using the Inflexahex Case-Conceptualization Worksheet" below). Include in-session avoidance too—though the form of in-session experiential avoidance will vary, of course. Now let's take a look at how one form of experiential avoidance may surface in session.

Therapist: Do you feel that our therapeutic relationship is growing stronger?

Client: I don't know.

Therapist: What are your feelings about our time together?

Client: I ... I just don't know.

We do not want therapists to get caught up in looking for I-don't-knows during therapy, because the functional approach does not judge a problematic behavior strictly on its form. However, any seasoned therapist, or anyone having intense relationship discussions, is very likely to have experienced that distancing "I don't know" phrase whenever a person wants to avoid a touchy subject. It is important to look at the function of that phrase and the context in which it is used. Perhaps the aforementioned client has a history of impoverished interpersonal relationships and doesn't have the ability to contact how the alliance is growing. More likely this client has an opinion about the relationship and is avoiding answering because it can bring up strong feelings or an aversive interpersonal discussion.

Discerning whether a client is engaging in experiential avoidance requires good observation and well-developed functional analytic skills. (For a review on functional analysis, see chapter 3.) Hayes et al. (1996) have conceptualized several diagnoses as instances of experiential avoidance, and it is prudent to continue to assess if your client's behavior is in the service of experiential avoidance.

Cognitive Fusion

When behavior is inflexible and influenced more by verbal networks than by experienced environmental consequences, we can say that the person is engaging in cognitive fusion. Hayes et al. (1999) use an interesting turn of phrase when discussing cognitive fusion; they say that verbal symbols and environmental events are "poured together," as if two separate things become one compound. Think about two different things being fused together as when soldering or welding metals together. Two disconnected items become one solid, rigid entity.

From an RFT point of view, cognitive fusion is defined by "the domination of behavior regulatory functions by relational networks, based in particular on the failure to distinguish the process and products of relational responding" (Hayes, 2006b). Technically speaking, cognitive fusion is demonstrated when a relational context dominantly governs behavior relative to the context of function. In other words, verbally related antecedents and consequences such as thoughts, feelings, and judgments have relatively greater influence over responding than directly contacted nonarbitrary contingencies. Simpler still, fusion is when people are guided by the literal content of their thoughts rather than by their direct experience with the world. Responding to fused content is like responding to descriptions rather than to the event described. We will continue to use the word "fusion" when referring to "cognitive fusion," as there is no appreciable difference in the terminology.

Fusion can play a large role in human suffering when the relational context of literality reigns over behavior. Let's see how this operates in the life of one man. When a private event arises, such as the thought "I am bad," and he is entangled in that evaluation as if it corresponded to a literal truth, he is relating his experience to his own self (the "I") as if it was coordinated with direct aversive properties ("bad"). When "bad" (an arbitrary stimulus) has a history of being related to things to be avoided—things that are malformed or behaviors that are socially punished—and the man has now coordinated "bad" with himself, he now shares some of the same stimulus functions as "bad." That relation can elicit and evoke reactions—such as shame, depression, and guilt, and something to be avoided—that are classically and operantly conditioned to "badness." Fusing with the statement "I am bad" can elicit mood states (such as sadness or dejection) that make valued action less probable. The mood state, as a motivational operation (MO), might narrow this man's behavioral repertoire by reducing the effectiveness of certain reinforcers and reducing the evocative effects of certain antecedent stimuli. In simpler terms, when he frequently tells himself, "I am a bad person," and believes or buys that thought (is fused to that thought), he is more likely to be in a bad mood, thereby not seeing opportunities for living a more vital life. He may also discount the positive things that happen to him.

In contrast, a man who can defuse from the thought "I am bad" might simply notice the thought, recognize it as a piece of his history brought to bear on the present situation, and go on with his current activity. Suppose the man who can readily defuse from his evaluative thoughts is playing soccer and misses a shot at the goal, or asks someone on a date and is turned down. He might have the thought "I'm bad" and recognize it as a thought that shows up when he performs in a manner he negatively evaluates. He does not buy the thought and quit the game (whether soccer or dating) or become very distracted; he notices the thought and goes on playing.

Additionally, and perhaps more importantly to ACT case conceptualization, when the man is fused with his thoughts, he may attempt to avoid the unwanted thought and/or situations that evoke that thought. If fused with the thought "I am bad," the thought can have aversive properties, and the experience of thinking "I am bad" itself becomes something to be avoided. An experiential avoidance agenda is set up, and the losing game begins, because any plans to avoid private content are likely to be followed by relatively unhelpful and inflexible behaviors characteristic of an experiential avoidance agenda. Suppose the man usually has thoughts of his "badness" when he goes to his house of worship or visits his parents. He may then choose to avoid practicing his spirituality or gathering with his family in the service of avoiding these thoughts, even when these aspects of his life are important to him.

Here are a few things to do—and not do—regarding cognitive fusion during assessment and conceptualization of your client's behavior:

- Look for instances where responding is guided by concretized evaluations and inflexible rules.

- Note the client's verbal responses and the effect they have on his behavioral rigidity in the Inflexahex Case-Conceptualization Worksheet. This part of building a case conceptualization could look like many other therapy worksheets, self-help forms, and thought logs where the clinician or client jots down "irrational beliefs" or "distorted thoughts." The similarity to ACT is only in form.

- Jot down the assessment data and use it to assess and then address the function of verbal events.

- Do not use these data in order to dispute the verbal events.

- Record the client's statements in order to individualize defusion and mindfulness interventions, note what private events the client avoids, and help elucidate what valued action should be encouraged.

As the end goal of ACT is to foster psychological flexibility, this area of case conceptualization investigates what verbal events the client is unhelpfully and rigidly following. We will further discuss assessment and treatment of fusion and defusion in chapter 13.

Attachment to the Conceptualized Self

In ACT it is useful to talk of three different senses of self that are related to self-knowledge:

■   The conceptualized self, also called self as content

■   Ongoing self-awareness, also called self as process

■   Self as perspective, also called self as context or the observing self

These are not meant to be construed as three different selves or as the only ways of discussing the self as they pertain to self-knowledge; they are merely a means of talking about three different ways in which we might experience our one unique self (Hayes et al., 1999, p. 181). The conceptualized self is the focus of this section while the other two senses of self will be discussed below in the context of weak self-knowledge.

The *conceptualized self* is the verbal content that we use to define and describe ourselves. As Hayes et al. (1999) describe it, "We humans do not merely live in the world, we live in the world as we interpret it, construct it, view it, or understand it. In technical terms, derived stimulus relations dominate over other behavioral processes" (pp. 181-182). Statements such as "I am a twenty-eight-year-old Latino man and Jorge's best friend," "I am an accountant and I used to be a good baseball player," and "I am a terrible mother and a rotten person" are all examples of self as content. Notice that some descriptions of self are relatively permanent (for example, one's gender or ethnic identity), while others describe one's activities (for example, accountant or baseball player), and others are evaluations that might remain relatively stable over time or might change over the course of hours, days, or years (for example, "best friend," "good," or "terrible"). When Shandra notes, "I dropped out of high school when I was seventeen and I never wanted to go to college," or Rick evaluates, "I am smarter than most of my coworkers," they are speaking of their conceptualized selves. People also often describe ongoing experience in terms of self, and instead of noticing that one feels tired, one might instead say, "I am tired" (or anxious or depressed). It is as if the experience becomes one with the conceptualized self. We might also say that one is fused with the conceptualized self.

Relational frame theory provides an account of why this occurs. An individual, through the multiple exemplar training that occurs in everyday life, comes to relate herself to other stimuli, including verbal descriptions, events, people, and places. Through transformation of stimulus functions, she herself may acquire stimulus functions of the thing with which she is in a frame of correspondence. For instance, the child who is told, "You are pretty," may evaluate herself as pretty and have, for herself, the stimulus functions of other pretty things. The child told, "You are ugly," has a similar experience.

A conceptualized self is useful; it allows us to participate in a verbal social community and answer questions such as "What is your name?", "Where do you live?", "Is that your son?", and so on. A conceptualized self is not itself problematic; rather, attachment to the conceptualized self can foster psychological inflexibility. When one rigidly holds onto descriptions that no longer apply, increase one's suffering, or lead to ineffective behavior, then one may be attached to the conceptualized self.

Now for a few clinical examples. First, consider Mark, a twenty-seven-year-old construction worker who came to therapy at the urging of his wife after she caught him kissing another woman. Mark's wife was seven months pregnant at the time. Mark described it this way: "I know I should have stayed away from other women, but I'm like 'Mark the ladies' man.' Women like me, they flirt with me, and I like it when they do. It was hard enough to be a husband, but I got married because I really love Krissy. But now a dad? Dad's aren't hot. Dads are boring. Women are never going to look at me the same."

Mark is describing attachment to his conception of himself as a ladies' man. His sense of self is inflexible because he isn't making room for changing circumstances and roles. He doesn't notice that, even while his life roles are changing, there is a fundamental way in which he is and always will be the same person he has always been. Notice also that Mark does not need to change his conception of himself; he needs only to relate to it differently.

We can also look at Shandra's attachment to her sense of herself as bad. Shandra struggles with this sense of herself as bad by trying to do good, which she defines as giving money to her kids. Through framing relationally, almost any event can trigger the thought "I am bad." When Shandra feels guilty, she has the thought "I must be bad." When her children get into trouble, she thinks about what a bad mother she is, and so on. Shandra's life seems geared to changing this evaluation of herself from bad to good. She acts to quickly alleviate feelings of guilt in the service of changing what she thinks. She flatters, pacifies, and acquiesces to others so they will tell her how good she is. There is a frantic quality to Shandra's behavior, as if she is chasing her own tail.

While there is nothing wrong with feeling good about one's self, Shandra's attachment to a description of herself as good or bad leads her to behave ineffectively and to do things that ultimately lead her to strengthen her sense of badness. For example, she gives her son money and she feels like a good mother, and then he buys drugs, and she is back to feeling like a bad mother. The problem is not that she thinks she's bad. The problem is that she is attached to her conception of herself and engages in behaviors to change that conception when it is "bad" and hold onto it when it is "good." And for Shandra, as well as many other people, such strategies are usually ineffective and lead to problems in her relationships, work, and leisure.

During the case conceptualization, the therapist should identify statements that demonstrate an attachment to conceptualized self. It would be helpful to look for statements such as these:

- I am too…

- If only I did … (or didn't …), then I …

- If I wasn't so (ugly, hated, stupid, and so on), then I;

- My problem is that I am…

- I am a (failure, loser, druggie, wimp, and so on).

- I am not (smart, pretty, strong) enough.

Persistent Inaction, Impulsivity, or Avoidance

In many ways, this—persistent inaction, impulsivity, or avoidance—might be the problematic domain that is most obvious to clients and influences them to seek help. This domain usually includes the obvious problems other people can see too. Now we are talking about the "symptoms" that are often measured in psychopathology studies and are addressed in the empirically supported treatments. When performing functional analyses on troublesome behavior, the B part of the ABC functional analysis is the clinically relevant behavior being addressed in this portion of the case conceptualization.

The clinical question in this domain might sound like this: "What is the client doing too much of or too little of, or doing in the inappropriate contexts?" During case conceptualization, the therapist is developing an understanding about what the person is doing in the service of experiential avoidance. Notice what the people in the following vignettes are doing too much of or too little of, or are doing inappropriately, and then notice the experiential avoidance and inflexible verbal behavior supporting the problem:

- A woman who is unwilling to have thoughts and feelings about contamination may impulsively wash her hands a few times an hour with bleach in order to avoid those private events.

- A man diagnosed with a mood disorder may be persistently inactive because whenever he attempts to live toward his valued ends, aversive private events arrive. He has thoughts of difficulty and feelings of failure, and in the service of experiential avoidance, he develops a repertoire of inflexibly avoiding these private events. He decides to sleep in, miss work, and refuse social interaction, then sets up an agenda that keeps him from these aversive events. By doing so, he sabotages a value-directed lifestyle.

- A young woman participates in a relationship with her abusive girl-friend. She claims, "I am dedicated to her, even if this is a star-crossed relationship."

In treating each case, we would first discuss with the client what behavioral goals might be most prudent for treatment, and then select the behavioral measure that might correspond with clinical improvement.

In chapter 1, we commented that the domain of committed action is where the rubber meets the road in psychological flexibility. This is where people are doing what they care about. Persistent inaction, impulsivity, and avoidance are where the rubber isn't meeting the road or where people are just spinning their wheels erratically. When using the Inflexahex Case-Conceptualization Worksheet, the persistent inaction, impulsivity, or avoidance section will be dedicated to recording the infrequent, excessive, or inappropriate responses that prevent the client from flexibly approaching his valued directions. Notice that with ACT case conceptualization, the concern is with changing the client's overt behavior, not changing the form of the client's covert behavior. With OCD, ACT therapists are interested in making the client's repertoire more broad and flexible, which can include reducing the number of times he washes and increasing the number of public places he goes. The ACT therapist is not interested in making his obsessive thoughts less frequent or more rational. The ACT approach with a person in an abusive relationship is not to reduce the number of times the client says, "But I love him and he really needs me," nor is it to make her statement more rational. Rather, the approach is to get the client to notice that thought and to change her overt dependent behaviors that continually put her in harm's way.

The section of the case conceptualization that considers inaction, impulsivity, and avoidance will include the ABC Functional Analysis Sheet (see appendix A) or Event Logs (see appendix C), and may include measures of clinically relevant behavioral dimensions (frequency, intensity, and so on) as well as other standardized assessments. Be mindful that inaction may be especially difficult to assess during therapy because it is based on what the client *doesn't* do. Oftentimes the empirically supported treatments will focus on ameliorating the concerns rated in this domain of the inflexahex. In this regard, it is prudent to measure "psychopathology" change for ACT clients in terms related to valued living rather than with symptom reduction per se. Bach and Hayes (2002) measured change in latency to rehospitalization and reduction in believability of psychotic events for people diagnosed with psychosis disorders treated with ACT. For people with type 2 diabetes given ACT therapy, Gregg (2004) measured improvements in self-management behavior and blood glucose levels. ACT outcome studies will include measures that may hint at an eliminative agenda. ACT for smoking cessation measures the reduction of cigarette consumption, and ACT for depression is interested in change in Beck Depression Inventory-II (BDI-II; Beck et al., 1996) scores. Influencing clients to do less of what they do too much of, or do more of what they do too little of, can be an ACT goal.

And at the same time, ACT is explicitly about helping clients develop broader and more flexible repertoires. The clinical direction engenders committed action toward vital living. Selecting a valued direction and maintaining that course is critical to the ACT approach. If clinical measures show a reduction in the number of cigarettes per day, a lowering of the BDI-II scores, or better maintenance of blood glucose levels in the service of valued living, then those measures are part and parcel part of our ACT treatment. Third-wave behavior therapy thoroughly embraces measuring inaction, impulsivity, or behavioral avoidance, and utilizing evidence-based interventions to treat those concerns.

Lack of Values Clarity

This domain on the Inflexahex Case-Conceptualization Worksheet focuses on the struggles and obstacles clients have regarding what they want their lives to be about. The therapist is looking for statements and behaviors indicating a lack of vitality or intention. When clients discuss indifference toward their own lifestyle, or that they feel aimless or like they are on a treadmill, the therapist can note the inability to contact personal guiding principles. Clients occasionally mention that they are not sure what their values are, and may not understand that their behavior is in service to an unclarified value system. Some clients can halfheartedly verbalize what they care about and still not fully show up to their ability to respond (response-ability) in contexts that supports those values. Identifying, recognizing, and becoming present with what one truly values is critical to the case conceptualization because it buoys the client's willingness for treatment and authenticates committed action.

Identifying Values

Some clients may believe that they don't have any values. Sometimes this occurs when a client verbalizes a value and then points out what a terrible job she has been doing at living this value and wonders if perhaps she doesn't really value what she values. For instance, a client who says she values being a loving parent and then recalls how she abused her son when she was drinking might wonder if she can really value being a loving parent if she has hurt her child. In this case, instead of evaluating the value, she is evaluating herself. With some defusion and acceptance work, she can get present with her values and with negative evaluations that might accompany contacting values. And then she can get moving in the direction of her values.

Some clients try to decide what they should value instead of exploring what they actually do value. Or they may be reluctant to verbalize values evaluated as "silly" or "not important enough." It's important that the therapist communicate that values aren't limited to acts associated with heroism, altruism, and saving the world. While these are fine values, almost anything that brings vitality to the client's life is valuable.

Other clients may struggle with identifying values because they've never been asked. Their personal experiences never put them in contact with questions about what their truest desires are. We can also speculate that their history is fraught with people who modeled behavior that was counter to the client's values, or people who punished values-directed behavior or discussions. It is not entirely necessary to know why clients have not developed an integrated value system, but it is important to start them on the course to explore their values.

Unrecognized Values

Another part of the case conceptualization is looking for client statements suggesting that they don't value anything. Often such clients have completely pushed values out of their awareness perhaps because of anxiety, resignation, or hopelessness, or because of being overwhelmed with negative consequences of past behavior. While people may easily become disconnected from values, it is unlikely that anyone truly values nothing. Wilson and Byrd (2004, p. 169) suggest contacting values with clients who deny them by asking questions such as "Was there a time when you wanted something, to be something, to do something?" or "In a world where you did care about something, what might that be?" During the case conceptualization, when looking for a lack of values clarity, these assessment questions are likely to come in handy.

Wilson and Byrd (2004) also point out that no one starts out life wanting to be anxious, depressed, or drug addicted, and that if we hang in there with the client and nudge her toward looking at her own history, she may reconnect with hopes and dreams and desires she gave up long ago. Recognizing one's own values sets the occasion for the person to be able to respond. She can have a responsibility to herself to move in that valued direction.

Values Conceptualization with Disabled Clients

Case conceptualization with so-called low-functioning clients, such as people with schizophrenia or low intellectual ability, does include values work. Clients with serious mental illness or intellectual deficits do not lack values; instead they have been denied the opportunity to explore values, often by well-meaning mental health professionals. For instance, many clients are told their treatment goals instead of setting their own treatment goals. (Therapists treating any clinical population must be mindful of this error!)

After years in mental health systems where clients see one provider after another and are given the same treatment goals year after year with little change in their circumstances (even after decades of treatment), many clients still do not know what they value and may not even know what a value is. Such clients are capable of doing values work. The therapist may need to start with some psychoeducation around defining and identifying goals and the relationships among goals and values. And once the client is on board, treatment can proceed as with any client (Bach, Gaudiano, Pankey, Herbert, & Hayes, 2005). These clients may have different specific goals than higher-functioning clients, and yet the values are similar and generally focused on important life domains such as family, relationships, education, occupation, health, and so on.

The Significance of Trivial Matters

Look for how the client reports being led around by the nose by trivial, inconsequential elements in life. When case conceptualizing with the inflexahex worksheet, record what circumstances in the client's environment push him into restricted, impulsive, or vitality-sapping behavior—and then note if the client even cares about those circumstances. If not—if those influences on that person's life are so inconsequential— the case conceptualization should include clarifying what will be consequential and vital for that person.

Values Clarity Through Pain

For many people, the discussions leading to a clarification of values can be troublesome or strenuous. Look for struggle and pain in therapy because often it is in that struggle that the values are whispering. In the pain, values can be found. For example, Carlota was devout in her faith and exhibited scrupulosity OCD concerns. She would frequently think that "God hates us all" and other thoughts she evaluated as sacrilegious. In her anguished tears while she told of her "symptoms," she said, "I just want to love God and serve him all my life, and I can't because of my sins." The first part of that quote is a strong values statement!

As another example, take Seamus, who reported he was "deeply depressed" and was lonely and estranged from his brothers and sisters. He sobbingly related to his therapist that his arrogant and disdaining past behaviors toward his siblings eradicated all familial relationships from his life. As Seamus put it, "I just wanted to be a part of their lives. I ached to belong, to mean something to them. And I was misguided in thinking if they looked up to me as powerful or cool or something, maybe they'd like me and want me in their life. I went about it is such a wrong way!" Those first few statements were genuine statements of his values.

Clarifying values has a large role in ACT case conceptualization because it establishes a context for just having difficult thoughts and feelings (defusion and acceptance), can be done in the present moment, and dignifies the difficult work sometimes involved with committed action. Values statements as augmentals—that is, as verbal rules that increase the reinforcing functions of various other behaviors—can motivate committed action and facilitate increasing psychological flexibility. For instance, the person who hears himself say, "It is so important to me to take care of my health," may find rising half an hour earlier in the morning in order to go jogging more reinforcing than the does the person who doesn't acknowledge such a value.

During case conceptualization, values clarification opportunities may arise when the clients makes statements like these:

- What's the point?

- Nothing matters.

- I don't know where I'm going.

- I don't know what to do.

- What should I do with my life?

- Everything seems meaningless … I feel disillusioned.

- Ever since (my divorce, my illness, I started using drugs, and so on), my life has been going nowhere.

Dominance of Pliance, Avoidant Tracking, and Problematic Augmenting

Pliance, tracking, and augmentals are useful. However, like most behaviors, they become problematic when they are excessive, inflexible, or practiced in contexts where they move one away from valued outcomes.

Excessive pliance can be problematic and indicate psychological inflexibility as it often occurs as behavior in the service of pleasing others at the expense of attaining valued outcomes. This is not to say that pliance is pathological. Pleasing others, obeying orders, and following social norms are often related to values in the context of family, romantic relationships, friendship, occupational goals, or community and spiritual values. Pliance is excessive when pleasing others and following rules dominates over a more flexible repertoire, and contacting direct contingencies is weakened or absent in some contexts. For example, Rachel, a depressed teen, quit the high school marching band and cheerleading squad and began using marijuana when her new high school friends ridiculed her hobbies and told her that "only nerds say no."

Peer pressure puts teens at risk for excessive pliance, and adults are not immune to peer pressure. Consider the following examples:

- Jonathan, a socially anxious adult, got a college degree in business in the service of pleasing his demanding father. He does not enjoy his job in middle management at a large company and dreams of what he would be doing had he followed his interest in studying archaeology.

- Karen remains in a loveless marriage because "it would kill my mother if I got a divorce."

- Mark wants to start a new business venture and hesitates because "if I did that at my age, everyone would think I'm having a midlife crisis."

Excessive pliance leads to inflexibility and movement away from valued goals and outcomes, and is often evidenced by a client's lack of vitality and joy in his activities and can often be detected in the client's verbal behavior about the importance of pleasing others.

Avoidant tracking occurs when a rule governs a person's behavior leading to escape or removal of aversive stimuli, and the avoidant behavior is detrimental to value-directed responses. For instance, Rick notices that when he speaks up in a business meeting he feels anxious. Privately he makes the rule "I will just stop speaking in meetings so I don't feel so flush and nauseated." He fails to notice that when he speaks up in meetings, his colleagues listen to his suggestions and he is regarded as part of a team, which are outcomes he cares about. When he rigidly follows this rule about avoiding his private events and does not speak up anymore, his colleagues stop asking his opinion and he becomes socially isolated at work. His tracking isn't necessarily wrong; when he stops speaking, he stops having anxiety. So there is correspondence between the rule and the way the world is arranged. It works in altering the contact with one set of stimuli; however, it is unhelpful to moving toward valued stimuli. While it may not always be costly to avoid unwanted thoughts and feelings, tracking is problematic when experiential avoidance dominates over attaining valued outcomes.

Problematic augmenting occurs when verbal behavior changes the capacity of certain events to function as reinforcers or punishers, and influences the person's behavior away from valued directions or increases inflexibility. When a person says, "This anxiety is unbearable," the statement can function as an augmental increasing the aversive functions of anxiety. Saying, "nothing is worthwhile in my life," can reduce the evocative and motivational properties of things that the person used to like to do, and the statement may diminish the reinforcing properties of such pleasant events. Again, the problem is not that people have these thoughts; rather, it is the fusion to these verbal events that can stultify value-directed living.

The ACT therapist should look for occasions where dominance of pliance, avoidant tracking, and problematic augmenting are discussed in session. Some examples of such events are when the client mentions the following:

- I always/never…

- Life is (unfair, perfect right now, upside-down, cruddy, and so on).

- Yes, but…

- I want to do (an important behavior), but if I do, then I will feel…

Weak Self-Knowledge

The conceptualized self was described above. In order to complete our discussion of the three senses of self that pertain to self-knowledge, we now turn to self as process and self as perspective.

Self as Process

A second sense of self, self as process or ongoing self-awareness, is experienced when we notice immediate behavioral events, public or private. We are self-aware when we say, "I am running on the track" or "I am typing a manuscript." This is also true with private events—for instance, noticing that "I feel tired" or "I'm having the thought that I should go home now" or "I am having a panic attack." The content in these verbal responses is less important than the process of noticing ongoing experience. It is useful to know what one is thinking, feeling, and sensing, thus many schools of therapy include interventions aimed at increasing one's ability to notice and describe ongoing experience.

Self as Context

The third sense of self has been variously called self as perspective, self as context, or the observing self. Self as perspective is often described in the context of religious and spiritual practices; we can also examine it empirically. This sense of self might best be described as "pure consciousness" (Hayes et al., 1999, p. 187) or as the self that is aware but does not think (Harris, 2007). As such, it is incorporeal and necessarily lacks verbal content. These qualities of self as perspective make it notoriously difficult to describe verbally, and we will endeavor to do so in spite of this slippery quality. *Self as perspective* is the sense of self we glimpse when noticing that we experience from a single perspective, and that while verbal content might change, and while we might encounter new people and things, and have different and ever-changing thoughts and feelings, the locus or seat of this experience is constant and always present. Put another way, the you that was present when you were two years old is continuous with the you reading this book at this moment. Even though you have had twenty-four hours worth of new experiences, the you that woke up this morning is, in a fundamental way, the same you that woke up yesterday. You might notice changing thoughts and feelings, and changes in your body as you age, and changes in your physical environment, and yet the person having those experiences, the perspective from which your life unfolds, remains constant.

Though additional senses of self could be described, these three share the feature of pertaining to self-knowledge (Hayes et al., 1999) and are most relevant to practicing ACT. Socrates admonished, "Know thyself," and there is no doubt that self-knowledge has its uses. In modern times, self-knowledge is not regarded as any less useful than in Socrates' time. Humans are socialized from an early age to describe the self verbally, first as listeners and then as speakers. As a listener, the baby hears comments like "You're Daddy's little girl," "Aren't you a big, strong boy," "You are so pretty," "You're so smart like your big brother," "Bad boy," and on and on with multiple examples. As beginning speakers, children are asked, "Are you hungry?"; "Do you want more?"; "Are you feeling sleepy?"; and so forth. These three senses of self will be discussed in more detail in chapters 7 and 11.

The Selves and Clinical Concerns

The ability to know and describe one's self is useful. Some psychopathology will arise when such self-knowledge becomes rigid and governs behavior in an inflexible manner. Other clinical concerns arise when there is underdeveloped ability in self-knowledge.

Weak self-knowledge may be evident when some small piece of the conceptualized self dominates. For instance, Janet owns a successful business and has two adult children who love her and who are succeeding in their own lives. She devotes time and money to community volunteer activities, is a formidable golfer, and is a good friend to many. In spite of the richness of her life, her self-concept is dominated by the conviction that she is a failure because "I couldn't make my marriage work." Janet has been divorced for twelve years and resists opportunities to date because "there's no way I'm going to go through that again." She does not enjoy her successes in many life domains and avoids the possibility of a successful romantic relationship out of fear of failure.

Weak self-knowledge may occur when skills describing the self as process are poorly developed. This may be evident in alexithymia, where the client cannot describe his feelings. Clients who show excessive pliance are often out of touch with their own thoughts and feelings. For instance, Shandra, focused on pleasing her children, usually answers with "I don't know" when she is asked what she would like to do, is asked for her opinion, or is asked how she is feeling.

Weak self-knowledge may occur when abilities in contacting self as perspective have not been learned or are immature. Clients with weak self-knowledge in this area are often at a loss to describe valued directions and life goals. Their behavior and experience may be characterized by a sense of aimlessness, inertia, and lack of vitality. Darren sought treatment for depression complaining that "the antidepressant medication my doctor prescribed isn't making me happy." Darren's youngest child had recently left for college, and Darren remarked, "Everything feels pointless. I get up and go to work, kiss my wife, feed the dog, and mow the lawn, and I feel dead inside." Though a devoted father, he seemed to see his role as a parent as a fait accompli rather than as a role that would continue with his now adult children, albeit in altered form. He could not describe any goals and exuded a sense of directionlessness. Weak self-knowledge often leads to an inflexible repertoire characterized by motionlessness in an individual who is not tracking actual and potential sources of reinforcement.

Dominating Concept of the Past and Feared Future

Many clients are fused with the verbally constructed past and future at the expense of contact with and effective behavior in the present moment. Thanks to arbitrarily applicable relational responding, participating in "now" can be a challenge. Words just seem to have a pull toward the future and the past, and often toward the "negative."

"A mind is a wonderful tool for detecting and evaluating external dangers and developing plans for adapting to these demands, but we cannot avoid applying these same processes to the content of our private world. When we do so, we both see and produce negativity" (Hayes et al., 1999, p. 71). Not only do constructed futures—such as "If I don't take a three-hour shower this morning, then something terrible will happen today"—have a tendency to pull people away from the present, evaluations of the past can also sully a perfectly good current moment as we will see in the section below.

Dominated by the Past: Man vs. Dog

Consider this: A man, whom we'll call Roger, arrives home in the late autumn as it is beginning to rain and realizes he has forgotten his house key. Both he and the family dog, Fido, are locked out and in the backyard. All his mind's problem solving doesn't work: the neighbors aren't home, there's no garage, and the tree house isn't providing much shelter. Besides, someone will be home any minute. Fido and Roger get drenched waiting. Time passes. At last, here come the headlights and a person with keys to the house is behind the wheel. After a few moments, the warm, dry house is open and the aversive cold and rainy environment is outside (there). Fido shakes off the rain, goes to the kitchen to lap up some water from the bowl and crunch on some kibble, and then finally saunters over to his nice warm bed. He circles around the cushion three times before finally, and contentedly, lying down to rest (here/now).

Roger does something similar, right? Wrong! Despite the cessation of the aversive stimuli, they are still verbally and psychologically present for him. Food, drink, and warmth could be easily attained. However, more than likely he will complain about how cold and wet he is, how stupid he is for forgetting his key, how angry he is at his wife for (of all things) being warm and dry, and how he's just too angry to relax and too upset to eat. When one is asked to have feelings, notice thoughts, and to commit to important behaviors, such as maintaining a good marital relationship, the person is not asked to do it someday but to do it now. How much different would life be for Roger if he were more in contact with the present moment of being in a warm, dry home with his loving wife than with more negatively evaluated moments there/then in a past already gone? This story may speak to your answer to the following famous Zen koan: "Does a dog have Buddha nature?"

Psychopathology and Lost Contact with the Present Moment

While Roger's experience described above may not be evidence of severe psychopathology, his fusion with past content at the expense of experiencing the present is not functionally different from clinically relevant behavior observed in treatment settings. Clinically relevant behavior typically diminishes psychological flexibility or corrupts valued living. Avoiding contact with the present moment sometimes occurs in the service of avoiding unpleasant private events, and is problematic because it is an instance of psychological inflexibility (reducing contact with the natural environment) and because unpleasant events—for example, anxiety, sadness, or physical pain—may naturally occur at times during a value-directed lifestyle. An extreme example of avoiding contact with the present moment is dissociation, where the individual is physically present but not psychologically in the present moment.

Experiential avoidance and fusion dominate when verbal behavior pulls the person from the present moment. (Can you see how the inflexahex domains also interact with each other?) Reconsider Roger coming in from the rain. His "now" has no directly aversive contingencies, but his verbal behavior (complaining) about what is already past makes what he evaluates as aversive so very present in his now even while he is warm and dry. Thus, while avoidance may "protect" people from unwanted feelings such as irritation or sadness or anxiety, it also prevents them from enjoying a potentially pleasant now while they are fused with an aversive past or feared future.

Dominated by the Future: Clinical Examples

Aversive events aren't the only clinical concern. Sometimes people verbally bring the absent "good" (past or potential reinforcers) into present problematic situations.

■ Case Study: Obesity

Consider Floyd, a morbidly obese family man who cares deeply about his children, and who also continues to binge eat despite frequent warnings from his doctor and family members. While the ice cream sundae is in front of him in the here and now, he can resolve to go on a diet tomorrow (there and then). We can only speculate about Floyd's learning history, and it is likely that a relation something like "eating ice cream now is bad in the context of my family and my health" is occasioned and transforms the stimulus functions of eating ice cream into something aversive. This verbal relation can be altered with further relations, such as "After I eat this ice cream (here/now), I will start to be healthy from then on (there/then)" or "This is my last ice cream sundae ever." He may also have history suggesting that the "last time" he does something, he gets to indulge heavily in it. The catch here is that despite all the verbalizing and rationalizing, there is still a high-calorie, high-fat substance being ingested into his medically frail body now.

Verbal relations here/now influence Floyd's behavior here/now as if they were governed by future direct contingencies over which he actually has no control. His verbal engagement with a rosy future there/then, with better living there/then, is putting his health in jeopardy here/now. Verbal behavior in this instance unfortunately engenders inflexibility: he falls into the same habit of satisfying his sweet tooth instead of just noticing the urge as it is. It also takes his focus off of his valued, present behavior of better living and being healthy for his family now, and helps put that off into the verbally constructed future. Floyd might avoid "feeling bad" now and might even "feel good" now as he verbally contacts that he is going to change his behavior as soon as tomorrow, even while he behaves in the same old destructive manner here/now.

■ Case Study: Pathological Gambling

We can also examine the behavior of a pathological gambler, Christopher, who wants financial health for his family. However, he also dreams (verbally constructs the future) of the jackpot there and then while putting what little money he has available here and now into a slot machine instead of toward paying overdue bills. Flexible behavior would be demonstrated if he could just notice that his mind is coming up with then-and-there verbalizations and then not respond to them, while using his money to improve his financial health now. Succumbing to the same urges he always has is inflexible; he follows the verbal rule "I could be rich on this next pull of the slot machine," which is what got him into the problem in the first place. Rather than inflexibly giving away his money on a low-probability investment, he might try just noticing what he is telling himself in the moment and contact the contingencies of the present moment now (lack of funds, abundance of overdue bills). He would then have more choices available toward improving his situation, such as reducing his debt rather than incurring more debt.

■ Case Study: Abuse Victim

We can also consider Michelle, a woman who stays in an unrewarding relationship while thinking of the day there and then in the future when her partner will stop being abusive. Or she may stay in the relationship while thinking of the past when he didn't act abusively. Michelle's behavior is governed by dominating concepts of the past or future, and that puts her in harm's way now.

The problem in each of these vignettes is not merely that the person is not in the present moment. The additional concern is that focusing on the past or future avoids the current problems of obesity, unpaid bills, and domestic abuse. Contact with the present may still be experienced as unpleasant at times, and one can behave more flexibly in that moment.

The Interrelation of the Inflexahex Domains

Note that there is overlap in the inflexahex domains and that, while they are discussed as separate processes, they influence each other. Put another way, ACT's core clinical concerns are not separate problems in any absolute sense, yet it is useful to discuss them as if they are distinct in order to get a foot in the door with certain treatment strategies. Note also that as mentioned in chapter 1, core treatment strategies often influence more than one clinical domain.

As an example of overlap, notice how experiential avoidance of one's physical symptoms of anxiety can overlap with fusion to thoughts that "anxiety is horrible," and both events may influence persistent inaction. Consider a situation where a woman's lack of contact with the present moment can overlap with her pliance, leading her to do what she's been told rather than what is best for her in that moment, and also to become less likely to contact immediate reinforcers related to vital life pursuits.

Assessing Inflexibility with FEAR

FEAR (Hayes et al., 1999) is an apt acronym for some of the processes just described and associated with psychological inflexibility:

- Fusion

- Evaluation

- Avoidance

- Reason giving

A simple algorithm for quick assessment is to look for the presence of FEAR in your client's behavioral repertoire. As explained earlier in the chapter, when direct experience becomes indistinguishable from thoughts, behavior may become less flexible and less value directed, thus the fusion part of FEAR plays a key role during the case conceptualization. The evaluation of private events in given contexts, and subsequent fusion to those evaluations, may lead to experiential avoidance and should also be noted during case conceptualization. Reason giving has not yet been fully explored in this chapter (it will be in chapter 9), and has to do with people justifying their behavior based on emotions or thoughts rather than on their values and the environmental events that have greater impact on their behavior. The FEAR acronym suggests a way at looking at this set of verbal responses in order to detect inflexibility. We will discuss this further in chapter 14.

Using the Inflexahex Case-Conceptualization Worksheet

During ACT case conceptualization, the therapist aims to assess which psychological processes influence psychological inflexibility. "Although every client probably exhibits some behaviors relevant to each of these processes, the therapist's job is to recognize behavior patterns that are particularly strong for the client that can have important implications for treatment planning" (Luoma et al., 2007, p. 232). One way to do this to use the following Inflexahex Case-Conceptualization Worksheet, which we introduced earlier in this chapter. In the boxes provided on the worksheet, record the client's clinically relevant responses corresponding to the problematic domain. In addition, ACT case conceptualization is coupled with functional assessment to assess the environmental events that govern the client's behavior. During the intake process and also throughout therapy, the clinician solicits and synthesizes information regarding the client's problem and the past situations that shaped the person's problem as well as the current situations that maintain this problem. By using the Inflexahex Case-Conceptualization Worksheet, the ABC Functional Analysis Sheet, and the Event Log, you as therapist will have the fundamental elements to develop a case conceptualization. As you become more familiar with ACT, you will surely develop a procedure consistent with the model presented that works most effectively for your clients and treatment setting.

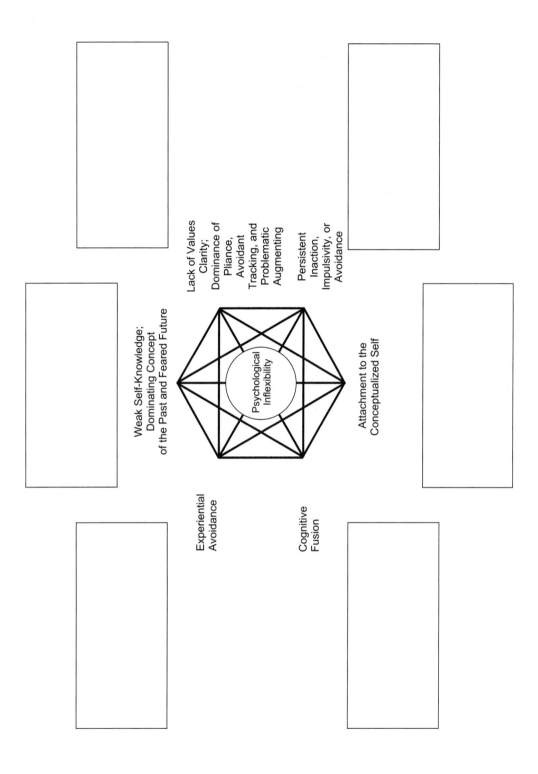

Lack of Values
Clarity;
Dominance of
Pliance,
Avoidant
Tracking, and
Problematic
Augmenting

Persistent
Inaction,
Impulsivity, or
Avoidance

Weak Self-Knowledge;
Dominating Concept
of the Past and Feared Future

Attachment to the
Conceptualized Self

Psychological
Inflexibility

Experiential
Avoidance

Cognitive
Fusion

ACT in Practice with Rick

Let's take a look at how the Inflexahex Case-Conceptualization Worksheet can be put to practical use as we assess Rick's struggles. While Rick has many complaints, use of the worksheet facilitates describing his concerns in terms of the ACT model of psychopathology.

Rick: I got stoned last night after staying clean for four days. We had a staff meeting and I wanted to suggest that new product again. I've been thinking about the thing for a year and can't get up the balls to talk about it… But then when I was even just thinking about speaking up, my hands started to shake and my face got all hot and my mind started going blank. I knew I wouldn't be able to say anything without looking like an asshole, so I just kept my mouth shut. And then while I was thinking about this stuff, I didn't hear the boss ask me a question and all of the sudden everyone was staring at me waiting for me to say something. I know I turned all red and I heard someone snickering when I had to ask the boss to repeat the question. And then I just mumbled something stupid. I wanted to just disappear. And then the real kicker—Adam suggested the product I was going to suggest and everyone said what a great idea it is. Now he, as usual, gets all the kudos while I'm the one who looks like a loser. I was driving home just thinking, "I'm such an asshole; nothing is ever going to change." And I couldn't stop thinking about that damn meeting. And then when some neighborhood kid asked if I wanted to score some good weed, I was like, "What the hell? Nothing's ever going to change." So I bought a half ounce and got real stoned. It felt great until I woke up the next day, and now it's still like nothing is ever going to change! I'm always going to screw up. What's the point in staying off of the marijuana? It's, like, the only thing worthwhile in my life. Why should I quit it just because some shrink thinks I should? No one else really cares if I smoke the shit or not. Why should I care?

Rick's statement, even while it has content unique to him, hints at processes ubiquitous to human struggling. His words are rich with content suitable for conceptualizing his behavior functionally in the following Inflexahex Case-Conceptualization Worksheet.

Rick's comments might serve as a framework for conceptualizing target behaviors with respect to nearly any of the processes in the ACT model of psychopathology. Rick's behavior is inflexible. This is seen not merely in the passage above, but also in his history and in his behavior in prior sessions. The case conceptualization exemplified in the worksheet is that Rick avoids anxiety and feared negative evaluation by minimizing his participation with others at work and in his limited and unsatisfying social life. He fails to keep commitments as he impulsively uses marijuana in the service of avoidance, and he keeps his work activity to a level that minimizes his exposure to the scrutiny of others. His values appear unclear: while he speaks of dissatisfaction with his life, he does not describe desired life directions. He is verbally entangled with his negatively evaluated conceptualized self and conceptualized future.

Rick disappeared during the meeting, not paying attention to the task at hand. He couldn't answer his boss and ruminated on the drive home. He repeats "I'm always going to screw up" and "Nothing is ever going to change." He gets high to escape the current moment.

Weak Self-Knowledge; Dominating Concept of the Past and Feared Future

Lack of clarity: There is little evidence of valued direction beyond referring to how others might evaluate him per the form of his behavior in the meeting and his marijuana use.
Pliance problem: He speaks of changing his drug use for what others, including the therapist, want him to do.
Tracking problem: He speaks of using marijuana to change the way he feels in the moment. He describes his behavior in the meeting in terms of avoiding aversive private events more than in terms of participating in the business at hand.
Problematic augmenting: He says, "Nothing is ever going to change" and "I'm always going to screw up."

Lack of Values Clarity; Dominance of Pliance, Avoidant Tracking, and Problematic Augmenting

Persistent Inaction, Impulsivity, or Avoidance

Rick is not taking action on his idea for a work product. He reports impulsively using marijuana as soon as it is offered in spite of his previously professed desire to stop smoking marijuana.

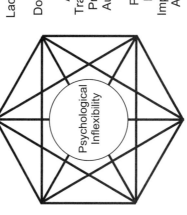

Psychological Inflexibility

Attachment to the Conceptualized Self

Rick repeats more than once that he is an asshole and that nothing will change. He seems to buy this concrete evaluation. These are themes he repeats in most sessions.

Experiential Avoidance

Rick mentions escaping his anxious feelings and avoiding increased anxiety by keeping quiet in his staff meeting. He also mentions smoking marijuana to change the way he feels.

Cognitive Fusion

Rick twice describes himself as an asshole and says that nothing is ever going to change. The thought that nothing is ever going to change is also consistent with dominance of the conceptualized future, as is "I'm always going to screw up." Fusion to "Why should I quit . . . ?" may support continued drug abuse.

The ABC Functional Analysis Sheet in Practice with Rick

In addition to the inflexahex worksheet, the therapist will use the ABC Functional Analysis Sheet to help in understanding what events in Rick's life are influencing his behavior. Rick was given a blank ABC Functional Analysis Sheet for homework and asked to complete it when he smoked marijuana.

ANTECEDENT What happened *before*?	BEHAVIOR What did you *do*?	CONSEQUENCE What happened *after*?
Day & Time: Friday, 11:00 a.m. In meeting, thinking about making suggestion. Hands started to shake, face got all hot	Got high on my lunch break	Felt paranoid that someone would smell it on me; told myself it was a dumb thing to do
Day & Time: Friday, 4:30 p.m. On my way home from work and had urge to smoke after a lousy day	Smoked a joint when I got home	Felt mellow for a while and kind of guilty and told myself what a jerk I am

With Rick's entries, we see smoking marijuana functions as escape from his negatively evaluated conditioned responses (CRs), and might suggest exposure and relaxation in the service of putting him in more functional contact with the broad conditioned stimuli (CSs) of feeling "more mellow" or "less paranoid." We also see that the consequences of smoking marijuana are immediate relaxation, feeling guilty, and negatively evaluating himself. At first glance, these latter consequences may look like punishers for smoking pot, but they may also reinforce his evaluation of himself as "a jerk" and therefore are likely to keep his relational network coherent. The reinforcement of negative self-evaluations give rise to those behaviors being occasioned again, and perhaps in their presence he will feel lousy and experience conditioned responses that he will attempt to escape from.

(Keep in mind that we look at the functional analysis not to develop a functional intervention for each and every row of ABCs that our clients portray but to look at the overall contingencies that influence their behavior.)

Day & Time: Friday, 6:00 p.m. Bad mood, thinking about problems from the day; dealer asked if I wanted to buy weed	Bought the pot and smoked it	Took me away from the problems

Here we see his bad mood as a motivational operation (MO), and the presence of the drug dealer and the dealer's question as a discriminative stimuli (S^Ds)for buying marijuana. This analysis allows us to see what events have stimulus control over his behavior, and can suggest that Rick take alternate routes home from work, erase the drug dealer's number from his cell phone, and take other measures to alter his environment so he does not interact with the dealer anymore. Eliminating such influences from his external environment can be helpful; however, one can't set up a similar eliminative agenda with his private events (the MO). Do not misconstrue that the aim is to avoid or get rid of the "bad mood" in the same way the drug dealer was avoided. With that part of the functional analysis, we are clued into using the ACT interventions that allow room for "bad moods" while still behaving effectively.

We also see that pot smoking is again negatively reinforced. Rick may need assistance in seeing the long-term loss in vitality when just pursuing these short-term "fixes." Values work can put him in greater contact with directions that will trump his inflexible and impulsive pursuit of immediate negative reinforcers. The values serve as augmentals that can increase the reinforcing properties of other, more important events, which can compete with pot smoking—and in turn make pot smoking less likely.

Day & Time: Saturday, 11 a.m. Woke up late for visit to Mom; partied too late last night	Got high	Felt mellow for visit, but missed lunch with Ma

Here we see Rick's inaction and experiential avoidance. The experiential avoidance and pot smoking is reinforced by "feeling mellow" during an aversive visit to the nursing home. The consequences of his inaction (sleeping late, missing lunch) are likely reinforced by the direct contingencies: he escapes from having to make an effort to do anything, which can be negatively reinforcing. His values are not clarified, so he is not contacting his inaction as aversive.

Event Logs in Practice with Rick

Alternately, when we are looking at avoided private events, we may use an Event Log (see below; also see appendix C), a variation on the ABC Functional Analysis Worksheet. When using the Event Log, the client monitors an event that is usually escaped or avoided or endured with great discomfort, such as a panic attack, an urge to use, worry, or obsessive thoughts. Different logs can be used for different clinically relevant behaviors. In Rick's case, instead of monitoring marijuana use, we might monitor urges to use marijuana using the following log.

Event Log

Name: _____

Target Problem: _____

In the chart below, write your observations about what happens during problem situations. In the When/Rating column, write the day and time of the event, and rate the problem from 0 (not present or not bothersome at all) to 10 (present all the time or most bothersome). In the Before column, write what you notice happening just before the event of concern. (For example, if you are struggling with panic attacks or urges to use alcohol, write down what happened just before you noticed the panic attack or urge.) In the After column, describe exactly what your behavior looked like after the event. (For example, write down if you endured the panic attack or drank three beers.) Then describe what happened next in the Consequence column. (For example, write down if the panic attack subsided and your friend asked if everything was okay, or if you became intoxicated and passed out.)

When? Rating	What happened just **BEFORE** the event?	What did you do just **AFTER** the event?	Then what happened? **CONSEQUENCE**
Day & Time: Rating:			
Day & Time: Rating:			
Day & Time: Rating:			
Day & Time: Rating:			
Day & Time: Rating:			

Let's take a look at how Rick responds to this Event Log during his homework.

When? Rating	What happened just **BEFORE** the event?	What did you do just **AFTER** the event?	Then what happened? **CONSEQUENCE**
Day & Time: Friday, 5:15 p.m. Rating: 8 for anxiety	Thinking it's gonna be a boring weekend and what a loser I am	Got high as soon as I arrived home	Nothing. I just fell asleep. Felt like shit on Saturday

Here Rick is describing the environment-behavior relationships related to his clinical problem, and rating his anxiety as an 8 on a scale of 1 to 10 as instructed in the Event Log directions. This piece gives us a clue about his cognitive fusion, lack of contact with the present moment, and failed attempts at experiential avoidance. On Friday evening, Rick is already living Saturday and Sunday, which he assumes will be boring, so he gets high now and the outcome is that he feels bad later. We can look for other instances of this sort of functional relationship occurring in other contexts, for example, when Rick stays home from work to avoid anxiety he anticipates later.

When? Rating	What happened just **BEFORE** the event?	What did you do just **AFTER** the event?	Then what happened? **CONSEQUENCE**
Day & Time: Sunday, 3:00 p.m. Rating: 8 for anxiety	Thinking that I have to work tomorrow and feeling anxious about a meeting	Got high	Felt less anxious

We again see that pot smoking is negatively reinforced. We might use this observation to ask Rick about the workability of avoidance. For instance, perhaps he felt less anxious and did not accomplish goals he set for himself for Sunday afternoon after he was high, or, after the high wore off, perhaps the anxiety returned and he felt angry with himself for smoking pot. The Event Log can be a springboard for further examination of the workability of an avoidance agenda.

When? Rating	What happened just BEFORE the event?	What did you do just AFTER the event?	Then what happened? CONSEQUENCE
Day & Time: Tuesday, 7:00 p.m. Rating: 8 for anxiety	Working on a computer program and smelled pot from neighbor's apartment	Kept working on the program	The urge went away

Here we notice that Rick sometimes resists an urge to use while he is engaged in an activity he enjoys. We might leverage this observation to point toward valued action and willingness to experience unpleasant private events and behave effectively. Alternately, we might point out the stimulus control and automaticity of private events in noting that even while he is enjoying a valued activity, just the smell of marijuana can be followed by an urge to use. And Rick can notice the urge and be willing to have it while continuing to engage in valued action. It isn't necessary that the urge go away, though eventually it will (as all thoughts, feelings, and sensations come and go).

These sorts of self-monitoring activities can facilitate functional analysis and increase the client's and clinician's understanding of variables—including stimulus control, contextual control, avoidance and escape behaviors, appetitive control, and competing contingencies—that influence the client's behavior. Beyond the functional assessment, Event Logs can be used to monitor change and to monitor the effectiveness of various interventions. Variants of the ABC Functional Analysis Sheet and Event Log are available in ACT books and self-help workbooks, at www.contextualpsychology.org, www.actinpractice.com, and in many CBT protocols.

A Functional Analysis with Shandra

We can also look at in-session behavior for functional assessment in terms of ACT processes. The following exchange occurred near the end of Shandra's third therapy session:

Shandra: (brusquely) Yes, yes—I can see where you are going. What should I do next?

Therapist: I noticed a change. I've been feeling a little bit disconnected from you the last ten minutes or so as compared to earlier in our meeting. And now that I think about it, I had similar thoughts and feelings at the end of last week's session. Do you notice anything similar?

Shandra: Um ... well ... to be honest ... I am late to a dentist appointment and I don't want to leave you early.

Therapist:	Do you mean that you have an appointment after our meeting?
Shandra:	Yes. I have an appointment with my dentist for the next three Tuesdays, and I am going to be late because it starts in ten minutes.
Therapist:	That doesn't work well.
Shandra:	*(blurting out and near tears)* I totally messed up! Now you are mad at me and he is going to be mad at me too. You said we should meet at 3:00 on Tuesdays and this therapy was important to me, so I agreed to it, and then my dentist said that he wanted to meet at the same time and now I am going to be late and he is probably mad at me too!
Therapist:	Having two appointments at the same time doesn't work well. What would you like to do right now?
Shandra:	I don't want you to be mad at me.
Therapist:	Let's see if we can make this work. I suggested 3:00 on Tuesdays as a time I have open and not as the only time we might meet.
Shandra:	*(interrupting)* I don't want you to be mad! I want to see you and see my dentist … I am screwing up again … See what I mean?
Therapist:	I would like to set a meeting time that works for both of us. If this time does not work, or does not work for the next few weeks, we might also meet on Tuesdays at 5:00 or 6:00 or on Wednesdays at 12:00, 1:00, or 2:00.
Shandra:	But I thought you only wanted to see me at 3:00 on Tuesdays.
Therapist:	I apologize if that is what I conveyed. My intent was to suggest that as the time I prefer rather than as the only time we might meet.
Shandra:	But I don't want to inconvenience you!
Therapist:	And I will let you know if I feel inconvenienced. Times that work for me are Tuesdays at 5:00 or 6:00 or on Wednesdays at 12:00, 1:00, or 2:00.
Shandra:	So you're not mad at me?
Therapist:	No, I am not mad.
Shandra:	You won't drop me as a patient?
Therapist:	We can make this work. How about you go to your dentist appointment now, and I will call you tomorrow morning to schedule a time that works better for you? And I think it's important that we discuss this further the

next time we meet when you are fully here and we have all the time we need.

Shandra: So you're not mad at me and you'll really call me and you're not just saying that?

Therapist: I am not feeling mad and I will call you tomorrow between 10:00 and 11:00 a.m.

Shandra's in-session behavior may be clinically relevant since it appears to be similar to the problematic behavior she exhibits with others. While we would need more information in order to be more certain, we might immediately suspect that Shandra shows excessive pliance. She opted to meet with both her therapist and dentist at times that were inconvenient for her, and she was concerned that both might feel angry if she didn't acquiesce to their suggested meeting times.

Based on Shandra's statements, we might also wonder about fusion with thoughts of being a screwup or avoidance of feeling distressed when she is asked to express an opinion, make a request, or deny a request. Finally, the therapist might speculate about how Shandra's behavior interferes with attaining valued outcomes. In the brief example above, Shandra was undermining both her dental and mental health treatment even while the conflict could have been easily resolved.

The preceding exchange was brief and took place early in treatment. The therapist would certainly want to follow up on the exchange in the next session and be attuned to other clinically relevant behaviors that might occur in session.

The therapist might opt to keep her own ABC Functional Analysis Sheet or Event Log of in-session behavior. This is written from the perspective of the therapist.

ANTECEDENT What happened *before?*	BEHAVIOR What did the client *do?*	CONSEQUENCE What happened *after?*
Day & Time: 3:02 Our session started late—I ran over time with the last client.	Shandra said, "How come you always end our sessions on time even when I am upset. I guess you like him better than me."	I felt annoyed and we processed her comment.
Day & Time: 3:20 I looked at my watch.	Shandra stopped talking and said, "I must be boring you."	I reassured Shandra that she was not boring me.

Here Shandra's responses to the therapist and the therapist's responses to Shandra provide useful information because Shandra likely responds to the therapist in a manner similar to how she responds to other people in her environment (see Kohlenberg, R. J.,

& Tsai, 1991). The therapist might, on the basis of the above, speculate that Shandra puts herself down and engages in excessive reassurance seeking with others. The therapist might also notice her own feelings of annoyance and speculate that others also sometimes feel annoyed by Shandra's self-deprecation and obsequiousness. In addition, this functional analysis helps the therapist see her own behavior (reassuring the client) as a consequence that possibly reinforces Shandra's problem behavior. Attending to the interpersonal process provides information critical for case conceptualization.

The ACT model of psychopathology guides the initial case conceptualization. While the above model focuses on inflexible behavior, the therapist will certainly note client strengths as well. For instance, both Shandra and Rick exhibit high treatment motivation, and both have identified some valued outcomes they would like to attain. The next phase of treatment requires moving to the ACT model of psychological flexibility and planning specific ACT interventions.

CHAPTER 7

Contacting the Present Moment and Perspective Taking

The hexaflex model and the Inflexahex Case-Conceptualization Worksheet (appendix B) can be helpful aids when conceptualizing an ACT case. They delineate the six domains where people can get stuck in their lives, and each domain has interventions to help loosen their "stuckness." From a functional contextual approach, a behavioral event is, of course, contextually bound, and it is also a unitary whole. A behavior cannot be defined or measured without a context, and neither is there a context without a behaving organism. Similarly, psychological events are not naturally divided into these six domains; all of the processes participate in behavior. So while we might talk about observed behavior in terms of one or more of the six core processes, we are not attempting to describe how the world really is, or to say that some particular behavior is contact with the present moment while another behavior is acceptance. Instead, describing behavior in terms of the core processes should be regarded as useful so far as it aids our case conceptualization and treatment planning. The hexaflex model gives us a convenient way of speaking about different influences on psychological flexibility and rigidity, but the processes are likely less helpful if thought of as naturally separate. They are all interdependent domains. As we will see, the six domains can be related to each other during applied endeavors.

We turn our attention now to the "poles" of the hexaflex model: the contacting-the-present-moment and perspective-taking processes. These domains share similar properties because of their orientation toward direct experience and transcendence as opposed to being rigidly governed by verbal, emotional, and physiological events. The interventions in these domains are aimed at having the client get in touch with what life is handing them right now and doing it from a perspective less influenced by verbal clutter and evaluations that occurred in the past. Helping clients connect with "the now" from a point of view or self, unencumbered by the weight of evaluations of the past and problem-solving schemes for the future fosters a stance of acceptance of thoughts and feelings, and a platform for stepping toward valued living. The committed action and values domains explicitly enlist verbal behavior to broaden the person's repertoire toward self-determined clinical gains and assist in living a life truly desired.

An immediate challenge faced when we begin considering transcendence and values with a client is that the very process of exploring the self and what the client truly desires her life to be about, and making plans to move forward on these desires, is inherently verbal. Language is embraced when the client is asked to delve into the question "What do you want your life to be about?" And the answers to such a rich clinical question provide a blueprint for what actions must be taken to walk the walk instead of just talk the talk. Committed action shares similar properties with values because language is also involved with goal setting and measurement of progress during behavioral commitments, and also during the use of evidence-based therapies. The interventions from these two domains put the client in motion toward psychological flexibility and a life worth living.

Acceptance and defusion processes assist the client in developing a different relationship with ever-present verbal, emotional, and physiological events. Acceptance interventions aim to remove the barriers clients have constructed to "protect" themselves from unwanted private events. Acceptance and defusion work to give clients the opportunity to have or take in what arises physiologically, emotionally, or cognitively when they interact with the world. As the ACT algorithm goes (Hayes et al., 1999, p. 246), they are invited to do the following:

Accept your reactions and be present.
Choose a valued direction.
Take action.

Defusion parallels acceptance through the invitation to just have, notice, take in, and contact thoughts and words and sensations. Clients learn the automatic nature of language through exposure and the experience of noticing their thoughts, and once willing to notice thoughts and other private events, they learn how to discriminate the usefulness of each evaluation and "problem-solving" strategy that arises. These interventions aim to undermine excessive literality. In other words, they prompt clients to merely notice verbal events and evaluations rather than to act from those events and evaluations. Therapists are cautioned not to consider thoughts and feelings as something to be completely ignored or rendered irrelevant. On the contrary, the idea is to help the client learn to *feel* better . . . not just feel *better* (Hayes et al., 1999, p. 77). In other words, we aren't aiming for the client to have more socially approved, "positive," and "better" feelings and thoughts; rather the aim is to embrace what is currently being felt without resistance. Working on perspective taking in therapy can lower a client's resistance against experiencing unwanted feelings and thoughts. In addition, experiencing such thoughts and feelings, whether "positive" or "negative," is a part of contacting the present moment. Let us now turn to the direct matter of this chapter: contacting the present moment and perspective taking.

Contacting the Present Moment

"Now" is always happening and has no beginning or end. Despite the inescapable nature of the present, human beings have an uncanny ability for moving away from their current experience. Thanks to the very useful tool of human language, people can evaluate the present moment against a past event or problem solve during the current moment in the hope that doing so will lead to a better future. In both instances, the person's present experience is filled with verbal stimulation about the past and future: "now" often becomes more about the past or future "then," and the present "here" becomes more about some verbally construed "there."

And hey, that's not necessarily problematic. Some very treasured moments in many people's lives are when they are reminiscing about the past or planning for the future. It is useful for people to suppose what the future might be like, anticipate problems, and develop solutions. Planning an upcoming vacation can be useful and enjoyable. Reminiscing with a loved one about a past shared experience can be pleasurable and facilitate closeness. Yet in the context of behavioral health, clinicians may want to look at how reminiscing and planning might take a turn for the worse (or, shall we say, a turn for the unhelpful). For instance, Shandra complains of being plagued with guilt about the abuse of her child by her significant other and also about her children's lack of self-sufficiency. In spending her currency on these verbal events (they aren't being experienced directly by her now), she is less likely to be in a position to notice opportunities to move forward in life on the basis of what she values. Of course one may protest that if a woman commits to a value of being a dedicated and loving mother, then worrying is a part of the game. However, a mother's worry becomes problematic when her aim is to get rid of the worry rather than to act in the interest of her children with or without worry. Shandra's worrying and guilt about there/then actually interferes with the flexibility that would be necessary to assist her children in the most efficient way possible here/now. Rick is caught in a similar trap. He says that "the future is bleak." The future is there/then, and his verbal construction of the future there/then is being brought to bear on his responding to current events here/now. Rick would be in a more behaviorally flexible position if he could contact what the present moment afforded him rather than be governed by his seemingly unhelpful rules and predictions. When talking about the clinical importance of the present moment, we need to talk about time. The next section is philosophical, and we believe it will help clinicians understand the relationship between present experience and verbal behavior, and how it affects people clinically.

A Functional Contextual View of Time

Time is a perplexing subject and is often oversimplified as something like a force that happens to people: "Time waits for no man" and "time is of the essence." From a functional contextual standpoint, we will look at time as simply a measure of change. Hayes (1992) suggests that we do not experience time but rather experience change, and that change is a process that inherently includes the prior changes. The changes are evolutionary, not in a Darwinian sense, but in the sense that the stimulus change events are cumulative. Hayes continues, "Change has only one direction, from now to now. No one has ever changed from now to not now (e.g., then), and if it did happen there would be no way to experience it, since any experience is an experience of now" (p. 113). In this very basic sense, all we have is the present moment.

And the present moment can be blemished by verbal behavior. As pointed out by the Grammy-winning classical guitarist David Russell, "The Present is a point just passed." This elegiac phrase suggests that the "present" in a verbal sense is beleaguered by the clumsiness of language. In other words, when a speaker says "now," by the time the listener responds, it will already be the speaker's future "then." The practical application of verbal behavior to temporal events taints the experience of the now, even when the speaker and listener are the same person (as in the case of thinking). When Augustine of Hippo muses, "What then is time? If no one asks me, I know what it is. If I wish to explain it to him who asks, I do not know" (397/2002, p. 224), he implies that there is a difference between experiential time and verbal time. There is a qualitative difference between direct contingency changes and verbally evaluated contingency changes. It is different to verbally evaluate at 8:00 a.m. that "I will be hungry by 11:00 a.m. if I skip breakfast" than it is to experience the sensation of hunger at 11:00 a.m.

Experiential Time

Experiential knowing about time involves behavioral responses determined through a direct history of environmental change (Hayes, 1992). The ubiquity of relational-framing behavior makes it difficult for verbally able humans to nonverbally experience change. Nonverbal organisms still respond functionally and predictably based on what has been experienced directly and through what has generalized (as demonstrated in basic operant research). For example, in a behavioral experiment with a rat, a light is presented (S^D), the lever is pressed (R), and food is eaten (S^{R+}). When this series of events happens several times, a temporal relationship is established among the sequential changes. The rat experiences changes in the environment, and its behavior is organized around these changes. Establishing a history of environment-behavior relations through experience can lead to an effective behavioral repertoire and is the crux of operant psychology. And the learning history includes experiencing change from event A to event B from the past. This change event correlates with cues about the future event probabilities. In the presence of the light (event A), certain responses reliably lead to food (event B) in the present context. Hayes suggests that "for a non-verbal organism time is an issue of *the past as the future in the present*" (1992, p. 113, emphasis in original). This is not to suggest that one can actually experience the future, but that nonverbal contact with the present maintains a historical context, and the current context is likely to influence emitting behavior functional in that past context as if it were to happen similarly in the present context. Events only happen in the present, and the responses are shaped by past experience and function *as if* the future is like the past's change of events.

Okay, so that last paragraph might have been too much like Carl Sagan meets Michael J. Fox in *Back the Future IV*, so let's make it a bit more concrete. The take-home point is that the behavior of both humans and nonverbal organisms is operantly conditioned. (Perhaps this is the oversimplification that was mentioned at the beginning of this section.) That bears repeating: human behavior is affected in the present by past consequences. Things become more complex when we include verbal behavior in the analysis. Behavior of verbal and nonverbal animals changes as a function of environmental changes, yet the ability to engage in verbal behavior changes change. Although life is just a series of "now," language can make "now" more like "then." We'll take a look at that next … er, now …

Verbal Time

By *verbal time*, we mean how and in what contexts humans relate the stuff in their world with frames such as temporal relations (before/after), and conditional and causal relations (if/then), and these are instances of behavior typically focused on changes in the environment. Many things and events can be related verbally, and overt and verbal behavior may be influenced by verbal relations among things and events (that is, verbal behavior is generative, and a whole host of contextual cues can influence transformation of stimulus functions and change behavior). People can learn relations such as "After having unprotected sex, you will contract a sexually transmitted disease," "If you get your degree, then you'll make a lot of money," or "No one cometh to the Father but by Me." Relational frame theory suggests that the events specified in these verbal relations do not have to be directly experienced in order for the person to behave in accordance with the relations. In other words, a person does not have to contact the contingencies of an STD through direct experience in order to have the verbal rule govern abstaining from some sexual behaviors or using a condom. Response dimensions (such as the frequency of behavior) can be altered by the temporal verbal relations even when verbally described consequences are not themselves experienced directly. In this sense, the future is constructed, and responses are altered by the language-based contingencies. Hayes (1992) forwards:

> Verbal time is behavior organized with regard to *the past as the constructed future in the present*. That is, based on a history of deriving temporal sequences among events (the "past"), the organism is responding in the present by constructing a sequential relation between at least two events. Again it is not the literal future that is part of the psychology of the verbal animal—it is the past as the future, but in this case the future is constructed by arbitrarily applicable relational responding. As with all psychological events, the event is happening in the present or it is not happening at all. (p. 114, emphasis in original)

Derived relational responding can alter the influence of direct contingencies. Although certain events may not have happened, arbitrarily applicable relational responding can set up a context whereby the person responds to the verbally constructed future as if there was a history of direct experience. For instance, a woman using a map or a global positioning system as she drives will turn right or left at the appropriate intersections even when driving in a city she has never visited. Note that she is not responding to future contingencies. She is still behaving in the present with respect to what was learned in the past. The past included multiple examples of relational responding that shaped up a verbal behavior repertoire and also included multiple instances of direct experience with certain events that participate in the relational frames pointing toward the constructed future (if/then, before/after frames: "If I follow a map, then I get where I plan to go"). She is still responding in the present moment (there are no other times to respond to), and the constructed future only exists in the present moment.

One may ask, "If a person can only experience the present moment, why does 'contacting the present moment' have to be a domain in ACT work?" Teaching clients to contact the present moment is important because behavior is multiply caused (that is, many stimuli influence human behavior). Typically there are several levels of contingencies influencing a person's behavior, including direct and verbal contingencies. For example, when John, a man with OCD, believes what his mind tells him—"If I don't take a three-hour shower this morning, then something terrible will happen today"— and then he rigidly adheres to the three-hour showering verbal contingency despite the other aversive contingencies that arise at the same time (for example, ire from his partner or skin irritation from excessive washing), then he is not fully contacting the present moment; rather, he is responding to a verbally constructed future, not one that has been directly contacted. This can be problematic if John values his interpersonal relationship with his partner. His showering behavior is under the specious governance of a verbal construction, yet he follows it rigidly rather than contacting the other events in his "now," namely the degradation of his relationship. ACT attempts to realign the person with what is currently happening. The ACT therapist invites the client to embrace that current event, fully and without defense (including anxiety and thoughts about something terrible happening) as it is (just thoughts and feelings) and not as what it says it is (something terrible happening) while moving toward what the person cares about—now.

Clinical Relevance of the Present Moment

While it may not be absolutely critical to understand time from a modern behavior analytic point of view, the upshot is to consider that while there certainly are direct contingencies brought to bear on human behavior, there are also verbal contingencies. A person following the verbal rule "If you get your degree, then you'll make a lot of money" may be pursuing financial reward inflexibly by pursuing a college degree only. There are several methods of making money, and not all of them require a college degree. Conversely, having a college degree does not entitle a person to make a good salary. A person following an "if you go to college, then you get money" rule isn't contacting other important environmental variables, such as entrepreneurial opportunities that may be more personally rewarding. She may even major in a subject that is regarded as being lucrative but actually find no personal joy in the pursuit. Because rules (contingency-specifying stimuli) can lead to a rigid response pattern (Catania, Matthews, & Shimoff, 1982; Wulfert, Greenway, Farkas, Hayes, & Dougher, 1994), helping the client contact the present moment can be a litmus test for workability. The client can be asked, "Right now, is following these rules leading you toward true desired life ends for you, or are the rules just making your actions narrow and less flexible? How are these words working for you?" This query incorporates the committed action and values side of ACT, and it also illustrates the "nowness" of ACT. The therapist is asking about right now, in the session—whether it is before an exposure experience or when talking about stepping toward desires or toward acceptance—right now, can the client be with that moment? Engendering such a wakeful stance may help clients see more lucidly what is happening in their lives and whether their behavior is moving them in a valued direction.

There may be obstacles to this piece. A client may have thoughts and beliefs that prevent contacting the present moment, current feelings he avoids, or no real motivation or forward direction, or he can't see that he is different from all the verbalized content he carries around. Each of these obstacles can be loosened by exercises in the defusion, acceptance, values, or self-as-perspective domains respectively. Remember that these domains are naturally unitary and not distinct from each other.

Present-Moment Exercises in Practice

All experience happens now, and time only moves from now to now. If our clinical work is aimed at having people behave flexibly with what life is handing them, it may be prudent to have people become more present with the present. Behavioral change and also acceptance are going to be more robust in the current moment. One cannot change past behavior outright, although in the moment it is possible to change the way one evaluates and responds to results of past behavior. For example, one might forgive a wrong from the past (even if it was one's own) or commit now to more functional behavior. A person can't directly change his own future behavior, although his current behavior can be aimed at altering the environment so that there is an alteration in future behavior, such as a smoker removing cigarettes from his house or a worker setting her alarm clock a bit earlier to help her get to work on time. So there are verbally planned actions that can be taken to influence events that happen there/then.

An ACT therapist is inclined to influence events occurring here/now. Doing so requires actions that are particularly more experiential and less verbal because of language's tendency to have people relate events from the past or future. The constant stream of verbal mind chatter and of consciousness itself is difficult to stop from happening. Mindfulness exercises may play a role in treating clients who are especially entangled with verbal behavior and/or clients who require a greater sense of the present moment. Mindfulness exercises, such as watching one's thoughts or counting one's breaths, can facilitate the process of noticing thoughts and sensations here/now as opposed to being caught up in or directed to there/then through verbal entanglement with thoughts and feelings. Contacting the "now" fluently is a skill and takes practice, and exercises in mindfulness are provided throughout section 3.

Case Conceptualization and Contacting the Present Moment

There are many clinically relevant behaviors that might suggest the client has difficulties related to contact with the present moment. We previously suggested that the six core processes are not completely separable. Avoidance, fusion, failure to make commitments now, lack of values clarity, limited perspective-taking skill—all may be related to difficulty contacting the present moment. Alternately, we might also say that contact with the present moment will facilitate acceptance, defusion, committed action, valued living, and self-as-perspective work. A lack of contact with the present moment decreases psychological flexibility and reduces self-knowledge.

The Clinical Relevance of Poor Contact with the Present Moment

When a client is dominated by thoughts of the future and/or the past, psychologically flexible behavior is less likely. Here are some examples of common problems related to weak self-knowledge and lack of contact with the present:

- People with substance-abuse problems may use drugs in the service of avoiding what might be experienced if one were fully present. Being in an altered state of consciousness reduces contact with the present moment. Excessive sleeping, going on a long drive, or zoning out are also avoidance moves that should be investigated in the case conceptualization.

- Clients may also fail to enjoy and be fully present with events now because they are thinking about the future. For example, consider a father not enjoying playtime with his child because he is thinking about work he will be doing later. Another example is when a person misses what a companion is saying now while thinking about what she should say later to her companion. A person who chronically worries also demonstrates clinically relevant behavior important to the case conceptualization relevant to contacting the present moment.

- Failure to be present now due to ruminating about the past can also demonstrate a problem such as is seen in a person who ignores a friend's offer of support while thinking about a failed relationship. Another problem with a dominant concept of the past arises when a person turns down a value-consistent opportunity while focused on past mistakes and "failures."

■ When a person continually justifies her actions using temporal, conditional, and causal relational framing, she is likely missing important information from right now. This might happen if a person says, "If I ask her out, then I might be rejected," "If my child drops out of school, then I will be a bad parent," or "I didn't succeed in losing weight then, so why try again now?" Each of these verbalizations may lead to ineffective behavior and may be influenced by missing opportunities to engage in important responses that may be helpful to personal values and goals.

■ For a more everyday example, consider times when people fail to notice what is happening nearby while focused on mind chatter about the past and future. These events happen to most people quite often, such as driving without noticing the scenery or participating in a social activity without connecting with others.

The antidote to poor contact with the present moment is practice in contacting the present moment through mindfulness. It is also facilitated by work on acceptance, defusion, committed action, values clarification, and experiencing self as process and self as perspective.

Perspective Taking

Perspective taking, which is the ability to conceptualize experience from multiple points of view, is a uniquely human ability and is a relatively more advanced verbal skill. It isn't demonstrated by young children, most developmentally disabled adults, or animals. Even normally developing adults bump into challenges related to perspective taking. Faulty perspective-taking skill limits one's psychological flexibility, thus perspective taking is a domain of interest in the hexaflex model.

Deictic Relations

Deictic is a fancy word for "demonstrative," for showing or pointing out directly. We demonstrate our perspective in our verbal and nonverbal behavior. No one can experience the perspective of another. We can only contact another's perspective through relating others' verbal and nonverbal behavior to our own perspective. For instance, if I were to say, "I love modern dance; I get completely caught up in the fluid movement and the music, and the rest of the world seems to recede. I enjoy the athleticism and grace and beauty of the dancers. It is almost as if I disappear while I am watching them dance and I feel so vibrant after the experience." You might be able to relate the previous phrases to some experience of your own, and you would not be able to experience what I experienced directly. Even if you enjoy dance, you cannot know exactly what I experience, because you do not share my experience or history. We always act from the perspective me/here/now, and at the same time, it is often useful to talk about or think about or act in terms of "me or you," "here or there," and "now or then." In one sense, we can say that the self is the perspective me/here/now; I exist here/now as the sum of my experience there/then and distinct from you/here/now and your experience there/then (Barnes-Holmes, Hayes, et al., 2001). Perspective taking can be viewed at once as a skill and as an experience, and with relevance to psychological flexibility.

Three Senses of Self

Three senses of self that pertain to self-knowledge are the conceptualized self, self as process, and self as context (or self as perspective), and were described in chapter 6. We will now revisit these senses of self in more detail as knowledge of each sense of self is necessary for grasping self as perspective, and for utilizing self-knowledge therapeutically.

The Conceptualized Self

Socrates's notion that self-knowledge is important has endured. Among more modern behavioral thinkers, Skinner pointed out that self-knowledge arises among members of a verbal community because other members of the community shape up a repertoire of self-descriptive behavior. People teach youngsters how to describe their own behavior because it is useful in community living: "Where were you when you saw the herd of deer?"; "Did you take my slingshot?"; and "Please show me where it hurts." Over time, the individual as both a member of a verbal community and as a speaker and listener inside his own skin, learns to speak and listen to himself (Skinner, 1974). In a post-Skinnerian account of language, we regard the act of knowing about or describing the self as a verbal process, and the verbal description—that is, the things or information known about the self—as verbal content. The conceptualized self is thus the verbal content generated through verbal processes in the context of self-knowledge.

The conceptualized self is regarded as rather thinglike; it is not the self, but it is a product of thinking about the self or behaving verbally in relation to the self in context. Some aspects of the conceptualized self might be rather static—for example, one's gender. Some might be changing yet consistent—for example, one's age changes, and it changes in a consistent manner relative to the verbal community's notion of time. Some aspects of the conceptualized self might change radically depending on the specific context—for example, one might feel talented in the context of artistic ability and incompetent in the context of athletic ability, or attractive in the context of spending time gazing into the eyes of one's beloved and unattractive in the context of watching the Mr. or Miss Universe pageant.

A conceptualized self of some sort will arise within any verbal community. A conceptualized self allows us to communicate with others. For example, "My name is Shandra, I am a vegetarian, I do not like cold weather, I do not speak Spanish, I am a native of California, I am allergic to cats, and I have two children." A conceptualized self allows us to make sense of our own behavior and the behavior of others. It also provides a vehicle for others to make sense of our behavior. For instance, if a person interacting with Shandra knows that she is a vegetarian, the person might not cook chicken for her dinner, and if a person knows that she does not speak Spanish, the person will know why Shandra ignored a question asked in Spanish. A conceptualized self is useful in many settings.

A conceptualized self can be more problematic with respect to evaluative content. Notice the difference between the content "I am a woman/vegetarian/Californian/allergic to cats" and "I am bad/smart/clumsy/pretty/athletic/fat." Content is problematic when a person becomes fused with it. Instead of seeing content as merely words—that is, verbal output that is an outcome of verbal processes and influenced by one's history as it is brought to bear on the present situation or context—the individual fuses with that content and sees the content as the self instead of as a product of verbal behavior engaged in by one's self. When a person is fused with negatively evaluated content, emotional avoidance is likely. If "I am bad" is my essential nature rather than merely a thought that shows up, then it becomes important to avoid contexts that evoke this negative evaluation. If "I am anxious" and "anxiety is bad," then it becomes important to avoid anxiety. One might be tempted to merely change one's evaluations—for instance, by replacing the thought "I am bad" with the thought "I am good." However, fusion with positive evaluations can be just as problematic. If it is important to maintain the evaluation that "I am good," a person may avoid taking risks and engaging in behaviors that might lead to rewarding experiences that also include the possibility of negative evaluations—for example, seeking a promotion, asking someone out on a date, or trying a new activity, all of which might be rewarding, and all fraught with the risk of rejection and/or negative self-evaluations.

Self as Process

Self as process has a more in-the-moment quality than does self as content. Ongoing self-awareness is the process of noticing verbal content. A person unaware of her thoughts, feelings, and sensations would not function very effectively in many contexts. An extreme example of the consequences of not noticing sensations is that of people with congenital sensory neuropathy (also known as congenital anesthesia). Because their nerves do not reach close enough to the surface of the skin, they do not feel the sensation of pain. To never feel pain sounds desirable, yet people who do not feel pain due to congenital anesthesia report many injuries. This problem is exacerbated by their inability to notice the early warning signs of danger and injury that pain provides. Such individuals experience frequent broken bones, cuts, and burns and may even bite off portions of their own tongues. Lack of self-awareness in this respect is problematic.

As a less extreme example, consider a man who as a child was told, "Boys don't cry," and as an adult is unwilling to cry and to contact sadness; instead of contacting tender feelings, he instead feels numb or perhaps even angry. The plight of the person who doesn't want to contact feelings and ongoing streams of thought is also bleak. Consider the example of a woman who, in trying to avoid thoughts and feelings related to a past trauma, may miss important current environmental cues that she is placing herself in a potentially dangerous situation. It is possible that a person who is repeatedly victimized is engaging in high-risk behavior because thoughts of warning signs and danger are being experientially avoided. Her unwillingness to contact her own thoughts about the past increases the chances of her being revictimized in the present. Our client Rick uses drugs in order to minimize or change the quality of his ongoing self-awareness of his behavior and feelings. Notice that while the individuals in the above examples are attempting to avoid verbal content, they are doing so by undermining the verbal processes involved in ongoing self-awareness.

Ongoing self-awareness is a form of contact with the present moment, and it often takes willingness and acceptance to notice painful content. Ongoing self-awareness can be brought into the treatment room through the therapist asking questions such as "What are you experiencing right now?" Similarly, when the client is lost in verbal content, the therapist can ask, "What are you experiencing right now?" and in most cases the client will notice avoidance or numbness and a lack of vitality in contact with the conceptualized self as compared to ongoing self-awareness. Defusion techniques can be used to increase focus on the process (for example, "I'm having the thought that …" while minimizing attachment to content.

Self as Perspective

Self as perspective (also called self as context), or the observing self, can be thought of as "the context in which private events such as thoughts, feelings, memories, and sensations occur" (Hayes, Strosahl, Bunting, et al., 2004, p. 9). As a context, self as perspective lacks content and does not have the same thinglike quality as verbal content. This transcendent quality makes it difficult to talk about the sense of self as perspective without getting lost in a tangle of words. Instead, the therapist facilitates experiencing the observing self through exercises, metaphors, and mindfulness practice. This sense of self is immutable and has no boundaries. It is the experience of self that has always been there, and where thoughts, feelings, and sensations are distinct from the "I" having the thoughts, feelings, and sensations (Strosahl, Hayes, Wilson, & Gifford, 2004, pp. 44–45). The sense of self as perspective is not unique to ACT. Other traditions have different names for it. It is integral to many religious and spiritual traditions, and is especially associated with Buddhism. ACT therapists often borrow metaphors and exercises from this tradition. For instance, Hayes et al. (1999, p. 187) use a metaphor of the relationship between the clouds and the sky borrowed from the writings of Baba Ram

Dass to describe the relationship between self as content and self as context. In this metaphor, the observing self is likened to the sky—it is always there even when we do not see it because it is obscured by clouds. Verbal content is like clouds that may be absent at times, or little and not very noticeable, or thick and big enough to completely obscure our view of the sky. Yet even though the sky isn't visible, we know that it is there and we don't need to move the clouds in order to know that it's there. Similarly, from the sense of self as context we can notice verbal content as well as notice verbal processes without being attached to them, needing them to change, or seeing them as the real or true self.

Buddhist nun Pema Chödrön describes the experience of self as context as "egolessness" and says (2000),

> The acknowledgment of egolessness, our natural state, is like regaining eyesight after having been blind, or regaining hearing after having been deaf. Egolessness has been compared to the rays of the sun. With no solid sun, the rays just radiate outward. In the same way, wakefulness radiates out when we're not so concerned with ourselves. Egolessness is the same thing as basic goodness or buddha nature, our unconditional being. It's what we always have and never really lose. (p. 62)

Her description nicely captures the transcendent nature of self as context and its contentlessness, and many (though not all) evaluate contacting the observing self as a pleasant experience.

Experiencing self as perspective is often powerful for clients and can be a boon to willingness and acceptance. Self as perspective is a safe place from which one can see content and experience it for what it is. From this place, content is less threatening as one can experience the distinction between content and the self as context. Negatively evaluated experience is less threatening when one can distinguish thoughts from the thinker and feelings from the feeler (Strosahl et al., 2004, p. 44). Acceptance is more likely when thoughts and feelings are viewed in this way because the individual feels

Checking In

- Notice that you are reading this book.

- Which sense of self is invoked in saying, "I am reading this book?"

- Notice that you are noticing that you are reading this book.

- Who is noticing that you are reading this book?

less pressure to avoid and struggle with negatively evaluated content when it is seen as merely content rather than as the essence of the self.

Self as perspective facilitates movement in a valued direction. When one contacts the self as perspective, she is more able to see the self as continuous and stable, knowing that whatever she does, whether or not she attains a desired goal, whether she experiences joy or pain, the observing self is not threatened and will remain complete (Hayes et al., 1999, p. 186).

Self as perspective increases psychological flexibility. As mentioned above, self as perspective is an experience quite different from self as content, which has a thinglike quality. As nothing, or no-thing, the observing self has no boundaries or limits. There is great freedom in a self with no limits, for the individual is not burdened or hampered by her limited descriptions of herself. Seeing content for what it is frees the person to try new behaviors, take risks, and act more effectively. As Hayes (2007) suggests, there is much about yourself that you do not know verbally. In a therapeutic context, this can help clients understand that all of the content with which they are encumbered are just teardrops in their ocean-sized self as context. This realization, as an experienced fact, frees one to behave more flexibly in the face of barriers to moving in a valued direction.

Of course we are unlikely to spend most our time experiencing self as context. One metaphor likens our experience of self as context to riding a bicycle and another to getting back on a horse after falling off (Hayes et al., 1999)—though we may be off balance or falling off, we can get back on at any time and over time we are moving

Stance of the Therapist

How long is a person's life? To answer, follow your breathing—comfortably in and comfortably out. You've just answered the question.

What is it about you that made you do that exercise? Breathe in as you answer, breathe out knowing your answer is incomplete.

forward. For now, as a personal introduction to self as context, spend a few minutes with the following exercise.

Case Conceptualization and Self as Perspective

Many client problems with the self have to do with attachment to self as content and limited ability to notice ongoing experience (self as process). Sometimes the clinical concern might also have to do with a client's limited experience with self as perspective. By now, you may be guessing that problems with perspective taking are related to avoidance, fusion, lack of committed action, poorly clarified values, and lack of contact with the present moment. Attachment to self as content and limited ability to notice ongoing experience lead to psychological inflexibility.

Certain client behaviors might suggest limited perspective-taking skill:

- Fusion with self as content—for example, a client who sees herself as little more than "a failure," "fat," "a drug addict," "a parent," "a student," and so on. It is as if the person is acting in a concretized manner. This can also happen with fusion with feelings, such as when a person says, "I *am* depressed," as if that were her totality.

- Unwillingness to try new behaviors. This can occur when a person says, "But I've always been this way" or "What's the use?" and acts in accordance with these verbalizations.

- Inability to describe ongoing experience. For example, think about the client who reports he doesn't know what he is thinking or feeling, and he is not just avoiding the feelings or reluctant to tell you. Rather, he really cannot label his emotions because he never learned how to do so. During the case conceptualization, it will be prudent to plan to help him discriminate his emotions and teach him how to describe and label his feelings.

- Lack of contact with the present moment (see above). Yes, when a client engages in behaviors indicative of lacking contact with the present, the client also demonstrates limited perspective-taking skill, as perspective taking is always experienced now.

In chapters 11 and 13, we will focus more on how to work with clients to undermine fusion with self as content, how to make constructive use of ongoing self-awareness, and how to experience the observing self.

CHAPTER 8

Values, Commitment, and Behavior Change Processes

Psychological flexibility is demonstrated by the execution of behaviors that are chosen by a person. By execution, we mean that a person actually does the set of responses that he cares about and doesn't just talk about it. When a person cares about a chosen direction, those directions are informed by his values. This link between values and committed behavior change is why we discuss them together in this chapter.

Values

The values domain can be considered the richest, most existentially complex domain in the hexaflex, and at the same time it is elegant in simplicity. Values may be the least researched process in the hexaflex model, yet for millennia philosophers and poets have been addressing values. Values clarification asks the client, "What do you want your life to be about?" It's about deepest desires, yearnings, and druthers. People often hear phrases like "Follow your heart," "Do what you love and love what you do," "You only get one shot; do not miss your chance," and "If you can dream it, you can do it." Parents, caregivers, and motivational speakers all try to influence others by fostering passion in the context of attaining long-term goals. We too can encourage our clients to take a "North Star approach" to life, suggesting that clients pick a bright, stable direction to help orient themselves and navigate through life.

A question about values can stop clients in their tracks. Take the following example about how a brief values examination shifted the boisterous behavior in a roomful of aggravated adults. During a court-mandated parenting class for adults going through a divorce, the din of conversation was unusually high, the interest in the material was low, and the body language of the attendees was very off-putting for the presenter. Then the presenter asked, "What do you really want your life to be about? When you reach the end of your days, will you look back with satisfaction because of a life well lived? Can you look forward to tomorrow being well lived? How about your life right now? Right now, can we make this time about learning the best way to care for your children during this rough time? Is it possible to make a little room in your life so that it can include vital, worthy things, and not be all wrapped up in the day-to-day grind of the divorce stuff? What if tonight's program could get you pointed toward where you truly desire to be?" The audience piped down halfway through those questions—and stayed attentive for another forty-five minutes during the lecture. Of course this is only anecdotal evidence, but it also seems as if starting a class with an orientation to values and how they add richness to life would be better received than most common introductions.

Consider that when we talk about values, it may seem rather "thinglike." However, far from being static and thinglike, values are vital and imbue even seemingly mundane behavior with vitality. Reorient yourself to think about this topic as "living valuably" or "valued behaving." Put the concept into action. When talking about values per se, the noun carries a motionless and solid feel. But even as a noun, it is a description of an ongoing process. It is not explicitly a formulation of a moral code, such as following "family values," although it can be influenced by culturally relevant moral codes.

Clarifying Goals and Values

When we talk about values, we're not talking about what gets achieved—that is, we're not talking about goals. We're talking about a direction people choose to head in with their lives. Let's take a look at a conversation (influenced by Hayes et al., 1999) between a therapist and Scott, a thirty-eight-year-old audio engineer struggling with hallucinogen abuse.

Scott: I really don't know what you mean about values. Like I don't really like everyone else's family values or my parents' good religious values, like they try to feed me.

Therapist: Okay. I get you. I'm not telling you to join up with some kind of code of conduct. Can we think about it differently?

Scott: I'm getting used to you asking me that. (laughs)

Therapist: (laughs) Okay. Let's just check this out. You get to choose what direction you want your life to take. Suppose you were to choose your life direction to be west—as in you will make your life about going west. You get to choose that. And as you head in that direction in life, you'll attain certain goals. You might get to California, and then you'll know that you are (pause) … more west than you were at a different time. And you can look at getting to California as achieving a goal, a certain marker on the way, but that doesn't mean you've arrived at west. There is always more west to go! You might need to be creative at times. To head west from California, you'll need a boat or plane, and if you value that direction, you are flexible with your travel methods. The next stop might be Fiji or Hawaii. You may eventually get to Asia, and with that goal attained, you know you've been headed in the valued direction, but you still aren't at west. There's more west to go. You can continue to travel west indefinitely. And even if you get slowed down, and you can't make those big westerly treks, if you still can take one small step west, you are traveling in your valued life direction.

Scott: And that's values?

Therapist: That is a way of talking about values. Values are what you do. Values are what you demonstrably care about doing.

Scott: (clarifying) Demonstrably?

Therapist: What I mean is, what does your behavior show that you care about? What are you demonstrating that you care about? Not what do you think you care about, or what you've been fed or told you should care about. We're not saying that you should decide to listen to society or your parents to "go west, young man!" We're talking about choosing to live—and by that I mean act—in the direction you deeply care about. And you can start now. Right here. We're talking values, and we're talking commitment. When you know the whys, you can figure out the hows.

Scott: (pondering) Hmm.

This value-directed living is still possible even when the options are limited. Scott has a broad spectrum of directions toward which he can aim his life.

Remember, values are defined in ACT as being *"verbally construed global desired life consequences"* (Hayes et al., 1999, p. 206, emphasis in original). Let's unpack that definition—term by term—in the next few sections.

Life Consequences

The term *consequences* relates to "results" or "outcomes," and in most situations suggests a circumscribed event or stimuli that could reinforce a particular behavior. For the most part, "consequence" has a certain time-limited and final tone to it. When talking about values as being consequences, note that we are talking about life consequences, that is, consequences which occur over a lifetime. Some are cumulative, some are daily consequences, and some are one-time consequences. Some life consequences have a single form and others take many forms. The ACT view of values as consequences allows one to contact the present moment and simultaneously move the usual goal-oriented future to here/now—values are lived now, and yet much of living is directed toward future outcomes. Values are an outcome of living and they are a process of living. Be aware that ACT's definition of "values" may be different than other definitions you have encountered.

The ACT phrase "Outcome is the process through which process becomes the outcome" (Hayes et al., 1999, p. 219) speaks to the enduring nature of valuing and living. Engaging in an ongoing stream of desired, personally worthy actions is a process, and it is also an outcome. Goal setting and achieving can be looked at as outcomes that are part of the process and as processes that precede the outcome of valued living. When a man is following values, he can get regular corrective feedback when he sets his sight on a value-directed goal, and then modify his behavior accordingly whether or not that goal is attained. A runner might set the goal of winning a race and train by establishing a program of running and cross training. Whether or not he attains the outcome goal of winning the race, he attains the process goals of exercising and caring for his health. As an outcome, he improves or maintains his health and perhaps socializes with other runners, and he might enjoy running "just because" even though he may or may not ever win a race. The person who wants more friends as an outcome may or may not attain that goal, and she might attain outcomes of meeting people, taking risks, and being kind and friendly to others as process goals that, as values, become outcomes in their own right. (Perhaps this is a bit too much self-disclosure, but late in the process of editing this volume, it was easy for us to get caught up in narrow goals such as "finishing the edits on chapter 8." At the same time, we were always heartened to catch sight of the real value behind our writing—disseminating and making ACT more accessible to others.)

Desired

Merriam-Webster's Collegiate Dictionary (11th ed.) defines *desire* as a "conscious impulse toward something that promises enjoyment or satisfaction in its attainment" (p. 338) and also implies something that is longed or hoped for. The dictionary wasn't written by behavior analysts, so there is a bit of structuralism and mentalism involved in that definition. To take another crack at it, we could say a *desire* is a verbally derived conditioned establishing operation involving appetitive stimuli—though that definition might be too much to digest to make it practical in therapy!

We are talking about a person's attraction toward participating in certain events: behavior that by its very execution makes the doing worthwhile. It isn't just something that a person "wants to" do. Hayes et al. (1999) caution against the using the word "want" to describe what a person values because "wanting" implies that something is missing and something must occur to fill the void. ACT supports taking an abundance stance (Wilson, 2006b), as if psychologically the client already has what he needs, and then moves forward from there toward desires—events that he longs for or hopes for. Wants are, by definition, not here/now. Values can always be lived here/now.

Global

Values are described with the qualifier "global" to denote how comprehensive the desired ends can be. People acting out of their values are not aiming for specific, confined results. For instance, when one values participating in his work environment, he usually isn't just shooting for an employee-of-the-year award (though that could be part of the greater plan). Valuing work participation might include aiming to foster work relationships, to make a difference in the community, to satisfy customers, to mentor subordinates, and to be an apprentice to his betters. It is an aim for all the experiences entailed in becoming employee of the year whether or not he ever receives the award. It is possible that a client might come to therapy and say, "I just want to win an employee-of-the-year award," or some other defined end goal. It isn't that an ACT therapist wouldn't be able to help her with this agenda; we could work on improving her social skills and enhance her productivity by helping her arrange contingencies with a well-developed performance management program. And the ACT therapist would also perform a functional analysis of her behavior with regard to achieving goal X:

- Why is such a circumscribed goal so important to this woman?

- What supports that agenda, and can it be construed to be more global and influenced by long-term experiential direct consequences rather than the satisfaction of a one-time "want"?

- Is this goal set up just to help her escape thoughts such as "I'm a rotten salesperson"?

- Is this goal intended to help her argue to her abusive husband or demanding parents that she is "worth something"?

Finding those verbally construed contingencies helps us look at a broader spectrum of clinical concerns. Looking for an experiential avoidance agenda can assist in promoting a more therapeutic interaction, and assessing for personal approach agenda items can help direct the purpose of the intervention.

Verbally Construed

Needless to say, something as complex and particularly human as values is going to be wrapped up in derived relational responding in one way or another. Note that the definition uses the word "construed," not "constructed." We are interpreting what we globally desire as outcomes in life. When we are defining a value, it is verbal. Valuing, however, is action. People value something. The only verb in that last sentence is "value"; valuing is something people do.

In therapy, when we talk about what we globally desire our life to be about, we need to be careful we don't get ensnared by the words we use. The process of clarifying values indicates that the client and therapist are communicating about the behaviors that are most meaningful to the client. Values clarification may have an augmental function. That is, when a person says, "I value being a loving parent to my children," that statement may function as an augmental increasing the reinforcing functions of any number of parenting behaviors and related consequences. However, we are not establishing rules, but helping the client focus on what he really cares to do in life.

When someone is engaging in value-directed behavior, he may be acting with the reasons discussed in therapy—but that person isn't doing it for those reasons. Values aren't rule governed in that respect. Flexible behavior is done with reasons but is not done for reasons (Hayes et al., 1999, pp. 212–213). That is, reasons may show up as derived relations and come along for the ride, and those reasons do not cause behavior. A person may have the thought "I'll forgo buying this expensive new handbag so I have more money to put into my retirement fund," but the thought does not cause her to decline the handbag. It is more likely that the same contingencies that give rise to her declining to purchase the handbag also give rise to the thought about it. (Reason giving is further discussed in chapter 9.)

Valuing is a choice. When a man chooses to act a certain way, the chosen actions are his values. Until they are executed or acted out, they are just verbal behavior. We don't know what a person values by what he says, but we might know it by what he does.

Clarifying and Specifying Values

Dahl and Lundgren (2006) forward ten different life domains that can stimulate discussion of values:

- Intimate relationships

- Parenting

- Family relationships

- Social relationships

- Work

- Leisure

- Citizenship

- Personal growth

- Health

- Spirituality

Discussing the client's values during sessions can help point the therapy in the most appropriate direction. Having your client complete a values assessment as homework or in session may also yield important assessment data and be worthwhile as an experiential exercise. The only caution is that since the assessment invites the client to consider values in a rather abstract verbal form, some clients may get caught up in wordiness and wonder about having the "right" values or filling every domain, and so on. When this occurs, the therapist can gently shift the work back to an experiential rather than abstract focus.

The Value of Values

The term "values" comes from Latin *valeo*, which indicates having power, strength, effectiveness, and meaning. If we were to talk as behavior analysts, we'd say that environmental and verbal stimuli related to human affairs—such as "meaning," "future goals," and "effective commitment"—would occasion our verbal response: "values." When a therapist says "values" in the context of ACT, it is verbally related to the repertoire of behavior a person exhibits that is governed by personally meaningful environmental, social, and verbal stimuli and that is consequated by the actual execution of the behavior, not solely by the confined achievement of a goal.

Values Are Defined Appetitively

ACT therapists can define global reinforcers as something to work purposefully toward (see "Purpose" in chapter 3 for a functional contextual discussion of purpose) or to make more abundant in order to sustain well-being and, in turn, sustain that class of behavior. With a values focus, behavior can become more abundant and sustain well-being.

■ Case Study: Parenting Values

Sarah values being an involved parent for her son. She can then move forward in choosing to be present in the child's life, reading to her son, teaching the boy how to make friends, and so on. The interaction between Sarah and her son is a reinforcer; watching his improvement in reading skills is a reinforcer; seeing him develop socially appropriate skills is a reinforcer. Sarah is likely to engage in behaviors more frequently because these consequential events make it more likely. Overall her execution of "mothering" is a reinforcer. The outcome of being an engaged mother unfolds in the process of the social behavior between mother and son. The process of helping her child's development and positive relating with her son is the reinforcing outcome. And being an involved parent is an outcome of the process of teaching her son, reading to her son, and so on. Sarah can never fully attain the outcome of being an involved parent, and at the same time there are ongoing moment-to-moment opportunities to attain being an involved parent as an outcome. Outcome is the process through which process becomes the outcome.

There is not a circumscribed, fully attainable end goal in parenting. To an adult who values parenting, being a parent is a lifelong process. Sarah, or any mother with this stance, does not simply dust off her hands after her son finishes blowing out the candles on his eighteenth birthday cake. Seeing a child into adulthood may be a goal along the way of parenting, but it is not the end goal. Mothering can happen throughout the child's life: as an adult confidante, as a caring grandmother to his children, and even as a model of dignity on her deathbed.

"Ah," one might protest, "but what if the child goes astray as a teen, and shuns his own mother despite his mom's commitment to her parenting values throughout his life? After all, a peer group can have a significantly stronger effect over an adolescent's life-style choices than a parent." This is certainly a concern for the boy and for his mom, yet it does not threaten her value-directed behavior. Parenting can include all the appropriate actions a mother can take to help her son even when he shuns her. She can continue to nurture the relationship, give good advice, and mete out suitable consequences for her son's behaviors, based on whether his conduct is proper or improper. If the young man stonewalls his mom or runs away, value-directed behavior need not cease. Engaged parenting also means knowing when to let go. Remember, value-directed behavior is not about achieving a circumscribed goal—for example, when the son completes high school, or expresses affection and tells her, "I love you." If these are not the outcomes of her mothering, the mother can, if psychologically flexible, still continue to engage in value-directed behavior. She can seek him out, offer him protection, and have an open-door policy for him. Or, if it's functional, she can just let him make his own mistakes, take his lumps, and present a tough-love agenda for his behavior.

For the mother with a teenage child who is shunning her and presenting with troublesome behavior, she may have a limited influence on the goals that she can achieve. At the same time, she also can be open to a broad spectrum of opportunities. Despite specific positively evaluated goals not being attained, she does not have to abandon her value of being a committed parent. Her son may choose to be a stonewalling runaway child, and many options for her as a parent may have been exhausted, but she can still value being a mother. With psychological flexibility, she can be present with her feelings of abandonment and just notice her thoughts of revenge or self-denigration, knowing she only has this moment and that she is not her life's content (not even the content of her identity as mother). She can also commit to loving her son and being ready for his return in the most appropriate way. She can still choose to maintain a westward-facing stance even if she just places her nose right up against the rocks of that stonewall.

Values Are Not Defined Aversively

Values clarification is about exploring what to live toward and for. Conversely, we might say that it is not focused on what to live away from or without. When talking about values, it is prudent to discuss a life that is eventful and abundant—a life direction toward which one can choose to move. Aversive contingencies, those that include negative reinforcers or punishers, suppress positively reinforced operant behavior. Avoidance decreases psychological flexibility, and we are trying to build a broader, more flexible repertoire.

Aversive contingencies can be problematic. Negative reinforcement and punishment carry with them some added effects, such as evoking aggressive responses or emotional responses similar to depression. A lifestyle defined by these types of global contingencies is not likely to be experienced as desired or vital. An avoidance agenda may increase experiential avoidance, and be less flexible. Put another way, the outcome of being rid of certain things becomes the process through which avoidance becomes the outcome. For instance, when Jillian becomes ever more reclusive so she won't have to experience the pain of losing a friend to relocation or estrangement, avoidance of friendship becomes an outcome. When Marcelo stops applying for jobs so he won't have to experience the pain of rejection, avoidance becomes an outcome and Marcelo's job-seeking behavior becomes less flexible.

A coherent lifestyle is more likely to develop when people choose where they want to go rather than where they want to get away from. It's more coherent to choose going west rather than "anywhere but east." Going west facilitates choice and moving forward; going anywhere but east may result in running away or going in circles.

Keep in mind that because values can be verbally described, they can be evaluated and also socially influenced. Most people learn their values through their participation in a verbal social community. However, values are also highly individualized, as language is generative, and verbal behavior is shaped by consequence for each individual with a unique reinforcement history. We can tell someone, "I think marriage and family are important," and we can't tell him that he should value marriage and family. One's values can't be fully evaluated by someone else, because the evaluator must do so from the context of his own values. What's valuable to one is not necessarily valued by another, and that's okay since each person is unique. There is no gold standard for values, and therefore they cannot be judged.

Values in Action (as If There Were Another Way!)

Values work often begins with verbal conversation in the therapy room and with written worksheets completed by the client as homework. Yet, as the old saying goes, "Talk is cheap." While the verbal behavior of values clarification is useful, action is where the rubber meets the road.

▪ Case Study: Agoraphobia

Melody reported having agoraphobia and living in her New York City penthouse for "either nine or eleven years." She reported that she actually couldn't remember how long it had been since she left her thousand-square-foot studio apartment. Melody presented as an articulate college graduate and had spent about a decade, give or take a whole year, in a room fifty stories above the streets of the Big Apple. She entertained biannual visitors (at Passover and Yom Kippur), but most of her time was spent reading, watching TV, and frequently and vividly recalling her panic attacks on the city streets. She was adamant about avoiding another attack, saying, "The panic attacks are too much to bear." That statement can be conceptualized as an augmental that increases the aversive functions of any stimulation related to panic attacks. Her isolative behavior was in service of avoiding another attack or events related to such an attack.

Let's just stop there and conceptualize the situation. From this vantage point, we can see what Melody values. She values living in isolation so that she does not experience extreme levels of anxiety. Values are not a feeling or a plan. Melody may dislike staying home, but she also values staying at home, as evidenced by her behavior. By definition, Melody values the agoraphobic lifestyle. It is what she has chosen to do with her life. The outcome of her lifestyle is the process by which she is living it. Using the inflexahex case-conceptualization model, in the domain of lack of values clarity, we can assess the conflicts she is having about what she really wants to do with her life. Now, back to her story ...

When Melody received a phone call from her daughter, who lived in another state and visited once a year at Passover, and learned that she was engaged to be married in a few months, Melody realized that her avoidance agenda was diminishing her participation in life. Determined to go to the wedding, Melody called a clinician to request treatment.

During her first session, Melody articulated a desire for a richer, fuller life, and an ability to be present as a mother at her daughter's wedding. Her values were unsolicited by the therapist, and her story just poured out. Melody clearly conveyed that she had not been living the life she wanted to live. Her articulation of the valued directions toward which she wanted to live her life gave way to a process of self-discovery, of acceptance and defusion moves. She said, "These walls are all I've seen for a lot of my life because I'm afraid of a panic attack. So my heart races? So I feel sick and dizzy? Jeez, who cares? That phone call from my daughter made me realize I've got worse stuff going on: I'm missing everything! I'm missing my own life! I'd rather go to the wedding feeling sick than stay home from the wedding feeling ... well, not really feeling much of anything." When she called the clinician to start her road to recovery, she engaged in committed action, which was influenced by both her recognition that her lifestyle was not vital and her new accepting stance regarding her panic symptoms. Her continued exposure treatment was also evidence of committed action, and her attendance at her daughter's wedding was a goal achieved on her road to valuing being a dedicated mother.

Committed Action

Commitment is an important aspect of ACT. At the core, committed action occurs in treatment when the client engages in clinically relevant behaviors suggestive of "improvement." When a client is given an orientation to committed action—defined as behavior in the service of values, defused from unhelpful rules and verbal events, executed in contact with the present moment, while accepting physiological and cognitive responses elicited during that situation—the client has a better platform from which to take her first step toward clinical improvement.

■ Case Study: Fear of Public Speaking

Lauren values pursuing lifelong learning and chooses the vocation of teaching young children. She also reports that her fear of public speaking impedes progress in this life direction. She says that she would like to be an educator, but fears the peering eyes of an audience. She also needs to pass an oral communication class to graduate from her university. A combination of certain behavior therapy interventions (for example, exposure treatment) and ACT interventions (such as acceptance, defusion, and mindfulness exercises discussed in section 3) will be helpful with this concern, yet the most important move of all is Lauren's actual, measurable progress toward speaking in front of the class. When she begins exposure therapy for public speaking by such seemingly small actions as raising her hand in her college courses, asking gas station attendants for directions, or taking other actions in order to contact the experience of public speaking, she is engaging in action that demonstrates commitment to her lifelong values. Even the tiniest overt baby step taken toward valued living is still committed action.

The therapist can get a lot of leverage out of linking values and committed action; when small steps are regarded as value-directed behavior, opportunities to engage in valued behavior are almost always present. Even if the would-be teacher isn't willing to be in front of a classroom, she can still do social phobia exposure exercises (for example, striking up a conversation with a stranger or announcing the time to a crowded bus every minute) in the service of being an educator.

Some ACT strategies aim to undermine destructive language processes. In contrast, committed action and values help to build positive use of language. Committed action engenders new behavior-environment relationships. In other words, it can be behaving in a new way (learning social skills) in old environments (at work or school) or performing well-developed responses (speaking) in new environments (in front of a boardroom or classroom). The newness of the environment-behavior relationships is in the service of the client's values, and also begins to foster greater psychological flexibility.

Willingness to Take Risks

Committed action unfolds in the context of willingness (see chapter 14). *Willingness* is a quality of behavior supported by the ability to accept emotional and physical events, and to defuse from challenging cognitive content. When one commits to a new behavior in an old environment or old behavior in a new environment, intended and unintended consequences arise. Willingness to contact those feared or unusual consequences supports the execution of important and vital committed actions.

When valued directions are articulated, the client has merely described an agenda verbally. All behavior and plans for behavior can still have inadvertent consequences. A client isn't always going to know what happens when the valued direction is taken. People can pontificate and problem solve, but they do so in the world of words rather than in the world of flesh and blood. Breaking the unhelpful agenda and flexibly finding out what other consequences are available in life can only happen when a person acts differently overtly. This is not an easy task, and when supported by willingness, fostered by acceptance and defusion, done in the service of values, and done right now by a person defused from verbal content, proactive behavior can flourish.

Flexibility and Commitment

An ACT client is made aware that the goal of therapy is psychological flexibility. *Psychological flexibility* includes acting in a new manner to meet new environmental demands. *Flexibility* means changing old strategies in some contexts, and in other contexts, it actually includes persisting in some behavior. When people can bend to meet the demands of a newly contacted valued direction, it is clearer that they are being flexible. The unwavering quality of some response classes is also a demonstration of flexibility. However, when a person meets the same old problems with the same old responses and this isn't directed toward valued living, we might consider that *inflexible behavior*.

If you have ever been to a hockey game, you will notice that before the game starts the goalie will get limbered up by stretching his muscles. This helps him be more physically flexible. During the game, when the opponents' sticks are shooting in close range and the puck is bouncing off of him, sometimes he can find himself doing the splits, holding his stick out in one direction, and moving his other arm in the other direction to prevent any points from being scored. He's showing new (topographical) responses as the environment changes. His flexibility literally helps him change position and move quickly in new ways to help him with his commitment to keep the other team from scoring. And sometimes he needs to not move at all. When a slap shot speeds toward the goalie at ninety-five miles per hour, his job is to persist in his position in front of the net. Think of the willingness and psychological flexibility it takes the goalie to not move in the face of a flying puck!

Niccolò Machiavelli noted, "Where the willingness is great, the difficulties cannot be great" (1532/1984). This is apropos whether a person is developing new responses or being resolute in a course of action in an ever-changing, always-tempting world. Willingness such as this is the fuel for committed action. The committed action in therapy is not simply verbalizing, "Yes, I'll change." It isn't just articulating a commitment—it is engaging in action. It is making clinically relevant, life-affirming change. It can include persisting in behavior or changing some dimension of behavior.

Committed Action and Empirically Supported Treatments

Changing behavior in therapy can be accomplished through empirically supported treatments. The therapist does not just verbally relay the wisdom of commitment and acceptance during sessions; the clinician integrates the approach with a functional analysis of the individual's behavioral concerns along with a treatment plan based on the latest applicable research.

Applied behavioral scientists have been cataloging the different therapeutic approaches that have been empirically evaluated for over a decade (Task Force on Promotion and Dissemination of Psychological Procedures, 1995; Chambless et al., 1998; Chambless & Ollendick, 2001; Nathan & Gorman, 2002). The empirically supported treatment (EST) literature gives clinicians an opportunity to select therapeutic approaches that have been shown to be effective with other clients with similar clinical presentations, and to develop a treatment plan for the particular client based on what has worked with others. When examining your functional analyses of the client's behavior and the area of the inflexahex case-conceptualization model devoted to persistent inaction, impulsivity, or avoidant behavior, see what behaviors need to increase or decrease in order to achieve valued ends. The therapist is encouraged to be familiar with the current literature on best treatment options for the clinical problem and to perform literature reviews when unfamiliar with the latest information on empirically supported practices. Then, using the EST literature, match the interventions shown to be effective in altering behavioral repertoires. This literature is large, and treatment matching for all clinical concerns is beyond the scope of this book. However, it is important to recognize that EST work (for example, exposure therapy for anxiety disorders) is a solid part of ACT work in the committed action piece of the hexaflex model.

Treatment Plans Integrating ACT and ESTs

One may ask, "If there are already evidenced-based treatments, why integrate ACT?" The literature is still young in this regard, and it is still worth considering that ACT has been effective with substance abuse, depression, skin picking, social stigma, and psychosis (see Hayes, Masuda, Bissett, Luoma, & Guerrero, 2004, for a review). The combination of ACT with habit reversal has also been effective (Twohig & Woods, 2004).

A small sample study showed ACT to be helpful with OCD as well (Twohig et al., 2006). One of the interesting aspects of the ACT for OCD study is that all the participants reported the treatment to be highly acceptable. This is a departure from typical responses of people being treated by evidence-based treatments for OCD. Exposure and ritual prevention (ERP) is the widely approved method for treating OCD (Abramowitz, 1997), yet approximately 25 percent of clients decline this therapeutic method, and 3 to 12 percent of clients drop out of ERP treatment (Foa, Steketee, Grayson, & Doppelt, 1983), mainly because the clients do not want to be exposed to their feared stimuli. Foa, Franklin, and Kozak (1998) suggest that unacceptability of treatment and diminished compliance from the client lead to poor treatment results. With these clients, we might assess that their willingness in treatment is low. Perhaps the ACT interventions that build willingness, including defusion, acceptance, and values clarification work, could be an adjunct to ERP. More research is required, but it may be that ACT alone or an ACT approach to ERP could help the therapy become more effective in treating OCD.

A client's ACT treatment plan can describe a treatment approach with tried-and-true interventions. When putting ACT into practice, not only does the orientation of the therapy change from topographical to functional, the scope of clinically relevant behaviors expands as well. In other words, an ACT approach will look for the environmental events that support the client's problematic behavior rather than just giving a treatment plan based on their *DSM* diagnosis without an eye toward behavioral functions.

Further, the clinician assesses for what experiences the client is avoiding. Does the client say that things or events have to be removed or altered before committed action can occur? Getting those answers from the client can assist with treatment planning. Therapy then, in addition to the evidence-based work, can be based on accepting those private, emotional, and cognitive obstacles to the therapy. The treatment agenda is not just eliminative. There is an understanding in the ACT work that certain psychological events are more readily contacted than altered or avoided. The ACT therapist's job is to promote clients' ability to experience life on life's terms, and also to help clients change their behavior so as to behave more flexibly in service of their values.

Case Conceptualization with Values and Committed Action

Values are fuel for committed action. Case conceptualization in these domains is best begun with values clarification followed by planning committed action aimed toward valued living. Some clients might present with high committed action and low values clarification. Take, for instance, the client who is committed to getting high on drugs with only a vague direction in life. Other clients might show high values clarification and low committed action. For example, consider the client who presents with great disappointment and frustration about failing to attain deeply desired outcomes and yet presents no agenda to move toward those outcomes. Some clients present with a mixture of a lack of clear values and a sense of aimless action and meaninglessness. Also note that many problems with values and committed action are likely to be related to problems with avoidance, fusion, contact with the present moment, and/or perspective taking.

Here are some examples of client behaviors that might suggest difficulty with values and committed action:

- Clients who report meaninglessness in their life, such as the client who says, "I don't know where I am or where I am going" or, more simply,

"I don't know" or "Who cares?" to many poignant questions about the direction of his life.

- The client who often says, "Yes, but…" during conversations about important goals and value-directed living. For example, consider a young man who says, "Yes, I'd like to go back to school, but it would be really hard" or "Yes, I want to be a better father, but my work is very demanding." During case conceptualization, note the lack of commitment (among other problems, such as emotional avoidance and fusion) to the directions he might care very deeply about.

- Clients who endorse other people's values as their own. Imagine a woman who says, "Mom and Dad really want to be grandparents, but I am not sure if I want to have children" or "Everyone assumes I'll be promoted to manager, but I am not sure I want to make it my career" or "My family believes in marriage, but I am not sure I want to stay married to him." In these situations, the person is partially being influenced by other people's values.

- A focus on goals rather than values—for instance, the client who cheated on a test or during a game in order to attain a goal. Another example is a man concerned more about the image others have of him as a good worker or father than about the actual behaviors consistent with being an effective worker or father.

- The client presenting with a sense of meaninglessness caught up in daily tasks while losing the values connected to those tasks (put another way, where process becomes the outcome rather than outcome the process). For example, consider the new single mother overwhelmed with late-night feedings and diaper changes who has lost sight of the joys of motherhood, or the student overwhelmed with studying and competition who has lost sight of the value of learning.

- The avoidant client who knows what she values yet fears the private events that might accompany committed action. Take, for example, the client who values rearing an independent child yet avoids allowing her teenager more independence because she fears it will be accompanied by worry and extra stress.

- Clients who often experience negative self-evaluation. Consider the client who has remained in an abusive marriage for twenty years and then feels like a fool for staying in the relationship. Also consider the client with schizophrenia who has avoided medication for many years and feels regret over years wasted, or the client who has stayed in an unsatisfying job for years who might feel angry over being treated like a doormat.

Values, Commitment, and Behavior Change Processes 157

Almost any problematic behavior can be construed in terms of problems with values clarification or problems with committed action. The major challenges for you as the therapist are to identify these behaviors and to be clear about the client's values as distinct from your own values.

CHAPTER 9

Acceptance Processes

There are two acceptance processes described in the ACT model—acceptance and defusion. Both acceptance and defusion facilitate psychological flexibility. Like the other four core processes, acceptance and defusion can be integrated with all other processes in practice.

Acceptance

To *accept* means to take in or receive an event or situation. *Acceptance* also means abandoning futile change agendas (Hayes et al., 1999, p. 77). Acceptance, however, is often misunderstood. Instead of being regarded as an action that might increase psychological flexibility, it may instead be seen as an evaluation (a judgment or opinion about events), as a passive stance toward events, or, worse, as an acknowledgment of defeat. Acceptance may be mistakenly understood to mean that accepting an event implies liking or wanting the event. However, acceptance as receiving or taking in an event or situation does not imply liking that event or situation. Acceptance may include taking in an event and accepting that one does not like it. For instance, Mike didn't want a grade of C in his chemistry class, nor did he like that he earned a grade of C in chemistry class. Even while he hoped to get a grade of A or B, he accepted that the grade of C was a fair evaluation of his work and that he was a C student in that class.

Alternately, some might view acceptance as a passive process. It's not unusual for clients to initially be aghast at the idea of accepting unwanted psychological events—for example, "You want me to just accept my anxiety attacks?" However, acceptance as taking in or receiving is not passive—on the contrary, it is often an active and even effortful process for the client. For instance, Alexis found it challenging to accept the idea that she might have a panic attack when she went to the mall. She entered treatment hoping that she might avoid shopping or find a way to guarantee that she would not have panic attacks before entering the mall. Acceptance may also be viewed as defeat where it is seen as equivalent to giving up (if, for example, Alexis just lived with the plan that she could never go to the mall again). This is not acceptance. However, taking in or receiving an experience can be regarded as the very opposite of giving up (for instance, Alexis noticing and acknowledging the private events related to anxiety rather than making attempts to avoid or eliminate her private events). Regarded this way, the only thing that might be given up as an outcome of acceptance is an unworkable change agenda.

Hayes and colleagues (1999, p. 77) point out that some degree of acceptance is implicit in psychotherapy in that the client and therapist accept that there is a problem that the client wants to do something about. What is often problematic is what the client wants to do to solve the problem.

Reason Giving, "Causes," and Avoidance

Much of human verbal behavior is in the service of making sense of human behavior, both one's own behavior and the behavior of others. *Reasons* are verbal statements offered in answers to a question such as "Why did you do that?" or "Why did that happen?" Reason giving has its uses; social discourse often requires that we give reasons for our behavior, such as telling our employer, "I will not be at work today because I have the flu." However, it can be problematic for clients seeking treatment when reasons are regarded as causes of events rather than as mere descriptions of events. As Hayes and colleagues point out (1999, p. 51), a client enters therapy with the belief that he has a problem, and that the problem is caused by something. Implicit in the belief that the problem is caused by something is an assumption that once we can identify the cause of a problem, we can then solve it. For instance, Alexis might believe that if she can figure out the cause of her panic attacks, they will then cease.

Social norms often dictate that people provide explanations for their behavior, and we are socialized to look for cause-and-effect relationships among events, including looking for causes of other people's behavior. There is much social support for reporting reasons as causes of behavior, and thoughts and feelings as reasons. For instance, imagine that someone asks Rick, "Why are you smoking marijuana?" He might respond, "Because I feel bored and frustrated." Rick's response suggests that boredom and frustration are causes of marijuana smoking. His response is more likely to be approved of by others than if he answered, "I don't know why I smoke marijuana" or "Because I feel like smoking marijuana." Further, if we asked Rick why he feels frustrated and bored, he might say, "I feel frustrated and bored because I am dissatisfied with my job," implying that dissatisfaction causes frustration and boredom rather than noting that boredom and frustration are evidence of dissatisfaction. We can even conceptualize that boredom and frustration *are* dissatisfaction, rather than outcomes caused by dissatisfaction. These types of faulty causal reasoning are pervasive.

Even before a child can speak, parents and other speakers in the environment provide reasons for all sorts of behavior. Frequently those reasons offer feelings as causes of behavior: "You hit your sister! You must be tired." "Look at her play; she must be feeling happy." "You're not smiling. Are you feeling sad?" Once socialized that emotions are reasons for actions, children start giving answers to why they did something with an emotion-based answer. Even at a tender age, children are socialized to look for and report emotional causes of behavior.

Therapist Exercise: Reason Giving

Rick said the cause of his marijuana smoking is that he feels bored and frustrated.

If we asked why he feels bored and frustrated, he might reply, "Because I hate my job."

In this exercise, your task is to brainstorm for a few minutes and generate as many reasons as you can for each of the behaviors described below—that is, why might the person behave in the manner described?

- Joanna ate an entire box of cookies.

- Martin started an argument with his wife.

- Maya yelled at her secretary for making a minor clerical error.

- Willie did not do the chores his father told him to do.

- Carmen drank to the point of severe intoxication while at a party.

Now look back over your responses and note how many of your responses referred to emotions as the cause of behavior—for instance, that the person in question was feeling bored, angry, sad, and so on.

If you are like most people, quite a few (but not all!) of your responses referred to thoughts or feelings as causes of behavior.

Keep your responses handy, as we'll refer back to this exercise again shortly.

Private Events and Reason Giving

Thoughts and feelings are likely targets as reasons or causes for behavior because thoughts and feelings often precede or follow important, memorable, or clinically significant events. Thus, the client reports that he is failing in school because he is depressed, or she is not enjoying satisfying social relationships because she feels anxious. We clinicians and mental health researchers are as guilty of this sort of reasoning as are our clients. We define, name, research, and treat disorders based on thoughts and feelings—for example, anxiety, mood, and thought disorders (Hayes et al., 1999, pp. 154–156).

Notice also that we tend to describe psychological disorders as causes of behavior. Look back at your answers to the reason-giving exercise above. Were any of your causes of the person's behavior psychological disorders? For example, did you indicate that Joanna ate a box of cookies because she has bulimia, that Carmen drank because she abuses alcohol, or that Willie didn't do his chores because he has oppositional defiant disorder? With those types of answers, instead of turning feelings into causes, psychological disorders are made out to be causes of problem behavior. However, the problem with this sort of causal reasoning is that we mistake a description of a set of symptoms for the cause of those same symptoms. It is not clinically useful to say that a person drinks too much because they have a substance-use disorder. Alcohol abuse doesn't cause excessive drinking; alcohol abuse is defined by excessive drinking. Similarly, bulimia doesn't cause bingeing and purging behavior: bulimia is defined by bingeing and purging behavior. Pay close attention to some of the conversation around you and to explanations for behavior offered in textbooks and research reports. You will notice just how pervasive the tendency is to describe feelings as reasons and reasons as causes of behavior.

We might regard the use of reasons as causes as just social nicety rather than as a problem to be concerned about. It is true that reason giving often smoothes social discourse. Reason giving becomes problematic when the individual believes that those reasons are causes of behavior, because if feelings cause problematic behavior, then getting rid of or avoiding those feelings is seen as a solution to the problem.

Think of a client or someone you know who complains of trouble with social anxiety. Most often people who describe an anxiety disorder as a problem have the aim of getting rid of anxiety. People with significant social anxiety tend to report problems with things like dating, going on job interviews, assertiveness, and social isolation. And such people rarely come to treatment saying something like "The problem is that I avoid social situations, I fail to seek promotions so I'm not advancing in my career, I do not extend social invitations to others, and I avoid or leave most social situations so I am now almost completely socially isolated." Though this might be a fairly accurate description of the problem, instead clients most often say something like "My problem is anxiety; if I could get rid of this anxiety, then everything else would fall into place." Nonacceptance of anxiety is implicit in this stance. And due to the very nature of anxiety, in contexts where anxiety is seen as bad and unacceptable it becomes very important to avoid anxiety, which leads to hypervigilance: being on the lookout for anxiety and dreading situations where anxiety might show up. And what is the outcome of this stance? More avoidance and, paradoxically, more anxiety.

In practice with ACT clients, be on the lookout for reason giving. Where you detect reason giving, look for avoidance, as they tend to go hand in hand. The antidote to avoidance is acceptance. In contexts where clients are willing to take in or receive an event or experience, the power it has over them is greatly diminished. If anxiety does not cause social isolation and anxiety can be taken in, then clients are in a position to truly do something about social isolation. If anxiety does not cause problem behavior, then, whether or not anxiety is present, they can extend a social invitation to another, attend a social gathering, or strike up a conversation with a neighbor. If clients can accept—that is, take in or receive anxiety when it does show up—then they can engage in whatever social behavior they choose when their anxiety is low as well as when it is high.

Reason Giving and the "and/but" Distinction

The tiny word "but" is used in many instances of reason giving. For example, the client who avoids anxiety might say, "I wanted to ask her out on a date, *but* I was anxious." Similarly, the lapsed substance abuser might say, "I wanted to stay sober, *but* I was too stressed out, so I got drunk." Hayes and colleagues (1999, pp. 166–168) point out that the word "but" is from a Latin word meaning "be out." It is similar to saying "I would have asked her out on a date, be out the feelings of anxiety," as if the anxiety could be out of the man's life. The event that follows the "but" undermines or undoes what comes before. This use of "but" puts thoughts, feelings, and actions in competition with one another, rather than acknowledging that two events are simultaneously present. It is more accurate to say that the anxious client wanted to ask her on a date *and* he was feeling anxious. Similarly, the substance-abusing client wanted to stay sober *and* she drank. ACT is aiming to shape up psychological flexibility, which includes a willingness to engage in value-directed behavior in the presence of clinically relevant private events, not despite them.

In ACT, this type of reason giving is challenged by instructing clients to use the word "and" where they have been inclined to use the word "but." It may take some getting used to, *and* this convention sets up a context that facilitates defusion and acceptance by weakening the imagined connection between private events and overt behavior. In other words, thoughts and feelings do not cause behavior; a person can feel one way and act another without having to change the feelings. There are other words that people can use that function as "be out" reason giving, such as "yet," "however," and "except for," so be on the lookout for such phrasing. And remember to look not only at the form of the verbalizations but also for the avoidant functions. (Notice that the "but" in the preceding sentence was instructive, not emotionally avoidant!)

Is All Avoidance Problematic?

You may be having some lingering questions about avoidance. Why not avoid anxiety? Isn't anxiety undesirable? Shouldn't we teach our clients distraction and relaxation training, and maybe suggest that they see a psychiatrist for antianxiety medication? Who wants to be anxious?

Considered theoretically from a functional contextual position, the reason that avoidance is unlikely to work with regard to feelings is that feelings cannot be controlled directly. We can only control feelings by changing the environments that elicit feelings. Techniques such as relaxation and distraction may work in some settings and when anxiety is mild, and probably will not be very effective in all settings or for severe anxiety. Usually if the goal is to eliminate a feeling, then one outcome is a shrinking environment—for instance, not going to crowded places or meeting new people, or perhaps only going where alcohol is available to numb the anxiety. These nonacceptance moves mean less psychological flexibility and often more problems. In contrast, acceptance allows clients to change what they do have the ability to change directly: their own overt behavior. When anxiety can be taken in, clients can receive it, and instead of trying to control feelings, they can choose to engage in new or abandoned forms of overt behavior and move in the direction of their values. In this way, accepting a feeling leads to a more expansive environment.

Thoughts are also behaviors that cannot be changed directly. Try not to think about a green giraffe. Of course you are now thinking about a green giraffe! Deliberately avoiding a thought doesn't work. Thoughts aren't rule governed; we can't simply follow a rule to suppress a thought such as "Don't think about your ex-wife." Paradoxically, attempts to suppress thoughts lead to an increase in those thoughts (Wegner et al., 1987). Some people, instead of trying to avoid thoughts directly, try to avoid all stimuli that might evoke an unwanted thought, which can lead to a less vital lifestyle. For instance, consider what life is like for a client who doesn't want to think about the boyfriend who left her, so she avoids places they had been together, their mutual friends, and music that stimulates thinking about him. Another client experienced an intrusive thought he wanted to get rid of. He would frequently have the thought "I hate myself," and he noticed that the thought often showed up after he made a mistake. His solution? He stopped trying anything new to reduce the chances of making a mistake. For both of these clients, the outcome of trying to avoid thinking a thought, like attempts to avoid unwanted feelings, was a shrinking environment, a paradoxical increase in thinking the unwanted thought, and less psychological flexibility.

In practice, many clients are not immediately receptive to the idea of accepting unwanted thoughts and feelings. The stance of the therapist is important in this part of the work. As an ACT therapist you model acceptance, and this includes accepting where the client is with her life, and accepting the person's clinical concern. This may also include accepting the client's nonacceptance and avoidance. This accepting stance can be cultivated by contacting your own avoidance. Yes, we suspect that, like us, you may engage in avoidance behaviors at some times and in some situations. No, we haven't been watching you, but we do know that you are a human being. This means that, like us and your clients, you were reared in this culture that makes reason giving important, that readily sees feelings and thoughts as causes of behavior, and that advocates avoidance as a reasonable response to unwanted thoughts and feelings. Putting ACT in practice with clients is always facilitated by putting ACT in practice yourself. And if you contact your own avoided content, be gentle with yourself just as you would be with a client. Acceptance isn't passive; it's an active process of taking in or receiving, and, though simple, it's not always easy!

Avoidance as a Trap

As we mentioned earlier, clients are not always open to accepting unwanted content. Willingness and creative hopelessness exercises (in section 3, Putting ACT into Practice, and especially chapter 10, on creative hopelessness, and chapter 15, on acceptance) assist in the active process of acceptance. Nonacceptance is often demonstrated in ACT as a trap or a loser's game. Hayes et al. (1999) discuss an exercise using Chinese finger cuffs, which are tubes of woven bamboo in which a person can put her left and right index fingers. Once inside, when the person tries to pull her fingers out of the tube, the cuff becomes more snug, and the harder the person pulls, the tighter the snare. Actually pushing both fingers together, an acceptance of being trapped, loosens the cuff, allowing the person more wiggle room and greater flexibility to find a way out of the snare. Acceptance of the situation is required.

An interesting metaphor is the Asian Monkey Trap Metaphor, which also can show the futility of struggle. A monkey trap is made from a hollowed gourd and is filled with fruits and nuts to bait a monkey. The gourd has a single opening just large enough for the monkey's hand to reach in and grab the bait. Once the bait is grasped, the monkey cannot remove both its hand and the fruit. The filled fist is too large to pass the trap opening. The trap is effective because the monkey refuses to let go of the bait, even as the trapper approaches it with a club. If the monkey would be willing to lose the reinforcer, it could slip its hand out and save its own life. If the monkey isn't willing to lose it, it's lost it! In other words, if the monkey is not willing to lose the immediate reinforcer, it loses all opportunity for further reinforcers. (See chapter 14, on willingness, for further exercises and explanation.)

Some clients may easily get on board with acceptance as an alternative to avoidance, since they have seen the futility of their own efforts at control. For the less willing client, we might try to use some of the willingness techniques described in chapter 14 or cultivate a sense of creative hopelessness, which is the subject of the next chapter. Or we can use defusion techniques, one of the two acceptance processes in this model of ACT.

Case Conceptualization and Acceptance

Problems with acceptance are likely to be detected very early in treatment, as most clients come to treatment with an explicit agenda of avoiding or getting rid of unwanted thoughts and feelings. However, problems with acceptance may also show up later in treatment as progress is made. For instance, a client who enters treatment with social anxiety may make progress on accepting anxiety, and as she commits to interacting with others, she may find new phenomena to avoid, such as fear of being rejected or fear of intimacy. She may not be willing to accept the discomfort arising from "making others feel bad" when she turns down social invitations that don't interest her. So while problems with acceptance are likely to show up early in treatment, the therapist—and the client—should be on the lookout for them at all times.

Client behaviors that might suggest difficulty with acceptance include these:

- Clients state the explicit goal of eliminating private events. Early in therapy, many clients say, "I don't want to feel sad (angry, nervous) anymore." A slightly broader eliminative agenda can also be suggested by the client, such as "When this depression goes away, then I can get on with my life" or, more perniciously, "I just want to be happy."

- Clients also explicitly state frequent avoidance behaviors justified by private events, such as "When I start feeling anxious, I have to leave."

- Clients describe thoughts and feelings as causes of behavior; for example, "I can't make a new relationship work because I can't stop thinking about my ex."

Defusion

Defusion is a term coined by Hayes and colleagues (1999) describing the attempt to reduce cognitive fusion, or the impact of the transformation of stimulus functions when a client is presented with a verbal event. The defusion process aims to disconnect (de-fuse) the person's behavior from the stimulus control of the words. Defusion practices are useful in their own right, and are often integrated into acceptance, contact-with-the-present-moment, and perspective-taking work. Cognitive fusion occurs when people fail to distinguish things from descriptions of things, including distinguishing themselves from their thoughts and feelings (see chapter 6). For example, instead of experiencing the thought "The future is bleak" as merely a thought, Rick is fused with the thought and regards the thought "The future is bleak" as if it were the same as the lived experience of a bleak future. Instead of experiencing "I'm a loser" as an evaluation, Rick experiences it as a truth about himself. He is fused with his thoughts.

Defusion means changing one's relationship to thoughts and feelings. From a functional contextual perspective, thoughts and feelings are seen as psychological content, and defusion allows one to distinguish oneself from that content (Hayes et al., 1999, p. 73). When not fused with his thoughts, Rick is able to see his thoughts as thoughts and evaluations as evaluations. They are mere verbal content that shows up in certain situations and that he has little control over. Though the distinction between being fused with a thought versus seeing it as content seems subtle, the difference can have a massive impact on how one experiences events. In Rick's case, when "the future is bleak" is treated as a definite statement that corresponds to the physical, nonarbitrary world, there is little incentive to change his behavior. From the functional contextual viewpoint, he has verbally cast his future as bereft of reinforcers, and the transformation of stimulus functions from this verbal event leads to a narrowed repertoire. When "the future is bleak" is merely received as a thought, Rick may be more willing to broaden his behavior instead of doing more of the same. With the defused stance, the transformation of stimulus functions of a bleak future does not govern his behavior.

Consider Rick's notion of a bleak future. The future, by definition, is not here now. And yet, when fused with "The future is bleak," Rick responds to events here/now in relation to the verbalized "bleak future" that isn't and can't be here now. This fusion can have destructive consequences. For another example, suppose a person we'll call Susan was fused with the thought "I have the winning lottery ticket"—that is, Susan responds to the thought "I have the winning lottery ticket" in same manner as if she actually held the winning lottery ticket. She might quit her job, go on a shopping spree, give away money, and behave with respect to her finances as if millions of dollars would be coming her way shortly. Contrast this with her behavior if she noticed that she merely had the thought "I have the winning lottery ticket." In that case, she might go to work, pay her bills, and budget her money while perhaps imagining what it would be like to actually win the lottery.

At a glance, this example may seem fanciful. No one would act as if they won the lottery just because they thought "I have the winning lottery ticket." Is it really that much different from what we see our clients do (and maybe what we secretly do) when fused with thoughts and feelings? Being fused with "The future is bleak," "No one likes me," "I will have a panic attack if I go to the store," "I can't stand this pain any longer," or "This depression is never going to end" is not substantively different from being fused with a thought such as "I have the winning lottery ticket." Fusion with more bizarre thought content, such as thinking "I have the winning lottery ticket" when one does not or being fused with thoughts such as "They are all out to get me" or "I am not really alive" may be what distinguishes delusional beliefs from merely odd thoughts that show up now and again (Bach, 2005). The experience of responding to a fused thought ("The future is bleak") as compared to responding to a defused thought ("I am having the thought that the future is bleak") is quite different. Similarly, fusion to "No one likes me" is qualitatively different from the defused "I am having the thought that no one likes me." Is the thought the problem, or is the client's relationship to the thought the problem? The following exercise provides some of the answer.

Therapist Exercise: Fusion and Mental Polarity

Think of a relevant self-evaluation that you struggle with. Perhaps you don't like your weight, or you think you should do a better job of housekeeping, or you wish you were more productive on your job. Now make that evaluation just a little more extreme. Next, if you are in a place where you can do so, say that evaluation aloud, or say it mentally to yourself; for example, "I am fat," "I am lazy," or "I am a slob."

What does that feel like? Do you buy it, or try to resist or avoid it?

Now, add the words "I'm having the thought that . . ." to your evaluation; for example, "I'm having the thought that I'm lazy." Notice how different that feels. You may notice that it's easier not to accept and take in the experience of "I'm having the thought that I'm lazy" than to have the experience of "I'm lazy."

Now let's add another step to this exercise (from Hayes et al., 1999, p. 189, Mental Polarity Exercise). Take the thought and make it more positive. For example, change "I'm lazy" to "I'm lazy sometimes." Now make it even more positive ("I work hard sometimes") and keep making it more positive until it is completely positive ("I am the most productive person there is!"). With each step, notice what your mind does.

Now start with the initial evaluation and make it more negative ("I'm very lazy") and work your way to extreme negativity ("I'm the laziest person on earth") and again notice what your mind does.

In the above exercise, did you find the positive or negative self-evaluations more difficult? If you are like most people, you probably found yourself resisting both the extreme positive and the extreme negative statements. And if you were able to have them all without resisting them, great, you are already good at defusion! Now say to yourself, "I am great at defusion" and "I am the greatest at defusion." The point is, when we get entangled with content, it doesn't much matter whether it is positive or negative. Fusion is fusion, and if a person is fused with thoughts, they are likely to struggle with positive and negative thoughts alike. For example, Shandra feels guilty when she thinks about her children's problems and blames herself for causing those problems. She even feels guilty when she notices that she has not been thinking about her children's problems because then she feels like a bad mother for not worrying more about their problems. She can't win at this level of content. Defusion is not about changing thought content; it is about changing the client's relationship to private events.

Defusion Is Not Cognitive Restructuring

In our experience, the distinction between changing content and changing context is so frequently made that it is worth saying explicitly that defusion is distinct from cognitive restructuring. In cognitive restructuring, the goal of the therapist is to change the client's irrational thoughts and to modify problematic feelings and desires (Ellis, 2003). The emphasis is on changing the content of private events. For example, "No one likes me" might be challenged and changed to "Some people like me" or "I am a decent person." Similarly, "I will have a panic attack if I go to the store" might be restructured to "I don't always have panic attacks when I go to the store" or "If I go to the store, maybe I will have a panic attack and maybe I will not." And if the thought "No one likes me" leads to feelings of despair, it is hoped that a change in the thought content will decrease feelings of despair. And if the thought "I will have a panic attack if I go to the store" is restructured, perhaps the change in thought will lead to decreased panic and an increase in going to the store. In contrast to cognitive restructuring, in cognitive defusion the emphasis is not on changing the content of clients' thoughts and feelings. The goal is instead to change the client's relationship to thoughts and feelings, regardless of whether the content itself changes. The client may continue to have the thought "No one likes me" and may or may not feel despair upon having the thought (and if present, she would notice and defuse from the despair). If no longer fused with the thought, she may have the thought and invite someone out for dinner even while having the thought "No one likes me." Similarly, she may have the thought "If I go to the store, I will have a panic attack," and she may or may not feel anxious, and may choose to go to the store while having the thought "If I go to the store, I will have a panic attack." There is no assumption that the client's thought content must change before feelings or overt behavior can change. Cognitive defusion and cognitive restructuring are so different that using defusion and restructuring at the same time is contraindicated.

The distinction arises because cognitive and functional contextual approaches have different assumptions about cognitions. Cognitive restructuring is based on the assumption that clients can choose rational versus irrational beliefs, and that changed beliefs lead to changed feelings (Ellis, 2003). In contrast, in a functional contextual approach, the assumption is that clients have little control over private events, and that thoughts do not cause some behavior. A single stimulus may precede both a negative thought and avoidant behavior. This is different from saying that negative thoughts cause negative behaviors. Thoughts and other private events are viewed as historically situated responses that cannot be changed directly. For example, Shandra has the thought "It's my fault" when she or her children have negatively evaluated feelings or experiences. Shandra might, through exploring her past, notice that in her history other people were quick to blame her when things went badly. Now in the present, Shandra continues to have the thought "It's my fault" in contexts where those she is close to experience negative events. She is not choosing the thought "It's my fault"; rather, the thought is viewed as a product of her history. As we saw in chapter 4, on relational frame theory, we cannot subtract from verbal networks, we can only add to them. From this perspective, it is impossible to replace one thought with another thought. In some cases, frequent exposure to a new thought might weaken the old thought. For instance, if Shandra experienced others frequently telling her that she is not to blame, she might eventually have the thought "It's all my fault" less frequently. On the other hand, it is just as likely that when someone tells her, "You are not to blame," she will respond by having the thought "It's all my fault," and she might vigorously argue that she is indeed to blame for current circumstances. In trying to change a thought, her struggle is at the level of content, and she is entangled with verbal notions of fault and blame. In practicing defusion, she might notice that she is having the thought "It's all my fault" and respond to cues other than her thoughts of blame as guides for action. If she is fused with her thoughts and feelings, it becomes very important to avoid feelings of fault or to change self-blaming. This limits her psychological flexibility because her available options are avoidance or the "mindy" behavior of arguing with herself. So in contexts where it is important to avoid self-blame, she might avoid all situations where she or others might assign blame, or argue with herself or others about whether or not she is really to blame, or kick herself while she's down by berating herself for feeling self-blame. Contrast this with defusion, where Shandra might notice that she is having self-blaming thoughts and feelings. She might be negatively evaluating her thoughts and feelings, and she can notice that she is evaluating her thoughts and feelings. She has more behavioral options at hand, as she might do any of the avoidant and fused behaviors, and she can choose to behave in alternate ways even though they might be followed by thoughts and feelings of self-blame. Self-blame no longer matters, or rather, Shandra no longer "matters about" self-blame. ACT therapists often say that "people matter about" things that are important to them. Consider that "mattering" is something people do. Events in the environment do not inherently matter; people make them matter. Individuals "matter about" or "make important" certain issues and situations (see chapter 12 for a further discussion of "mattering" as a verb). One might say Shandra chooses to no longer blame her blame; that is, she does not avoid thoughts and feelings of guilt and blame if action that might be followed by guilty feelings or thoughts is consistent with some valued outcome.

Shandra's experience of blame illustrates the interrelationship of acceptance and defusion. Sometimes acceptance is followed by defusion, sometimes defusion facilitates acceptance, and sometimes defusion is acceptance. The client who is willing to have an unwanted thought can get close enough to be able to defuse from it. The client who defuses from an unwanted thought may be more willing to accept it. The act of defusing from it may be an act of acceptance.

Case Conceptualization and Defusion

Fusion might show up anytime in treatment. Often where there is avoidance, there is also fusion. For instance, clients who avoid anxiety are often fused with beliefs such as "Anxiety is bad" or "I can't have a panic attack."

Client behaviors that might suggest difficulty with defusion include these:

- The client's evaluations of himself are stated as facts rather than as evaluations. For example, a client says, "I am a loser," instead of something more qualified, like "Sometimes I think that I am a loser."

- The client's avoidance is related to a fused belief, such as a client with chronic pain who says, "I can't take the pain anymore, so I stay in bed most of the time."

- The client espouses rigid beliefs about how the world is or how other people should behave, and doesn't acknowledge them as only his opinions. Consider a client who says, "Premarital sex is wrong," rather than "I believe that premarital sex is wrong" or "I want to wait until I'm married to have a sexual relationship."

Acceptance and defusion processes also play a role in the other four processes—contact with the present moment, self as perspective, values, and committed action—which will be touched on the next few chapters, and we will consider more about putting acceptance strategies into practice in chapter 15.

SECTION 3

Putting ACT into Practice

CHAPTER 10

Creative Hopelessness:
When the Solution Is the Problem

As odd as the phrase may sound, "the solution is part of the problem" can often be a profound realization for the person who suffers. Most clients who present for treatment have been trying to solve "the problem" for some time. It is unusual for someone to immediately attempt to solve a problem by seeing a psychotherapist. More often individuals try to solve their problems on their own first: they ask for the advice of family and friends and then from paraprofessionals, they read self-help books, they seek medication or self-medicate, and so on (Hayes et al. 1999, p. 94). Finally, after months, years, or decades, some seek psychotherapy on their own or by referral from another.

The notion that "the solution is part of the problem" sounds strange to many new clients and might be a hard sell at first. After all, clients' "solutions" for their problems are not likely to be perceived as the problem. By definition, a solution solves the problem at hand and therefore does not appear to be part of the problem. And when "the solution is part of the problem" is considered functionally, it is likely to resonate with clients' experience. "The solution is part of the problem" is a useful concept when looking at the Inflexahex Case-Conceptualization Worksheet, for directing your functional assessment, and for planning ACT interventions. As an assessment device, it directs you toward avoidance behaviors and is a starting point in understanding functional relationships among client behaviors, both verbal and overt. As an intervention-planning tool, the idea that "the solution is part of the problem" helps you and, more importantly, the client grasp how past attempts to solve problems have themselves been problematic. The notion that "the solution is part of the problem" is central to understanding creative hopelessness.

Defining Creative Hopelessness

Creative hopelessness is the stance of the client when contacting the experience that past attempts to solve a problem are actually part of the problem. Having this perspective on clinically relevant concerns influences the person to be ready to try new change strategies. Creative hopelessness is an often misunderstood concept. In fact, some ACT therapists have suggested that it instead be called creative hopefulness. The misunderstanding arises out of confusion about what is being described/evaluated as "hopeless." The client is not hopeless. The possibility of more effective living is not hopeless. The client's past change agenda, however, is hopeless. The client has been trying to control events that can't be controlled and/or avoiding events in the interest of avoiding unwanted private events in a way that decreases psychological flexibility and keeps the client from attaining valued outcomes. Adhering to this fruitless and bleak change agenda for controlling private events is doomed for failure. Now that's hopeless!

Therapist Exercise: Attempting to Control Feelings

That controlling feelings is difficult is easily demonstrated. Try right now to feel really angry. Or really sad. Or afraid. You can't do it. In ACT training, we often use the following example: "I will pay you a million dollars if you fall in love with that person over there." Most trainees will laugh and several will, in jest, volunteer to fall in love with a stranger for the payout. And then we ask if they would really be in love with the person or if they would merely be performing overt behaviors consistent with feeling in love, for example, spending time together, being physically affectionate, and saying the words "I love you." The overt behaviors are easily controlled—the feeling of being in love is not.

Control agendas often work just fine in the context of overt behavior. The utility of our ability to control things in the physical world is evident in all the wondrous human creations that surround us. We can control gross and fine motor movements in ways that allow us to drive a car, build a computer, play the guitar, carry on a conversation, perform microsurgery, and so on. The driver or surgeon will also think and feel while performing activities; the driver might mentally anticipate the next curve in the road or the surgeon might feel nervous about an upcoming surgery. These private events are more difficult to control than motor activity. In short, control works well for driving, surgery, and thousands of other activities. However, in contexts of thought and emotion, control does not work so effectively. We cannot easily will ourselves to stop thinking about something or to feel a particular feeling; the driver can control whether or not he turns, and he cannot control whether or not he thinks about the turn. The surgeon can control the activities she performs in the operating room and not the feelings she feels in the operating room.

Controlling Emotions

Are you convinced that control doesn't work for private events, or are you having the thought that you can directly change feelings of anxiety or anger? If you are thinking such thoughts, all we can say is "Of course you are!" These thoughts, like all thoughts, are a product of your history. And your history, if you were raised in Western culture, most likely tells you that people can and should control their feelings. We are told, for example, things like "Don't you get angry with me," "Don't be afraid," or "It's not funny! Wipe that smile off of your face." This is just an extension (generalization) of aspects of the change agenda that do work: if the alarm clock disturbs you when you want to sleep, you can get rid of it by hitting the snooze button; if the room is too dark, you can get rid of your eyestrain by turning on lights; if your poison oak rash itches too much, you apply an ointment. Through multiple experiences, people develop a negatively rein-forced avoidance repertoire that is effective in some contexts. In other words, people learn that they can often get rid of discomfort.

Clients often come into therapy with the goal of learning how to better control discomfort or negatively evaluated feelings (or how to bring about positively evaluated feelings, for example, "I should feel happy"). They also bring with them a change agenda that goes something like this: "If I can get rid of feelings A and B, then I will be able to do X, Y, and Z." That verbal relation between a behavior and its consequence works wonders in domains of overt behavior; for example, "If I can control my spending, then I will be able to buy a home" and "If I control how often I golf, then I have more time to work." And this change agenda gets generalized to private events. The concern here is that the client has a wonderful tool for the physical world that isn't as handy in the world of thoughts and feelings. If the only tool someone has is a hammer, then everything starts looking like a nail. Ouch!

Clinical Examples of Problematic Solutions

Problems with anxiety can be easily conceptualized as unworkable attempts to control unwanted thoughts, emotions, and other private experiences. The person with social anxiety avoids social events in the service of avoiding anxiety despite the fact that participating in these events might be useful for attaining desirable social or occu-pational outcomes. The client with panic disorder avoids many activities (for example, driving or going to crowded places like the mall) in the service of avoiding panic attacks. The person with OCD performs compulsive behaviors in the service of avoiding the thought content of obsessions. Yet the individual presenting for treatment usually sees anxiety, rather than avoidance, as the problem preventing him from attaining valued outcomes. In addition, unwanted feelings and thoughts are seen as reasons for negative life outcomes.

Avoidance

While anxiety is most easily conceptualized in terms of avoidance, other common problems can also be conceptualized in terms of avoidance. Take the following example.

■ Case Study: Worrying

Martha brought her sixteen-year-old son, Michael, in for treatment of drug addiction. He had been caught using a prescription tranquilizer his friend stole from a relative. As punishment for the transgression, his parents had him undergo monthly drug testing, which he paid for from earnings at his part-time job. He was also punished with a 9:00 p.m. curfew and was not allowed to visit friends deemed untrustworthy. Martha brought him in for treatment after he began staying out past curfew and skipped school to spend time with his new girlfriend. He got really mad when she made his curfew even earlier in order to punish those behaviors. Michael reported that he had never used drugs before or since the incident in question and indeed his drug tests had all been negative. He reported that he felt "like a prisoner" and that his friends no longer invited him out because he could not stay out past 8:00 p.m. He was angry with his mother and acknowledged responsibility for breaching her trust. Martha reported, "I feel bad for keeping him in and I am worried that he will become an addict like his no-good cousin. When he is away, I am afraid he is using drugs and getting into other trouble, and I worry every minute he is gone. I want him to go to college and have a good life." While her spoken agenda was in the service of the valued end of helping her son succeed, she also had an unspoken agenda of controlling her feelings of worry. This control agenda became clearer in the next few sessions. When Martha felt worried, she restricted her son's activity. This worked in the sense that she felt less worried when he was home. It didn't work in that her son began disobeying the rules and became less open with her, which led her to trust him less and worry more. Instead of allowing him opportunities (within limits) to earn back her trust, she focused on decreasing her own feelings of worry and ended up trusting him less and worrying more. Her solution is part of her problem.

Reason Giving

Reason giving is another problematic solution. Formally, reasons may be verbal descriptions of relations between events; for example, "He has no money because he lost his job." ACT therapists conceptualize excessive reason giving as a problem rather than a solution when thoughts and feelings are seen as reasons for or causes of behavior (Hayes et al., 1999); for example, "I couldn't go to the meeting because I was too anxious," "When I get rid of this depression, then I can find a job," "I was too angry to call her," and "I got drunk because I was upset." Though the relationship isn't immediately obvious, excessive reason giving is related to unworkable control. When thoughts and feelings are viewed as causes of behavior, then it becomes important to control those unwanted thoughts and feelings based on the assumption that behavior can only change after thoughts and feelings change. The formulation is turned around somewhat in ACT: when behavior changes, thoughts and feelings might change—or they might not. But really, the point is the behavior changed, and changed in a manner consistent with moving in a valued direction.

Ways Solutions Can Be Part of Problems

This way of thinking—that solutions can be part of problems—might be new, so for practice consider some ways in which the solution can be part of the problem: where the "solution" creates more of the same problems it's intended to solve.

■ Case Study: Problem Drinking

Artie consumes alcohol in order to feel more socially competent. Using alcohol will solve the problem in some contexts in that he usually feels more socially competent after consuming alcohol. And at the same time, his excessive alcohol consumption decreases his social competence as he behaves inappropriately when intoxicated, and his anxiety increases as he notices negative social evaluations from others. As he prepares for the next social event, he might "lube up" with a few drinks to "calm his nerves" because he's going to see those people who saw his drunken behaviors last time and he wants to be inebriated in order to face them. On and on the story goes. Sometimes when the client comes up with new control "solutions," the ACT therapist might reflect, "Is this 'more of the same'?"

Short-Term Reinforcers vs. Long-Term Reinforcers

What is so insidious about this cycle is that people are seduced by short-term reinforcers and cannot contact long-term, and perhaps more valuable, reinforcers. These "contingency traps" (Baum, 1994) can contribute to a good deal of human suffering, such as drug addiction, poor achievement, anxiety, and depression.

Taking "liquid courage" in the face of his anxiety is Artie's solution, but really it is the problem and is perpetuated as "more of the same." These clinically relevant "solutions" just aren't workable in most contexts: Artie tries hard to control social anxiety, and in order to do so, he attends vigilantly to internal anxiety cues and attends to social cues that others might be negatively evaluating him. These behaviors may cause him to feel additional anxiety and to miss important social cues, and his behaviors decrease his social competence and increase his social anxiety.

Now depending on how we look at the situation, Artie's drinking surely does work. In the context of altering physiological sensations called "anxiety," imbibing copious amounts of alcohol works like a charm. In the "I have to get rid of these sensations" context, alcohol is a workable solution (no pun intended). But honestly, the client isn't likely to come to therapy just because of the physiological symptoms or because of the alcohol consumption per se. The client likely entered therapy because frequently getting drunk is causing social, occupational, or health problems. Put another way, frequently getting drunk is inconsistent with what is valued in other contexts. So boozing sometimes works in the short-term and likely doesn't work in the long-term to promote quality living.

■ Case Study: Workaholism

As another example, consider A.J., a father who wants to earn more money to be a more effective parent, yet he occasionally neglects his children in the service of working more to earn more money. Working more allows him to be a better provider, which is one aspect of effective parenting, and it gets in the way of spending time with his children, another aspect of effective parenting. In the short-term, his behavior is effective, yet if he values effective parenting, then his limited repertoire isn't functional in the direction of that long-term value. ACT assists in engendering psychological flexibility and broadening one's behavioral repertoire. It's not that earning more money is bad. However, in the context of this client who values parenting, being a good provider is problematic when it isn't balanced with other parenting behaviors. Expanding behavior repertoires is at the heart of increasing psychological flexibility.

The Cost of the Solution

To reiterate, sometimes the client's "solution" works, and the cost is reduced psychological flexibility. Consider a woman who does not want to think about a past trauma and abuse and who uses drugs to cloud her mind. Her solution works in the sense that she spends less time thinking about the past trauma, and her behavior becomes inflexible as drugs become the only solution for managing unwanted thoughts and feelings. Her drug use negatively affects many areas of her social and occupational functioning as well.

Notice that all of the above examples of a solution as part of the problem could be interchanged. That is, in each example, one could observe that the solution works in some contexts. However, it also makes the problem worse, causes additional problems, and decreases psychological flexibility. Most presenting complaints are like that, and can be assessed with the ABC Functional Analysis Sheet and the Inflexahex Case-Conceptualization Worksheet. Once such problems are identified and formulated functionally, the next task is how to present these hypotheses to the client.

Conveying Creative Hopelessness

When presenting the formulation to the client, it's important that it resonates with the client experientially and not merely as a matter of logic. In ACT, this is where the therapist uses familiar phrases such as "Don't believe me; believe your own experience," or "What does your experience tell you?" The goal is that the client contacts the futility of the change agenda at the level of experience rather than considers it logically as one more reason for more of the same unworkable problem solving. The ACT therapist looks for evidence of unworkable change agendas while listening to the client's presenting complaints, and directs the client to his experience in order to convey creative hopelessness.

■ Case Study: Panic Attacks

Joan reported that she began having panic attacks "out of the blue" two months ago and she was no longer driving at the time she began treatment. Later a pattern that was less out of the blue emerged. Joan's panic attacks began shortly after her sister moved thirty miles away. Her sister had provided much care to their elderly and infirm father, and Joan's sister and two brothers expected Joan to take over caring for him since she now lived in closest proximity to their father. Joan's father had been a heavy drinker and had physically abused his wife and verbally abused his children when drinking. Joan did not want to take care of him and acknowledged feeling angry that her siblings expected her to do so. In session, she wondered aloud if the panic attacks could be occurring because she did not want to care for her father. Further exploration of Joan's formulation suggested that, whatever the "cause" of her first panic attack, her panic disorder allowed her to avoid seeing her father without acknowledging that she did not want to. She could avoid feeling guilty because she could not control her panic attacks, so she had a "good reason" for not assisting her father. This formulation resonated with her experience. Though her panic attacks did not immediately disappear, they did slightly decrease in frequency and she began talking more about past experiences with her father. This helped her to recognize that spending time with her father was followed by memories of his past abuse and intense anger at him, followed by guilt "because that's in the past; he's sick now and he needs me."

Joan's initial treatment goal was to decrease panic attacks. Then she accepted that she couldn't control her panic and instead focused on controlling guilt and anger. Eventually—as she accepted that the guilty and angry feelings were showing up as her history was brought to bear on the present situation, and she became more accepting of these unwanted feelings—she became better able to say yes to taking care of her father on some occasions and also more able to say no on other occasions. After a period of time, she initiated a discussion with her siblings. Together they developed a plan to hire in-home health care workers to provide most of the care for their father, and they agreed to take turns visiting him regularly. Joan was willing to visit him more often than the others because of her closer proximity and reported that she felt like she was choosing to do this rather than feeling as though she "had to."

Choosing to visit (as opposed to having to visit) appeared to decrease her anger about the situation. Joan didn't make these connections as a matter of logic—there was very little that was "logical" about her panic attacks. The formulation made sense to her at an experiential level. She experienced creative hopelessness when she recognized that her attempts to escape her anger were futile. She felt angry at her father and siblings when she felt they were making demands, and when she refused their demands she felt angry with them "for making me feel guilty." When she could accept feeling guilty and angry, the feelings lost their power because they were not experiences that had to be avoided; instead she experienced them as both unpleasant and not necessary to avoid. The recognition of the hopelessness of gaining mastery over her anger gave way to creative alternatives.

Therapist Exercise: Unworkable Change Agendas

George has been diagnosed with depression. He was laid off from his job six months ago and has not worked since. He has recently been drinking more, consuming six or more bottles of beer four or five nights a week, and he reports that drinking "helps me sleep and then I don't lie awake thinking about what a failure I am." He reports that he can't look for a job when he has a hangover and feels so depressed because "No one will hire a negative person." He came to therapy because his wife of twelve years threatened to leave him if he didn't do something about his drinking and about finding a job.

As you consider George's case, consider these questions:

- What are some possible problematic sources of George's avoidance and/or control?

- How might the "solution" be part of the problem?

- What additional information would you want in order to fill out the Inflexahex Case-Conceptualization Worksheet?

Take a few moments to think about George's case and respond to the questions above. Next, compare your responses to our answer below.

Our answer: George is using problematic reason giving in saying that he can't look for work until his depression remits. He is drinking to avoid feeling bad, yet he describes feeling bad most of the time and that hangovers prevent him from looking for work. Also, his drinking is affecting his marriage. We would want to explore possibilities about the relation between drinking and the state of his marriage. Perhaps he is avoiding feeling bad about his unemployment and depression by drinking, which is negatively affecting his marriage and his ability to look for work. This is then followed by more bad feelings and has not, in the long term, alleviated his depression.

When clients get the ACT formulation of the problem as an unworkable change agenda, they may experience a sense of insight. They may then understand what the problem is differently and find behavior change relatively easy. Others experience hopelessness about changing unwanted experiences and may respond, "Are you saying I can't get rid of the anxiety?" or "Do you mean I'll always be depressed?" Some feel that they themselves are hopeless: "I can't seem to do anything right" or "I am a failure" might come up. When this happens, it is important that the therapist communicate that it is the change agenda that is unworkable and hopeless, and that the client's predicament is understandable, and even inevitable, given his history. We feel what we feel and think what we think in specific contexts because of our unique histories. At one time or in some contexts, dysfunctional behavior worked or the client would not be engaging in that behavior. Everything we do is an outcome of our history. The therapist's stance is not that clients are defective, bad, or to blame for their predicament. To the contrary, the therapist might see exactly how someone with a particular history might have a particular presenting problem.

When clients contact that it is the change agenda (rather than they themselves) that is hopeless, then they can move into a more creative space. This psychological space is more creative because it is more flexible: clients do not have to be beholden to verbal rules and evaluations. This is what is meant by creative hopelessness; there is hopelessness about the initial presenting change agenda, and that gives birth to willingness to try a different approach.

Creative Hopelessness Metaphors

Metaphors may be a useful way for the client to contact creative hopelessness experientially rather than as a matter of logic. The Feeding a Baby Tiger Metaphor is useful to undermine an unworkable change agenda where the client's behavior makes the problem worse. Take, for example, an excerpt from one of Shandra's early sessions:

Therapist: So what you're describing is kind of like feeding a baby tiger. The tiger might be kind of scary when it growls, so you feed it to make it stop growling.

Shandra:	You mean like when my son is in trouble and I help him so he won't get into more trouble?
Therapist:	Exactly! You feed the tiger, but what happens to a baby tiger when you feed it?
Shandra:	It gets bigger.
Therapist:	And scarier, so you feed it more. Guilt scares you, so you feed it by bailing him out of trouble. Worry about others evaluating you worries you, so you feed the tiger by avoiding former friends.
Shandra:	But doesn't feeding it work? It stops growling…
Therapist:	And what happens after it stops growling? After your son is bailed out of trouble, after your boyfriend moves back in, after the guilty feelings subside—what happens to those tigers?
Shandra:	(dejectedly) They're quiet for a while and then they start growling again.
Therapist:	Right on. And they're bigger. And the "tiger chow" you're feeding those tigers is pieces of your life: your self-respect, your vitality. You give away the money you've saved for a home so you won't feel guilty about your son's latest problem, you give away your social group so you don't have to worry about what they might be thinking, and you give away your self-respect to avoid feeling lonely.
Shandra:	And the tiger gets bigger and bigger. And now it's like I'm running out of tiger chow.

A different metaphor might be used to convey that acceptance and willingness are alternatives to struggling with the unworkable change agenda. In the Tug-of-War with a Monster Metaphor, the client's struggle and unworkable change agenda are likened to—you guessed it!—playing tug-of-war with a monster (Hayes et al., 1999, p. 109). The monster is very strong and the client is tugging and pulling and struggling. There is an apparently bottomless pit between the client and the monster. Losing the struggle means falling into the pit. The therapist can either provide the solution or gently use Socratic questioning to nudge the client toward dropping the rope as an alternative to continuing the struggle. Instead of struggling with thoughts and feelings, the client might let go and be willing to have them.

A risk at this point is that the client might misunderstand and engage in "pseudo-acceptance." That is, the client might formally describe willingness and acceptance, while functionally intending acceptance and willingness as another form of avoidance. The client in this position might say something like "You mean if I accept the anxiety, then it will go away?" or "If I'm willing to have urges to drink, then the urges will stop?" These are just more instances of the same old change agenda where the solution is part of the problem. Imagine the client who is formally trying to accept anxiety experiences: "I will accept these feelings. I will *accept* these feelings. I *will accept* these feelings! Did they go away yet? No! I'll accept them harder. Oh no! The feelings are still there! This isn't working! Maybe I'm doing it wrong! Maybe nothing can help me."

Stance of the Therapist

Finally, the solution can be part of the problem for the therapist as well as for the client. The stance of the therapist in ACT is one of radical acceptance and respect for the client (Hayes et al., 1999, p. 274). This means acceptance of the client's experiences and acceptance of one's own experience. In a process often referred to as countertransference, therapists have reactions to the presentations of clients. Case conceptualization and functional analysis allow the therapist to see that clients are influenced to act and think certain ways based on their history and current environment. Given the prevailing contingencies, conceptualizing the client's perceived abnormality as actually a normal response can facilitate this radical stance. In addition, seeing one's own judgments as verbal events and as automatic, idiosyncratically and culturally influenced arbitrarily applicable relational responding can also aid the therapist in seeing the person and not the problem. Acceptance of one's own experience means acknowledging that we therapists are in the same boat as our clients. We all experience the human condition. We too are vulnerable to cognitive fusion and to uncomfortable thoughts, emotions, and avoidance behaviors. The positive side of this radical acceptance and of placing ourselves on an equal footing with clients is that it allows opportunities for modeling acceptance, mindfulness, and willingness. It also increases our empathy for the predicament of our clients.

Clinician's Mistakes with "The Problem"

Therapists can also get caught in the trap of "the solution is part of the problem" while providing therapy. Usually this is reflected in behavior intended to decrease one's own discomfort. The examples below are not uncommon forms of avoidance and unworkable change agendas in the behavior of the therapist.

Discomfort with silence. Kaye's therapist noticed that Kaye was not talking much, and there were several long silences during session. The therapist, feeling uncomfortable with the silent periods, began filling them with question after question. As the session went on, the therapist began feeling increasingly distant from Kaye. Eventually the therapist noticed what was happening—that she was not fully responding to the client and was instead responding to her own discomfort. She stopped the questioning and allowed the silence to be present. Near the end of the session, the therapist remarked, "I'm experiencing you as difficult to get to know." Kaye visibly relaxed and said that she was feeling somewhat nervous and generally took a while to get to know someone. The shift in the human connection was palpable.

Solving the problem. James complained that he'd tried everything to get his son to change his behavior and was at a loss about what to do next. The therapist and client began to try to solve the problem with the therapist coming up with solutions that James negated (for example, "I already tried that" and "Yes, but my wife wouldn't go along with that"). Instead of sitting with James's stuckness, and her own, the therapist was trying to solve the problem.

Discomfort with the expression of emotions. Donna was discussing a recent upsetting event and began crying. The therapist immediately handed her a tissue and then offered words of comfort. The direction of the intervention changed to another subject. The therapist realized that he was reacting to his own discomfort at Donna's distress, and instead of modeling acceptance of discomfort, he tried to change Donna's distress in the service of lessening his own. Donna was glad to oblige and to move on to a less distressing topic.

Persuading the client to see problem our way. Another way therapists might use excessive control and reason giving is in handling client resistance. Resistance is often a sign that we are not accepting the client where he is and are instead following our own agenda. In order to decrease client resistance, we might inadvertently begin arguing with or persuading a client in order to get him to see the problem our way. Of course such a strategy is likely to be experienced as invalidating and to further increase resistance. For example, a client named Diane stated that she intended to drop out of school. She disliked school and was in college because her parents insisted that she go to college. For Diane, this was a move in a valued direction of becoming more independent and making decisions without excessively seeking advice. The therapist thought this was a bad idea and began presenting Diane with reasons she should remain in school. The client initially argued, then got quieter. The therapist caught herself and acknowledged trying to force her own agenda on Diane instead of trusting Diane to make a choice. Diane then acknowledged that she might very well decide to return to college sooner or later. This admission was easier to make when the therapist was experienced as being on her side instead of being another person trying to persuade her to go to college.

Persuading the client that the solution is part of the problem. Even trying to verbally persuade a client that "the solution is part of the problem" can become an instance of "the solution is part of the problem" if the client doesn't contact this experientially.

There will be times when even the best therapist falls into attempting to avoid his own experience in session. Mindfulness is the antidote. Mindfulness may not prevent all such experiences. It will, however, allow us therapists to catch ourselves more quickly and get the session back on track. And at times, acknowledging our own avoidance or control moves can be a powerful intervention. We are all swimming in the same stream.

Checking In

- Are there ways you inadvertently try to control or avoid private experiences in sessions with clients?

- What feelings and situations are most difficult for you?

- Are they likely to become instances of the solution becoming part of the problem?

CHAPTER 11

Bringing Mindfulness to Clinical Work

Mindfulness and self as perspective are concepts the client may be unfamiliar with. It's easy to get very "mindy" about mindfulness and to lose perspective in self-as-perspective work. The key to keeping your work moving is to keep it experiential and to stay mindful yourself.

Mindfulness in ACT

To some people, mindfulness is synonymous with meditation. We take the position that while meditation is a form of mindfulness practice, mindfulness is broader than meditation. The relation is hierarchical, with meditation as member of the class "mindfulness practices."

Mindfulness has many definitions with none universally accepted. The features of mindfulness definitions most consistent with ACT include describing, acting with awareness, and accepting without judgment (Hayes & Shenk, 2004). Mindfulness practice is linked to every process on the hexaflex model. A single exercise might bring any or all of the other processes into the present moment. Mindfulness is most linked to contact with the present moment and the idea of experiencing the world now as opposed to living in your head in the derived verbal world of "mindiness." Mindfulness is also related to self as perspective since the observing self can only be experienced by the self in the present moment here/now. Mindfulness may facilitate committed action, and for many clients mindfulness practice itself is a form of committed action. Mindfulness facilitates defusion and even while not explicitly described as such, many acceptance and defusion exercises have a mindfulness component to them (for example, the Physicalizing Exercise; see chapter 15). Mindfulness practice facilitates acceptance within mindfulness practice itself as the person practicing accepts—or perhaps notices that he is trying to control or avoid—thoughts, feelings, and bodily sensations that show up during mindfulness practice. Mindfulness practice can help the client with values clarification simply by helping her mindfully contact her own in experience in order to notice what is most vital to her.

The Mindfulness Tradition Today

Mindfulness is hardly a new idea. Because virtually every religious and spiritual tradition includes some type of mindfulness practice, there is a three-thousand-year record of various mindfulness exercises. There are plenty of modern books and CDs that offer practice in meditation or that guide one through various kinds of mindfulness exercises. Some approaches to mindfulness have a spiritual slant while others are completely secular. While books and other media may be useful for some, they are by no means necessary. Unlimited opportunities for mindfulness practice exist, as it can be done anytime and anyplace. Yet for some reason, instead of jumping for joy over the plethora of available mindfulness resources, it seems that many clients (and therapists!) become paralyzed when asked what mindfulness is or how to do it.

Mindfulness as Unattached Embracing

We think mindfulness only looks scary when it is made unnecessarily complicated. It's really fairly simple in practice. While there are many variations, most mindfulness practices ask participants to focus attention on and carefully observe something. One type of meditation asks that the person observe something they are doing—such as breathing, eating, walking, driving, or even doing the dishes. When the mind wanders, they are asked to notice this and return to observation. When body sensations show up, the person notices these also and returns to observation. During mindfulness practice, many people have urges related to body sensations, such as an urge to stop the exercise or to change posture. These too are noticed and attention is gently shifted back to observing. In some mindfulness practices, the participant may also say covertly or aloud a word describing in what way they were distracted from observation. For example, while observing his breathing, a participant might label the private events: "thinking," "urge to stop," "bored," "knee ache" (Baer, R. A., & Krietemeyer, 2006). There is some difference in how emotions are handled in various mindfulness practices. In some traditions, the individual focuses on feelings that arise and carefully observes them and notices how and if they change, while in other traditions emotions are merely noted in the same way thoughts are, and the individual returns to observing.

Mindfulness as Noticing

Another variety of mindfulness exercise invites the person to focus awareness on a single stimulus. The stimulus may be auditory, such as a ticking clock, a meditation gong, or a mantra, a syllable the client repeats. Or the stimulus may be visual, such as focusing on a candle flame, an object, or a single spot on the floor. In this type of practice, the person is instructed to bring attention back to the sound or object as soon as he notices that his mind has wandered. This practice is slightly different from the practice described above in that the person does not notice the nature of the distraction, only that he has been distracted (Baer, R. A., & Krietemeyer, 2006).

Another type of mindfulness exercise has the individual focus attention on the environment and observe the sights and sounds and smells and textures. For example, one might go for a walk in the park and notice thoughts and feelings that arise without trying to change them and without evaluating them while also attending to the park. The person is instructed to have a curious, open, and accepting stance while observing (Baer, R. A., & Krietemeyer, 2006). A client practicing this might notice clinically relevant experience. For instance, Shandra went on a walk. Afterward she reported, "I noticed that when I saw a young couple walking hand in hand, I felt sad and had the thought that I'll never have love like that in my life. And then I felt mad at myself for feeling sorry for myself and not being able to enjoy the park. I mean birds were singing and it was a beautiful day, and I was stuck in my head thinking about how miserable my life is. I guess I need more practice at this mindfulness stuff." Over time and with practice, Shandra found that while on a walk, she spent more time in the park and less time in her head.

Client Exercise: Guiding Mindfulness

Observing the environment can also be done in session. Described by Hayes and colleagues (1999, pp. 162–163), Taking Your Mind for a Walk is a mindfulness exercise aimed at having the client experience how much our minds (our ongoing stream of verbal responses) chatter on and on, how much of that chatter is evaluative, and how much our minds interfere with making contact with the present moment. Since the therapist plays the role of the client's mind, it is easier for the client to defuse from verbal content. The therapist introduces the purpose of the exercise and then asks the client to go for a walk. The client may go wherever she chooses and the mind will follow and chatter on and on. She may not talk back to the mind. She must listen to the mind and try not to "mind" the mind. This exercise should last around five minutes and be followed by debriefing. It is best done out of doors but can also be done indoors. An interesting twist is to agree before the exercise that the person will execute some type of response, such as going out to her car and touching her license plate or finding a certain page in a magazine. The mind's job is to talk the client out of doing a fairly simple action. The therapist, in the role of the mind, should evaluate, judge, analyze, compare, make predictions, tell the client what to do, comment on things in the environment, talk about the future, and so on. For example (while walking on a residential street), "Look at that car; I wish I had one of those. That reminds me, you need to get an oil change, and you need to go to the store later too; you'll never get everything done. Hey! Why are you going that way? The other way would be better. Turn and go the other way. You never listen. The other way is more interesting. Look at the dull scenery here. You'll probably miss out on something fun. That lady is looking at us. I'll bet she thinks you're crazy. I hope she can't hear us. This exercise is getting dull. But it's not as dull as sitting home watching reality TV…" The mind should talk steadily until five minutes ends. The client is then instructed to walk alone for five minutes and the therapist also walks alone away from the client, and the client is asked to notice that she is still taking a mind for a walk. In debriefing, the client shares her experience of the exercise. She may report things like feeling annoyed with the mind, wanting it to stop talking, or finding it difficult not to do what the mind says—for example, wanting to turn around and go the other way when the mind said to. The therapist should also note that when the client walked alone she was still talking a mind—her own mind—for a walk and ask her what she noticed while taking her own mind for a walk. This is a clinically useful tool because it demonstrates that the client has thoughts and isn't beholden to the thoughts. Taking your mind for a walk is also intrinsically related to defusion work.

Mindfulness as Insight

Another mindfulness practice is insight meditation. Here the individual is instructed to notice when unwanted feelings arise and to "breathe them in." The content attached to the feeling is ignored, and instead of avoiding an unwanted feeling, the individual breathes it in and accepts it. This exercise can be expanded upon to include breathing in the pain of someone the client knows who is suffering, to breathe in the suffering of others in the same predicament as the client, or to breathe in the suffering of all. In some Buddhist traditions, this practice is called *tonglen* (Chödrön, 2000). The "breathing in" is an acceptance posture, is done fully and without defense, and is exposure to stimuli otherwise experientially avoided.

■ Case Study: The Tea Ceremony

When talking about mindfulness exercises, Leonard said:

I read about mindfulness in college and I actually do that stuff. But not like they say. I know, I'm supposed to get a special teapot and tea and a cup, and then purposefully make the stuff a special way and watch the tea spread out through the water and be mindful of that and not get caught by other things. And then drink the tea and stay with the experience. Well, I sort of do that. I get my packet of instant oatmeal, mindfully put it in a plastic bowl, and attend to what I am doing as I place it in the microwave. I listen mindfully to the whirring motor and watch the bowl spin in the oven. I used to read the newspaper for that one minute while the oatmeal was heating up, but I wasn't paying attention to what I read, and when the food was done, I'd just read the rest of the article with a glance while scarfing down my breakfast. But now I just watch what I'm doing while prepping and pay attention to what's going on during that minute it's cooking, and stay with that. (*laughing*) I totally bastardized this billion-year-old sacred practice: my tea ceremony is microwaving instant oatmeal in a plastic bowl and eating it at my breakfast nook. But whatever ... it works for me.

Now this client appears to be putting mindfulness practice into effect in his world. Other than calling it a "billion-year-old sacred practice"—it started only in the ninth century AD, but his point is well-taken—his purpose of being attentive to the making and eating of his oatmeal is a basic example of the crux of mindfulness. In an essay entitled "Chanoyu, the Art of Tea," we are told about the discipline of the tea ceremony and that "awareness is the aim here, the means and the end" (Urasenke Foundation, n.d.). Often people introduced to mindfulness and meditation will begin to get hooked by the "stuff" involved in the practice. Certain retail outfits exploit this market with special candles, mats, and mindfulness garb. That stuff can be really neat and maybe even helpful to some folks. However, there is a greater point beyond the stuff: mindfulness is done in the now with what you have.

Implementing Mindfulness in Practice

Clients are often initially confused about mindfulness practice. Often they wonder if they are supposed to feel something in particular or feel nothing at all, or if they should try to think about what they are focusing on or try not to think. Clients may also wonder if they should have some sort of spiritual experience or if something should happen while they are practicing mindfulness. They may wonder how they will know if they are practicing correctly. These questions may arise because, while practicing mindfulness is easy, actually being mindful is difficult. Ironically, our minds get in the way of mindfulness as it is difficult to be present without all sorts of verbal events cluttering the experience.

One purpose of mindfulness is to experience directly how verbal events, when we fuse with them, interfere with being fully present in the moment. Clients may also notice that experiential avoidance interferes with mindfulness; one cannot make contact with the present moment as a fully conscious human being and avoid content at the same time. Another purpose of mindfulness is to attend to the processes of thinking, feeling, and sensing while paying little attention to content. This aids in defusion, acceptance, and contacting the observing self. In this sense, mindfulness is a skill that improves with repetition and practice. Over time, regular mindfulness practice enables one to be less distracted by verbal events that prevent contact with the present moment. This in turn allows for more awareness of other features in the environment that might regulate one's behavior. This outcome facilitates committed action and may be useful for

© 1994 Tsai Chih Chung, translated by Brian Bruya. Reproduced by permission from Tsai Chih Chung and B. Bruya, *Zen Speaks: Shouts of Nothingness* (New York: Anchor, 1994), p. 49.

Therapist Exercise: Mindfulness

Choose one of the mindfulness practices described in this chapter and practice it for twenty minutes.

After your practice, reflect on what the experience was like. Use the following questions to guide your reflection:

- Did you find mindfulness easy or difficult?

- Did your mind wander, or were you able stay focused?

- What sorts of processes distracted you from observing?

- Did you get caught up in thought content, or were you able to gently let go of the distracting process and return to observing?

- Did you complete the exercise?

- If not, what stands between you and completing the exercise?

- If you do not already practice mindfulness, do you see yourself practicing regularly?

- Why or why not?

values clarification, and is synonymous with increased psychological flexibility (Hayes & Shenk, 2004).

You may have experienced that mindfulness, as we mentioned above, is at once simple and not very easy. The question of whether or not ACT therapists should regularly practice mindfulness is a frequent one. There is no right or wrong answer to that question. We find that mindfulness practice benefits us personally and professionally. Personally we attain the same benefits that clients do, namely increased acceptance, defusion, and psychological flexibility. Professionally, mindfulness is sometimes useful for modeling and rapport building, identifying barriers to mindfulness practice, discovering more mindfulness exercises, and creating new exercises. There is a sense in which one can regard mindfulness like any other learned skill. For instance, imagine learning how to play a sport—say golf—by reading books about golf, watching people play golf, observing professionals on television, and then attempting to teach someone else how to golf. It probably wouldn't be very effective, because watching and reading isn't enough. In order to learn to play golf, you have to swing golf clubs and hit golf balls. While you may decide not to practice mindfulness regularly or continuously, we do suggest you first do any mindfulness exercise yourself that you intend to use with your clients.

Therapists often ask whether or not clients should be asked to meditate or practice other forms of mindfulness on a daily basis. This is entirely up to the therapist and client. Mindfulness practice is likely more helpful when used functionally, and could be misused if it is being done to avoid or escape private events. There are some ACT protocols that prescribe daily meditation and others that include no mention of mindfulness outside of what is done in session. We find that we prescribe daily practice to some clients for a period of time, and do less mindfulness work with others. Generally we encourage clients to practice mindfulness without necessarily prescribing it. Clients seem more receptive to the idea of regular practice when treatment includes different mindfulness practices in session.

Mindfulness might be described as the easiest intervention of all since every moment presents an opportunity to be mindful. A person can practice mindfulness while walking, driving, eating, working, playing with children, exercising, making love, washing the dishes, and completing tax forms. On the other hand, the same could be said of all ACT processes. In every moment, we are afforded opportunities to accept, defuse, be present, act, and value from self as perspective.

Self as Perspective

The observing self is not discovered by description, by logical reasoning, or by talking about it. Self as perspective is experienced, so ACT work in this domain is primarily experiential work. The observing self is difficult to talk about because of its lack of "thingness." While difficult to talk about, it is easy to talk a lot about it in trying to explain and describe something so difficult to explain and describe.

You may recall from chapter 6 that three senses of self that pertain to self-knowledge are considered in ACT. The conceptualized self is the self as content; it is all the descriptions, evaluations, and other things we might say about ourselves. The conceptualized self is the self that one evaluates and avoids and is fused with. Self as process, or self-awareness, is the sense of self in which one notices private events such as feelings, sensations, perceptions, and ongoing streams of thought. Self-awareness is necessary for purposeful and effective behavior. Identity is best tied to self as perspective because when the self is the locus of experience, private events are experiences one has; they are not the self (Hayes et al., 1999, pp. 187–188). In contrast, when the conceptualized self dominates, evaluation and experiential avoidance are likely. Self as perspective is the sense of self in which one notices that one notices. It is transcendent in that it has no boundaries. It can be described as "pure consciousness."

Self as perspective is associated with spirituality, yet it is not religious in nature. It is spiritual in the sense that self as perspective is transcendent; it transcends definition by words and form. It is that experience of self that is the context for all experience, and it does not have boundaries (Hayes, 1984). It is not religious in that there is no content to it, religious or any other kind; like spirituality, it is experienced, while religion is a matter of belief rather than experience (Hayes et al., 1999, p. 199). Many mindfulness and observing-self exercises have been described in texts of a religious nature. Such material is acceptable to use so long as the client is comfortable with it. There is nonspiritual material available as well.

We'll use a dialogue between Shandra and her therapist to illustrate this work. The exercise used in the session is adapted from the Chessboard Metaphor by Hayes and colleagues (1999, pp. 190–191).

Shandra: I know I'm supposed to accept this stuff and I just want it to go away. I'm sick of feeling sad all the time. I have so many regrets for the way things have turned out for me.

Therapist: And is that who you are? A person who's filled with regret and worry? It's a funny thing about regret and worry—regret is about the past and worry about the future. What happens to the now?

Shandra: I guess it's just kind of blah.

Therapist: Exactly. When you're in your head thinking about the past, that isn't here. And the future—that isn't here either. It's kind of like there's no room to experience now.

Shandra: I'm sorry. I hope you're not mad. But I really am trying.

Therapist: Now you're worried about what I'm thinking and feeling. Isn't that just like you? (*smiling*)

Shandra: (*sighing*) ... I guess so.

Therapist: I want you to imagine that there's a chessboard like that one there [points to chessboard on nearby table], except imagine that it goes out in all directions beyond the table. It has red and black squares on it [points to the squares] and a set of black and white chess pieces [picks up pieces while talking]—the kings and queens, knights, bishops, castles, and pawns. Imagine the white pieces are your bad thoughts and bad feelings and bad memories and bad sensations. And the black pieces are your good thoughts and good feelings and good memories and good sensations. And they're battling it out: the black pieces against the white pieces. It's as if you are caught up in that battle and winning that battle is terribly important. Can you connect with that?

Shandra: I can almost feel the war.

Therapist: So a white knight might attack with "Shandra, you're a bad mother" and along with that comes "feeling guilty," so you send out the black queen with "I'll help my children do better" and the white bishop attacks with "Charles doesn't really love you" with fear and sadness on his flank, and you fight back with the black knight, "I'll leave him!" and the white queen counterattacks, "No you won't! You always go back to him," and on and on the battle goes.

Shandra: Yes. That's exactly what it's like in my head!

Therapist: It's a war game; opponents fight against their enemies. And the problem with this battle is that your experience is on both sides of the war. When you are battling with your thoughts and feelings and memories, your own experience becomes your enemy. No matter which side wins, part of you loses. And because you are right out there with the pieces, it seems as if they are as solid and real as you are. The more you fight, the bigger the battle becomes, and more and more of your life is spent fighting this war against pieces of yourself. The more important it is to win this war, the harder you try to knock the pieces off of the board. You think that if you win, the fighting will stop even while your own experience tells you that the pieces never fall off of the board, and the harder you try to win, the bloodier the battle. The more convinced you are that you must win this battle, the harder you struggle against the pieces and the more hopeless the prospect of winning the battle feels, and the more distant and disconnected you feel from life outside the war zone. You've been living on a battlefield for a long time, and that's no way to live.

Shandra: And what I am I supposed to do? It seems like the war just goes on all by itself.

Therapist: I'm not surprised that it feels that way; you've been in the battle for a long time. I want you to consider the possibility that you're not the chess pieces. Think about it. If in this metaphor you aren't the chess pieces, who might you be?

Shandra: I guess I could be the person playing since I'm the one moving the pieces.

Therapist: And does the player of a chess game care about whether the white pieces or the black pieces are winning the battle?

Shandra: Yes, the player wants his team to win.

Therapist: Exactly. And besides, who would you be playing against? We're right back to the pieces battling it out. So who are you if you are not the player and you are not the pieces? What's left?

Shandra: The chessboard?

Therapist:	Bingo! If you look at it that way, your relationship to the battle changes. The board holds the pieces. If the board wasn't there, there would be no battleground for the pieces to occupy; they'd have no place to go. Those pieces—the good thoughts and feelings and the bad thoughts and feelings—can't even exist without you there to hold them. And also notice that from the board's point of view, the battle isn't very important. The chessboard isn't invested in whether the white team or the black team wins. The battle can go on or the battle can stop, the pieces can be black or white or red or blue and it doesn't matter to the board. As the board, you can hold those black and white thoughts and feelings and notice when they are battling and when they are not battling, and as the board you are not invested in one side or the other winning. You contain the pieces, and the pieces are not you. You contain your thoughts and feelings, and they are not you. When you're at the same level as the pieces, they seem bigger and more important and it feels like you really have to win. At the board level, when you are the board, when your thoughts feelings are not you, it's not so scary to be close to them. You are a locus or perspective, you are like the board containing the pieces. When you are in the battle, fighting the pieces takes a lot of effort. When you are the board, holding the pieces doesn't take much effort. You contain your thoughts and feelings, and you are not your thoughts and feelings.
Shandra:	I think I get it.
Therapist:	Suppose you want to remove one of the pieces; how would you do that?
Shandra:	I'd just get on the board and take it off.
Therapist:	And if you get on the board?
Shandra:	Then I'm back in the battle.
Therapist:	Right, you're back at the piece level. Back in the battle. Suppose that, as the board, you want to go somewhere. What happens to the pieces?
Shandra:	They go with the board.
Therapist:	Yes, and since the board isn't in the battle, taking the pieces along isn't any effort.
Shandra:	So I just have to put up with that junk in my head, and if I let it just be there, then I can do other stuff, the really important stuff.
Therapist:	And you've been practicing that.

Shandra:	The mindfulness exercises.
Therapist:	Yes, and when a thought you struggle with shows up in mindfulness practice, what do you do?
Shandra:	It usually takes me a minute to notice that I'm in the thought, and then I catch myself and go back to mindfulness.
Therapist:	And in this scenario, it's like going back and forth between the piece level and the board level. You are not your feelings, and sometimes it may seem like you are your thoughts and feelings, and you can go from piece level to board level any time you notice that you're at piece level.
Shandra:	That makes sense.
Therapist:	It makes sense maybe in a logical way, and what does your experience tell you?
Shandra:	That I'm never going to win that battle with my thoughts and feelings!

The struggle with the conceptualized self is often an ongoing battle. It's easy to get caught up in relating to content as if one is defined by verbal content. Self-as-perspective work done as experiential work allows the client to exit the battle and experience the self as perspective rather than as content. As Deikman describes,

> The most important thing about the observing self is that it is incapable of being objectified. The reader is invited to try to locate that self to establish its boundaries. The task is impossible; whatever we can conceptualize is already an object of awareness, not awareness itself, which seems to jump a step back when we experience an object. Unlike every other aspect of experience—thoughts, emotions, desires, and functions—the observing self can be known but not located, not "seen." (1982, pp. 94–95)

Self as perspective is nonthreatening because it is outside of private experience even while it holds private experience. Self as perspective cannot be evaluated. At the same time, it is the locus where evaluating and feeling and thinking unfolds. Self as perspective does not change. The unchanging nature of the observing self allows for a stable sense of self. Content changes. People have new experiences and new memories that are added to old ones. Even our bodies change throughout our lives. Self as perspective does not change; whatever our content, whatever our environment, the same continuous observing self that has always been there is still there to observe and experience. The continuity of the observing self, coupled with the freedom from content, makes self as perspective a peaceful and safe experience.

Once the observing self has been experienced, it can be leveraged in work with many client concerns. Take Jean, for example, a client who had made some progress through defusion and acceptance work, and was concerned about losing her identity. Even though her conceptualized self was very negative, she feared that "I won't know who I am if I'm not sad and lonely and wishing I had a different past." With self-as-perspective work, she was able to experience continuity even while her conceptualized self had less of a hold on her sense of identity.

Another area where self as perspective can be helpful is with the client who is distressed about unwanted life changes that completely change her conceptualized self. For example, Lauren had divorced, lost custody of her child, and relocated to start a new job. She was feeling depressed and complained, "I don't know who I am anymore. I used to be a New Yorker, a wife, a mother, and an employee for a different company. Now I'm not any of those things." Self-as-perspective work enabled Lauren to experience the continuity of herself, even while her life roles and environment were changing. After doing some observing-self work, she was more willing to consider values and committed action, and she did so from a more solid sense of self instead of from the fragile conceptualized self.

A third area for self-as-perspective work is with the client who believes he is a fraud (Hayes et al., 1999, pp. 198–199). For example, Geoffrey, who struggled with social anxiety and wanted to date more, believed that "if others got to see the real me, they would see what a jerk I am. I can keep up the act from a distance, but if I get close, then they'll see the real me. It doesn't seem worth the trouble when I know they're going to leave when they see the real me." The therapist can ask Geoffrey which self is evaluating his behavior and which self is predicting the future, and then gently bring him back to experience and the observing self.

One of the biggest dangers for the clinician is the ease with which one can fall into talking about self as perspective as content. The easiest way to avoid this trap is to stay focused on experience and experiential work. The client's observing-self work will be apparent less in how the client talks about the observing self and more in behavior change, such as increased willingness and acceptance of unwanted private experience, the ability to laugh at one's self, and noticing when one is caught up in struggling with content. These are signs that the client is ready to move forward with values work and toward a more vital direction in life.

CHAPTER 12

Values Work

A focus on values is a defining feature of ACT. Values work begins the moment the client walks in the door and never really ends—and is likely to be a major clinical focus throughout the course of treatment. There are many pitfalls the therapist must watch for in doing values work, and yet values work can be most enjoyable for both therapist and client as moving in a valued direction is an ultimate goal of treatment.

Why Work on Values?

One ACT slogan goes this way: "Work to control your feelings and lose control of your life" (Strosahl et al., 2004, p. 45). When a client walks in the door for treatment, she has often given up hope, has abandoned dreams, sees little to look forward to, and feels stuck in the morass of an unworkable change agenda. She may not tell you that her troublesome behavior is in the service of avoiding unwanted feelings and thoughts, and although she may be unable to articulate what she values, surely she values something. How can we be so sure? If she is a human being, she values something—even if she has lost her compass and gotten off track, even if she cannot verbalize what she values, and even if she has abandoned valued activity. This is good news for the therapist, because values work is the heart of ACT. Behavior in the service of values dignifies the pain that sometimes accompanies acceptance work. Values are fuel for willingness and committed action. Values create meaning and direction in life, and helping the client identify values and confront barriers to valued action directs the therapist's work with the client (Hayes et al., 1999, p. 205).

Defining Values

The ACT therapist spends considerable time undermining unworkable change agendas and defusing language. However, values are one area where the therapist encourages verbal influence of behavior. Why? Because doing so works! In chapter 8, you read the Hayes et al. definition of values as *"verbally construed global desired life consequences"* (1999, p. 206, emphasis in original). While many verbal events can have destructive effects on behavior, as verbally construed consequences, values help individuals act in the service of consequences that may be very distant and even for outcomes that may never be attained (Hayes et al., 1999, p. 207). For instance, a peace activist may spend a lifetime working for an end to war even while wars always rage on. A grandfather may start a college fund for his grandchildren even while he will not to live to see them go to college. A scholar will set out to understand some aspect of the world even while she can never know all there is to know about her subject matter. While some consequences or outcomes are remote or improbable, values are lived now. Even though the activist can't end war, he can do something to make the world more peaceful now. Even if the grandfather can't see his descendents' future, he can contribute to it now. And while the scientist can't learn everything, she can learn something now.

One of the most rewarding aspects of values is that even while the consequences values specify may be remote or improbable, the opportunity to move in a valued direction is available in every moment. The verbal and remote nature of values makes them naturally flexible. The "nowness" of values gives them their vitality.

Guiding Values Work

Though rewarding, values work can also be challenging to therapist and client alike. Fortunately it is relatively easy to notice when values work has gone astray. Perhaps it has become too intellectual and less experiential, or maybe avoidance has crept into the work. Just take the pulse of the therapy session and if the vitality is low, it is probable that the values work has gone off course. If the work feels alive and vital, chances are better that the values work is on track.

Values can be considered in the context of many important life domains, such as family, work, education, leisure, friendship, health, community, and spirituality. Below are two clinical examples of values work in the domains of parenting and work.

Exploring Values: The Example of Parenting

Read the transcript below of part of the values work with Shandra and decide whether Shandra is on or off track.

Therapist:	How would you know that you're moving in a valued direction as a parent?
Shandra:	I guess my children wouldn't get in trouble so much.
Therapist:	Hmm … so if your son stays out of jail, then you are an effective and loving parent, and if your son goes to jail, then you are a failure as a parent?
Shandra:	Maybe. (*pauses*) I'm not sure. Now I'm confused.
Therapist:	What if you locked Jim in the basement so he couldn't do anything that would get him put in jail? Then would you be an effective parent?
Shandra:	Well … no … of course not. But he keeps getting into trouble no matter what I do.
Therapist:	You seem to be saying that being an effective parent depends on what Jim and Karen do. If being an effective parent is not determined by what you do and instead it is determined by what your children do, then it seems that you may never have the opportunity to be an effective parent.
Shandra:	Well, that's not exactly what I mean.
Therapist:	What could you do today to be a loving parent?
Shandra:	I guess I could give Jim some money… He's broke and he's been asking me for some money. Except he probably wouldn't use the money to buy groceries or pay the phone bill… He'd probably spend it on drugs and get into even more trouble.

Can you feel the deadness in Shandra's values work? She's falling into the trap of measuring her goal attainment with her son's behavior as the outcome. This type of behavior shows a lack of clarity in her values and can be written down on the Inflexahex Case-Conceptualization Worksheet as a reminder to the therapist about what needs to be addressed during therapy. If a parent believes she is only effective if her children are successful adults, then she is likely to engage in any of several avoidant or dysfunctional behaviors. For instance, she may push her child in a direction he doesn't want to go so that she can hold on to her evaluation of herself as a successful parent. She may avoid the unsuccessful child because being around him leaves her feeling ineffective. She may focus her energy on her more successful children while paying less attention to her less successful child, thus sending him a subtle message that her love is contingent on his success. Or she may do as Shandra is doing, and bail him out at any sign of trouble so she doesn't have to contact the thoughts "My son is in trouble" or "I am a bad parent." Meanwhile, he doesn't have the opportunity to attain success by getting himself out of trouble.

Exploring Values: The Example of Work

Contrast Shandra's effort at values work with this sample of Rick's values work.

Rick:　　　　I guess my computer programming is one of my values.

Therapist:　　I'm not sure what you mean. Can you say a little more about it?

Rick:　　　　Well, first off, I like it. I can spend hours at it and not even notice the time going by.

Therapist:　　Great!

Rick:　　　　And I hate to say it, but I guess I'm kind of a show-off because I like it when people like my programs.

Therapist:　　Okay, so what if no one knew you designed a program and they liked it?

Rick:　　　　Oh, that's easy; that already happened with my shareware. Lots of people use it and none of them know that I wrote it.

Therapist:　　None of them?

Rick:　　　　Nope, and it was great when I overheard some college kids talking about it. They were like, "This program is great; it really helps me get my work done."

Therapist:　　Wow!

Rick:　　　　Yeah, I was like, "Wow! People are using this stuff in actual work … and I wrote it."

Therapist:　　(*laughing*) Well, you're full of surprises today. A few minutes ago you were telling me what a selfish bastard you are and now you're telling me you like making a difference.

Rick:　　　　(*sheepishly*) Yeah, I guess so. I guess I really do. But don't tell anyone! (*laughing*)

Therapist:　　(*joking*) Your secret is safe with me.

Rick comes alive when he talks about his work. The dialogue above was mildly shocking to the therapist because Rick was usually dour and negative. Recall when we first met Rick, he was saying, "I hate my job … but at the same time … I won't quit … The future is bleak." These are statements that we'd put on the case-conceptualization worksheet as inflexible and unhelpful. As Rick and the therapist discussed values, he became suddenly animated and even started laughing. A good rule of thumb is that you are on the right track when you can feel the vitality in the room. You don't intellectually connect with values, you experience them. And when the client is in contact with values, there's energy and vitality in the room, and usually both the client and the therapist can feel it.

Rick contacted values related to making a difference in the community and to creative expression. The next task in his treatment was helping him bring this value alive in more life domains. For instance, Rick complained often about his "dead-end" job. He wasn't bringing any of the vitality in his creative ability to the job he was getting paid to do. After much more work, Rick realized that he was afraid that if he was more successful on the job, he would receive more attention from others and that more attention would lead to more social anxiety. Rick was contacting a barrier to moving in a valued direction. The next phase of work was going back to acceptance, willingness, and committed action with respect to anxiety.

Rick's case nicely illustrates how values dignify acceptance work. We don't want our clients to feel anxiety, shame, guilt, or sadness because we see something intrinsically useful about feeling painful feelings. We want our clients to be willing to feel painful feelings when painful feelings stand between them and moving toward valued outcomes. When a client begins living his values, he may experience emotional pain as he works through barriers to valued living, and at the same time he is also likely to experience more vitality.

Walking the Talk

Values work is lived in what we do. Even when we cannot verbalize what we value, we value something. Looking at overt rather than verbal behavior, or at the discrepancy between them, is often more useful in doing values work than is having an abstract conversation about values. For instance, Bobbi said that she valued "getting along with others." And over the course of a few sessions (and not necessarily sessions involving values work), she described a family feud and reported that she no longer speaks to her sister because her sister is "mean and will never admit she's wrong." She also described quitting her volleyball team over a conflict with a teammate because "if we can't get along, then there is no point in being on the same team." A short time later, Bobbi reported that she asked a member of her book club to leave the group because she found the woman "annoying—always trying to hog the conversation." While Bobbi verbally described that she valued getting along with others, her behavior seemed more consistent with a value of avoiding conflict or being right or only spending time with people she liked or agreed with. Her behavior was not directed toward getting along. It was in the direction of avoiding conflict.

Are Values Reflected in Behavior?

Some people verbalize one set of behaviors while doing the opposite. Others say they do not value something when their behavior says otherwise. For example, Steven, who is twenty-eight years old, denied valuing learning and education because he did not go to college even though he had a scholarship offer when he finished high school. However, while denying that he valued learning and education, he was a regular at the public library, checking out all sorts of nonfiction books on a variety of topics. He watched documentaries about history and science, and he used the Internet and reference books to answer questions that puzzled him. He clearly valued learning, and his denial of this may have been in service of avoiding negative social evaluation for not going to college or perhaps avoiding negative evaluation for valuing education if he had a history where higher education was viewed as being "for snobs and sissies." (Of course, the clinician must do a functional analysis in order to determine that.)

Everyone values something, and what is valued can be observed in what people do with their feet—where do they get up and go to? Values work can create a space for observing where one is headed, for assessing how well moving in that direction is working, and for mindfully choosing a direction.

Is the Behavior Based on Feelings or on Values?

A common point of confusion in values work is the distinction between valuing as a feeling and valuing as an action. For instance, Rick says that he values a loving relationship with his mother. Then he says that he does not visit her often because she has senile dementia and "half the time she doesn't know who I am, and even when she does, she tells the same stories again and again. And that nursing home is gross; I almost feel sick to my stomach it smells so bad." Rick is confusing having loving feelings with valuing a loving relationship. In any relationship, warm feelings are not always going to be present.

If feelings dictate our behavior, values could not be easily sustained. For instance, people would quit projects, end relationships, and end creative and athletic endeavors with high frequency if engaging in those activities was determined by feelings alone. Unfortunately Western culture supports the notion that a person's feelings are good reasons for behavior. You may notice that this point resembles some of the comments on reason giving and avoidance in chapter 9. As Hayes and colleagues (1999) put it, "The cultural context that supports the association between feelings of love and acts of love is the same cultural context that supports the client with agoraphobia staying home in the presence of high anxiety and the alcoholic's drinking in the presence of strong urges" (p. 209).

Client Exercise: Putting Values into Practice

One way to help clients distinguish the difference between values and feelings as guides to action is to have them consider values in the context of something they do not care about. Consider the exercise Rick completed (adapted from the Argyle Socks Exercise in Hayes et al., 1999, pp. 210–212).

Rick: I don't get it. How can I value going to the nursing home to visit my ma if I think it is gross and bums me out?

Therapist: Let's try something that has nothing to do with your values—a kind of silly way to get it.

Rick: I'm game.

Therapist: Okay, I want you to feel strongly that it's very important that your colleagues begin writing with green pens instead of with blue pens. I want you to believe it deeply. (*pause*) Can you feel it? It's very important that your colleagues write with green pens. Can you believe it and feel it?

Rick: That's stupid. Who cares what they write with?

Therapist: Try to care!

Rick: I can't. That's too dumb to care about.

Therapist: Okay, even though you can't make yourself care about this, I want you to imagine how you could make your colleagues care about writing with green pens even if you don't feel strongly about it. For example, you could hang a sign that says, "Green pens rule." What else could you do to make writing with green pens important to them?

Rick: I don't know… This is weird.

Therapist: Can you have the thought that it's weird *and* imagine ways to make writing with green pens important to your colleagues?

Rick: (*smiling*) I knew you'd say that! Okay … I could give away green pens.

Therapist: Yes! What else could you do?

Rick: I could put boxes of green pens in the office supply cabinet and take out the blue pens.

Therapist:	There you go!
Rick:	I could ask the boss to give everyone who uses green pens a bonus. Or I could give everyone I see using a green pen a dollar.
Therapist:	Now you're on a roll! And notice that if you did all those things, you could really make writing with green pens important to your colleagues. And can you also notice that none of your colleagues would know that you think it's "too dumb to care about"?
Rick:	Uh-huh.
Therapist:	If you did all those things, would you be valuing writing with green pens?
Rick:	I guess so.
Therapist:	You'd be valuing writing with green pens even though your feeling is that it's a dumb thing to matter about...
Rick:	So it's about what I do more than what I think or feel about it.

Guiding behavior with values. Valuing with your overt behavior will always be more effective than valuing based on feelings. Overt behavior is under more conscious control (that is, the behavioral dimensions can be altered by verbal events) than are feelings. In Rick's case, he might visit his mother at her nursing home even while having the thought that he doesn't want to, and even while feeling frustrated and annoyed that his mother cannot recognize him, and even while feeling guilty for feeling frustrated and annoyed. Earlier in therapy, he was reporting that he was not living according to his values because he sometimes did not want to visit his mother. Today he experiences his visits as somewhat less aversive, not because his mother is different in some way, but in part because he is less entangled with private events and also because he notices that he has a choice about going to visit his mother. Having a choice is empowering.

Making choices based on values. Values work is important in part because it helps clients choose among alternatives. Each day we have the opportunity to make thousands of choices. Some are big ("Go to college or not?" and "Say yes or no to the marriage proposal?") and some are trivial ("Pizza or salad for lunch?") and some are very trivial ("Watch a television rerun or the ball game?"). While some might confuse values with feelings, others may confuse values with judgments. For instance, a person who chooses salad instead of pizza because salad has fewer calories is making a judgment. The person who chooses salad and has the thought that salad has fewer calories than pizza is making a choice. The distinction is clearer when put into action.

Client Exercise: Making Choices

The therapist can make this distinction apparent to the client by asking him to make a choice—for example, by holding two objects, say a pen and a piece of paper, and saying, "Quick! Choose one." And when the client chooses one or the other, ask him why he made the choice he did. He probably won't have an answer. And if he does provide a reason, such as "I chose the paper because I thought that was the one you wanted me to choose," then point out that he made a judgment and not a choice, and then repeat the exercise.

The point is, make the client aware of choice and the possibility of making choices with reasons rather than for reasons (Hayes et al., 1999, p. 213). The distinction between choosing with reasons rather than for reasons is related to the work on acceptance and defusion. The reasons show up as verbal events, and as private events, they do not cause choices, though they may participate in choices as judgments.

Judging or Choosing?

This is not to say that people should not make judgments. We make judgments all the time— for instance, one might use judgment and base a decision to take an umbrella to work on an evaluation of the weather. Or someone might analyze the housing market to decide whether or not to sell his home. There is nothing wrong with judgments per se; however, judgments are problematic when confused with values. Colloquially one might say that we judge with our heads and value with our hearts—and our actions.

In conversational speech, one might also say, "Public safety is important and matters to me." In ACT phraseology, we say that people "matter about" things that are important to them. We invite people to think about it this way: public safety (and world hunger and global warming) don't matter—that is, those issues are not doing the "mattering." It is individuals who "matter about" or "make important" issues like public safety, world hunger, and global warming. People do the "mattering" or the "importanting." What matters is arbitrary, and what any individual "matters about" is determined by her history; it is her chosen values brought to bear on the present context.

Outcome Is the Process by Which Process Becomes Outcome

The ACT emphasis on values turns the usual outcome/process distinction on its head. In many treatment settings, a treatment goal and "good outcome" might be something like decreased drug use, increased treatment adherence, and/or decreased compulsive behavior. In ACT, these would be regarded as process goals rather than outcome goals. The client doesn't stop using drugs, adhere to a program of treatment, or reduce the frequency of compulsive behaviors with these behavior changes as ends in themselves. She changes her behavior in the service of something, and that something is values. Choosing to reduce the frequency of drug use or other compulsive behaviors is an example of removing barriers to valued actions. There would be little reason for clients to change behavior just for the sake of changing behavior.

Values as a source of motivation. Values work provides an incentive for behavior change as the client notices behaviors, such as drug use or compulsions, that stand between her and moving in a valued direction. Values work also energizes the hard work of committed action. For example, when in contact with values, going to a Narcotics Anonymous meeting is no longer in the service of stopping drug use; it is in the service of being a loving parent and partner, being an effective employee, or living a healthy lifestyle.

Focusing on vitality. Any attempt to consider behavior in terms of what the client is not doing is likely to be lifeless. In fact, a program of change focused on what the client should stop doing has been derisively called "the dead man's program" (Lindsley, 1968) because even a dead (or lifeless) person will not drink, perform compulsive behaviors, swear, yell at others, and so on. As a clinician, be on the lookout for the client, or even you yourself, focusing excessively on extinguishing behavior. If the client or you find yourself moving in this direction, then steer toward what the client wants his life to stand for and what he wants to do more of rather than what he wants to do less of.

The journey is the goal. One metaphor for getting in contact with the outcome-process distinction is the Skiing Metaphor (Hayes et al., 1999, pp. 220–221). Ask the client to imagine going skiing, and then just as she is poised at the top of the hill to ski down, a helicopter hovers overhead and the pilot says, "I see you want to get to the bottom of the hill." He plucks her off of the hill and flies her to the bottom. Ask her why she might object to the pilot's action. Hopefully she will say that the pilot is missing the point, that the purpose of skiing isn't just getting to the bottom of the hill. Skiing and getting to the bottom of a hill illustrate how outcome is the process by which process becomes the outcome. The purpose of skiing isn't to get to the bottom of hills; getting to the bottom of the hill is an outcome of that process and it isn't the point of the thing. Going from the top to the bottom of a hill is the process by which we attain the outcome—skiing. This is similar to the relationship between values and acceptance, and between values and committed action. In one sense, acceptance and committed action might be regarded as outcomes. And in another sense, they are processes for attaining the outcome of moving in a valued direction. Values increase willingness for acceptance and committed action.

Stance of the Therapist

The stance of the therapist in ACT is a stance of radical respect (Hayes et al., 1999, p. 274). This is as true in values work as in any other domain of treatment. There are several ways in which we therapists can undermine the integrity of treatment if we do not stay mindful of this. Some of the danger zones in values work are:

- Pushing clients toward our own valued direction rather than toward their own
- Judging the client's values
- Excessive intellectualizing
- When our values are at odds with client values

In this last case—when our values are at odds with the values of our client—it is critical that we stay focused on the values of the client lest we undermine treatment.

■ Case Study: Ethics and Values

Consider Justin, a gay male college student, who did not want to report to the police that he was the victim of a sexual assault and that the perpetrator was someone he knew. Justin's friends and family felt he should report it, and part of the reason he was in therapy was at the urging of his parents and close friends. The therapist also felt, based on her personal values, that he should report the assault. Instead of sharing her evaluation, she explored Justin's values and what not going to the police was in the service of. His response was that reporting it to the police would make him uncomfortable because he would have to see "my attacker and my friends regularly" and "everyone would know what had happened." Justin did not report the sexual assault and continued work in other areas, including depression and low motivation for school, work, and social activities. Then several months later, seemingly out of the blue, he reported that he was going to file a police report. Justin said he realized that, whether or not he filed a report, he would regularly encounter the perpetrator and that he didn't want what happened to him to happen to anyone else, even if that meant that "everyone would know what had happened." It took lots of work on his part in the areas of acceptance, defusion, values, and removing barriers to values. Once this work was sufficiently done, Justin, on his own, chose a course of valued action. At the end of treatment, he thanked the therapist for not urging him to go to the police.

Values "Traps" for Therapists

ACT trainees often ask, "What if the client values doing something completely immoral, such as pedophilia or stealing from others to have more money? Then do I have to support him in those values?" The answer is yes and no. To be ACT consistent, the therapist does have to respect that those are the values of the client. On the other hand, since the therapist also acts on the basis of values, he may choose not to treat the client and refer him to another treatment provider. That said, it's also important to note that we have never heard, nor has any ACT therapist we know of described hearing, a client articulate values around harming others. When given a choice, most people choose to move in a benign direction and move toward personal growth rather than toward destructiveness. Be careful not to fall into the trap of feeling you cannot work with a client because of a conflict of values until you know what the client truly values.

Therapist Exercise: Overcoming the Habit of Judging

How old were you when you decided to become a therapist? Did you have any other career goals earlier in your life?

Think back to an earlier time in your life when you had "unrealistic" goals. Maybe you wanted to become a movie star, major-league athlete, prima ballerina, or something similar. Really feel what it was like to have that goal.

Now imagine telling that child or young adult that this goal is unrealistic.

What does that feel like, to be told your goal is unrealistic? What does it feel like in your body? Notice how your posture changes after being told that your goal is unrealistic. What thoughts do you have after being told that your goal is unrealistic? It's discouraging!

Now imagine supporting your younger self. Smile at him or her and say how wonderful it is that he or she has identified this goal. Ask how you can help.

Notice how you feel.

Judging a client's values and goals is another trap the therapist should avoid. For example, consider Josh, who valued artistic expression, especially music, and had a goal of becoming a rock star. The therapist did not think this was a very realistic goal, and yet he worked with Josh on removing barriers to moving in a valued direction. Josh was initially diagnosed with social phobia, and by the end of treatment, he had increased many social activities he had previously avoided in the service of obtaining musical instruction and making social connections. While Josh was not yet a rock star, he formed a band and was earning money performing in local clubs. Think about how many of us never attain goals we set, yet the goal setting helps us clarify values and may be followed by unexpected experiences that shape our lives and move us in the direction of our values.

Another potential trap for the therapist is intellectualizing values. It can be challenging to talk about values in a manner accessible to the client. It is all too easy to get caught up in talking about values and easily move toward rationalizing choices, in effect switching from values to judgments. If you notice that you are doing a lot more of the talking than the client is, or that the client is verbalizing about what he is thinking rather than contacting his experience, then you may be intellectualizing. Notice this and move in a more valued direction in the therapy room. Our experience is that clients notice this and even appreciate it when the therapist says something like "Oops, I just caught myself evaluating again. Let me rephrase that last question..."

Values Are Perfect

A final aspect of values work is recognizing that values are perfect in that they are perfectly one's own. Put another way, no one can judge the values of another because one can only make such judgments from the perspective of one's own values. The client can feel the acceptance of the therapist—it permeates the room. The client can also feel nonacceptance, which will create distance rather than connection.

Values are personal in that they arise through one's experience in the world. They are part of what makes each person unique. There is no need to explain why or how one values what one values. Values stand alone. Saying "I value X" is enough. There is no need to justify or explain what one values. It is not unusual for clients to share hopes and dreams they have never uttered aloud. This makes values work very intimate. It is moving for the therapist to be present with clients as they share who they are. It can be equally moving for clients to be accepted fully while being true to themselves and truly being who they are with the veil of experiential avoidance lifted.

CHAPTER 13

Defusion and Deliteralization

Imagine being able to experience some of life's events without language—without description or evaluation. While this is an impractical and even undesirable aim because of the immense utility of language, defusing from language can be an important clinical move when "languaging" interferes with valued life directions.

Sometimes people witness magnificent or horrific things, and when asked to tell about it, they say, "Words fail." Like personally experiencing an automobile collision in slow motion or being present at the birth of your own child, there are times in a person's life that transcend language. These are uncommon life events, and we can conjecture that these rare events present such inimitable contexts that verbal behavior is not evoked: there are fewer words to describe them, and the direct event is so intense that a broad spectrum of responses, including evaluating and problem solving, is suppressed for a brief period of time. The mind's page is blank.

Daily events may also transcend language at times: watching a sunset, observing one's child peacefully sleeping, gazing into the eyes of a loved one. However, as we shall see, it is difficult to completely blank one's mind on purpose, but we can have words and thoughts and not get sucked in by their meaning.

Lorem ipsum dolor sit amet, consectetuer adipiscing elit, sed diam nonummy nibh euismod tincidunt ut laoreet dolore magna aliquam erat volutpat. Ut wisi enim ad minim veniam, quis nostrud exerci tation ullamcorper suscipit lobortis nisl ut aliquip ex ea commodo consequat. Duis autem vel eum iriure dolor in hendrerit in vulputate velit esse molestie consequat, vel illum dolore eu feugiat nulla facilisis at vero eros et accumsan et iusto odio dignissim qui blandit praesent luptatum zzril delenit augue duis dolore te feugait nulla facilisi.

Nam liber tempor cum soluta nobis eleifend option congue nihil imperdiet doming id quod mazim placerat facer possim assum. Typi non habent claritatem insitam; est usus legentis in iis qui facit eorum claritatem. Investigationes demonstraverunt lectores legere me lius quod ii legunt saepius. Claritas est etiam processus dynamicus, qui sequitur mutationem consuetudium lectorum. Mirum est notare quam littera gothica, quam nunc putamus parum claram, anteposuerit litterarum formas humanitatis per seacula quarta decima et quinta decima. Eodem modo typi, qui nunc nobis videntur parum clari, fiant sollemnes in futurum.

What happened when you hit the last two paragraphs? Ironically those paragraphs might be the best way to get what defusion is all about. Like the "lorem ipsum" paragraphs above, verbal content can unfold, yet the events do not have a direct meaning or influence on the person's behavior. (In RFT terms, we would say that there is no transformation of stimulus function.) Those lines beginning with "lorem ipsum" have the formal qualities of language but have no meaning to an English speaker. It is highly unlikely that you read every word in the two paragraphs above in the same way you've been reading the other pages of this book. (We hope!) It was textual stimulation, yet it probably did not evoke a reading response because the stimuli did not participate in frames of relating from your conditioning history. We'll bet you may have tried to read the text and soon found yourself skimming most of the passage, until you were presented with text that did participate in frames of relations with which you have a history.

Incidentally, the "lorem ipsum" passage is simply industry standard mock text used in printing and Web-page designing. Phrases similar in form to those above have been used since the fourteenth century to mimic what a page would look like once the printing press work was completed. The printers wanted their layout laborers to be productive yet not distracted by meaningful passages. These Latin phrases had similar appearance to normal language, and the words did not participate in relational frames for the workers. They didn't transform any stimulus relations, so the worker was less likely to read the passage. The wonderful irony here is that this extremely popular dummy text used worldwide in the media business is an ACT-friendly phrase. The phrasings (those actually used in the print business rather than those seen above) are derived from Cicero's *De finibus bonorum et malorum* (*On the Ends of Goods and Evils*), and part of the translation (45 BC/1914) reads as follows:

> No one rejects, dislikes, or avoids pleasure itself, because it is pleasure, but because those who do not know how to pursue pleasure rationally encounter consequences that are extremely painful. Nor again is there anyone who loves or pursues or desires to obtain pain of itself, because it is pain, but because occasionally circumstances occur in which toil and pain can procure him some great pleasure. . . . The wise man therefore always holds in these matters to this principle of selection: he rejects pleasures to secure other greater pleasures, or else he endures pains to avoid worse pains. (pp. 35-37)

It is too bad that vast numbers of people have happened across these wise words about accepting pain as part of a greater commitment, but they couldn't experience a transformation of stimulus functions because it is in Latin! Now that we've had this little historical aside concerning lorem ipsum, let's get back to the task at hand: defusion and deliteralization.

Defining Defusion

The processes on the hexaflex and the inflexahex represent two sides of the same coin. As such, in order to properly discuss *defusion*, we are required to discuss cognitive fusion.

Fusion Revisited

Recall that cognitive fusion occurs when responses are guided more dominantly by verbal events than by environmental events. The "pouring together" of experiential stimuli and verbal events leads to cognitive fusion. This can be a clinical concern because the immediate verbal event may govern behavior and make the person less sensitive to more value-laden, long-term consequences. Also problematic is when the verbal event is poorly constructed or unhelpful, such as "I am a bad person." People who are fused may behave in a dysfunctional manner either because they buy this thought as if it were gospel truth or because they want to avoid this thought outright because of the discomfort it stimulates.

Fusion to "Good" Thoughts Can Be Problematic

Even fusion with more "positive" thoughts can present a clinical concern. First, working toward promoting one's own positive thoughts promotes the fusion agenda. It is as if the person is saying, "There is an important literal truth to my thoughts," which by itself is not likely a functional way to approach language in the long run. Second, in the context of function, sometimes the context of relation will not hold up. If a man considers himself worthwhile (in the context of relation) by saying, "I am good because I work for a nonprofit organization," and then loses his job because of budget cuts (the context of function), where is his goodness now? Third, attempts at focusing on just the "good" things might eventually evoke some "bad" things. We see this in the following comments related by a client with social phobia:

Client: Right before my sales call, I told myself, "I'm okay here. I am in control. Staying cool. Not going to have a panic attack. That dreadful panic attack. No! Not thinking about that. Gotta keep it cool, not like last time." After saying that to myself, I noticed my heart started racing and I could hear my pulse in my ears, because—guess what? I'm thinking about last time! I turned right on my heel before going into the meeting and said, "I'm gonna keep it cool. I'm not going in there, but I am gonna keep it cool."

Fusion to Thoughts Doesn't Have to Be Problematic

Not all verbal behavior is fusion and not all avoidance is necessarily the enemy of a life well lived. Or we could say, it is bad to say that avoidance is bad! Context is everything. If you are hungry and given directions to a restaurant, you don't want to have an "empty mind" or relate to the directions as if they were the "lorem ipsum" words earlier in this chapter. When you get to a crossroad on the way to the restaurant and the verbal directions say, "Make a left at the intersection," merely noticing the words as "only a thought" won't be useful in this context because you'll just be standing there noticing ... and not eating!

During evaluation of external events, responding to the context of relating may be more efficient than the context of function (see chapter 4). For instance, it is likely more helpful to avoid a yard with the sign "Beware of Dog" rather than to go into the yard and actually get bit by the dog in order to know to avoid it next time. It can also be functional to use verbal problem-solving strategies, as long as they procure reinforcement, such as using the verbally mediated assembly instructions included in most do-it-yourself furniture kits. That context of relating is likely more efficient than trying to build the desk by trial-and-error in the context of function. (Males have a bad reputation for being defused from assembly instructions.) Popular recreation activities such as watching movies just aren't as interesting without verbal transformation of stimulus functions. If people watching a movie are only experiencing the event as changes of visual and audible stimuli on the screen, bereft of meaning and language, then they are missing the point of going to the theater!

The examples in the last paragraph show effective results guided by verbal events. It appears that a distinction between helpful and unhelpful forms of relating involve the matter of choice. The moviegoer chooses to suspend disbelief (somewhat—she is scared by King Kong and she doesn't run out of the theater). The person reading "Beware of Dog" chooses to heed the sign; if the fusion were complete, he might fear the sign as well as the dog. And the person following instructions chooses to read the directions and relate the verbal instructions and the object to be assembled to her own behavior.

Fusion and Values

The area of values is another example of positive use of language. In values work, overt action is in a frame of coordination with verbally construed life consequences. The ACT community debates whether or not valuing is positive fusion with language. While the theoretical account of values work in ACT is coherent, to date there is a lack of process research to definitively answer the question of whether or not valuing is fusion. It is our opinion that valuing is usually not fusion because people choose to move in the direction of their values. They know that they are distinct from their values and that they can choose to move in another direction at any time. In contrast, people who are fused do not experience the opportunity for choice and instead exhibit rule-governed insensitivity, impulse, or compulsion.

For example, early in treatment Shandra said that she values helping her children. However, when one of her children asks for a particular type of assistance, Shandra does not fully assess how she can most appropriately help or whether fulfilling the request is an instance of "helping my children" behavior. Instead she mindlessly fulfills the particular request, which is usually for money. Granted, there is an outside chance she doesn't know that she isn't actually helping her children by granting their every request, and we might provide psychoeducation in order to best assist her. After being given that psychoeducation, there is likely a continued emotional or rule-governed obstacle interfering with her exacting the tough love approach that is really called for. Shandra is likely experientially avoidant of the potential guilt, harassment, and personal effort that comes along with ceasing to reinforce her children's problematic behavior.

We might say that she values helping her children by helping them financially. However, when a functional assessment of her financial helping behavior is conducted, Shandra reports that she feels anxious when her children ask for her help, that she has given her children money knowing that they would use the money to purchase illegal drugs, and that she does not contact her children very often because she fears they will ask her for help. Shandra is "helping her children" in relational contexts where "helping her children" is in a frame of correspondence with "giving her children money when they ask for it." However, based on her own description of her helping behavior, she is helping her children maintain their substance abuse, escaping her own anxiety, and minimizing/avoiding situations where she might be asked to help. This does not resemble someone who values helping her children! In the context of direct contingencies, Shandra's "helping behaviors," such as giving her children money, function as avoidance. Her use of valuing language appears to be reason giving in the service of justifying her helping behavior rather than moving in a valued direction.

Shandra might value avoidance. However, since values are verbally construed outcomes, if she valued avoidance we would expect her to say something like "I give my children money and avoid calling them in the service of avoiding anxiety" rather than saying, "I value helping my children so I give them money when they ask for it." Shandra is fused; however, she is not fused with values. The confusion arises because Shandra uses the language of valuing in some relational contexts.

More on Fusion

Strosahl, Hayes, Wilson, and Gifford (2004) either cleverly or serendipitously model defusion while also explaining the problem of fusion in the following excerpt:

> There are three particularly pernicious forms of fusion that you will attack in this component of treatment: 1) Fusion between evaluations and events they are tied to; 2) Fusion with the imagined toxicity of painful events; 3) Fusion with arbitrary casual relationships that, collectively, form the client's "story"; and 4) Fusion with a conceptualized past or future. (p. 40)

If you got fused with the word "three," you may have had a bit of trouble absorbing all the important details of their point. As Shunryu Suzuki quixotically states, "The secret of Zen is just two words: not always so" (Chödrön, 2002, p. 119).

Returning to the main point of the Strosahl et al. quote above, ACT clients may require assistance for several reasons. As previously mentioned, when a person is fused to personal evaluation, such as "I am bad," that person may actually engage in behavior akin to depression because she buys the thought rather than just noticing the thought; the literality of the thought actually controls the behavior. Memories and bodily sensations can have "imagined toxicity," as if flashbacks of a trauma in the present literally bring that traumatic event totally into the now. Through exposure, clients can experience that such private events are just words and images, and that it is okay to just have them—and that having flashbacks, while painful, does not make them "broken" or unable to move in a valued direction. Further, fusion can be problematic when it comes to one's conceptualized self or life story. During the development of relational framing ability, people learn to keep their framing coherent. We learn that stories need to make sense and be consistent. Making sense is reinforcing.

For example, if a man's own life story is that he is always independent and self-reliant, it can be disheartening and depressing to sustain a traumatic leg injury requiring nursing care. The literality of his story, which he grips very tightly, is unraveling. His fusion to his story prevents him from being flexible enough to accept that while his behavior is dependent and reliant on others, he himself is not dependent. A person who values living independently will aim to move in that direction and may even choose to be temporarily dependent on others for care and treatment in the service of being more independent in the long run. In contrast, the person fused to "I am independent" will behave inflexibly in contexts where independence and dependence are psychologically relevant. He will likely engage in experiential avoidance moves. He may become angry and aggressive to those who try to help, and then become lonely and unable to manage. His solutions to maintain the fusion to self-concept actually can create even thornier problems. Now he is angry about his injury, his incoherent story, and his anger. Not only is fusion to one's story problematic, but Strosahl and colleagues (2004) suggest that people can struggle with fusion to the past or future. The aforementioned injured man demonstrates his conceptualized past, and he might express fusion to evaluations about his conceptualized future like this: "I am supposed to win marathons" or "I can't be a coach of my son's football team anymore," therefore "there is nothing to look forward to and without those things I am nothing." Being fused to the evaluations of the future in this way may influence the person to behave as if the bleak future was an inevitable, nonarbitrary feature of his life, and may lead to a depressive repertoire.

Defusion

So now we've got our work cut out for us. When clients talk about their "story" about who they are, what their past was, and what should happen in the future, we want to be on our toes for how fused they are with the verbal content. Same with their evaluations about the world, their self, or any of the events they experience. As clinicians, we can intervene in the relationship between private events such as thoughts and feelings and the client's overt behavior. We're defusing, or pulling apart, the connection between language-based contingencies and direct contingencies. When doing cognitive restructuring in CBT work, the aim of the intervention is to change the content of private events in the hope that new content will be followed by new and/or different behavior. In defusion work, the aim is to change the relationship between content and behavior. Instead of changing content, the context is changed. The context of literality selects fusion with private events. The context of mindfulness selects noticing the process of thinking instead of the content. Specific defusion exercises provide the experience of distancing the self from self-generated content.

The goal of defusion is to undermine the problematic control that words can exert over behavior. The term "undermine" is used frequently in the ACT community to describe what is happening in defusion. It is a poetic and apt description. By talking about language as the root of suffering and then tunneling under the person's constructed reality, we are digging a hole right through the foundation of language and looking at the structure of the world created by words.

Undermining the literality of words is done so that the person can contact the direct contingencies in her world, rather than being guided solely by the rules, evaluations, and problem-solving agendas that can make the behavior less sensitive to natural contingencies. As mentioned earlier, this is not to say that all rules, evaluations, and problem solving are problematic, and yet these verbal events can contaminate living a vital life. Strosahl and colleagues (2004) propose that there are at least four levels of intervention to consider when doing defusion work. The authors suggest discussing (1) the automaticity of language, (2) the speed of fusion, (3) the arbitrariness of evaluation, and (4) the process of thinking rather than the product of thinking.

Automaticity of Language

One way to introduce defusion is by talking about the automatic nature of language. Once a child learns how to frame events relationally, direct and social contingencies reinforce the development of a fluent verbal repertoire. Evaluations and descriptions can and do occur at a high rate—so much so that almost all experiences are tinged with a verbal component, and relational framing occurs during most waking moments. These verbal events seem to happen automatically. Adults in therapy are likely to have contacted the idea that it is difficult to stop thinking, and it can still be helpful to point it out in the context of the therapy.

Pointing out the automaticity of language is fairly easy thing to _____. Fluent speakers are typically able to engage in closure, and if you leave out a few words in a sentence, a client will probably be pretty good at filling in the _____. Speaking with coherent relational networks is regularly reinforced, and speaking with incoherent networks is regularly punished, so when words are strung together, chaining will likely evoke a workable and coherent response.

Client Exercise: Automaticity of Language

Depending upon the context, almost any common phrase can be used in an experiential exercise for the automaticity of language; for instance, "What goes up must come _____" or "A picture paints a thousand _____." With some clients, you might choose to be more provocative: "Nothing is certain but death and _____," "Houston, we have a _____" or "Money is the root of all _____." The take-home point in the beginning of defusion work is the automaticity of language; provoking automatic verbal and emotional responses may be useful later in therapy.

The Speed of Fusion

Another aspect of language worth discussing is how quickly concepts can be verbally framed. The ease with which relations can be learned can suggest just how arbitrary or even useless some verbal events can be. The What Are the Numbers? Exercise can be effective in demonstrating this concept. It is often used in ACT workshops and is discussed in the printed literature (Hayes et al., 1999; Strosahl et al., 2004), and perhaps the most interesting description of it is found on the website of the Association for Contextual Behavioral Science: "Teach a simple sequence of numbers and then harass the client regarding the arbitrariness and yet permanence of this mental event" (Gifford, Hayes, & Strosahl, 2005).

Client Exercise: What Are the Numbers?

During the exercise, the therapist tells the client that if she can remember certain numbers a few years from now, she'll be awarded a million dollars. The numbers are 1-2-3. The playful harassment comes in by showing that by presenting certain contextual variables (the presence of the therapist and the query "What are the numbers?"), the client is going to be hard-pressed not to automatically respond, "1-2-3." This is the case even after just a short "training," and even though there are no worthwhile reinforcers for recalling those numbers. (The context makes it quite obvious that a million dollars is not at stake.)

This demonstration of how quickly a relation can be established may give pause to taking the related events so seriously. The response "1-2-3" is probably going to be relatively permanent with the right stimulus control, and it is such a useless thing to have. Maybe lots of our verbal behavior is as hollow.

The Arbitrariness of Evaluation

Language evolved with human beings because of its value to survival. When early hunter-gatherers foraged for edible plants, the group that was able to evaluate vegetation as poisonous was able to avoid dangerous consequences without actually contacting the direct contingencies. Even with only primitive language, if one man survived the very aversive contingencies of going into a bear cave, he could simply point to the cave and say "bad" to the other members of the tribe who had been reared in a social community relating "bad" to other punishing consequences. Comparisons of certain stimuli against previously encountered stimuli or a verbally derived ideal is a widespread behavior in today's world, and it can serve a purpose for survival and well-being.

And it can become problematic. In some contexts, "bad" might be usefully related to a dangerous cave and poisonous plants; it might also be usefully related to a mathematical formula, an election campaign, or the blueprints for a skyscraper. But "bad" is not usefully related in a context of literality to an individual's personhood, bodily sensations, memories, or other private events. It isn't necessarily that the relating is inappropriate. Rather, what is inappropriate is having the relation actually govern behavior so that these "bad" private events are avoided in the same way as other things that are usefully related to "bad" are avoided.

"Bad" is, after all, an arbitrary stimulus just like all the other words in language. It is only true insofar as it is useful. And the "badness" of something is a human evaluation. Consider this variation on the Bad Cup Metaphor (Hayes et al., 1999, p. 169) in the therapeutic exchange below.

■ Case Study: Depression and Evaluations

Arnold, qualified for a *DSM* diagnosis of major depressive disorder, severe, has a history of being sexually abused by clergy members as a preteen, and has been to several therapists over the last decade.

Arnold: Everything is just rotten. Outright rotten. The thing with the wife. My lawsuit against the church. My job. I say everyday, "I gotta get outta here." I mean, man, it's … it's rotten. Life is rotten. [Client consistently denies suicidal ideation. He uses these verbalizations to indicate his interest in escaping his situation by running away to another country but has no thorough plans.]

Therapist: Rotten?

Arnold: It is. My whole life is rotten. And don't tell me that there's always some good stuff going on. I'm not really interpreting this stuff all wrong. I hate that silver-lining crap.

Therapist: Okay.

Arnold:	When people give me that "It can't be all bad" stuff and whatnot. Hate it.
Therapist:	Okay, can we try something else?
Arnold:	Mmm. *(frowning—consenting and skeptical too)*
Therapist:	[standing up and pointing to his chair] Is this a rotten chair?
Arnold:	*(rolling his eyes, breathing out a disdainful chuckle)* Uh … no. You sit in it all the time. It's fine.
Therapist:	See, now I disagree. This chair is rotten. I mean, yeah, I sit in it all the time, so I oughta know. Here. You sit in it. [they change positions.] Whatta ya think?
Arnold:	Hey, hey! I'm in your chair. Ha. You ever been on the couch before?
Therapist:	Plenty of times! Now, what about that rotten chair?
Arnold:	See, now … don't be stupid. I know what you are trying to do. You say it's "rotten," and then I grab the chair and tell you all the things that are good about it. More silver-lining stuff.
Therapist:	Hmm. Not what I'm driving at. See, I know you aren't gonna convince me about that rotten chair. I'm not gonna convince you either, right? About your rotten life? Convincing is not my game. I know you're wise to that trick, and I'd like to have you tell me why it's not a rotten chair anyway.
Arnold:	It's not rotten because it has no rips. It's got a good cushion. It rolls and swivels. I can sit on it!
Therapist:	It's also got no lumbar support, and it can't really lean back far enough. The arm rests are also scraped up from banging into the desk.
Arnold:	I see. You can say the chair is rotten, but it's not the chair that's rotten.
Therapist:	Boom. Right there. You've got your words about the chair, I've got mine. Where's the rottenness come from?
Arnold:	You're trying to tell me that my life isn't rotten—it's just the way I look at it. But guess what? I'm not gonna wake up one day and start saying my life is great.
Therapist:	I am with you on that first part. Rottenness is an evaluation. It isn't that your life is rotten—you evaluate it as rotten. And I am not trying to tell you to think different thoughts about it. But I am asking you to think differently.

Arnold:	Okay?
Therapist:	Arnold, what if it was more like this? It's not a push or pull between the right and the wrong thoughts. The great and the rotten. Having one side win over the other isn't the game. Here. What if we both left the room—and left the chair in here? What would happen to the rottenness?
Arnold:	*(pauses ten seconds and shakes his head)* I … I really guess I don't know.
Therapist:	Is the chair still rotten?
Arnold:	It's not even rotten now. You only say it is.
Therapist:	Uh-huh. And when I leave the room, the "rottenness" leaves altogether. The rottenness is not in the chair and it's not in me; it's a quality of my interaction with the chair. So when I leave the room, when the chair is not present, then I'm not thinking about or noticing the chair. Let me repeat that: the rottenness is not a quality of the chair; it is a quality of my interaction with the chair.
Arnold:	Hmm. So you're saying water isn't wet when you aren't there to feel it.
Therapist:	I don't want to get too far afield yet. And to answer the question, there are two things to consider. One, water is what it is. A fish wouldn't call it wet. But more importantly, Arnold—and I think that was a good point—but more importantly, you just described the water. It wasn't an evaluation.
Arnold:	*(assenting with a nod)* Gotcha.
Therapist:	Alright though. Where are we with this?
Arnold:	Well, I am in your seat. And it isn't rotten, and it isn't not rotten. Those are evaluations. Evaluations are part of the person, not the thing.
Therapist:	Not the thing being evaluated.
Arnold:	What does that do with my life being rotten?
Therapist:	You tell me.
Arnold:	It's not that my life is rotten. It's not even that I should try to see my life as good. You're trying to say that they are just plain old evaluations. That maybe my life isn't outright rotten. It just is.
Therapist:	I think that is a useful approach. We'll see. Now, can I have my seat back?
Arnold:	I thought you said you didn't like it. I even think you said it was "rotten" [emphasis made complete with "finger quotes"].

Therapist:	Uh-huh. I did evaluate it that way. It's my stuff; I'm willing to own it. And I am willing to have it. And I can have it 'cuz it's my only chair. 'Cuz from there I can do the work I care about, even if I am saying it's rotten. [They switch chairs in silence.] Right now, I am sitting in this chair, noticing I am telling myself that it is rotten. That it's terrible. And it's from here that I'm gonna continue to do what I care about … thoughts of rottenness and all!
Arnold:	(contemplatively) Hmm.

The Process vs. the Product of Thinking

While Arnold was learning that thinking and evaluating can be arbitrary, he was also learning that thinking and evaluating are a process, not just static thinglike products as are thoughts and evaluations. The stream of consciousness gets treated as a thing, but understand that it is something that is streaming. It is instructive for the client to catch the thinking process "in flight." Instead of looking at thoughts up close, "in the nest," and taken for granted, we can also examine from a distance thoughts in action.

Noticing thinking can be facilitated by mindfulness practice. Mindfulness puts us in contact with the human condition—that is, it makes it clearer that there are contexts of function and contexts of relating. Exercises such as seeing thoughts as clouds floating across the sky, soldiers marching in a parade, or words crawling across a teleprompter put thoughts in a new context. (There are many variants of this exercise. For one example, see Hayes et al., 1999, Soldiers in the Parade, pp. 158–162.) In these exercises, thoughts are being seen, not seen from. The typical way of thinking is in the context of relation (also known as the context of literality). In this context, when a person verbally frames stimulus A in coordination with stimulus B, and stimulus B has reinforcing properties, stimulus A will likely have reinforcing properties too. However, in the context of function, stimulus A and B are responded to distinctly by their natural properties and the event of relating is also noticed as another stimulus event, yet no transformation of stimulus functions occurs. As you might predict, staying only in the context of function is extremely difficult if not impossible, as relational framing is such a fluent behavior, and all experiences are eventually evaluated verbally.

The difference was once was explained to a client in this way:

Therapist:	We struggle with thoughts because we buy them, we get hooked by them … as if they are reality. It is as if the sounds or sights that we call words and images … the stuff that happens between our ears and behind our eyes … we treat it like the "prime directive." We have a thought and, bam, we listen to it, we follow it. But heck, just because we think something doesn't make it so. If you think you're a purple banana, do you turn into a purple banana? If you had that purple banana thought, you'd

likely say, "Where'd that come from?" And you'd likely move on. What if you could treat all thoughts like that? You don't get hooked by the craziness or the weirdness, you don't buy into the so-called importance of the thought. You just kinda … notice it … for what it is—sounds and sights—not for what it says it is: something that pulls you this way and that … and sometimes off course from your valued directions.

Remembering Language Is Powerful

Discussing fusion and defusion can put the clinician in a one-up position. As ACT therapists, we would do well to remember that we are, more often than not, swimming in the same stream as the client. The defusion conversation may be better received when it unfolds in conversation and during experiential exercises that both client and therapist can do concurrently. Lecturing will not have much sway, not only because people zone out at lectures, but also because "as ye sow so shall ye reap." A whole bunch of words telling the client not to get hooked by their own bunch of words is just plain ineffective modeling.

When teaching defusion, a humanistic stance is prudent. Clients might feel that their fears and concerns are being misunderstood or maligned when they are asked just to notice them. Letting the client know that you get it and have been there with the heaviness and perceived hazards of words, and also that you continue to go there quite often, would be beneficial. Reiterate that there is automaticity to language and that fusion happens very quickly. Notice in the next dialogue what the therapist is driving at when he starts talking about lemons.

Lambs, Lemons, and Broken Copier Machines

The defusion ideas can be rolled up into a coherent discussion during one session and then revisited over time. Here is a session transcript utilizing variations on several ACT standards.

Dave reports that he frequently worries that he is going to get terrible stomach diseases and fears becoming nauseated. He is in his third session and has already been through creative hopelessness interventions.

Therapist: So you are having a hard time stopping yourself from thinking about getting really sick from contamination. Okay. What do you do when you think you are contaminated?

Dave: Wash.

Therapist: Wash, okay, right. Does that help?

Dave: I mean, yeah. For a while. But no, it doesn't make the thoughts go away. Nothing does.

Therapist: Sure, right. And like, how are you going to truly stop thinking something? Your mind has a mind of its own. You can't stop thinking about something if the world sets you up to think it. Right? Watch. Mary had a little...

Dave: Lamb.

Therapist: Good. Now, this time, don't think lamb. *(pause)* Mary had a little...

Dave: *(laughing)* A little skirt.

Therapist: *(laughing)* Nice. A little skirt. Good choice. Why did you pick "skirt"?

Dave: 'Cuz it was funny.

Therapist: And it wasn't...

Dave: Huh? It wasn't? Oh, it wasn't, it wasn't "lamb."

Therapist: Yeah. So by just trying to not think "lamb," to try to think anything else but "lamb," you had to at least at some point check it with yourself and say, "What isn't lamb?" And by asking that, you've just thought...

Dave: ...Lamb.

Therapist: Eenie, meenie, miney...

Dave: Moe.

Therapist:	This time don't think "moe." Okay. Ready? (*pause*) Eenie, meenie, miney…
Dave:	Curly?
Therapist:	No idea why you picked it, though I imagine that it is because it is not "moe." By virtue of you trying not to say, "moe," you had to at least say, "What isn't moe?" and then pick something unrelated.
Dave:	Yeah. Hmm. And the weird thing is, it's totally related.
Therapist:	I don't follow you.
Dave:	Moe. From the Three Stooges. Moe, Larry, and Curly.
Therapist:	(*laughing*) Right. So even when you want to not think about something, your attempt to pick something else to think about might still be related to the thing you're trying to avoid. So the world sets you up to think "moe" or "lamb," and you do all you can to avoid it, and it doesn't really work out, huh?
Dave:	Hmph.
Therapist:	Now lamb and moe are simple. And I get it… Your thoughts are quite a bit heavier. Just follow me here. Imagine you've got this lemon. [gesturing]. You're holding this ripe, bright yellow lemon, and you can smell the citrus as you put it on the cutting board. And with a knife, you cut right through and the juice sprays up and then leaks out on the cutting board. And then you take that lemon wedge right up to your mouth and just squeeze the juice out and swallow the lemon juice. You got that. Are you salivating?
Dave:	Yeah. A lot.
Therapist:	Me too. And here's the thing: There isn't a lemon for at least a quarter mile from here. Not a single one in this building. Man, words can be powerful. Just by talking about it your glands start producing fluids. That can happen with a lot of things.
Dave:	Like talking about scary movies gives me the chills.
Therapist:	Right! Even in broad daylight! Same with me and talking about roller coasters. Just talking about it gets you all hyped up; you even get goose bumps. So wow, just the mere discussion of things can make you feel all different kinds of things. Words can make you salivate. Words can make you feel scared, excited. Lots of things.
Dave:	Yeah.

Therapist:	*(deliberately)* And it does that without the … actual … things … present. Weird, huh?
Dave:	Yeah.
Therapist:	Let's try something else. Ready? Just go with me now. [hand up to an ear like trying to listen for something] Lemon, lemon, lemon…
Dave:	*(simultaneously)* Lemon, lemon, lemon…
Therapist:	Louder! Lemonlemonlemonlemonlemon … [after twenty seconds, makes nonverbal gesture to stop] Lemon.
Dave:	*(laughs)*
Therapist:	Weird right. What happened to it?
Dave:	It started to sound like a broken copier machine!
Therapist:	*(laughs)* Right. Just noise. Sounds. And a few minutes ago, we were talking about "lemon" and you were salivating! So yeah, words are powerful. And they sure don't have to be!
Dave:	You're gonna tell me that this has to do with my obsessive thoughts.
Therapist:	Well, I don't know. Why don't you tell me how it relates?
Dave:	That you can't, well, I can't… I can't just stop thoughts. They happen, uh … automatically. And that even though they upset me, uh … they don't have to 'cuz it's just sounds. Yeah, but … it sounds too good to be true.
Therapist:	Okay, I gotcha. We'll work with that. I don't want you just to believe what I am saying. Let's try it out. Let's try it out. We'll see what happens. I just wanna plant that seed there.
Dave:	Yeah, I mean, it seems interesting, ya know.

When looking at the case conceptualization, understand that defusion is just a piece of the puzzle. It is not the cure. It is not intended to be a panacea. We wouldn't recommend doing a nauseanauseanausea exercise for Dave. That seems to set up an eliminative agenda and may not generalize the concept of defusion. The defusion exercises direct the therapy toward psychological flexibility. For Dave, the nascent ability to see that he has thoughts, that they are automatic, and that they don't have to have a major influence on his action can dilute their potency. And the intervention does not stand alone. The defusion work is in the context of assisting him in accepting feelings of nausea and the anxiety about becoming nauseated. His verbal behavior tied to not wanting to get sick, evaluations of how "horrible" being sick would be, and the solutions he could come up with to not get sick could all be just experienced, instead of adhered to, in the service of acceptance. When Dave clarified his values as desiring to fluidly and fully connect socially with the people in his life, then he could summon up his defusion skills in the service of living out those goals instead of buying his thoughts about illness and contamination. During his exposure therapy, and more importantly during his ecologically valid broadening of his daily repertoire (see the descriptions of FEEL exercises in chapter 14), he could just notice thoughts while committing to valued action. His mindfulness practice, which interestingly had to do with mindful eating meditations, helped him contact the present moment and his self as perspective. Learning that there is only "now" diluted the evaluation of becoming sick in the future, and seeing himself as the context of his thoughts rather than the content bolstered his defusion skills because he could notice that they were ephemeral evaluations and worries.

Seeing Things Differently (or Alt Erna Tivew Aystod Odelite Ralizat Ion)

Alternative ways to do deliteralization and defusion in session offer greater flexibility to the clinician. (By the way, did you notice how the gibberish in the heading above was meaningless at first? And did you notice how the last sentence was meaningful? When you see things differently, it aids defusion. The first five words of this paragraph are the gibberish in the heading.) Some ACT moves might not be as effective with some folks during therapy, and it pays to have a few different methods that engender deliteralization. Defusion teaches the client to notice that verbalizing occurs rather than being muscled around by the tyranny of verbalized content. This is can be done using different verbal conventions, and it entails overexposure to words and/or weakening the context of literality through increasing attention to process.

Presenting the client with alternate perspectives on their own provocative words and phrases may loosen the stimulus control these verbal events have over experiential avoidance repertoires. There are several ways this can be done, and we present only a few. However, it might be really helpful to the client-therapist dyad to develop their own exercises. The ones we give below will give you an idea of how to start creating your own exercises.

Looking at Verbal Behaving

The Lemonlemonlemon Exercise demonstrates how words can start out as very provocative and then be rendered powerless when viewed differently (in this case repetitively). Simply exposing anxious clients to certain words can be a step in the right direction for defusion, especially if reading the words provokes an anxiety response. We call this the Card-Shooing Exercise. The clinician can consider writing feared phrases on an index card and tossing them on the lap of the client. The client can try to shoo them off his lap while the clinician barrages him with more "thoughts" from her stack of provocative thoughts. Next, the client can be instructed to just let the cards rest on his lap, fully and without defense, and not sweep them off. As they stack up, he may realize that it is less effort for him to just have the cards rather than continually work at not having the cards.

The Card-Shooing Exercise was once rejected by a client with severe OCD because the man reported that he could not stand to have the exposure cards on his lap. The therapist wrote out, "Ridd Ledwit Haid Snow," on a card and showed it to the client from a distance. Seeing that it meant nothing to him, he reached out and grabbed the card and put it on his lap. When the contingencies of the context of literality were contacted, so too were the contingencies of the context of function. In other words, when he figured out that the words said, "riddled with AIDS now," he also figured out that they are, after all, just words. He startled at first, and then sat still, resigned to keep the "contaminated" card on his lap.

Changing the audible form of the words can be as instructive for some clients as changing the text. Sl-l-low-l-l-l-y saying the words may untangle the stimulus control of the verbal behavior and can also put the literal meaning in the stark light of functionality. Imagine a client particularly hooked by the phrase "I am a total failure." He lives his life as if he actually, nonarbitrarily is a total failure and refuses to be convinced otherwise, which is just fine by the ACT therapist, who isn't in the business of convincing anyway. And the clinician asks for permission to proceed with an exercise: "Let's see how that phrase sounds in slow motion: Ieeeeee aaaaaammmmm aaaaaa tooooo-taaaaalllll faaaaaaaalyerrrrrrr." It is an exercise in taking the literality out of the words. Singing thoughts aloud is not only a good defusion exercise, it is also an opportunity for willingness too! However, care must be taken that the therapist isn't shaming the client for having the thoughts and rather is facilitating relating to thoughts differently.

Recall the previously mentioned caveat: while the Lemonlemonlemon Exercise may be useful for defusing from the word "lemon," this exercise is not useful for complex verbal networks. It would probably not be very useful, and might be experienced as invalidating, to have a client say, "iwillneverhaveanormallifeduetomyhistoryofsexuala-buseiwillneverhaveanormallifeduetomyhistoryofsexualabuse." On a related note, some clients are tempted to use the Lemonlemonlemon Exercise as a new form of avoidance: "If I say it over and over, then it will go away." The point of the exercise is to have the client experience defusion with nonthreatening stimuli.

Looking at the Context of Verbal Behaving

In chapter 11, we discussed the Taking Your Mind for a Walk Exercise (Hayes et al., 1999, p. 163), in which the therapist takes the position of feeding the client verbal behavior as the client's own mind. This ACT convention is a stimulating example of how to engage in behavior while being defused from what the mind is jabbering about. The exercise helps the client to have verbal content and also to note that the content is fostered by a source much different than where value-directed action comes from.

In one clinical situation with a man with social phobia, it was made very clear that when the therapist said "Go!" the man was to touch the waiting-room doorknob no matter what else the therapist (as the client's mind) said. The man said that he would definitely be able to do this, no matter what the therapist said. After the therapist said, "Go!" the man stood up and stepped toward the door, physically unimpeded. The mind sat in the chair and said, "Man, do I look stupid doing this exercise. I hope there is no one in the waiting room that might see how dumb I look!" The man sat down. After a review of the Lemonlemonlemon Exercise and his previous self-as-perspective experiences, and a reorientation to valued commitment, they tried the "mind walking" exercise again. After "Go!" the therapist repeated social evaluations and descriptions of how stupid he looked doing this exercise. More pressure was added by the mind, with phrases such as "All that values stuff is baloney. These thoughts are real! I need to shut this mind up and go back and sit down," but the man persevered and touched the doorknob.

In addition to reducing the strength of words, making the client aware that the words are a not reality can assist in defusion. Just using the ACT convention "Thank your mind for that!" relays to the client that some of our verbal behavior is automatic, unhelpful, and more rule based than value based. (See below for more on "Thank your mind for that!")

Take off your glasses. A clinician can illustrate how folks are separate from their thoughts using a pair of sunglasses as a prop.

Therapist: Have you ever been wearing sunglasses for such a long time that you've forgotten that you are wearing them? [Therapist puts glasses on.] It's like you just see the world in this newly colored or shaded way. It isn't the way the world really looks if you could experience it directly. [Therapist takes glasses off, looks around, and puts them back on.] When you see the world through evaluation and other thoughts, the world takes on a tint. It can be a dimmer and, depending on the type of glasses you wear, more distorted view of the world. And you get really used to it! The neat thing is, you're learning that you can take them off. Your words, thoughts, these evaluations that you have are not the direct world around you; they are like filters through which you view the world. Like these glasses. What if you could take 'em off. [Therapist takes off glasses and looks at the glasses.] Notice, "Hey, I am wearing glasses. The world actually looks a bit different when I take them off." That's what we're driving at here. Notice that you are looking at the world through evaluating glasses. Take a look at the fact that you evaluate.

Quite obviously, we know that the "glasses" do not stay off for long. We're all subject to the overlearned behavior of thinking and evaluating. But we can foster this skill of taking off the glasses happening a bit more as we waltz through the hexaflex model. When clients are aware of their values and living a value-directed life, the thoughts that can veer them off the path become a bit more obvious. When committing to important action, the flow and motivation trumps the content from being fused. Mindfulness practice helps one contact the "now," and as clients integrate this into their lives, they are more able to notice how evaluations and problem solving are more about the past or future, and this tempers the pull of thoughts. The self as perspective is made of no-stick Teflon, and fused content cannot adhere to the context where experience unfolds. An acceptance stance toward physiological events supports defusion as well. When a person learns to accept events fully and without defense, the evaluations of feelings and sensations become impotent.

Checking In

ACT has a lot of neat experiential exercises. If you are so inclined, you may want to purchase a shoe organizer to match the decor of your office. In each cubbyhole, you can keep the ACT exercise artifacts, such as sunglasses (from this chapter), 3 x 5 cards (both blank and any used ones for each client), Chinese finger cuffs (chapter 9), and your "Bad Cup" (Hayes et al., 1999, p. 169). Having these and other props ready may make therapy more seamless, and you might actually use the physical examples more often.

Thank your mind for that. Discussing the mind as separate from valued directions and direct contingencies is a main aim of the sunglasses exercise. The "word machine" can be such an insidious source of suffering that showing the distance which can be put between the never-ending stream of verbal content and the pursuit of vital living can be a powerful intervention. This is why we sometime treat the mind as a separate "person." Taking your mind for a walk and saying, "There are four of us in this therapy room—me and you and your mind and my mind" (Hayes et al., 1999), puts this concept directly in the conversation. The tried and true "Thank your mind for that" response on the part of the therapist consequates verbally entangled experiential avoidance moves and illuminates the difference between the client's statement and her valued direction. Consider the following examples:

- A person dealing with OCD says, "Probably the best way to stop obsessing about my coworkers' lifestyles would be to stop going to that job."

- A person who abuses alcohol and struggles with depression says, "Gettin' sauced is my only option... I don't have the social skills you want me to use."

- A teenager struggling with sexuality issues says, "I'm just gonna go join a convent ... leave all this stuff behind!"

You can say to each one, "Thank your mind for that!" They are evaluations and "solutions" that are extremely likely to come from the almighty verbal change agenda and not from a principled choice or commitment to values. As you conceptualize your case with the inflexahex model, record what kind of change agenda plans are common for the client, and then refer back to the case conceptualization sheet as a reminder of the client's typical change agenda plans. Listen for them, as they are bound to crop up from time to time. Any types of distortion of experiences or inappropriate plans to avoid certain experiences are a target for defusion generally and the specific move of thanking one's mind for a thought.

I am having the thought that... Another standard ACT exercise is teaching the client to say, "I am having the thought that..." The purpose of this move is to describe that private events are occurring. Fluently learning to say "I am having the thought that 'I am no good'" is highly likely to take the teeth out of the statement "I am no good." Just look at the simple difference in words: "I am having" already shows a distance from "I am." "Having" is holding or retaining something and is used (that is, this verbal response is occasioned) in situations of relative impermanence. Forms of "being" (for example, "am" or "is") are about existing and living a certain way, and are used to describe something more permanent. "I'm having the feeling of ..." distances the person from the feeling, creating some wiggle room or flexibility to just experience it directly as it is. People usually know, or at least can learn, that feelings are transient, so saying, "I'm having the feeling of anger," may reduce the struggle with the emotion compared to saying, "I am angry."

Stance of the Therapist

One difficulty of being a behavioral health practitioner is that, in many ways, you already get it. That is to say, if you work with people with anxiety concerns, you might be apt to lose a bit of patience with teaching defusion exercises day after day. Please keep in mind that it is extremely likely that your client may never have considered just noticing thoughts, never have done a defusion exercise, and never have learned that going toward certain scary things is a better way to deal with them than running away from them. Also be careful of the arrogance that might interfere with the relationship. This is new stuff for many. Perhaps once you learn it, it loses its profundity, but really try to connect with the first time you did a mindfulness exercise. You are now bestowing very profound considerations on your client, and this is best couched in a respectful tone and manner.

Mindfulness and Defusion

Diminishing the stifling impact of fusion with private events and increasing the experience of direct nonverbal contingencies can facilitate more value-directed living and is a major part of ACT. The exercises about mindfulness discussed throughout this book are not only useful for contacting the self as perspective and the present moment, but also for untangling and defusing the person's behavior from unhelpful rules, evaluations, and "solutions." When the woman addicted to alcohol says, "I have to drink to get through the day," she can be invited to mindfully notice that thought crawling across a teleprompter. That simple move touches upon all six domains of the hexaflex, especially defusion and self as perspective. A man who evaluates himself by saying, "I am not handsome enough to ask out a woman for a date," can be invited to see those words floating on a leaf in a stream. In family therapy, when a mother of a girl with anorexia says, "I'll just have to hold her to higher standards," and it is the pressure of high standards that the girl is responding negatively to, the mother can be asked just to have that problem-solving idea mindfully and not act on it. Each family member can thank their mind for those thoughts, use the previously mentioned defusion strategies to loosen up their control over their lives, and then connect fully to the direction they want their lives to take, which can distill the values from the residual verbal dregs.

This chapter is not intended to be an exhaustive inventory of all the defusion exercises available. Strosahl et al. (2004) list thirty-five different defusion interventions, and more are posted on the website of the Association for Contextual Behavioral Science (Gifford, Hayes, & Strosahl, 2005). The multiple exemplars used in this chapter should offer enough variability and direction so that you can tell yourself that you are able to make up your own interventions. And if you tell yourself that you can't do it, thank your mind for that thought, and notice the thought for what it is and not what it says it is!

Checking In

What are the differences between a second-wave cognitive therapy approach and an ACT approach when it comes to thoughts that a client is struggling with?

Our response:

Cognitive therapy affects problematic relationships between private events and behaviors by changing content through cognitive restructuring and disputation. In other words, bad content is changed to good content and then the problematic behavior stops.

ACT, in contrast, aims to change the relationship between private events and behavior by undermining the context of literality where events and descriptions of events have the same or similar functions. In a deliteralized context, thoughts are descriptions and not the things they describe.

What is a difference between disputation and defusion?

Disputation challenges thought content in an attempt to alter behavior in the context of literal meaning. Defusion focuses on noticing the process of thinking rather than altering content. The context of function is primary.

CHAPTER 14

Willingness

Imagine two girls with a zest for life and a desire to experience all the fun that child-hood has to offer, and they both are given the opportunity to go roller-skating. Both girls are afraid to fall down, and each girl soon learns that the slightest shift in her body weight in one direction calls for an adjustment in her feet the other way, and then, in the spirit of just trying to stand still, legs and arms start flailing, and they plant their derrieres on the floor just by standing still. In many ways, learning to move forward in a chosen direction will actually minimize the frequency of falling down in the long run. But much more importantly, when one of the girls is willing to move (and therefore willing to fall), she has actually started roller-skating. The other girl, choosing to stand still is actually just roller-*wearing*.

"Ah!" one might say, "but the second girl who chose to stand still only falls down. The first girl, who is actually doing the skating, falls down and forward, and definitely hits much harder. She's much more likely to get injured!" To which someone with a passing understanding of value-directed living might reply, "Yes, but remember, only one of the two is skating! Pain is a potential for both, but suffering only happens to one, and not the girl who fell harder!"

If the would-be skater is not willing to fall, down she'll go—both physically on her rump and conceptually as not being a skater. Think about it. A girl willing to fall down in the service of learning to skate is less likely to fall down in the long run. She may learn ways to lessen the blow of falling, and will have practice in getting up after a fall. The girl unwilling to fall continues flailing noncommittally or just sits rinkside. Worse, because of the lack of reinforcers, she may eventually avoid skating, skating rinks, people who skate, and so on. Worse yet, with that kind of agenda, she may just avoid any context where she may fall or fail.

The roller-skating girl is, of course, a metaphor. With clinical concerns, the question is "Are you willing to move forward with your life in your valued direction, and carry the thoughts of falling and the fear of failing with you?" In therapy, the concern is not so much that the person will fall from time to time; it is that he is so experientially avoidant that there is no movement at all. This is why experiential avoidance is the target for much of the ACT approach, and willingness is part of the antidote.

Avoidance vs. Unwillingness

A Gaelic proverb states, "Nothing is easy to the unwilling," and Nobel-prize-winner Helen Keller tells us that "[a]voiding danger is no safer in the long run than outright exposure." In a sense, both are telling us that avoidance and unwillingness can be problematic for human beings.

Avoidance Revisited

Willingness has been discussed in the context of the six ACT processes, and it is an important enough treatment concern to merit discussion in its own right. The relationship between unwillingness and avoidance is slippery. *Avoidance* is a technical term in behavior analysis that can be summarized simply as "the prevention of an aversive stimulus by a response" (Catania, 1992, p. 364; see chapter 3). All organisms eventually develop a repertoire for avoiding painful stimuli that they have contacted in the past. A cat can be trained to press a lever in order to avoid shock, and natural contingencies also influence the cat to clear its throat in order to prevent a coughing fit or other aversive hair-ball problems. Clearing your own throat to prevent a coughing fit is a brief and usually innocuous avoidance move on your part. Turning on a lamp when entering a room can be considered an avoidance move too. Given the technical definition of avoidance (and the scope of one's analysis), people engage in forms of avoidance countless times every day. So keep in mind that avoidance is not inherently pathological. In fact, it can be quite adaptive. Remember that we are looking at the act-in-context.

Unwillingness Visited

Unwillingness is a verbal event where the relations involved participate in establishing or maintaining avoidance responses. We can say it is derived relational responding that alters the functions of stimuli and thereby increases the probability of avoidance responding. Said more plainly (and less precisely), unwillingness is a decided reluctance to do something.

Unwillingness, like avoidance, is also not inherently pathological. An individual can verbalize a rule stating that she is unwilling to work for a bigoted employer, even if she never had such an employer, and then follow that rule by quitting her job if she learns the boss is a bigot. She can also be unwilling to climb a thirty-foot ladder to fix a streetlight. She may have never contacted the direct consequences of bigotry or the dizzying effect of being up high on a ladder, but verbal relations about the consequences can contribute to an avoidance strategy. Unwillingness, like other behavioral events, is contextually bound, something a person exhibits not globally but in the presence of certain historically relevant events.

■ Case Study: Agoraphobia

Unwillingness is often at the core of a client's unworkable change agenda. Consider Gloria, a woman with agoraphobia, who lives her life with this kind of rule: "I don't want to have the shortness of breath and the memories I have of the time when I had a panic attack out on the street—so I'll just stay here in the house where it is safe. That way I won't have to have this problem anymore." Her statement articulates a change agenda showing unwillingness; she is unwilling to have memories about and symptoms of prior panic attacks. Her verbal plan aims to change something in her world that is massively difficult to change: the frequency of certain thoughts and feelings. And this verbally governed avoidance of the private events exacerbates her clinical presentation in three ways.

First, Gloria's unwillingness supports the negatively reinforcing consequences of avoiding, thereby increasing further avoidance. (Yeah, that's a bit twisty there, but stay with us). When she relates her shortness of breath (dyspnea) and memories to "bad" and "don't have them," these relations alter the function of the dyspnea and memories, increasing their aversive properties. Staying inside her home is negatively reinforced not only by the avoidance of the shortness of breath but also by the avoidance of the verbally derived functions of the shortness of breath and memories of the panic attack.

Second, her unwillingness (her derived relational responding that alters the function of stimuli that evoke avoidance) strengthens the stimulus control that the memories and shortness of breath have over her agoraphobic behavior. Gloria plans to get on with the business of living only in the absence of dyspnea and the memories. In other words, she will get on with the business of living so long as she does not experience any symptoms of panic. And her repertoire is narrowed in the presence of the interoceptive cues and memories symptomatic of panic disorder. The shortness of breath and memories are discriminative in that their presence occasions responses that result in their removal. If her verbal responding—that is, her unwillingness—maintains the aversive function of her dyspnea and memories (that they are "bad"), then they will continue to have discriminative functions that maintain avoidant behavior: agoraphobia.

Third, unwillingness exacerbates her clinical problem by keeping her from accessing a broad assortment of potentially available reinforcers. We do, of course, have to assess rather than assume that living the isolated lifestyle of an agoraphobic is not what she values. In her rule-governed avoidance of what she evaluates as problematic feelings and thoughts, she is not only maintaining the agoraphobia "symptoms," she is also engendering another insidious problem: a life lacking in flexibility and, most likely, lacking in vitality.

Her rules of living govern her overt responses and keep her indoors. Her rule-governed behavior repertoire is limited and rigid, and unfortunately she most likely continues to experience symptoms of panic because panic attacks are verbally present and linked to many thoughts, feelings, and bodily sensations even while she stays indoors. While she is sitting indoors thinking about the possibility of having a panic attack, she is missing opportunities to have other potentially valuable experiences. Research on behavior influenced by following rules suggests the responses may be less sensitive to changes in prevailing contingencies than behavior acquired by shaping (Baron & Galizio, 1983; Hayes et al., 1986; Shimoff et al., 1981; Skinner, 1969) and that sensitivity only occurs when the behavior contacts the change in contingencies (Galizio, 1979).

Approaching the doorway and eventually going outside puts Gloria in contact with the contingencies through exposure to her feared stimuli. This might lead to classical extinction of the anxiety responses, and may also put her in contact with a breadth of other reinforcers—probably the ones related to her values. Situational in vivo exposure is an evidence-based treatment (Barlow, 1988; Jacobson, N. S., Wilson, & Tupper, 1988) for agoraphobia, and can help Gloria reduce her physiological reactions and reinforce her for getting closer to the door.

ACT can support her treatment for agoraphobia (see Carrascoso Lopez, 2000) by engendering a willingness to get involved in the therapy—by showing that her verbal evaluations are just words; that her physical symptoms are normal and able to be experienced fully and without defense; that she is not her thoughts, feelings, or sensations; and that there are broad, process-based reinforcers available to her now by committing to living a value-directed life. Willingness exercises in ACT attempt to reduce the influence of the negative reinforcement contingencies, sway stimulus control to valued events, and put the person in the presence of valued reinforcers.

Willingness

So we have an idea what unwillingness looks like, but what is willingness? Defining it will be a daunting task. Wilson, Hayes, Gregg, and Zettle (2001) point out that "[t]here just aren't good words for what it is like to have … willingness" (p. 234). Willingness is not a necessarily a verbal process, even though it may be supported by verbal processes. Much like the discussion of reason giving (chapter 9), willing behavior can be done with rules but not likely done for rules. *Willingness* is an outcome of abandoning useless change agendas.

Let's continue with the analogy of the two girls who want to learn to skate: Both girls engage in behaviors to avoid the aversive stimulation of forcefully contacting the floor with their body parts. But they are each going about it differently. One girl's attempts to avoid falling down include actually taking manageable steps toward learning to skate, like holding someone's hand or staying close to the wall. Periodically, until she learns better, she still flails her arms and legs in attempts to balance herself. Those are all avoidance moves, and they are done in the service of skating. There is a willingness quality to the behavior. While avoiding falling, the girl may acquire better balance skills that help her skate, and she will also learn to fall. Incidentally many sports—such as skiing and the martial arts—include practice in falling as part of the basic training. Skating includes falling. A person who isn't exposed to falling isn't skating. When looking at her complex, moment-by-moment behavior, the skater might be following rules to avoid falling; for example, "Okay, keep my hands in front and look forward. Alternate pushing both legs, and make sure to coast." These moment-by-moment rules are also in the service of skating; she isn't following rules to avoid skating.

The other girl's attempts to avoid falling down include standing still, maybe even sitting down, or, worse, unlacing her skates. Those are all avoidance moves, and they are done in the service of not falling down, not in the service of skating. While avoiding falling in this manner, the girl never acquires balance skills and never learns how to fall—and, sadly, she never learns to skate. She might even acquire avoidance of thoughts and feelings related to skating. This girl isn't exposed to falling, and therefore isn't exposed to skating—and, for the purposes of the analogy, isn't contacting her personal, global, and desired life consequences of experiencing all the fun that skating has to offer. In the context of learning to skate, outright avoidance of falling and avoidance of thinking about falling are untenable.

Functions of Avoidance Depend on Context

So avoidance per se is only judged to be problematic given a context. For a new example, in a context of valuing a healthy lifestyle, a person does well to avoid entering an abusive relationship or getting in a car with a drunk driver. Those avoidance moves are perfectly functional.

Context gives avoidant behavior clinical relevance. For example, there is nothing particularly pathological about a person wanting to steer clear of contacting vomit in public places. The problem occurs when the emetophobic client brings his valued life directions to a standstill in the service of avoiding this situational stimulus. And even more importantly, he avoids the thoughts and feelings related to vomit. The emetophobia problem is maintained by fusion with the rule "I must avoid all puke" and an unwillingness to accept the nausea he feels when he goes out in public. With this agenda, he is rarely contacting the present moment but rather is caught up in future vomit threats or past vomit memories. He may not have fully realized that his life is about vomit instead of about something more vital. He is likely unwilling to commit to exposing himself to vomit or the potential threat of vomit, despite the benefits of exposure exercises. In these ways, he is living in an inflexible psychological space, and it is robbing him of living a life he might appreciate more if he clarified his goals and was willing to have all that life had to offer. (Yes, the vomit too.)

Remember that context makes the avoidance problematic. Take our client Rick, for example. There isn't anything wrong with his agenda of wanting to avoid embarrassing situations and turning red faced in front of peers. To Rick, there isn't anything particularly edifying about making a fool of himself in front of people. It seems reasonable and functional in most contexts that one's social repertoire follows a rule such as "Don't do anything embarrassing."

The concern is the context and what gets sacrificed as the rule is followed. When folks are able to hold lightly the rule "Don't do anything embarrassing," they may have a greater willingness to make a presentation at work or ask someone out on a date. In both of those contexts, it is almost impossible to avoid the natural emotion of embarrassment. An ability to defuse from the rule and a willingness to have periodic embarrassment feelings shows a flexible repertoire that may make value-directed living more tenable. For Rick, who is fused with "Don't do anything embarrassing" and who won't accept any feelings of embarrassment, not only will the fear remain, but also the forward movement toward his life's goals will be thwarted. It's this type of avoidance that is so insidious.

Unwillingness is a quality of avoidance behavior. Avoidance becomes clinically relevant in situations where the rule-governed behavior reduces the person's contact with their personal, global, and desired life consequences. In the skater example, the girl's unwillingness to fall, or to think about falling, might reduce the aversive experience of falling down, but she does so by sacrificing learning how to skate. Did you catch that? Unwillingness does reduce aversive experiences—but often it brings along other aversive situations, like not living a vibrant life! In that particular context, the solution is part of the problem.

Language and Unwillingness

The ACT approach endeavors to engender psychological flexibility for the client so that a vital valued life can be lived. Unwillingness is an obstacle to this aim. When clinically relevant behaviors occur because of unwillingness to remain in contact with psychological events, it is important for the ACT therapist to not only functionally analyze the environment with respect to classical and operant conditioning influences, but also to analyze the influence of the client's verbal behavior. In other words, if a dog-phobic client is avoiding parks and friends' houses because of the presence of canines in those environments, the therapist needs to do more than just a two-factor analysis of the classical and operant approaches. Of course it is important to look at counterconditioning the physiological, classically conditioned responses of anxiety. It is also helpful to positively reinforce braver and braver approach attempts to intervene on the negative reinforcement paradigm maintaining the operant avoidance.

In addition, the ACT therapist will investigate the participation of relational frames that influence the avoidant behavior. They need to look at ineffective pliance, avoidant tracking, and problematic augmenting, as seen in the inflexahex mode. Clients may believe thoughts such as "I'll get rabies and die if I get bit!" or even have images of themselves being disfigured by a dog bite.

The verbal behavior on the other side of the coin needs investigation too. The therapist assesses whether or not the client has developed verbally construed global desired life consequences that will support attempts at psychologically flexible behavior in the presence of canines. Treating a client's experiential avoidance (standing still instead of skating, steering clear of the park where dogs might be present) will not only encompass utilizing established behavior therapy techniques but also incorporate attempts to alter the impact of verbal behavior through defusion, mindfulness, and acceptance.

Unwillingness in Case Conceptualization

Author and professor Leo Buscaglia once said, "What we call the secret of happiness is no more a secret than our willingness to choose life." What might it look like to let our clients in on the secret of willingness? (Are *we* even in on the secret all the time?) What can be done with human language to increase an individual's willingness in treatment?

A new relationship with words and thoughts can help detangle people from their experiential avoidance agendas. In this respect, the ACT approach would include acceptance and defusion work. In fact, willingness is called "the goal of deliteralization" (Hayes et al., 1999, p. 170).

■ Case Study: The Impact of Verbal Behavior with Depression

Let's meet Ken, a middle-aged electrical engineer who is dealing with depression. Ken frequently thinks to himself and says aloud in therapy, "I'm just not good enough" or "It would be terrible to be unsuccessful," especially in the context of asking for a raise or a promotion, or when forwarding a new idea for his company. Ken is not only unwilling to fail, he is also unwilling to think about failing. He evaluates himself poorly, buys the thoughts that he is not good enough to be listened to by his boss and coworkers, and gives reasons why he should avoid such circumstances.

To the ACT-trained eye, fusion, evaluation, avoidance, and reason giving—aptly denoted in the acronym FEAR—are present in those verbalizations. With the methods of undermining FEAR (see chapter 6), a foundation of willingness can be started. When Ken experiences defusion exercises, he can begin to notice that the teeth are removed from those "reasons" for standing still in his life. He can learn that "I'm just not good enough" is a string of words he tells himself, and that he doesn't have to be pushed around by this evaluation. He can learn that he is not the content of his evaluations, and that such evaluative talk is contacting the past or the future but not the present moment (see chapters 1 and 6 for why that is). His reason giving is a weak argument for not moving forward with his desire to be a respected and contributing engineer. "I am not good enough" is not a valid reason to not contribute to his industry. Further, and more ACT consistent, that reason is only a verbal formulation and not worth stultifying his value-directed behavior. When the "reasons" for not doing something are diminished, there is more room for doing something. Ken responded well to the Shrinking Room Metaphor (see below), which aims the FEAR assessment toward decreasing the unconstructive impact of relational framing on willingness. With this exercise, the client can experience the loss of flexibility and loss of access to a broad environment because of fusion to unhelpful words. The Shrinking Room Metaphor might be introduced to a client who describes avoiding private experiences such as thoughts and feelings.

Client Exercise: The Shrinking Room Metaphor

Therapist: It seems that if this room was your world, and there are some things in your world that you are not willing to have, you have a lot of adjusting to do to make sure you don't have to see or encounter that stuff. It looks like this: Suppose that bookshelf over there is "I'm just not good enough." And you aren't willing to have that because that evaluation is just so true about you. You want to completely avoid it. So come over here [motions to client] and maybe you can just turn your back on it, and look at the other 80 percent of the room. Who needs that 20 percent related to that "I'm just not good enough" thought anyway? Well, don't forget that the lamp over there is the "It would be terrible to be unsuccessful" thought. Well, you could do what worked for you before. Turn your back on all that stuff that provokes that thought. I'm sure it will work just fine. Now you're looking at about 60 percent of the room, and that's just fine. And here's the thing. Don't both those thoughts relate to something. I mean in one way or another, the rest of the room that you see here is eventually going to remind you of what you've turned your back on. The rug is touching both the lamp and the bookshelf—it's related to those bad thoughts—so because of that you can climb up on the couch. Well, the light from the lamp is cast on all the four walls. So because of that, why not climb in the corner and cover your eyes so you don't see any of the "It would be terrible to be unsuccessful" lamplight—as good of a reason as any. And what if you were able to just have it? Have the light, see the bookshelf, touch the rug. What would you have? You'd have your life back!

Another influence on experiential avoidance might be the lack of developed values. Ken might also be standing still in life because he doesn't know why he "laced up" in the first place. A client will be more willing to fall down when he has a purpose in skating! Why did he become an engineer? Values clarification might be a good adjunct intervention from the other side of the hexaflex. Contacting what draws him to contributing to the profession in the first place can put defusion exercises in a different light.

When people talk of "everyday heroes," they usually talk about people who are willing to sacrifice short-term gain, comfort, and sometimes even their lives because their actions are value consistent no matter what thoughts and feelings show up. Firefighters, soldiers, and police come to mind as "everyday heroes" for many people because of their willingness to experience aversive events in their lives while valuing a common good. But when people are asked to describe their personal heroes, they usually don't talk about civil servants who engage in high-risk occupations. They usually talk about their parents or a family member, a teacher or a coach—someone who was willing to forgo creature comforts in order to nurture something worthwhile in that individual. A mom who comes home exhausted from work and is willing to play ball with her little girl is also willing to notice feelings of muscle fatigue and aching ankles and to accept thoughts such as "Doesn't this rug rat know I did enough for her already today?"

These may not be heroic acts, but cumulatively these small acts make for personal heroes. And that kind of willingness, the willingness to forgo instant gratification in the service of a greater good, is inherently verbal. Verbal behavior can support willingness.

If You're Not Willing to…

If the clinician conceptualizes the client's "solution as the problem," the clinician can expect that the client is unwilling to have something. Exploring the futility of avoidance of private experience can facilitate willingness.

If You're Not Willing to Have It, You've Got It

Rick smokes marijuana to avoid feeling guilty about (among other things) not visiting his mother. Then once he is high, he feels guilty for being high instead of seeing his mother. His solution (getting stoned) participates in his problem (reduces the likelihood of visiting his mother and maintains an illegal, unhealthy habit). Getting high is an experiential avoidance move aimed to reduce guilt, and it begets more guilt and experiences that are additionally aversive and not value directed.

Shandra also demonstrates unwillingness in several areas of her life that leads to an insidious change agenda. She says that Charles is abusive and creates an unhappy environment for her, yet when he is gone she is unwilling to feel lonely, so she invites his abusiveness back into her life. Additionally, she is unwilling to have the feelings that come from her children's lack of success and their guilt trips. Her solution is to continue to buy herself out of the guilt by giving them money. This reinforces their dependent behaviors and contributes to the problem through the guise of a solution. In both these cases, Rick and Shandra exhibit an unwillingness to have some private events, and as the ACT saying goes, "If you're not willing to have it, you've got it!"

If an anxious client is unwilling to be nervous, then the first sign of arousal will provoke nervousness. The verbal agenda of controlling anxiety sets up a system of hypervigilance and an infinite feedback loop. Unwillingness puts the person on the lookout, and then any arousal on the radar is reacted to with an intensity that actually maintains the arousal. Anxiety tends to grow and grow as it is fought off. Rick is unwilling to feel guilty and have thoughts that he is a loser; in order to escape these thoughts, he smokes an illegal drug and avoids his mother. This problematic cycle is obvious to us here in black and white, and we invite you to be aware of this in the therapy room and as you are developing your case conceptualization. This kind of unwillingness can lead to the most incongruous change solutions.

If You're Not Willing to Lose It, You've Lost It

An interesting variation on this theme of unwillingness is this: if you're not willing to lose it, you've lost it. This can apply in a number of situations, and especially in contexts where the person is unwilling to lose people's respect. Take the example of Tom, a musician who worked very hard to gain the admiration and respect of other local musicians and critics. Tom's playing and his songs were well received, yet he also developed performance anxiety. He was fused with evaluations and worry, and was so scared about losing the admiration and respect that he was given that he avoided playing music to audiences. When they asked Tom why he wasn't playing, he gave half-baked reasons and then stopped going to places where he might be asked why he wasn't playing. Ultimately he became fused to the belief that the other musicians continued to admire him and his past music performances, even though he was no longer playing. And he was entirely mistaken. The respect and admiration were actually lost in his effort not to lose them.

The Similarity of Experiential Avoidance Among Clinical Problems

The verbal agenda behind different kinds of experiential avoidance moves are all fairly similar at the core. What is a surefire way for a depressed person to avoid social punishers and denigrating self-talk? Going back to sleep might "work" for some, or avoiding people outright could "work" too. What is the best way for a compulsive checker to douse the worry that he left the toaster oven on at home? He can go back and check and check again! How can an agoraphobic man stop panic from attacking? He can stay home for weeks on end. Are hangovers showing up for the alcoholic? Taking a nip from the hair of the dog before work seems like a solution to that problem. If these "control" behaviors continue, we can see these as instances of negative reinforcement for clinically relevant behaviors. Notice the word "reinforcement," as in "increases the likelihood of responses" (Catania, 1992, p. 391). A response (going back to sleep/going home and checking/staying inside/doing a shot of whiskey) that takes away an aversive stimulus (denigrating self-talk/worries of a toaster catching fire/dread of a panic episode/having shaking hands) is more likely to be occasioned in the future in the presence of the aversive stimulus. The bitter irony is that the negatively reinforced behavior may actually beget future presentations of the stimuli originally avoided. In some contexts, when a person sleeps all day, he may also be more likely to be shunned by his social group or denigrate himself for "wasting" his day. The "checker" may continually miss work because of the checking, which sets up a work environment that keeps him perpetually worried and anxious, which eventually leads to more checking. Consider how this problematic change agenda is perpetuated for the client with agoraphobia and the client that abuses alcohol.

Checking In

What if the people in the four examples above—depression, OCD, agoraphobia, and alcohol abuse—were willing to have their challenging experiences without trying to change them? Pick one client and consider the ACT approach to that client's problem.

Perhaps it would be instructive for the client to learn that she can have thoughts and feelings from an unchangeable enduring self that isn't comprised of verbal content, and that all the private events that arise are happening in the "now." With such a mindful stance established, perhaps that person could orient toward her deepest desires. If that happened, she might then commit in this moment toward seeking that end, which might, just might, mean noticing the thoughts and the problem "solutions" and evaluations that are arising—and simply see them as words, not commands from the almighty dictatorial mind. And with this orientation, the feelings and bodily states can be noticed as natural reactions to the world in the moment. And they are "have-able" because they are distinguishable from the self and established valued living. It doesn't matter if we're talking about the person with depression, OCD, agoraphobia, or alcohol abuse. The functions of the poorly adaptive behavioral choices are to avoid certain experiences, and the aim of ACT is to engender the psychological flexibility to have those experiences so that avoidance behavior is no longer supported and valued living is.

Stance of the Therapist

■ What shows up for you when you are feeling stuck as a therapist?

■ Are you plagued with imposter-syndrome thoughts?

■ Do you perhaps have disdainful thoughts about, your client, who seems so challenging, so recalcitrant, so … so much like everyone else on the planet?

■ Are you willing to have the thoughts—even the judgmental thoughts about your client, even the denigrating thoughts about you and your own skills—and continue in a valued direction in the vocation of clinical work?

Willingness for the Sake of Unwillingness

During sessions, and while considering the case conceptualization between sessions, be watchful for a client expressing verbal willingness for the sake of experiential avoidance. The most obvious example of this happens quite frequently early in therapy when the client says, "So if I accept the urges/thoughts/cravings/heart palpitations/feelings, will they go away?" This is a reasonable question. Eliminative agendas abound in the culture, and clients who are not yet savvy to the ACT approach are probably in therapy in order to get rid of their discomfort.

If you are willing to have experiences in order to make them go away, just how willing are you to have the experience in the first place? There is an important nuance here. The client has to be fully willing to have the symptom, thought, urge, or feeling. The nuance is that he doesn't have to suffer it in the context of relating, that is, he doesn't have to buy the thought or get swallowed by the symptom as if it were the most treacherous of realities. The client needs to accept the experience as it is, not what it says it is or is evaluated to be. When the client reports being willing, but only in the hopes that these symptoms will go away, that inconsistency will not work in his favor! If you're only willing to have it so that it goes away, wanting it to go away means you are still fused to the evaluations and unaccepting of the events. The verbal entanglement is still there.

We might imagine our client Rick's reaction when he is prompted, "Can you just have the thought 'The future is bleak' and not try to rid yourself of that thought?" The mainstream culture that Rick was reared in usually tries to root out such "causes," to not accept them, so we might expect him to resist this acceptance-based notion at first. And recall what we learned about "causes" in chapters 9 and 10. The bleak future is not here and now, it is simply verbally derived. Defusion and acceptance moves can clarify for Rick that words can just be "had," and that all thoughts are not the be-all and end-all instructions for living. If Rick has contacted the point of the Lemonlemonlemon Exercise and the Bad Chair Metaphor, if he has contacted the point that thefut ureisble ak (the future is bleak), then he can see "The future is bleak" in a new light and be willing to have it.

Willingness and Values

Willingness is not encouraged in a vacuum. The context is critical. Discomfort and pain are not ends in themselves, and ACT is not a sadistic/masochistic endeavor. ACT therapists don't go to the dentist and say, "No Novocain for me, thanks. Who needs the stuff?"

Values dignify the willingness to have aversive situations. Willingness without values can lead to self-imposed hardship. Yet valuing without willingness is naive and short-lived. If you aren't willing to have obstacles, challenges, and barriers, it is highly unlikely that you're moving in a vital direction with life. Challenges are always bound to appear, and a willingness to have barriers paradoxically allows value-directed living.

■ Case Study: Low Motivation

Consider Calvin, a freshman in college who is plagued by thoughts of worthlessness. He reports being unwilling to go to classes and social functions because of these thoughts. Now this is where case conceptualization takes careful attention. One could attempt to defuse the thoughts of worthlessness and reason giving in order to increase willingness, which might be a worthwhile approach—as long as a functional analysis was done. The therapist needs to ask, "What are his evaluations and avoidant responses a function of?" There are many possible influences on his thinking: It could be that Calvin is avoidant in college because of a measurable skills deficit, or perhaps he has no personal motivation for success in college. Perhaps he has weak motivational operations (MOs) to support studying and fraternizing with college kids. The therapist might revisit with him why he "laced up" for college in the first place.

Calvin completed a values assessment in therapy, and the therapist discovered that he has a deep desire to start his own entrepreneurial endeavors. His attempt at college happened because he was following rules that said to go to college, rules set out by his parents and guidance counselors; he doesn't value this direction. Thankfully the therapist did a good assessment and did not go right for defusing his thoughts of worthlessness.

The values work (chapters 8 and 12) is critical for the case conceptualization in the willingness realm. If Calvin is at college to fulfill his parent's wishes at the sacrifice of his own values, he might easily be plagued with thoughts of worthlessness, as he is a stranger in a strange land. So consider this as you conceptualize the case of Calvin: is it better to help him defuse from thoughts such as "I am worthless" and "I don't fit in at college" in the service of helping him fit in at college, or is it more useful to defuse from "I have to please my parents" and "I need to get a college degree to be successful" in the service of following his values?

Willingness and Committed Action

Willingness in the ACT context is about behaving with value-directed purpose in the face of psychological obstacles. One exercise for contacting barriers and willingness is to join the client in the Eye Contact Exercise (Hayes et al., 1999, pp. 244–245).

Client Exercise: Eye Contact

In this exercise, the therapist sits directly across from the client, almost knee to knee, and says, "For the next few minutes, let's make eye contact and be fully present with one another in silence." While beginning to make eye contact, the therapist points out how difficult this exercise is, and might notice what the client does in the service of avoiding being fully present. For example, perhaps the client starts looking away, wringing her hands, laughing or suppressing a laugh, talking, and so on. The therapist can say, "Notice how difficult it is to be fully present with another human being. And are you willing to be present with me and with your discomfort?" After a couple of minutes, the therapist might break the silence and say something like "Notice how incredible it is that you are present with another human being, and that another human being is present with you." The therapist then debriefs by asking the client about her experience. The therapist also points out that even being present with another person for three minutes brings up barriers to committed action and that the client was willing to have those barriers. This is similar to how the client will experience all barriers to committed action. Clients often feel discomfort, but they can still choose to have that discomfort and be present and act.

The point of the exercise is not to feel discomfort for its own sake. Nor is the purpose to desensitize the client to anxiety. (In fact, many therapists continue to feel their own discomfort while doing this exercise even after years of practice.) This stance reframes traditional behavior therapy exposure treatments. The data are clear that in vivo exposure is a worthy intervention for anxiety disorders (Barlow, Raffa, & Cohen, 2002; Dougherty, Rauch, & Jenike, 2002), and the prevailing goals of exposure therapies are to reduce symptom dimensions. Many behavior therapists aim to reduce the client's subjective units of distress scale (SUDS) as a dependent measure in office-based treatment. This is to be expected, as the therapy is informed by the culture's typical eliminative agenda.

The concern here is that symptom reduction as a main treatment goal can actually give power to the private emotional and cognitive events. They are assessed as something to reduce rather than to have. As seen in earlier chapters, some private events are difficult to get rid of and can become much like a tar baby—the more you try to flick it off and get rid of it, the more you realize how tenaciously it stays despite your efforts. It's the verbal evaluation of these natural physical and emotional events that makes them clinically relevant. The agenda of eliminating private events can give these events greater aversiveness; they are something to be gotten rid of.

ACT also employs exposure methods, and the subjective distress measures may decline; that, however, is not the primary objective. Eifert and Forsyth (2005) explain that "exposure exercises within ACT are framed in the service of fostering greater psychological flexibility, experiential willingness, and openness. They are about growth and are always done in the service of client values and goals" (p. 82). They go on to mention, as we noted earlier, how exposure methods aim to have the client learn to "*feel* better (i.e., become better at feeling), not to feel *better* (i.e., feel less anxiety)" (p. 82, emphasis in original). The authors also reframe exposure as exercises to broaden the client's repertoires and to redefine the approach by calling them FEEL (feeling experiences enriches living) exercises:

- Feeling

- Experiences

- Enriches

- Living

Consider the possibility that the exposure treatments that have worked based on first- and second-wave eliminative case conceptualizations worked not only because of the extinction process related to frequent presentation of the conditioned stimulus and also the greater degree of reinforcement for braver and braver responses; perhaps they also worked because of the development of a broader repertoire in contexts that previously narrowed the response classes. Of course, the traditional behavior therapy principles are in play, and when a human being is put into this situation, the therapist can also capitalize on his verbal abilities and relational conditioning principles in addition to classical and operant conditioning principles. A values-based intervention embraces a therapeutic move toward breadth of experience rather than the removal of a circumscribed obstacle. The two case examples below illustrate the use of values-based interventions.

■ Case Study: Fear of Contamination

To illustrate the FEEL (feeling experiences enriches living) approach, take Martin as an example of a client with contamination OCD. His ACT therapist conceptualized the exposure and ritual prevention treatment in the service of broadening his willingness to participate recreationally and socially in public places. He wanted his life to be about becoming worldly with an understanding of other cultures and spending time interacting with other people. Martin also reported fear of contamination, and so he did not travel because he would have to use public lavatories and eat in restaurants. He also avoided shaking hands. The exposure procedure is fairly obvious: he would eat in public, and meet strangers and shake their hands. The treatment plan also included touching doorknobs in public places and using public toilets. The exposure design here is values based rather than eliminative. The clinical concern is conceptualized as "How can Martin's typically narrow repertoire be expanded? What can he do more of in service of his desired life consequences?" The aim is not to drive down the frequency of aversive obsessions. The exposure is not to get rid of the compulsions. When he uses a public restroom urinal in the presence of previously influential thought content, such as "I will get AIDS from touching things in a men's room," and is doing so to expand his repertoire of behavioral flexibility, he is showing willingness. He can touch the toilet in the presence of an elevated heart rate and nauseated feelings, and also just notice his private verbal rules about avoiding contamination.

Martin can be assisted in getting to this point in therapy through getting present in the current moment, noticing the self as perspective and not content, accepting bodily sensations, and defusing from verbal content. With the valued purpose of being able to contact all that life hands him, including the urinal in this FEEL exercise, he may begin to expand his repertoire in the service of being able to expose himself to other noxious stimuli. Martin is willing to touch the urinal (CS) even though it previously participated in a frame of coordination with "disgusting" or "contaminated," and those words are likely to have aversive functions. The traditional behavior therapy principles and process are certainly contributing to his improvement, and influencing his relational conditioning is moving him toward worthy therapeutic goals as well.

■ Case Study: Guilty Feelings

Nelson is a Native American man dealing with the aftermath of having committed a series of serious sexual criminal offenses on his reservation. He has become entangled with the courts, has lost his job, and has been ostracized from his family and his tribe. He said that his sexual assault rampage was significantly influenced by heavy alcohol use and his intense interest in prurient pornography. Nelson chose to go to therapy; it was not court mandated. Through his work with ACT, Nelson began to foster a willingness to accept his urges for alcohol and pornography, and to defuse from his negative self-talk, which often spiraled him into depression. In therapy, he clarified his values about family, intimacy, citizenship, and vocational pursuits. He committed to stop drinking. He also began to rebuild his relationship with his long-time partner, who was hurt in many ways by his criminal actions. These gains were facilitated by in-therapy discussions and mindfulness practice.

A therapeutic sticking point centered on his feelings of guilt. The meetings with court and tribal officials and loss of social contacts, including immediate family, not to mention many other specific reminders about his criminal behavior, all served as constant reminders that he was guilty of a heinous crime. But also important, these all exacerbated his feelings of guilt. Nelson evaluated the feelings of guilt in this conversation with his therapist in which the Heavy Computer Bag Exercise is used:

Nelson:	How long do I have to feel guilty? I'm tired of feeling guilty for all this. [Despite his willingness in other areas, the repertoire of acceptance had not generalized to his guilt feelings.]
Therapist:	How are you going to get rid of it?
Nelson:	Well, I can tell myself I've got nothing to be guilty about … [silence from therapist, seeing if the change agenda would become apparent]
Nelson:	Uh … but as soon as I tell myself not to feel guilty, I'll probably think of that night and feel guilty again… (pause) And hell, even if I did succeed at talking myself out of not feeling guilty … I'm bound to see that as a justification for going back to the porn. Like … not feeling guilty … like … that's not really the goal here, huh?
Therapist:	What could you do to help you not feel guilty?
Nelson:	Get the fuck out of here. Just … just fuckin' go.
Therapist:	That's really going "off the reservation," huh?
Nelson:	(smiling wryly) You think you're funny. Nah, man. I just don't want this shit.
Therapist:	How are you going to get rid of it?
Nelson:	No, I know. I'm not. You mean it's like the depression [referring to a therapy session from the previous week]. It's natural for me to feel guilty, so have it … that bit. Yeah? But … [recognizing the "but" convention] oh, wait … and this guilt is heavy, man.
Therapist:	And it's heavy. Like you're going to have it, and it is also heavy for you. Heavy like this thing? [pointing to a very large laptop case and picking it up by the shoulder strap] Heavy like this? Look how heavy you can make this bag. Let's say the last thing I want is this bag anywhere near me,

and that there was nothing I could do but carry the bag, 'cuz, well, there are certain things in life that come with you wherever you go. Now I gotta carry this bag, and I want to keep it away from me. In fact, I don't even want to look at it. [Therapist awkwardly lifts the heavy bag with an extended straight arm as far out to the side as possible. Therapist takes a few steps while continuing.] So now I gotta live life like this. (sarcastically) That's pleasant. I'll really get life going like this, huh?

Nelson: (sarcastically) Uh, yeah.

Therapist: Okay, so what do I gotta do to approach life as fully as possible?

Nelson: Use the shoulder strap.

Therapist: [slides strap over head] Bingo! [claps hands and puts them out front in a ready position] Look at me now, man—walking around hands free, able to take on what comes my way, and to make things happen. But oops—I got this thing close to me. I don't want it near me. But when I let go of that thought, that evaluation, that "badness," and I have it—I let myself come in contact with it—man, it is not nearly as heavy when I just strap it on. Just have it.

Nelson: (chuckles, attempts to get off topic for a few minutes) …

Therapist: [The therapist redirects.] Okay, so about the heaviness of the guilt. What's up with that? What did that say to you?

Nelson: Well, yeah. Like … it's like … the porn. I escape my guilty feelings and depression by getting into the porn. It's like intoxicating. When I am looking at porn, I am not focused on me … and I have done a good bit of boozing in the name of escaping my guilt too. If I am drunk, I am keeping the guilt at arm's length … which usually just ends up with me doing something while drunk to be guilty of the next morning.

Therapist: If you're not willing to have it…

Nelson: I know … I've got it.

Therapist: And Nelson, there's a bit more here. Why do you want to get rid of this guilty feeling?

Nelson: It just feels bad.

Therapist: [silence, seeing if client notices the evaluation] You mean like, it is bad. Like "Bad Music"?

This metaphor reprise was particularly apropos because Nelson is a professional musician, and a version of the Bad Chair Metaphor making use of music was used in a previous session. We'll return to Nelson's case after discussing this metaphor.

Bad Music Metaphor. When someone calls something "bad," that person might actually treat that object as if it had natural, directly conditioned aversive properties. This might be helpful at times, but what if the evaluation of "bad" is completely verbal?

Some people say some types of music are "bad," but those same types of music aren't "bad" to some other people. You may despise country-and-western music, classical music, or heavy metal music, but we assure you, there are thousands of people who will extol the virtues of heavy metal music, the inherent greatness of classical compositions, and maybe even a tiny handful of country-and-western fans who can actually find it passably tolerable. All kidding aside, a person can call music good or bad, but if that music is still playing when that person leaves the room, the "badness" of that music does not remain—it leaves when the person leaves. It is a quality of the interaction the person has with the music.

Badness is an evaluation. This can be seen similarly in the Bad Cup Metaphor (Hayes et al., 1999, p. 168) and the Bad Chair Metaphor from chapter 13. The "badness" of anything leaves when the evaluator leaves. Let's return to Nelson's progress:

Nelson: Ain't no such thing as bad music.

Therapist: Okay, so … can you have "This feels bad" and notice that feeling without trying to get rid of it? Have that feeling for what it is and not for what you evaluate it to be? Of course, you are going to think, "This feels bad." You've had a lifetime of evaluating things—and sometimes evaluation is a great thing, and sometimes it's not. Here, I wonder. Where is buying this evaluation, "It feels bad," going to take you?

Nelson: Heh. It's taking me off this reservation … and that's not really what I want. So you're not saying that I need to let myself feel *bad*; you're asking me to let myself *feel* … just feel. Like … like *feel* the feeling.

Therapist: Well, I am not asking you to do that … life is. What is your alternative?

Note that one of the most validating aspects of the Heavy Computer Bag Exercise (which can also be done as the Ball and Chain Exercise by referring to what the client struggles with as a ball and chain rather than a computer bag) is that the clinician can point out that the client does in fact have a heavy load to carry. Nelson has a lot of difficult situations to deal with in his life. The therapist is not suggesting that by holding those legal and social problems close the client's burden will become weightless. The therapist is suggesting that the burden will be easier to carry than when he buys into the verbal relational context that they are burdensome, leading to an avoidance of these events.

Assessing Willingness in Case Conceptualization

When developing the case conceptualization using the inflexahex model, be on the lookout for the FEAR (fusion, evaluation, avoidance, reason giving) processes as they relate to clinical concerns, and assess how the FEEL (feeling experiences enriches living) approach can help. (One pithy way of conceptualizing ACT is an aim to FEEL the FEAR.) Let's take a look at Martin's struggles with the FEAR approach.

Fusion

Fusion is evident when Martin responds to the words "I will get AIDS from touching things in a men's room." It is clear this statement influences his avoidance of public wash-rooms, and it would be prudent to write this on the Inflexahex Case-Conceptualization Worksheet. Part of Martin's clinical concern is that he is fused with unhelpful and distorted rules about community living and communicable disease. It's not that having the thought is dangerous or problematic; it isn't even problematic that he occasionally gets fused to content. The concern is the fusion to that problematic content. It reduces flexibility, as can occasionally happen with fusion, and it interferes with valued living for Martin, as can happen with distortions.

Evaluation

Evaluation can also interfere with important willingness moves. Putting an evaluation on the naturally occurring emotions, urges, or bodily states changes how readily someone will contact that event. The difficulty catching one's breath during an anxiety attack can be evaluated as bad, terrible, and horrible. The physical symptom (cardiovascular stress) is put in a relational frame with a verbal event, "bad," which is in a frame with aversive events. The verbal appraisal of the anxiety state now makes that physical event something to escape from or avoid, and not something one is willing to have. And here is an ironic twist: difficulty catching one's breath is actually pursued and called "good" by some people. In fact, every morning thousands of people do aerobic exercise that leads to a similar experience. The evaluation of such private events in given contexts, and subsequent fusion to those evaluations, makes it difficult to be willing to have those private events.

Avoidance

Avoidance is an underlying theme of this chapter, and when using the FEAR magnifying glass to look for willingness, experiential avoidance is obviously an absence of willingness. However, avoidance may not always be obvious. During the conceptualization, make sure to assess for willingness in the service of avoidance. Listen for clues during the FEAR assessment that the client is willing to have certain content as long as that means the content will eventually go away. In Martin's case, he initially asked, "If

I am willing to think about germs, then does that mean that I won't be contaminated?" That is the opposite of willingness. Pema Chödrön (2001) relates a neat story about a monk whose house is invaded by demons. Needless to say, the monk is bummed out at first, and then, in monklike fashion, invites them to stay and starts teaching them compassion. Of course, most of the demons leave. Except one. That one saw a loophole in the monk's "willingness in the service of getting rid of" routine. The monk was now in a position to really have to live with this one, and he did so fully and without defense as he put himself in the mouth of the demon and said, "Go ahead and eat me up." And with that final and true act of willingness, the demon spit him out and left. Willingness needs to be fully embraced and not fraught with underlying avoidance.

Reason Giving

Reason giving can present evidence of unwillingness when the context is explaining behavior as caused by private events. For example, Martin says that he avoids using public restrooms so he will not have to feel disgusted. Shandra explains that she gives her children money to allay her guilt, and Rick says that he smokes pot so that he doesn't feel like a loser. All three—Martin, Shandra, and Rick—are reason giving. They are justifying their clinically relevant behavior based on their thoughts and feelings. The explanations seem ingenuous, yet they are incomplete and distorted. They engage in problematic behavior because of various environmental influences, the reason giving being fairly impotent in comparison. The important consideration is that when the clinician hears the client justifying certain clinically relevant actions, there is likely an unwillingness to have certain private content. The FEAR acronym suggests a way of looking at this set of verbal responses in order to detect unwillingness. The FEEL acronym helps develop the treatment plan so that the client can feel experiences in order to enrich living.

Skating Away

Consider the roller-skating girl again. She isn't likely fused to evaluative content, isn't avoiding, and isn't giving her reasons for avoiding. She has no FEAR, so to speak. She's willing to skate, and her willingness participates in the global, values-based agenda of living life to the fullest. What would the ACT therapist do with the nonskating girl? Her avoidance is obvious, and we're sure you can imagine that her verbal reports would be fraught with fused content evaluating the downside to skating and the reasons she isn't on the rink. Suffice it to say, that if there was an ACT-oriented roller-skating coach, she would use direct skills training and contingency management to teach the girl to skate, and she would certainly use defusion, acceptance, and value-directed motivation to support the girl when private obstacles threw her off balance.

We're all reared in environments that give us tools to solve certain problems. When there are dust bunnies on our carpet, we aim to eliminate them with a vacuum. When we needed to get across a river, we learned how to swim, build boats, and eventually build bridges. When we needed to eliminate debt for all the costs of maintaining the bridges, we invented tollbooths. In many ways, our language helps us arrive at eliminative solutions for many aversive situations.

Problem solving becomes a fluent behavior. The problem solving is available quickly and in many situations. And sometimes we are faced with aversive states that are private. As we said before, when your only tool is a hammer, everything begins to look like a nail. When a private event arises, we begin to "solve" the "problem" with an elimination agenda: Get the vacuum cleaner! Build a bridge! In emotional situations, a person might feel angry and then want to punch someone to justify or reduce the anger. During times of depression, a person can sleep all day or "drink to forget." The fretful person with anxious thoughts can try to think of something else. Will these eliminative external strategies work to solve these internal problems? Why not?

For the angry person whose hitting is well reinforced, his urge can become more frequent, seeing that hitting "works" so well in removing people that anger him. The alcoholic person might feel bad about sleeping or drinking, so he'll go back to sleep or get drunk so he doesn't feel bad for a little while. The anxious person can't think of another thing for long—and just by virtue of testing whether or not her change agenda is working, she asks, "Am I thinking about X anymore?" And she is! So the "solution" is part of the problem here.

Stance of the Therapist

Sometimes the client needs to realize the automaticity of verbal events, and sometimes it is the clinician who needs reminding. Language makes us such good problem solvers, and some solutions are impossible, exacerbate the problem, or are downright against our values. What could a client say that would be "too much" for you to deal with?

Consider the experience of parents who learn that their child is disabled: when parents receive the news that their child has been diagnosed with a developmental disorder, many automatically go into problem-solving mode. The problem solving might be eliminative, such as "How can we get rid of this disability?" and "Is there a cure?" This is a natural reaction. In this situation, some parents actually wish for their own child's death (Price-Bonham & Addison, 1978), and this too is a natural reaction, as it comes from natural language processes. In many ways, this may be difficult for you to read; imagine how hard it is for the parents to experience these thoughts! Can you see the automaticity here? Actually, of course their mind thinks that. The mind is trained to eliminate problems.

As a therapist, can you develop the willingness to be present with clients who have those thoughts? Can you be present and compassionate with your client when an eliminative agenda is brought into therapy? Your job as an ACT therapist is to teach your client to have that thought, see it for what it is, realize the power of the words, and help take the teeth out of its bite. Can you be willing to have your own evaluations and "solutions" and still be present with that other human being, who is swimming in the same soup?

CHAPTER 15

Acceptance and Change

Acceptance and change are alternatives to avoidance and control. Acceptance or change is a part of virtually every ACT intervention. Acceptance and change, at a glance, seem like opposites; one accepts circumstances or changes them. Yet for many clients, acceptance is a profound change, and acceptance functions as a context for change. In this chapter, we will focus on using acceptance and change strategies in clinical practice.

Control vs. Acceptance

It's an ACT tenet that "control is the problem, not the solution" (Hayes et al., 1999, p. 116). We are socialized to the idea that control works because it is effective in the domains of overt behavior. For instance, we can control the lighting in a dark room by flicking a switch and thereby avoid the punishment of walking into objects. Also, we are told from an early age that we should be able to control our feelings, as when a child is instructed, "Don't you get angry with me!" or "Wipe that smile off your face; this is not funny." When people grow up hearing these types of phrases, it may be hard to convince them that it is difficult to control private events. You do not have to convince your client only with verbal argument. You can create an experiential exercise by using humor and saying something like "Imagine I am holding a gun and pointing it at you and then I say, 'Stand up or I'll shoot.' You would be able to do it, right? And what if I said, 'Do not think about the gun I'm holding or I'll shoot' or 'Do not feel anxious about this gun or I'll shoot. Don't have an increased heart rate or I'll shoot.' Would you be able to control your perceptions, thoughts, and feelings?" (adapted from Hayes et al., 1999, Polygraph Metaphor, pp. 123–124). The use of metaphor as opposed to persuasion allows your client to experience the impossibility of controlling private events.

Control strategies are useful in behavior change and committed action. Making plans to increase and decrease habits, and setting up the environment so that the behavior change is supported can work very well. However, there are many situations in which control is not very useful:

- Control is not useful when the process of control contradicts the outcome—for example, when deliberately trying to suppress a thought.

- Control is not useful when the process is not rule governed. For example, while a dieter can control whether or not she eats sweets, she cannot control whether or not she likes sweets.

- Control is not useful when it leads to unhealthy forms of avoidance. For instance, a person might control panic attacks by remaining inside his home and consequentially will miss out on many opportunities for positive reinforcement.

- Control is not useful when the event is not changeable, such as when a divorcée refuses to accept that her ex-husband has remarried.

- Control is not useful when the change effort contradicts the goal of the change effort. For instance, if people want to feel more self-assurance or more humility, they are unlikely to attain those outcomes directly. Why? Because checking in to see if one feels self-assured is not an act of self-assurance, and noticing how humble one is, is not humility (Hayes et al., 1999, pp. 65–68).

Talking to Rick About Control and Acceptance

In practice there are many techniques for facilitating acceptance. In chapter 12, we saw Rick explore his guilt and ambivalence about visiting his mother at the nursing home. In addition to values work around visiting his mother, he also explored control and acceptance in relation to visiting his mother.

Rick: When I don't visit my mom, I feel bad because I know she's all alone. And she was pretty good to me. But when I visit, I feel bad because I'm thinking I'd rather be doing something else and what a drag the nursing home is. No matter what I do, I feel bad. And I can't even tell you the rest. I'm such an asshole.

Therapist: It's up to you, what you tell me.

Rick: Okay ... No matter what I do I feel bad ... I ... sometimes I ... I think if she would die and get it over with, then I wouldn't have to visit or not visit, and it would just be over with. (*softly, hanging his head*) I'm such an asshole.

Therapist: I can see you're really struggling with this. And I notice that in the midst of all this struggle, you are visiting your mother regularly. What shows up

	after you have the thought "If she would just die, then the struggle would end?"
Rick:	I shouldn't feel this bad about visiting my mom, and I shouldn't think those terrible things about her. And then I get mad at myself, really pissed off, like I want to hit something. And I get stoned so I can chill out.
Therapist:	Are you saying that you shouldn't feel bad?
Rick:	Yeah. Before I go, I tell myself that I should try to be in a good mood, you know, for her … because she's my mom.
Therapist:	And does it work?
Rick:	Nope. Never.
Therapist:	What if you can't control what you think and what you feel? And trying to control what you think and feel not only doesn't work, it also makes you think about and feel more the very things you are trying not to think and feel?
Rick:	That sucks. It means I'll always feel bad about Mom. And I'll always have those terrible thoughts.
Therapist:	And why wouldn't you feel bad about your mom? Who wouldn't feel bad about his mother being in a nursing home and having dementia so severe she doesn't even know her own son?
Rick:	Okay, I think I see what you're getting at. But that's no excuse for those terrible thoughts.
Therapist:	And what happens when you try not to think those "terrible thoughts," as you call them?
Rick:	I tell myself, "Quit thinking that. It's wrong."
Therapist:	And do you check in with yourself to see if you are having those thoughts?
Rick:	Yeah, I do that.
Therapist:	And what happens when you check in with yourself and ask yourself, "Rick, are you thinking about Mom dying?"
Rick:	I don't see what you're getting at.
Therapist:	What do you think about right after you check in with yourself, after you ask yourself, "Are you thinking about Mom dying?" What do you think about next?

Rick:	I think about Mom dying! And I feel like a piece of shit.
Therapist:	So trying not to feel bad doesn't work and trying not to think bad thoughts leads to thinking bad thoughts and feeling like a piece of shit.
Rick:	But isn't it wrong to think about my mom dying just so I don't have to visit her?
Therapist:	I don't know if it's right or wrong. And I ask you, not as a matter of right or wrong, and instead as a matter of looking at your own experience, does it work for you to try not to feel bad and to try not to think about your mom dying?
Rick:	I guess not… No. It doesn't work.

Rick, like many clients, was acting from the stance that the problem is bad thoughts and feelings, and that in order to solve the problem he has to get rid of those bad thoughts and feelings. Seeing negatively evaluated thoughts and feelings as something to be gotten rid of increases the sense of "badness" about them, and increased vigilance makes the client even more likely to pay a great deal of attention to the unwanted thoughts and feelings. This sort of process leads to the outcome that "if you're not willing to have it, you've got it."

Clean Discomfort and Dirty Discomfort

Here the clinician might introduce the client to the concept of clean versus dirty discomfort (Hayes et al., 1999, p. 136). The therapist might describe *clean discomfort* as the discomfort that shows up in the course of living life and having painful and unwanted experiences. Clean discomfort can't be gotten rid of by trying to control it, and some amount of clean discomfort is inevitable in any life. In contrast, *dirty discomfort* is the unwanted thoughts and feelings that show up as an outcome of trying to control clean discomfort. When our control agenda goes awry, we set the occasion to have dirty discomfort.

In Rick's case, he wanted to control feeling bad and control thoughts he evaluated as unacceptable. So, what is Rick's clean discomfort? What is Rick's dirty discomfort? We'll answer these questions in the next section.

Rick's Experience with Clean and Dirty Discomfort

In Rick's case, it would be surprising if he felt good when visiting his sick mother in a shabby nursing home. It's clean discomfort to feel bad when a loved one is ill and for an adult child to feel bad that his mother doesn't recognize him and that she must live in a relatively unpleasant environment in order to get adequate nursing care. The dirty discomfort arises when Rick tries to control his negatively evaluated thoughts. To some degree, Rick's bad feelings do not show that he doesn't love his mother; instead they are an outcome of his love for his mother. He feels bad as an outcome of caring about her. The therapeutic goal isn't that Rick feel good when he visits his mother or that he stop thinking about her death or think about it differently. From a functional contextual perspective, control works in the physical world with respect to overt behavior, and in the realm of thoughts and feelings, control is useless and even makes the problem worse (Hayes et al., 1999, pp. 123–124). The goal also isn't that Rick change his evaluation of his thoughts—for example, that he thinks it is okay to feel bad about her death or that he stops thinking, "I'm an asshole," after he thinks about his mother's death. The goal is that he experience the futility of trying to control his thoughts and feelings, that he experience that control is the problem and not the solution, and that perhaps he will be more willing to try acceptance. This is not a matter of logical reasoning to a conclusion; it's a matter of demonstrating that control doesn't work, and the evidence for that unworkability is in one's own experience. If Rick sees this, then he may be willing to have clean discomfort, to have his thoughts and feelings as they are and not as they say they are.

Client Exercise: Physicalizing

Once Rick was willing to abandon the agenda of controlling his unwanted thoughts, the therapist used the Physicalizing Exercise to facilitate defusion and acceptance (Hayes et al., 1999, pp. 170–171). Clients can also use this exercise on their own as a type of defusion or willingness practice.

Therapist: Close your eyes, get comfortable, and see if you can be present with that thought you have about your mother, the thought that if she died it would all be over and your struggles would end.

Rick: (*pained*) Okay, I'm noticing that thought.

Therapist: Imagine that you could put that thought out in front of you and look at it. Can you see it sitting in front of you?

Rick: Sort of…

Therapist: If that thought had a color, what color would it be?

Rick: It's really dark … black.

Therapist: Good. Can you give it a form or shape?

Rick: It's just dark and big; it fills the whole room.

Therapist: Okay. Does it have a texture or feel to it?

Rick:	It's heavy, like when it's really humid and muggy outside.
Therapist:	Now look at it—the thought that "if she would just die and get it over with, then I wouldn't have to visit anymore and my bad feelings would go away." Look at that large black, heavy, cloying mass filling up the room. Are you looking at it?
Rick:	Yeah, I can see it.
Therapist:	Now, I want you to imagine picking up that mass and setting it to one side. Can you do that, can you set it aside in your mind's eye?
Rick:	Okay.
Therapist:	Now that you've set aside that thought, what thought or feeling shows up next?
Rick:	I feel angry! Really pissed!
Therapist:	Okay, now I want you to set that anger out in front of you and notice what it looks like.
Rick:	It's red.
Therapist:	What else?
Rick:	It's red and it's got white spots like when you have spots in front of your eyes... It's like it's zipping around all over the room. It doesn't sit still.
Therapist:	Anything else?
Rick:	It's hot, like it's sizzling.
Therapist:	Can you take that anger, that red-hot thing that's zipping around the room, can you, in your mind's eye, pick it up and set it off to the side?
Rick:	Okay … I feel something … big and I don't want it.
Therapist:	Are you willing to look at what shows up when you set the anger aside.
Rick:	(*tearfully*) I don't want her to die. I don't want my mom to die. She doesn't even know who I am. She's gonna die and I can't even tell her that I love her.

When Rick was willing to be present with unwanted thoughts and feelings, he was able to make contact with other thoughts and feelings that he had been avoiding even more strongly than anger and thoughts about his mother dying. Physicalizing can be useful because it is experiential in a way that talking about thoughts and feelings is not. It brings the feelings and thoughts into the room, while mere talk about thoughts and feelings can be misused to keep them abstract and distant. Although some clients find it difficult to visualize thoughts and feelings, it can be a useful exercise with those who are willing to try. In Rick's case, the exercise enabled him to contact painful and tender feelings about his mother's death, which ultimately led to a reduction in his sense of "badness" about his thoughts.

Acceptance and Pseudo-acceptance

While changing clients' evaluation of their thoughts is not a goal of acceptance, it is often an outcome of acceptance. However, there is an important caution. Clients' negatively evaluated thoughts and feelings may decrease as they give up control and begin practicing acceptance, yet this is not always the case. Often they continue to have panic attacks, urges to drink, obsessive thoughts, and so on. It's fine if unwanted content decreases in frequency. Yet an occasional side effect of early success with acceptance is that it puts the client at risk for pseudo-acceptance. When clients believe that accepting a feeling will make it go away and they practice, say, accepting anxiety in the service of decreasing anxiety, then this is not acceptance at all, and it will not work. The clinician should be on the lookout for this.

Avoidance and control can be misperceived as strategies for decreasing unpleasant, unwanted private events. Sometimes avoidance succeeds in the short run—for instance, a person with social anxiety who stays home from a party will probably feel less anxiety than if she went to the party. A few shots of vodka may also temporarily reduce anxiety. Staying in bed may feel better than going to work.

Who are we to say that avoidance is bad? Verbally convincing a client that control doesn't work is not often an effective way to promote acceptance. As clinicians, the most effective way to facilitate acceptance is to point to clients' own experience. If they are in treatment, they are most likely experiencing the futility of control. In some cases, the control is not working and the client is having unwanted thoughts and feelings in spite of control strategies. In other situations, the control strategy is working in the service of controlling some thoughts and feelings while simultaneously leading to negative consequences in other life domains, or the client is avoiding some feelings while missing out on opportunities for positive reinforcement and is left feeling numb and empty. There's little need to use verbal persuasion; the client's experience is the best yardstick for measuring the success of control and avoidance strategies.

Acceptance and the Clinician

Acceptance is a process for the clinician as much as for the client. Clinicians who do not accept their own thoughts and feelings in session are likely to be less effective and will also be poor at modeling flexibility. Also, clinician acceptance can be beneficial to the client as modeled behavior. We might have titled this section "ACT in Practice in Practice."

Therapist Nonacceptance

It's not unusual for therapists to have thoughts and feelings in response to client behaviors. Some of these thoughts may have content that the therapist evaluates negatively.

■ Case Study: The Judgmental Intern

A therapy intern, Alan, reported in supervision that he felt disgusted by his client because the client, diagnosed with substance dependence and bipolar disorder, had poor hygiene and smelled bad. Alan thought the client was lazy because he did not complete his homework or lost the assignments. He also believed the client was not trying hard and could get better if he wanted to. Supervision might focus on psychoeducation—for instance, how homelessness rather than laziness might contribute to the client's difficulties with hygiene and homework, and perhaps provide reading on bipolar disorder and substance abuse. This type of approach might lead to change in the intern's beliefs about his client and perhaps to increased empathy; this approach emphasizes changing the thought content of the intern.

In this supervision case with Alan, the supervisor combined psychoeducation with an ACT approach. When the readings were assigned, the supervisor said, "These readings might change your thinking, and since you have been trained in ACT, I don't have to tell you that thoughts show up in contexts where they show up. We can't always control our thoughts, so even if your thoughts change, those old thoughts can still show up in certain contexts." The supervisor also asked Alan what happened when he had these thoughts. Alan reported that he felt angry with the client for not trying and that he feared he would be negatively evaluated by other clinicians at his work site because his client was not getting better. Alan also noted that when he got caught up in his angry feelings, he didn't listen as well and lost track of his goals for the session. The supervisor suggested Alan use ACT practices in relation to his own behavior: notice his thoughts and perhaps use the strategy of saying, "I'm having the thought that my client is lazy" or "I'm having the thought that I will get a poor evaluation" or "I am feeling angry with my client."

The supervisor also recommended that the intern begin doing regular mindfulness practice himself. The outcome for this trainee is instructive. Alan reported that as he noticed and accepted his thoughts during the sessions with his client, he found it easier to stay focused on the client and he was less fused with his own thought content about his client. He also reported that he tried to practice mindfulness daily and that he wasn't succeeding. In fact, he was not doing any mindfulness practice on most days. And he said, "It maybe didn't make me more mindful, and it made me see that we ask a lot of our clients. Why should I be upset with my client for not doing his homework when I can't do my own homework?" Finally, in one session when the client shared that he felt like a failure because he wasn't getting better, Alan shared with the client his own thoughts and fears about failing and they had a productive session on defusion and accepting evaluations as mere evaluations. Alan told the supervisor that he thought it was a serendipitous coincidence that the client would bring up unwanted thoughts of failure just as Alan himself was working on his own struggle with thoughts of failure. He was quite surprised when his supervisor referred him to audiotapes of prior sessions in which the client had referred to his thoughts about failing several times. Alan's own increased self-awareness enabled him to become more aware of his client's struggles too.

Alan's case may seem extreme, yet it's not so unusual. When we're fused with our own thoughts, it is much more difficult to be fully present with our client. As a result, we may miss much content that could be important to adequate case conceptualization, or we may fail to connect with our clients in ways that enable them to feel our presence and our alliance with them.

While the case of Alan illustrates one potential therapist problem with acceptance, another type of problem occurs when a therapist has a negative thought about a client, and while she doesn't buy the thought content, she negatively evaluates herself for having the thought and trying to control it. Take, for example, a therapist who has thoughts such as "I don't want to see this awful borderline client!" or "Substance abusers lack self-control" or "This client is such a baby—I wish she'd just get it together," and then tries not to think the thought because she knows that it's "bad" to have such "politically incorrect" thoughts about her clients. Research on using acceptance and commitment training with clinicians (Hayes, Bissett, et al., 2004) suggests that it is not at all uncommon for clinicians to have negative thoughts about their clients. Further, clinicians who practiced defusion and acceptance with respect to their own negatively evaluated thoughts reported higher job satisfaction and less burnout as compared to clinicians who tried to change their thought content. The lesson here is that what's good for the client is good for the clinician.

One of the themes of ACT is that we are not all that different from our clients. As verbal human beings living in the same culture as our clients, we are subject to the same verbal and social processes that support fusion and avoidance. It may feel disempowering to give up the notion of a strong, organized therapist treating a weak, confused client. In our experience, the ACT stance of radical respect and equality between therapist and client begins with radical self-acceptance. Whether you notice it or not, the client experiences your stance.

Therapist Exercise: Acceptance vs. Control and Avoidance

Consider a problem you have struggled with. Now write down all the strategies you have used to solve the problem. Brainstorm—think of everything you have tried. Make a note about how well each strategy worked.

Now look at your list of strategies and note any that might be avoidance or control strategies. How effective are the avoidance and control strategies as compared to other strategies?

Sample: Problem is being disorganized.

Solution: Use a different organization system.

Did solution work? No, new system is disorganized.

[Notice how the new solution was avoidant. The person is trying to *feel* less disorganized instead of actually being less disorganized.]

Another solution: Read self-help books.

Did solution work? Yes and no, some strategies useful.

[Notice a partially avoidant strategy. The person chose reading a book about organizing instead of actually organizing her office.]

Another solution: Consulted with efficiency expert.

Did solution work? Yes, she had some great ideas that worked.

[Notice that this was not avoidant because work was actually executed.]

Another solution: Committed to clearing desk every day.

Did solution work? Yes and no, it worked for a while and then instead of truly clearing the desk, I merely put stuff on top of the desk into the desk, so I guess it only looked like it was working.

[Notice that this was sometimes avoidant, and there is also a commitment to continue practicing organization.]

Now, one by one, go through each of your control or avoidance strategies and see if you can use an acceptance strategy in its place.

Modeling Acceptance

The therapist may use acceptance and defusion and all other ACT processes in order to remove barriers to being an empathic and effective therapist. And that's not the only way in which practicing ACT may benefit the clinician. Using ACT processes yourself provides opportunities to model ACT processes in session. For example, when feeling anxious or distracted, you can remark on these events in a way that models an acceptance of them and defusion from them. Don't be afraid to say, "Wow, that silence felt uncomfortable!" or "I'm sorry, I got distracted for a moment. Could you repeat that?" or "I struggle with the same thing at times. It's impossible to be mindful all the time." Or, after getting off track, you might say, "I almost bought that thought too! Let's back up" or "Well, that wasn't very effective was it?" Although we may fear that we will look incompetent when we acknowledge shortcomings and mistakes, clients are likely to experience our confessions as refreshing and therapeutic. Good modeling is good relationship building.

CHAPTER 16

Pulling It All Together

We've been describing the ACT processes separately as if each stands alone. In practice, the processes are not so neatly distinguished. A single exercise might involve acceptance, defusion, committed action, and willingness. Also, the processes are not linear. Instead of moving from one process to another, therapy moves back and forth among the core processes. In this chapter, we will explore what treatment looks like when all the processes are considered together.

Where to Start

Get present. Get present with the other human being in the room with you—the person who is more similar to you than different from you.

Get present. Get present with your own humanity that goes everywhere you go, even in the therapy room.

Get present. Get present with life, the environment, and the human condition as it is in the room with you and your client at this moment here and now.

As you consider where to begin therapy, look the person in the eye. See that this person knows suffering and joy—and that this person is just like you. Greet that person with compassion and connect with warmth. Note what Rogers (1961) teaches:

> I have found that the very feeling which has seemed to me most private, most personal and hence most incomprehensible by others, has turned out to be an expression for which there is a resonance in many other people. It has led me to believe that what is most personal and unique in each one of us is probably the very element which would, if it were shared or expressed, speak most deeply to others. (p. 26)

Listen closely with care and kindness, and recall Jung's teaching: "Learn your theories as well as you can, but put them aside when you touch the miracle of the living soul" (Jung, Baynes, & Baynes, 1928, p. 4).

Getting Practical

The ACT therapist's dedication to reducing suffering comes from a tradition that is dedicated to improving life for all of humankind. It also comes from a tradition firmly rooted in scientific principles. A great deal of research needs to be done to get a better sense of precisely how to initiate ACT therapy. However, research and clinical experience have shown that proper assessment is an important initial step in therapy (Hayes et al., 1987; Haynes & O'Brien, 2000), and that comprehensive assessment can be therapeutic (Clees, 1994; Rothbaum, 1992). Connecting with the client, rapport building, psychological assessment, and functional analysis comprise much of the first few sessions, and they are ongoing processes. The understanding that "we're all in the same soup," that suffering is ubiquitous for all of us, and that the struggle with normal language processes influences this suffering will position you to truly interact with the person sitting in the room with you.

Clients will present with different concerns, and it would be wonderful to have clear instructions on where to begin; yet it would be inconsistent with ACT for us to say, "Start here." At the same time, it's ACT inconsistent to throw worthwhile verbal rules right out the window. The aim in ACT is psychological flexibility, and this is true for the therapist as well as for the client. With that in mind, we offer a few general guidelines—but always with the caveat that each client is unique. There are as many variables that influence the decision for where to start as there are clients. Two general considerations are these:

- Look for experiential avoidance and how it is presented.

- Consider the value-directed motivation of the client to change.

Starting with Creative Hopelessness

For a client electing to come to therapy and prepared to make a change in his life, creative hopelessness can be a fine way to start therapy. Because the client is motivated to enter therapy, he is prepared to talk about what he has tried in order to change his behavior and to discuss more fully the influences on his suffering. He likely has a purpose, a verbal plan for a future outcome, and the clinician's guidance toward that end can reinforce the development and execution of further purposeful, value-directed behavior. Of course, values work will become a part of the therapy; it's just that the motivation that comes along with values work does not have to be foremost at this point. The client's values may still be poorly integrated and unclear to him at the beginning of therapy, so don't misunderstand—we're only talking about where to start because addressing all points of the hexaflex is difficult to accomplish in one session, especially the first one.

The model of suffering. Clients with high treatment motivation are often motivated by their own suffering. They come to treatment because they are in distress, either the subjective distress of unwanted thoughts and feelings or distress secondary to the consequences of their own behavior, such as failed relationships and work. Clients with this sort of presentation are likely to find creative hopelessness as well as acceptance and defusion work to be a useful beginning.

Values work. ACT work is incomplete without assisting in values work, and for a client in this context, this work can often usefully commence after the exercises in creative hopelessness, defusion, acceptance, and mindfulness. In this situation, as obstacles to acceptance and defusion arise, the subsequent values orientation can dignify that difficult work. Hold this advice lightly as a therapist, and consider that the client's willingness and receptivity to other ACT approaches is likely to be higher when the client chooses to come to therapy.

After the client is less fused with his thoughts and feelings and has a more accepting stance toward private events, he may be prepared to work on perspective taking, values, and committed action. Since the six processes are inseparable, to some extent work on defusion and acceptance is committed action and facilitates perspective taking and values clarification.

Starting with Values and Committed Action

Although the ideal treatment candidate may be one with high treatment motivation, many of us see clients with low treatment motivation. Involuntary clients in inpatient settings are one example of clients who often have low treatment motivation. Some clients are ordered to treatment by the legal system, employers, social services agencies, or frustrated significant others who say, "Go to treatment or else." For example, clients with substance-use disorders, chronic pain, or anger management problems are often referred by others and may feel forced or coerced into treatment. Adolescents are usually not self-referred and may display little interest in participating in treatment. In couples and family therapy, often only one of the clients in the dyad or family has high treatment motivation. In these sorts of cases, it may be useful to begin by considering values and committed action (Bach et al., 2005).

Motivational Interviewing

Motivational interviewing is one approach that can be used for increasing clients' motivation for treatment begins with considering the clients' stage of readiness for change and uses various strategies to enhance motivation for change (Miller & Rollnick, 2002). ACT work on values may be regarded as a way to increase motivation for change, and, in another sense, values work *is* change.

Imagine starting with creative hopelessness when the client is not interested in therapy. A client involved in court-mandated therapy or coming to treatment under duress is not likely to play along when invited to think about her "problems" from the perspective of acceptance metaphors. Trying to metaphorically discuss clinical concerns as if they were like wearing Chinese finger cuffs might actually be like wearing those finger cuffs for the clinician. The new ways of thinking might be rejected by the client not only on their form but also because of their function. If the client isn't interested in therapy, how much success will the therapist have with the Lemonlemonlemon Exercise? The client is unwilling in more ways than one, and working on making the client more willing is likely to be perceived as old hat.

Values work as a motivator. Leading with values-directed work may loosen the difficult situation. The personal relevance of values, a focus on what the client wants rather than what those who have "forced" her into treatment want, may be an invitation to begin working together. "What do you want your life to be about?" may more effectively motivate conversation for the involuntary or "semivoluntary" client than will discussing how suffering needs to be accepted and distressing cognitions need to be defused from. Orienting therapy as a space for open discussion about living a broader and more vital life may be a better place to start, all things considered.

Changing the expected agenda. Beginning treatment using values work with less motivated clients is a strategic move on the part of the clinician. Involuntary clients or those who otherwise feel coerced into attending treatment expect to be told something like "Your behavior is bad, and you should change it, and I am going to show you how to change it." Values work may be very novel for the involuntary client in that it begins with the question "What do you want your life to be about?" and puts the client in the driver's seat in setting the treatment agenda. Instead of the therapist telling clients what to do and how to do it, a focus on values asks the clients:

- "What do you want?"

- "How successful have you been in attaining what you want?"

- "Can you consider exploring your barriers to attaining your valued outcomes?"

Acceptance and defusion. Once barriers to attaining valued outcomes are on the table and perhaps have been discovered to be related to experiential avoidance and psychological inflexibility, the therapist has an opening to shift the treatment focus to work on acceptance and defusion processes and do so with the implicit consent of the client. Clients are more likely to be on board with the new treatment agenda when it is developed in the context of personal values rather than in the context of others forcing their change. Many times the same issues that brought the client to treatment against their wishes are issues related to values, and in this latter context they may be more willing to participate in treatment.

Starting with Mindfulness

Now you might ask, "What about beginning treatment with mindfulness and self as perspective?" We are not aware of any literature on this topic, and we would suggest that clients who benefit from beginning treatment with work on mindfulness and perspective taking are likely to fall into two categories:

■ Clients who have previously participated in psychotherapy and have made treatment gains and want to move further along a path of self-discovery, recovery, and change

■ Clients who do not have substantial problems with avoidance and control, are somewhat clear about their values, and are interested in mindfulness for self-improvement and life enhancement

Ultimately, though, wherever you begin treatment you are likely to use all of the processes on the hexaflex.

ACT is not linear. It would be rare to see a course of treatment where each process in the model is used systematically in sequence and treatment concludes once the sixth process is completed. In practice, it is more likely that you and the client will shift back and forth among all of the processes and revisit old processes as new issues are confronted in treatment. For instance, suppose a client with substance abuse problems is taught to be mindful of his unworkable change agenda, accepts urges to use drugs, and defuses from thoughts related to drug use. He goes on to continue practicing mindfulness and makes contact with self as perspective, and completes a values assessment. And while implementing behavior change strategies to move in a valued direction, he encounters anxiety related to all this change and he begins avoiding, so treatment goes back to an acceptance focus, and more defusion, and then back to committed action, and so on. Even within a single session, you may use interventions from a few domains of the model, or you may use a single exercise that encompasses a combination of the domains.

Individualizing the exercises. Please understand that the name of an exercise does not determine the process involved in the exercise as lived and experienced by the client. Take, for example, the Physicalizing Exercise:

- This guided experience may be utilized by the clinician to facilitate contact in the present moment with unwanted thoughts and feelings.

- It may be used in the service of defusing from thoughts or feelings.

- It might serve as part of values exploration and clarification.

The exercise also requires mindful attention on the part of the client and therapist. We can't simply say that problem A calls for intervention B, and problem C calls for process number 1. The hexaflex model is only a way of talking about ACT. Doing ACT is much richer than a simple model can convey. With practice and supervision in functional analysis and case conceptualization, your ACT repertoire will become flexible enough that you can easily and functionally shift from one process to another.

Expanded Metaphors: Passengers on the Bus

The hexaflex processes are interrelated, and there are certain interventions that target flexibility in each. For instance, the Bad Cup/Chair/Music metaphors are typically used for defusion from evaluations. And these metaphors can be used for self-as-perspective work as well, by showing not only that words are arbitrary, but also that evaluation of the self is observed as weak and empty content rather than truth about the self. Some therapeutic contexts may give space for a broader application of a metaphor. We're not advocating metaphor abuse, which is what happens when clinicians just throw metaphors at the client without looking at using the exercises functionally. In fact, sometimes therapists mistakenly (or perhaps sometimes unmistakenly) use metaphors as their own avoidance moves when they're not sure how to work with a particular client or situation. We are saying that sometimes, when it's working for a client, skills in all of the domains can be fostered through an expanded application of an exercise or a metaphor. One metaphor that is apt for all the domains is the Passengers on the Bus Metaphor.

Defusion and Acceptance

In the Hayes, Strosahl, and Wilson (1999) description of this metaphor, the client is asked to suppose that she is a bus driver, and the bus is filled with passengers, such as thoughts and feelings. These are not merely businesspeople commuting to work, there are also passengers that are scary; they are the negatively evaluated content our client would rather not look at. The passengers come up and distract the driver, and tell her to go this way and that. They threaten to make things uncomfortable unless the driver does their bidding. And every so often, the bus driver fights with the passengers, and she tells them to sit down and be quiet so they don't bother her. And when she does that, she has to stop moving in order to give them her full attention, so she is no longer driving the bus in her valued direction. This shows how the attempts to control the passengers actually lead to a greater loss of control. The client is invited to notice that no matter how much the thoughts and feelings threaten, the passengers are mostly powerless to make her do something against her will. They are the passengers, not the driver.

Values

In the previous metaphor, the aim of defusion and acceptance can be seen. Thoughts can be noticed and feelings accepted as things that inevitably travel with people through life, but they do not have to change the course of one's life. And if using this metaphor is fruitful, it can be expanded toward other processes, such as values. A therapist could explain it like this:

Therapist: Okay, so we've established you as the bus driver, and the stuff you are struggling with can be compared to the passengers. Let me ask you, what is the route like? Who chooses the direction of the bus? Prior to jumping into the job of bus driver, you get to choose the route you are going to take. Heck, just getting on the bus shows you have some values in some direction. And planning your route is a values-directed process. Staying on that route demonstrates commitment and living your values. And as the bus driver, you are the boss. No one can criticize whether you drive the local or the express. As bus driver, you can't be criticized for driving a small route in your community or taking a cross-country trek. Your hands are on the wheel and foot on the accelerator. Where have you been driving? Where are you going to go next? When you are the driver, you get to choose. The meanies in the back might come up and try to talk you out of your valued direction, and yet you have the wheel. You don't have to hit the brakes just because the passengers say so. And when you are a bus driver, you drive the bus. Driving well is both an outcome and a process.

Contact with the Present Moment

Mindfulness exercises are typically used to contact the present moment, and if the Passengers on the Bus Metaphor is aptly established, the therapist might bolster this skill by saying something like this:

Therapist: Purposeful driving is a mindful endeavor. You drive in the moment. Sure, everyone knows the experience of driving on the highway for long periods of time and totally forgetting what went on during those miles. It's probable that you've missed an exit or gotten completely lost because you've lost contact with the driving moment. Is that the way to live a life? Missing important events and mindlessly coasting through? Let's face it. The bus driver can only drive that bus with purpose if it's being done in the moment. When does the bus driver make a left turn? Do you do it yesterday or tomorrow? You can only do it now. Driving happens now.

Self as Perspective

Likewise, self as perspective usually is contacted with mindfulness exercises, and the Passengers on the Bus Metaphor can assist. The metaphor can be expanded to make clear the relationships among the driver, the passengers, and the bus.

Therapist: We've established that the passengers' mutiny can be experienced, it can be had, and it doesn't have to change how and where the driver drives the bus. Let's also note that the bus and the passengers are nothing without the driver. Without the driver, the bus doesn't move. And notice that the driver is not the bus and is not the passengers. You might think that the bus driver would be interested in kicking off all those creepy guys in the back of the bus. That's the kind of agenda we might get from a driver who mixes up what the passengers say and what the valued route is all about. Notice that the driver can simply have the passengers. No matter who is on the bus, the driver is unchanged.

Committed Action

Psychological flexibility is best seen when clients change clinically relevant behavior in the direction of their values. The bus metaphor is all about movement.

Therapist: The forward movement of the bus is key. The bus driver is chiefly concerned with getting moving on a valued route. When the passengers scream, "Stop, or I'll keep yelling and hassling you," it is worth noting that it is the bus driver who has a foot on the gas pedal. When the route is chosen and valuable, and the passengers are noted to be occasionally difficult and yet "have-able," driving forward gets done right now by a driver separate from all the passengers and their wishes and wants. The driver is committed, by virtue of climbing on the bus and starting the engine. The driver is committed to that route, in the presence of any of the obstacles and jeers from the peanut gallery. The driver can continue to step on the accelerator.

Metaphors should be used judiciously—this depiction of the Passengers on the Bus Metaphor may not be useful with all clients. If any of these pieces of the metaphor appear functional, it may be worthwhile. Note also that some clients might find these examples a bit wordy. The therapist should be mindful of talking on and on. The last thing the metaphors should do is get the client more entangled. Watch for being too wordy or talking in circles! Mostly the metaphors and exercises should meet clients where they're at.

Creating Your Own Metaphors and Exercises

Baseball analogies are vastly overused in the mainstream, and we'll thank our mind for that evaluation, and proceed. Even if it is the billionth time a therapist uses an ACT metaphor or an analogy throughout a career, it may be the first time the client hears it and applies it to his own life. It is important to notice if you are becoming jaded. If so, commit to what is effective for your clients.

ACT is not a string of metaphors and exercises applied haphazardly. In fact, approaching clinical work from a formal point of view without an assessment and a plan is likely to go nowhere. It can be very helpful to tailor the ACT approach to fit the client's background and abilities. The following are examples from a series of sessions where the clinician is bringing ACT to the client at the client's level and letting the client shape the form of the dialogue to meet clinically relevant functions.

■ Case Study: Painful Shyness

Ted is a seventeen-year-old high school student, and an accomplished athlete who is painfully shy around female peers and almost all adults. The behavior therapy treatment will include exposure to social interaction at the shopping mall. The following ACT discussions were taken from several different sessions, and they were aimed at helping him move toward his value of, as he put it, "Being more open to all the great things life has to offer."

Baseball Metaphor: Avoidance and Acceptance

The following dialogue took place during a discussion on the concept of acceptance. Notice that the metaphor is functionally similar to other metaphors that have appeared in this volume even while being formally distinct.

Ted: I remember as a kid learning to hit a baseball. It started out fine, learning with plastic Wiffleball bats and aluminum bats at first, but then I started to use the wood bats as I got better. And when I moved into wood bats, the pitchers were also getting better. Throwing faster. Harder.

And I'll never forget the first few times I connected with a fastball with a wooden bat. Man, once you connect, you feel this shock in your hands. This stinging pain all the way up to your shoulders. It's like electricity zapping your arms [aversive direct contingencies]. And I remember thinking, "Wow, these wood bats hurt when I hold them." And then I started holding them looser and looser. I wouldn't tighten up on the bat because I didn't want to hold something too tight if it hurt. [avoidance of direct contingencies] And guess what? That made it hurt more. So I started wanting to bat less and less in this traveling Little League. I didn't even go to batting practice for a few days [experiential avoidance]. My coach said to me, "You gotta grip that thing. Wrap your hands around and squeeze" [acceptance intervention]. It seemed so opposite of the thing to do, but I tell ya, it's true. It worked.

Therapist: What do you mean, "it worked"?

Ted: Well for one, I hit better, and it also didn't hurt as much.

In this scenario, Ted is grasping the ACT approach by connecting it to previous experiences. From an RFT point of view, his analogy is bringing to bear the previous avoidance contingencies from his baseball experience to his social interaction experience. One verbal network is being put into coordination with another one, and with transformation of stimulus functions, the social network may be governed by those baseball contingencies. This analogy is personal for him, and perhaps more likely to assist in the transformation of stimulus functions better than the popular metaphor about how struggling with anxiety is like struggling in quicksand (Hayes et al., 1999; Dahl & Lundgren, 2006), since he has no direct experience with quicksand.

Baseball Metaphor: Values, Willingness, and Committed Action

Taking the "go with what you know" approach, the therapist later brings up baseball to Ted again when talking about values and willingness. Ted also begins to chime in more on the metaphor building, which is likely to assist in the metaphor being helpful outside of therapy.

Therapist: Ted, did your coach teach you to grip that bat tighter because he wanted to take away your pain or because he wanted you to hit better?

Ted: Hmm. Not sure.

Therapist: Mind if I guess? [Ted shakes his head.] My guess is that he wanted you in the game playing as well as you could. If all he cared about was getting rid of the pain, he could have given you lots of other advice. I mean, you could have just stopped stepping up to the plate! Stopped batting altogether. That would ease your stinging hand pain.

Ted: Hmm. So you're saying it wasn't to get rid of my pain…

Therapist: Perhaps partly, and heck, it worked for that. I'd venture to say that he asked you to try something new [engendering behavioral flexibility] to help you get you on base [goal oriented, metaphorically value directed]. You can't hit it out of the park with that wimpy grip that you had. You had to really grip it [committed action] even when your mind said (*falsetto*), "Hold it wimpy!" [defusion]. You know, again, if the only important thing was avoiding hand pain, he could have benched you. That would have worked. How is this like what you are dealing with when it comes to talking to new people and adults?

Ted: (*pause*) I'm only half-steppin' it. If I want to get anywhere with anyone, I have to step up to the plate. Even if it doesn't feel good.

Therapist: [Therapist could have shifted more toward acceptance of things that don't feel good, but instead introduced values so that it could be connected to acceptance later.] You step up because you care about baseball. I know you do. If you didn't care about getting on base, you wouldn't have tried to firm up on your grip on your bat. We're not doing the FEEL exercises at the mall for the heck of it; we're going to do them because you care about opening up your life to something more. It's not like all the exercises are just plain old embarrassing. It's not even to get rid of the feelings of embarrassment. It is in service of opening yourself up to life. All of it.

Ted: Hitting it out of the park.

Therapist: Well, hitting it out of the park in due time. No one does that at first. Let's get a single, then a double, and, if it makes sense, then someday I hope you will swing for the fences. And let's just focus on small steps now. Getting on base is still part of the game. If you focus only on home runs, then you'll be unsatisfied with a single. [Small steps can be value directed; unwavering obsession with home runs given certain contexts might be problematic rule governance.] If the bases are loaded, no outs, bottom of the ninth, and the score is tied, it might be better to focus on a solid base hit rather than a grand slam.

Ted: [nodding his head in agreement] Yeah! It all depends on the situation [demonstrating verbal understanding of the need for flexibility].

Baseball Metaphor: Contact with the Present Moment and Defusion

Therapist:	Do you swing at pitches that haven't been thrown?
Ted:	No.
Therapist:	How useful is it to swing based on the last pitch thrown?
Ted:	It could help. If he threw a curve, he probably won't throw another right after. I also need to know how much heat his fastball has.
Therapist:	Okay. Fine. Learning from the past is fine. I'm talking about thinking about the last pitch during the windup and the throw of the new pitch being thrown to you. Even if he just threw a curveball, he could throw another one. Hitting requires focusing on this pitch [contact with the present moment]. Or am I wrong?
Ted:	No, you're right. Like Yogi Berra said, "Don't think. Hit."
Therapist:	Good point! Funnily enough, he also said, "I never said most of the things I said," but good point. [It didn't make sense to correct the client during the therapy session. Yogi actually said, "Think! How the hell are you gonna think and hit at the same time?"] If you're thinking about the pitch, or even worse, about how badly you gotta hit this pitch, or worse yet (breathlessly), "Oh man I really gotta gotta hit this pitch or everyone will laugh and I will suck and that would be the worst ever!"—how would that work out?
Ted:	If you sweat it like that, you'll strike out.
Therapist:	And what are you going to do? When you are at the plate, can you force yourself not to think about all the crummy stuff that happens when you strike out?
Ted:	Nah.
Therapist:	What you can do is notice that you are having that stuff come up and not get hooked by it. Ya know? It's like the Mary had a little . . . and the lemonlemonlemon stuff from last week. The world sets you up to think, "lamb"—you can't help it. And . . . it's just a word, like lemon or anything else. Stepping up to the plate sets you up to think, "Oh man, blah blah blah blah" and you don't need to get hooked by all that jazz! Same with talking with people...

Ted:	Yeah, I used that! This week, right before talking to my new gym teacher, I just watched my thoughts about how this new teacher was going to make fun of me. I just let it go ahead like the word machine we talked about... It was just my own words.
Therapist:	Great! [reinforcing his use of defusion]
Therapist:	[after a few minutes of conversation about his gym teacher] Can we go back to something? [Ted nods.] Earlier you said you don't swing at pitches that haven't been thrown, and there is only limited use in thinking about past pitches.
Ted:	Uh-huh.
Therapist:	To the batter, all there is, is right now. This pitch. We swing in the moment. That's how it was with your gym teacher. That was the time to talk with him. You didn't spend time focusing on how things went bad with the past gym teacher, and when you did spend time thinking about how many bad things might happen if you did talk to this new guy, you just noticed that stuff. You made your actions about the present. Right then. Good for you. That's how it is. Think about that when you are in the lunchroom or at a party: your mind will throw you curveballs that get you to focus on the past or the future. When you are faced with a situation, be in it—not all up in your head about "What if..." or "Last time..." If your mind starts racing like that, notice it, and come back to what your life is about. Openness to experience. Of all kinds.

Baseball Metaphor: Self as Perspective

As we've said before, all of the domains of the hexaflex are interconnected. The therapist and Ted work together to help shape a more flexible perspective on his self, and this agenda is supported by work on defusion and acceptance.

Ted:	All the guys on the team get together, and they go to the diner, and they meet girls there. I keep saying, "I can't go. I'm too shy. They won't like me. I'm not like the other guys." I try to tell myself to chill out, that I'm alright, but I can't shake it.
Therapist:	That's your mind talking. You're heaping all these words on yourself ... these evaluations. It's like these words are weighty, man. They are, after all, just words.
Ted:	Yeah, but ... I am shy.

Therapist:	You behave shyly at times. It's like "the weight of the words is on your shoulders." You label it, boom, you're it. Take the approach of your hero, Yogi Berra, again.
Ted:	What do you mean?
Therapist:	Yogi said once, "Slump? I ain't in no slump… I just ain't hitting." He was deflecting the weight of the word "slump" and describing the behavior. Shy? You ain't shy… You just ain't acting assertive.
Ted:	I know, but sometimes that (*mockingly*) lemonlemonlemon just doesn't cut it. Those things are about me. It's not like I can be like, I'mshyI'mshyI'mshy.
Therapist:	Okay. I am not sure why not, and I'll take a different swing at this. What if all that stuff you heap on yourself—shy, unlikable, all that stuff [pointing out self as content]—what if it wasn't you. I'm mean, Ted, that isn't you. Not the *you* you. I mean, is "shy" and "unlikable" your totality? Like … (*joking like a carnival barker*), "Step right up and see Ted, the entirely shy and unlikable human being!" I mean, there is a core you that is indefinable with words and evaluations. And it's been there your whole life [developing a view toward self as perspective]. It was there on your fifth birthday, it's with you at school, when you're with your mom, while you feel sick or feel fine, or feel surprised or feel angry, sad, happy. There is a core you that is unchanged by all that stuff. That's a you I want you to know. It ain't all wrapped up in stuff like "shy" or "unlikable." As soon as you call that *you* something, isn't there a you, a perspective, that notices that these things are happening? This you is where you can experience life.
Ted:	(*questioning*) Okay…?
Therapist:	Here man, try this. You got this ball game going on. It's the Toledo Shys versus … versus the Atlanta Braves. (*Both laugh, but mostly the therapist.*) No actually, let's start the game over. It's the Unlikables versus Convincers. And it's all happening up here [points to his head]. This game will go into extra innings. They can play for hours, days, even years. Part of your mind will root for the Unlikables and the other part will pull for the Convincers. I mean, isn't that always the game? The unlikable thought arises and says (*falsetto*), "I am shy and unlikable" and the convincing thoughts compete (*gruffly*), "No, I'm not," and the battle goes on and on.
Ted:	Alright.

Therapist:	Okay, so this game gets played and you're waving your Convincer's pennant, and you're in the dugout trying to get the right convincing thoughts to win this game. And that's been the game for years at this point right, Ted? [He assents with a nod.] So what if we looked at this a bit differently?
Ted:	Root for the Unlikables?
Therapist:	Hmm. Not what I was driving at. How about taking a different perspective on the whole game? How about not taking a side at all! Can you try to see your role—as the playing field?
Ted:	I'm the field?
Therapist:	Exactly. You are the diamond, the mound, the outfield. You are where the game gets played out. The field doesn't care who wins, doesn't root for a team or directly involve itself in the game—it lets the game play out though. Without it, there's no game. Put yourself there. Look up, like you're the foundation of this stadium. See the Unlikables versus the Convincers. See that you have those "I'm unlikable" thoughts … evaluations rather. And the convincing thoughts that you are not unlikable. All the stuff you say to try to shake the unlikable thoughts. And they are in the epic battle, and you experience this battle, and yet you are not in this battle.
Ted:	Hmm.
Therapist:	So what does this mean with what you're dealing with?
Ted:	My shyness isn't me. *(long pause, no intervention by therapist)* That I am not shy. I can see that I think I am shy.
Therapist:	Nice—let's try something else. [Therapist does informed consent for the Observer Exercise and continues with that move (Hayes et al., 1999, pp. 193–195).]

Ted's therapy progressed well in the context of good rapport and a willingness to think in new ways about his problem. The hexaflex domains, all the core processes, were touched upon for a few weeks prior to the actual exposure experiences. He and the therapist eventually went to a local mall and had him talk to patrons and store clerks. The exposure included conversing with attractive women and intimidating-looking adults. Ted reported his obstacles to each exposure, and would reorient to the now, his self as perspective, and his abilities to defuse and accept to assist his journey in a valued direction. His committed action was never done with the eliminative agenda as typified by traditional exposure therapy. In other words, the therapy was not to reduce anxiety feelings—that type of approach would put the teeth back into anxiety. The approach to exposure-based therapy in ACT is not aimed at reduction of private events; it is the pursuit of a valuable life. This is the FEEL approach (Eifert & Forsyth, 2005) mentioned in chapter 13. To hearken back to his coach, Ted needed to grip the bat to get on base, not to stop the sting.

The aim of all exercises is to meet clients where they are. The baseball metaphors and exercises were apt for Ted. For your client, it might be the "housecleaning metaphor," the "cooking metaphor," the "going on a road trip metaphor," or the "going fishing metaphor." As you become more familiar with ACT exercises and metaphors, think functionally and meet clients where they are. With this approach, you and your client will create useful metaphors and exercises in practice.

How Do I . . . ?

While learning the ACT model, therapists often ask, "How do I do values work? How do I start defusion work?" and so on. These aren't simple questions to answer. ACT is not a series of choreographed dance steps. It isn't a prearranged routine. It looks different every time the two partners meet, with a different tempo and rhythm, with the partners alternating who takes the lead. And yet, the partners can dance their way through the hexaflex, waltzing in and out of each of the domains. Any one step can lead to movement in a new direction In the following section, we explore how any one point on the hexaflex can be supported or arrived at by virtue of working on the five other points.

How Do I Get to Values?

Values work might be done near the beginning of treatment or after doing some work on other processes, such as acceptance or defusion. Values work helps the client choose specific committed actions, and it can increase willingness to accept unwanted thoughts and feelings when the unwanted experiences are related to valued outcomes. The therapist can begin values work by inviting the client to answer key values-related questions:

■ "What do you want your life to be about? Don't decide based on feelings of comfort, or thoughts and reasons for the behavior. You don't need to decide based on your roles, and you don't have to decide what you value because you are your father's son or because you live in a certain area."

■ "Notice that you are the place where all your experiences happen, and that from this place, you act in a committed fashion—empty of content and full of commitment. What's next?"

■ "Where do you choose to go?"

How Do I Get to Acceptance?

Therapists aiming to help clients increase acceptance might start by inviting them to move into a position of clarifying what they want their life to be about and see that there can be a course of committed action now. Invite them to see that they have a perspective where they are not content. Help them to notice that they have thoughts and evaluations, and like lemonlemonlemon, these are just arbitrary sounds. Ask these questions:

- ■ "Can you then just have the feelings, urges, and pressures as they show up without trying to get rid of them or changing them?"

- ■ "Why get rid of them?"

Help them notice and experience that these private events are inherent in their value-directed, committed actions. If there is resistance to having the feelings, urges, thoughts, and so on, perhaps the following discussion points would be helpful:

- ■ "These things you are experiencing are your 'now,' a time and experience that just is."

- ■ "You aren't changed by these feelings, urges, or pressures. You just evaluate them with your words, which don't have to hold sway over you. They are just more content."

- ■ "So when unwanted private events arise, can you be willing to have them?"

How Do I Get to Defusion?

Defusion is a part of many ACT exercises. For instance, a client may be more willing to accept content she is defused from. A client may encounter fused thoughts when making commitments or exploring values—for example, "I can't accomplish that; I will fail." The client contacting the present moment will most likely find the task more difficult the more fused she is with private events. In facilitating defusion, you can query:

- ■ "Can you thank your mind for those thoughts? In the pursuit of a vital life, thoughts, like feelings, will arise that may stand as a barrier between you and moving in a valued direction, because that is what language does: it evaluates and problem solves. And can you notice them as you act and move with vitality in a valued direction?"

- ■ "In the service of your values, can you just notice the thoughts, feelings, and sensations that arise and move forward anyway?"

How Do I Get to Contacting the Present Moment?

Contacting the present moment may be a struggle in some therapy interactions. Using the other domains, it may be instructive to influence clients with acceptance and defusion exercises to recognize that thoughts don't have to govern all their behaviors, and that physical and emotional responses can be had fully and without defense. Using self-as-perspective moves, suggest something like:

- "You are not your thoughts, memories, roles, sensations, and so on. Mindfully recognize that you are not your content."

Ask the client, through values work and committed action, to:

- "Go ahead and care deeply about a direction for life and commit to that lifestyle."

From there, contacting the present moment becomes more possible. Ask your client to do the following:

- "Notice where and when your behavior unfolds."

- "Notice that the past and future aren't where you act and care."

Help clients notice they are less pulled into unworkable and inflexible change agendas, and also less pulled by language when they are fully contacting the "now."

How Do I Get to Self as Perspective?

Again, developing workability in the other five domains will be helpful with this task. Once clients notice the struggle with private events and are willing to "let go of the rope in their tug-of-war," experience the present struggle (acceptance, defusion, and contacting the present moment), and do things they find vital (committed action and values), ask:

- "Can you notice your private experience right now?"

- "Can you notice that you are not your thoughts, evaluations, and feelings? Notice who is noticing those thoughts and feelings that come and go."

- "Even while your body, your roles, your thoughts, feelings, beliefs, actions, and even your values have changed over time, can you experience that there is a place, a locus, a perspective, the you that you call *you*? Can you experience that *you* which transcends space and time?"

- "Can you experience this perspective as a safe and enduring place from which both to move forward and to remain you, perfectly you?"

How Do I Get to Committed Action?

Influencing committed action can result when clients identify both valued directions and barriers to moving in those valued directions. Then you can ask:

- "Are you willing to have barriers?"

- "Are you willing to accept the unwanted thoughts and feelings that will certainly show up when life hands you whatever life hands you?"

You may also query:

- "Are you willing to have self-doubt as you step into new territory and to notice that any self-evaluations are not you?"

These questions increase flexibility in the other domains and lead to specific committed action opportunities, about which you may ask:

- "With your values as a compass, can you accept, choose, and take action (ACT)?"

- "What can you do now in the service of what you really care about? Can you move in that direction even in the presence of any obstacles that show up for you?"

Committed action can come from a practical execution of clients' values and identification of barriers to committed action through empirically supported treatment plans. For example, in treating OCD, a therapist may set therapy up to help the client behave in relation to this question: "In the presence of your feelings of anxiety and thoughts of avoidance, and in the service of getting out into life the way you really care about, can you, right now, touch the doorknobs in this public place?"

Notice that assisting a client with a particular domain can be done both with the functional application of the many exercises used throughout the book and also by developing skills in the other areas of the hexaflex. Each one of the bulleted points above specifically addresses that section's domain, and it is also done in the context of the other domains.

Hints and Suggestions: The Suggestaflex Diagram

The metaphors and exercises discussed throughout this book are meant to be used flexibly. When we discussed the Feeding a Baby Tiger Metaphor in Shandra's case, we used it to help her with creative hopelessness and acceptance. This same metaphor can be invoked when discussing committed action: we can talk to Shandra about what she can do—such as execute assertive responses when dealing with her children—besides "feed the tiger." This metaphor also helps clarify values when the therapist discusses the question "Do you want your life to be about feeding this tiger?"

We discussed using the Chessboard Metaphor with Shandra in order to help her contact self as perspective. It is also possible to use this metaphor in defusion and acceptance moves, as in noticing that the black and white pieces are words and feelings that battle each other and that they do not have to govern the person noticing them. In the Green Pens Exercise with Rick, in which he was asked to act like he cared about using green pens, he was learning that values are different than feelings. This exercise also loosens up cognitive fusion and broadens repertoires despite strong emotions. The exercise gives an alternate view that people can act in certain ways even when their feelings and thoughts may not be directly supportive.

We would like to stress the flexibility of these exercises and metaphors, and at the same time, we would like to present hints and suggestions for which exercises may have the most influence over certain hexaflex domains. As you examine your clients' Inflexahex Case-Conceptualization Worksheets and begin to get a picture of which processes are influencing them to remain stuck, the following Suggestaflex diagram (see also appendix D) may help you recall which ACT exercises may be used to address the troublesome processes. These are just suggestions and the list is not exhaustive. Until further research can tell therapists exactly which therapeutic exercises they should use with each client for each clinical concern, this diagram can serve as a reminder of which metaphors are likely to have the most impact on a problem area.

It bears repeating: ACT is not a cookie-cutter approach. If you are dealing with a client struggling with experiential avoidance, you should not use this diagram as an arsenal where you just keep using each metaphor until they run out. The diagram is simply a heuristic to assist in case conceptualization and treatment planning. Also keep in mind that the diagram is certainly not a complete list of all possible interventions, and none of the exercises or metaphors are exclusively for only one particular domain. This Suggestaflex includes selected exercises discussed earlier in this book and in the Hayes et al. (1999) book.

Defining Values
Values Narrative
Skiing Down a Hill
Green Pens
Epitaph/Lifetime Achievement
Deciding vs. Choosing
Outcome Is the Process…

Eyes On Exercise
EST Protocols (Exposure)
Gripping the Baseball Bat
Carrying the Ball and Chain Forward
Relapse Recognition
Jumping from Paper
Garden Metaphor
Joe the Bum
Take Your Keys

Lack of Values
Clarity;
Dominance of
Pliance,
Avoidant
Tracking, and
Problematic
Augmenting

Persistent
Inaction,
Impulsivity, or
Avoidance

Meditation Exercises
Leaves on a Stream
Toy Soldiers Carrying Thoughts
Watch the Teleprompter
Tin Can Monster
Feeling *Right Now*
Just Noticing

Weak Self-Knowledge;
Dominating Concept
of the Past and Feared Future

Psychological Inflexibility

Attachment to the
Conceptualized Self

Discuss the Three Senses of Self
Chessboard Metaphor
The Observing Self Meditation
Mental Polarity Exercise

Experiential
Avoidance

Cognitive
Fusion

Two Scales Metaphor
Feeding a Baby Tiger
Tug of War; Let Go of the Rope
Chinese Handcuffs/Monkey Trap
If You're Not Willing to Have/Lose It…
Man in the Hole; Stop Digging

Physicalizing
Bad Chair/Bad Music/Bad Cup
Mary Had a Little…
Cutting a Sour Fruit
Lemonlemonlemonlemon
Looking *Through* vs. *At* Sunglasses
Taking Your Mind for a Walk

Stepping Into ACT Work

The aim of this work is to open options for value-directed therapy. As the mission statement of the Association for Contextual Behavioral Sciences states, the ACT community aims to create a psychology "more adequate to the challenges of the human condition." For you the therapist, we hope this book has been instructive for case conceptualization in ACT and that it will assist you in being a more effective therapist. We believe the community at large will benefit from a cohesive and effective therapeutic approach, and this wave of behavior therapy is flexibly moving in that vital direction. To this end, we invite you to put ACT in practice.

EPILOGUE

Saying Good-Bye to Shandra and Rick

Rick terminated treatment after he stopped smoking marijuana, started dating, and involved himself more at work. He returned eighteen months later for a "tune-up" therapy session. He had continued his abstinence from smoking marijuana and was moving in a valued direction with respect to his professional life. He was struggling with feeling unmotivated and depressed after his mother died. After five additional therapy sessions, Rick reported that he felt back on track.

By the time Shandra terminated treatment, she had an improved relationship with her daughter, and had joined a bowling league and a book club to have a social life again. She also left her boyfriend for good. Her son moved in with her so she could help him get back on his feet after he completed a drug rehab program in lieu of jail. She insisted he work, pay rent, and have a plan for moving out within six months.

On the whole, Shandra and Rick have lived happily—and anxiously, and guiltily, and joyfully, and sadly, and hopefully, and willingly, and flexibly—ever after.

APPENDIX A

ABC Functional Analysis Sheet

In the chart below, write what happens during your observations of problem situations. In the Antecedent column, write what you notice happening before a particular behavior of concern. (For example, if you are struggling with anger, write what was going on before you had an outburst.) Describe exactly what the problem behavior looks like in the Behavior column. Then describe what happens after the problem behavior in the Consequence column. (For example, did your anger outburst make people leave the room? What did you tell yourself and how do you describe your feelings?)

Name: _____

ANTECEDENT What happened *before?*	BEHAVIOR What did you *do?*	CONSEQUENCE What happened *after?*
Day & Time:		
Day & Time:		
Day & Time:		
Day & Time:		
Day & Time:		
Day & Time:		
Day & Time:		

Inflexahex Case-Conceptualization Worksheet

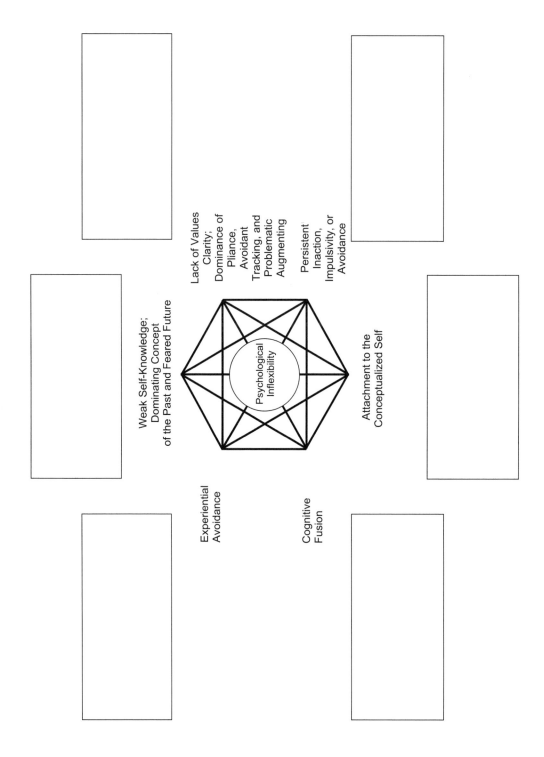

Lack of Values
Clarity;
Dominance of
Pliance,
Avoidant
Tracking, and
Problematic
Augmenting

Persistent
Inaction,
Impulsivity, or
Avoidance

Weak Self-Knowledge;
Dominating Concept
of the Past and Feared Future

Attachment to the
Conceptualized Self

Psychological
Inflexibility

Experiential
Avoidance

Cognitive
Fusion

APPENDIX C

Event Log

Name: _____

Target Problem: _____

In the chart below, write your observations about what happens during problem situations. In the When/Rating column, write the day and time of the event, and rate the problem from 0 (not present or not bothersome at all) to 10 (present all the time or most bothersome). In the Before column, write what you notice happening just before the event of concern. (For example, if you are struggling with panic attacks or urges to use alcohol, write down what happened just before you noticed the panic attack or urge.) In the After column, describe exactly what your behavior looked like after the event. (For example, write down if you endured the panic attack or drank three beers.) Then describe what happened next in the Consequence column. (For example, write down if the panic attack subsided and your friend asked if everything was okay, or if you became intoxicated and passed out.)

When? Rating	What happened just **BEFORE** the event?	What did you do just **AFTER** the event?	Then what happened? **CONSEQUENCE**
Day & Time: Rating:			
Day & Time: Rating:			
Day & Time: Rating:			
Day & Time: Rating:			
Day & Time: Rating:			
Day & Time: Rating:			
Day & Time: Rating:			

APPENDIX D

Suggestaflex

Defining Values
Values Narrative
Skiing Down a Hill
Green Pens
Epitaph/Lifetime Achievement
Deciding vs. Choosing
Outcome Is the Process…

Eyes On Exercise
EST Protocols (Exposure)
Gripping the Baseball Bat
Carrying the Ball and Chain Forward
Relapse Recognition
Jumping from Paper
Garden Metaphor
Joe the Bum
Take Your Keys

Lack of Values Clarity; Dominance of Pliance, Avoidant Tracking, and Problematic Augmenting

Persistent Inaction, Impulsivity, or Avoidance

Meditation Exercises
Leaves on a Stream
Toy Soldiers Carrying Thoughts
Watch the Teleprompter
Tin Can Monster
Feeling Right Now
Just Noticing

Weak Self-Knowledge; Dominating Concept of the Past and Feared Future

Attachment to the Conceptualized Self

Discuss the Three Senses of Self
Chessboard Metaphor
The Observing Self Meditation
Mental Polarity Exercise

Psychological Inflexibility

Experiential Avoidance

Cognitive Fusion

Two Scales Metaphor
Feeding a Baby Tiger
Tug of War; Let Go of the Rope
Chinese Handcuffs/Monkey Trap
If You're Not Willing to Have/Lose It…
Man in the Hole; Stop Digging

Physicalizing
Bad Chair/Bad Music/Bad Cup
Mary Had a Little…
Cutting a Sour Fruit
Lemonlemonlemonlemon
Looking Through vs. At Sunglasses
Taking Your Mind for a Walk

This Suggestaflex includes selected exercises discussed earlier in this book and in the Hayes et al. (1999) book.

References

Abramowitz, J. S. (1997). Effectiveness of psychological and pharmacological treatments of obsessive-compulsive disorder: A quantitative review. *Journal of Consulting and Clinical Psychology, 65*, 44–52.

American Psychiatric Association. (2000). *Diagnostic and statistical manual of mental disorders,* text revision (4th ed.). Washington, DC: Author.

Augustine of Hippo. (2002). *The confessions of St. Augustine.* Translated by A. C. Outler. New York: Dover. (Original work written in AD 397)

Ayllon, T. (1963). Intensive treatment of psychotic behavior by stimulus satiation and food reinforcement. *Behavior Research and Therapy, 1*, 53–61.

Ayllon, T., & Azrin, N. H. (1964). Reinforcement and instructions with mental patients. *Journal of the Experimental Analysis of Behavior, 7*, 327–331.

Ayllon, T., & Azrin, N. H. (1968). *The token economy: A motivational system for therapy and rehabilitation.* New York: Appleton-Century-Crofts.

Azrin, N. H., & Nunn, R. G. (1973). Habit reversal: A method of eliminating nervous habits and tics. *Behavior Research and Therapy, 11*, 619–628.

Bach, P. (2005, May). Impaired perspective taking in persons with psychosis. Paper presented at the Association for Behavior Analysis Annual Meeting, Chicago, IL.

Bach, P., & Hayes, S. C. (2002). The use of acceptance and commitment therapy to prevent the rehospitalization of psychotic patients: A randomized controlled trial. *Journal of Consulting and Clinical Psychology, 70*(5), 1129–1139.

Bach, P., Gaudiano, B. A., Pankey, J., Herbert, J. D., & Hayes, S. C. (2005). Acceptance, mindfulness, values, and psychosis: Applying acceptance and commitment therapy (ACT) to the chronically mentally ill. In R. A. Baer (Ed.), *Mindfulness-based treatment approaches: Clinician's guide to evidence base and applications* (pp. 94–116). Burlington, MA: Elsevier.

Baer, D. M., Wolf, M., & Risley, T. R. (1968). Some current dimensions of applied behavior analysis. *Journal of Applied Behavior Analysis, 1*, 91–97.

Baer, R. A., & Krietemeyer, J. (2006). Overview of mindfulness- and acceptance-based treatment approaches. In R. A. Baer (Ed.), *Mindfulness-based treatment approaches: Clinician's guide to evidence base and applications* (pp. 3–27). Burlington, MA: Elsevier.

Baer, R. A., Smith, G. T., & Allen, K. B. (2004). Assessment of mindfulness by self-report: The Kentucky Inventory of Mindfulness Skills. *Assessment, 11*, 191–206.

Baer, R. A., Smith, T., Hopkins, J., Krietemeyer, J., & Toney, L. (2006). Using self-report assessment methods to explore facets of mindfulness. *Assessment, 13*, 27–45.

Barlow, D. H. (1988). *Anxiety and its disorders: The nature and treatment of anxiety and panic.* New York: Guilford.

Barlow, D. H., Raffa, S. D., & Cohen, E. M. (2002). Psychosocial treatments for panic disorders, phobias, and generalized anxiety disorder. In P. E. Nathan & J. M. Gorman (Eds.), *A guide to treatments that work* (2nd ed.). New York: Oxford University Press.

Barnes-Holmes, D., Hayes, S. C., & Dymond, S. (2001). Self and self-directed rules. In S. C. Hayes, D. Barnes-Holmes, & B. Roche (Eds.), *Relational frame theory: A post-Skinnerian account of human language and cognition* (pp. 119–139). New York: Plenum.

Barnes-Holmes, D., O'Hora, D., Roche, B., Hayes, S. C., Bissett, R. T., & Lyddy, F. (2001). Understanding and verbal regulation. In S. C. Hayes, D. Barnes-Holmes, & B. Roche (Eds.), *Relational frame theory: A post-Skinnerian account of human language and cognition* (pp. 103–117). New York: Plenum.

Baron, A., & Galizio, M. (1983). Instructional control of human operant behavior. *Psychological Record, 33*, 495–520.

Baum, W. (1994). *Understanding behaviorism: Science, behavior, and culture.* New York: HarperCollins.

Beck, A. T. (1963). Thinking and depression: Idiosyncratic content and cognitive distortions. *Archives of General Psychiatry, 9*, 324–333.

Beck, A. T., Rush, A. J., Shaw, B. F., & Emery, G. (1979). *Cognitive therapy of depression.* New York: Guilford.

Beck, A. T., Steer, R. A., & Brown, G. K. (1996). *Beck Depression Inventory manual* (2nd ed.). San Antonio, TX: Psychological Corporation.

Beevers, C. G., Wenzlaff, R. M., Hayes, A. M., & Scott, W. D. (1999). Depression and the ironic effects of thought suppression: Therapeutic strategies for improving mental control. *Clinical Psychology: Science and Practice, 6*, 133–148.

Bentall, R. P. (2001). Social cognition and delusional beliefs. In P. W. Corrigan & D. L. Penn (Eds.), *Social cognition and schizophrenia* (pp. 123–148). Washington, DC: American Psychiatric Association.

Berman, P. B. (1997). *Case conceptualization and treatment planning: Exercises for integrating theory with clinical practice.* Thousand Oaks, CA: Sage Publications.

Bijou, S. W., & Baer, D. M. (1961). *Child development: A systematic and empirical theory. Vol. 1.* Englewood Cliffs, NJ: Prentice Hall.

Bond, F. (2006). *Acceptance and action questionnaire* (2nd ed.). Unpublished manuscript. Retrieved October 18, 2007 from http://www.contextualpsychology.org/acceptance _action_questionnaire_aaq_and_variations.

Borkovec, T. D., & Roemer, L. (1994). Cognitive behavioral treatment of generalized anxiety disorder. In R. T. Ammerman & M. Hersen (Eds.), *Handbook of prescriptive treatments for adults* (pp. 261–281). New York: Plenum.

Brown, K. W., & Ryan, R. M. (2003). The benefits of being present: The role of mindfulness in psychological well-being. *Journal of Personality and Social Psychology, 84,* 822–848.

Brown, R. A., & Lewinsohn, P. M. (1984). A psychoeducational approach to the treatment of depression: Comparison of group, individual, and minimal contact procedures. *Journal of Consulting and Clinical Psychology, 52,* 774–783.

Calkin, A. (2005). Precision teaching: The standard celeration charts. *The Behavior Analyst Today, 6*(4), 207–215.

Callaghan, G. M., Naugle, A. E., & Follette, W. C. (1996). Useful constructions of the client-therapist relationship. *Psychotherapy, 33*(3), 381–390.

Carlson, L. E., & Brown, K. W. (2005). Validation of the Mindful Attention Awareness Scale in a cancer population. *Journal of Psychosomatic Research, 58*(1), 29–33.

Carr, E. G. (1977). The origins of self-injurious behavior: A review of some hypotheses. *Psychological Bulletin, 84,* 800–816.

Carr, E. G., Landon, M. A., & Yarbrough, S. C. (1999). Hypothesis-based intervention for severe problem behavior. In A. Repp & R. H. Horner (Eds.), *Functional analysis of problem behavior: From effective assessment to effective support* (pp. 9–31). Belmont, CA: Wadsworth.

Carrascoso Lopez, F. J. (2000). Acceptance and commitment therapy (ACT) in panic disorder with agoraphobia: A case study. *Psychology in Spain, 4*(1), 120–128.

Casacalenda, N., Perry, J. C., & Looper, K. (2002). Remission in major depressive disorder: A comparison of pharmacotherapy, psychotherapy, and control conditions. *American Journal of Psychiatry, 159,* 1354–1360.

Catania, A. C. (1992). *Learning.* Englewood Cliffs, NJ: Prentice Hall.

Catania, A. C., Matthews, B. A., & Shimoff, E. (1982). Instructed versus shaped human verbal behavior: Interactions with nonverbal responding. *Journal of the Experimental Analysis of Behavior, 38,* 233–248.

Chadwick, P., Hember, M., Mead, S., Lilley, B., & Dagnan, D. (2005). *Responding mindfully to unpleasant thoughts and images: Reliability and validity of the Mindfulness Questionnaire.* Unpublished manuscript.

Chambless, D. L., Baker, M. J., Baucom, D. H., Beutler, L. E., Calhoun, K. S., Crits-Christoph, P., et al., (1998). Update on empirically validated therapies, II. *The Clinical Psychologist, 51*(1), 3–16.

Chambless, D. L., & Ollendick, T. H. (2001). Empirically supported psychological interventions: Controversies and evidence. *Annual Review of Psychology, 52,* 685–716.

Chödrön, P. (2000). *When things fall apart: Heart advice for difficult times.* Boston: Shambhala.

Chödrön, P. (2001). *Start where you are.* Boston: Shambhala.

Chödrön, P. (2002). *The places that scare you: A guide to fearlessness in difficult times.* Boston: Shambhala.

Chung, T. C., & Bruya, B. (1994). *Zen speaks: Shouts of nothingness.* New York: Anchor.

Ciarrochi, J., & Bilich, L. (2006). *Process measures of potential relevance to ACT.* Unpublished manuscript, University of Wollongong, NSW, Australia.

Ciarrochi, J., & Blackledge, J. T. (2005). *Social values survey.* Unpublished manuscript. Retrieved October 19, 2007 from http://www.contextualpsychology.org/personal_values_questionnaire.

Cicero, M. T. (1914). *De finibus bonorum et malorum.* Translated by H. Rackham. Cambridge, MA: Harvard University Press. (Original work written in 45 BC)

Clees, T. J. (1994). Self-recording of students' daily schedules of teachers' expectancies: Perspectives on reactivity, stimulus control, and generalization. *Exceptionality, 5,* 113–129.

Cloud, J. (2006, February 13). Happiness isn't normal. *Time, 167*(7), 58–67.

Cooper, J. O., Heron, T. E., & Heward, W. L. (1987). Applied behavior analysis. Upper Saddle River, NJ: Prentice Hall.

Dahl, J. C., & Lundgren, T. L. (2006). *Living beyond your pain: Using acceptance and commitment therapy to ease chronic pain.* Oakland, CA: New Harbinger.

Dahl, J. C., Wilson, K. G., & Nilsson, A. (2004). Acceptance and commitment therapy and the treatment of persons at risk for long-term disability resulting from stress and pain symptoms: A preliminary randomized trial. *Behavior Therapy, 35,* 785–802.

Davis, M., Eshelman, E. R., & McKay, M. (2000). *The relaxation and stress reduction workbook.* Oakland, CA: New Harbinger.

Deikman, A. J. (1982). *The observing self: Mysticism and psychotherapy.* Boston: Beacon Press.

Dobson, K. S., & Khatri, N. (2000). Cognitive therapy: Looking forward, looking backward. *Journal of Clinical Psychology, 56*(7), 907–923.

Dougher, M. J., & Hayes, S. C. (2000). Clinical behavior analysis. In M. J. Dougher (Ed.), *Clinical behavior analysis* (pp. 11–26). Reno, NV: Context Press.

Dougherty, D. D., Rauch, S. L., & Jenike, M. A. (2002). Pharmacological treatments for obsessive-compulsive disorder. In P. E. Nathan & J. M. Gorman (Eds.), *A guide to treatments that work* (2nd ed.). New York: Oxford University Press.

Eells, T. D. (1997). *Handbook of psychotherapy case formulation.* New York: Guilford.

Eifert, G. H., & Forsyth, J. P. (2005). *Acceptance and commitment therapy for anxiety disorders: A practitioner's treatment guide to using mindfulness, acceptance, and values-based behavior change strategies.* Oakland, CA: New Harbinger.

Elkin, I., Shea, M. T., Watkins, J. T., Imber, S. D., Sotsky, S. M., Collins, J. F., et al., (1989). National Institute of Mental Health Treatment of Depression Collaborative Research Program: General effectiveness of treatments. *Archives of General Psychiatry, 46*, 971–982.

Ellis, A. E. (1958). Rational psychotherapy. *Journal of General Psychology, 59*, 35–49.

Ellis, A. E. (1962). *Reason and emotion in psychotherapy.* New York: Lyle Stuart.

Ellis, A. E. (1975). How to live with a "neurotic." North Hollywood, CA: Wilshire.

Ellis, A. E. (2003). Cognitive restructuring of the disputing of irrational beliefs. In W. O'Donohue, J. Fisher, & S. C. Hayes (Eds.), *Cognitive behavior therapy: Applying empirically supported techniques in your practice* (pp. 79–83). Hoboken, NJ: John Wiley.

Emmelkamp, P. M. G., Bouman, T., & Blaauw, E. (1994). Individualized versus standardized therapy: A comparative evaluation with obsessive-compulsive patients. *Clinical Psychology and Psychotherapy, 1*, 95–100.

Eysenck, H. J. (1964). *Experiments in behaviour therapy: Readings in modern methods of treatment of mental disorders derived from learning theory.* New York: Pergamon Press.

Feldman, G. C., Hayes, A. M., Kumar, S. M., & Greeson, J. M. (2004). *Development, factor structure, and initial validation of the Cognitive and Affective Mindfulness Scale.* Manuscript submitted for publication.

Foa, E. B., Davidson, J. R. T., & Frances, A. (1999). Treatment of posttraumatic stress disorder: The expert consensus guideline series. *The Journal of Clinical Psychiatry, 60*(16), 1–76.

Foa, E. B., Franklin, M. E., & Kozak, M. J. (1998). Psychosocial treatment for obsessive-compulsive disorder: Literature review. In R. P. Swinson, M. M. Anthony, S. Rachman, & A. Richter (Eds.), *Obsessive-compulsive disorder: Theory, research, and treatment* (pp. 258–276). New York: Guilford.

Foa, E. B., Steketee, G., Grayson, J. B., & Doppelt, H. G. (1983). Treatment of obsessive-compulsives: When do we fail? In E. B. Foa & P. M. Emmelkamp (Eds.), *Failures in behavior therapy* (pp. 10–34). New York: John Wiley.

Follette, W. C., Naugle, A. E., & Linnerooth, P. J. (2000). A functional alternative to traditional assessment. In M. J. Dougher (Ed.), *Clinical behavior analysis* (pp. 99–125). Reno, NV: Context Press.

Forsyth, J. P. (2000). A process-oriented behavioral approach to the etiology, maintenance, and treatment of anxiety-related disorders. In M. J. Dougher (Ed.), *Clinical behavior analysis* (pp. 153–180). Reno, NV: Context Press.

Forsyth, J. P., Palav, A., & Duff, K. (1999). The absence of relation between anxiety sensitivity and fear conditioning using 20% and 13% CO_2-enriched air as unconditioned stimuli. *Behavior Research and Therapy, 37,* 143–153.

Freud, S. (1953). Fragment of an analysis of a case of hysteria. In *The standard edition of the complete psychological works of Sigmund Freud: Vol. 7 (1901-1905). A case of hysteria, three essays on sexuality and other works* (translated by J. Strachey, pp. 1–122). London: Hogarth Press.

Freud, S. (1963). From the history of an infantile neurosis. In *The standard edition of the complete psychological works of Sigmund Freud: Vol. 17 (1917–1919). An infantile neurosis and other works* (translated by J. Strachey, pp. 1–124). London: Hogarth Press.

Friman, P. C., Hayes, S. C., & Wilson, K. G. (1998). Why behavior analysts should study emotion: The example of anxiety. *Journal of Applied Behavior Analysis, 31*(1), 137–156.

Galizio, M. (1979). Contingency-shaped and rule-governed behavior: Instructional control of human loss avoidance. *Journal of the Experimental Analysis of Behavior, 31,* 53–70.

Geiser, D. S. (1992). *A comparison of acceptance-focused and control-focused psychological treatments in a chronic pain treatment center.* Unpublished doctoral dissertation, University of Nevada, Reno.

Gifford, E., Hayes, S. C., & Strosahl, K. D. (2005). Cognitive defusion. Retrieved November 23, 2007, from www.contextualpsychology.org/cognitive_defusion_deliteralization.

Goldman, A., & Greenberg, L. (1992). Comparison of integrated systemic and emotionally focused approaches to couples therapy. *Journal of Consulting and Clinical Psychology, 56,* 962.

Greco, L. (2006). *Revised Avoidance and Fusion Questionnaire for Youth* (AFQ-Y). Retrieved October 18, 2007, from http://www.contextualpsychology.org/revised_avoidance_fusion_questionnaire_for_youth_afq_y_greco_murrell_coyne_2005.

Greco, L., Murrell, A., & Coyne, L. W. (2005). *Avoidance and Fusion Questionnaire for Youth* (AFQ-Y). Retrieved October 18, 2007 from http://www.contextualpsychology.org/revised_avoidance_fusion_questionnaire_for_youth_afq_y_greco_murrell_coyne_2005.

Gregg, J. (2004). *Development of an acceptance-based treatment for the self-management of diabetes*. Unpublished doctoral dissertation, University of Nevada, Reno.

Hackman, A., & McLean, C. (1975). A comparison of flooding and thought stopping in the treatment of obsessional neurosis. *Behavior Research and Therapy, 13,* 263–269.

Harris, R. (2007). *The happiness trap: Stop struggling, start living*. Wollombi, NSW, Australia: Exile Publishing.

Hayes, A. M., & Harris, M. S. (2000). The development of an integrative treatment for depression. In S. Johnson, A. M. Hayes, T. Field, N. Schneiderman, & P. McCabe. (Eds.), *Stress, coping, and depression* (pp. 291–306). Mahwah, NJ: Erlbaum.

Hayes, S. C. (1984). Making sense of spirituality. *Behaviorism, 12,* 99–110.

Hayes, S. C. (1988). Contextualism and the next wave of behavioral psychology. *Behavior Analysis, 23,* 7–23.

Hayes, S. C. (1992). Verbal relations, time, and suicide. In S. C. Hayes & L. J. Hayes (Eds.), *Understanding verbal relations* (pp. 109–118). Reno, NV: Context Press.

Hayes, S. C. (1994). Content, context, and the types of psychological acceptance. In S. C. Hayes, N. S. Jacobson, V. M. Follette, & M. J. Dougher (Eds.), *Acceptance and change: Content and context is psychotherapy* (pp. 13–32). Reno, NV: Context Press.

Hayes, S. C. (2004). Acceptance and commitment therapy, relational frame theory, and the third wave of behavioral and cognitive therapies. *Behavior Therapy, 35,* 639–665.

Hayes, S. C. (2006a, July). Beginner workshop. Workshop presented at the meeting of the Association for Contextual Behavioral Sciences World Congress II, London, England.

Hayes, S. C. (2006b). Theory of psychopathology. Retrieved October 10, 2007, from http://www.contextualpsychology.org/theory_of_psychopathology

Hayes, S. C. (2007, July). The state of the ACT evidence. Address presented at the ACT Summer Institute III, Houston, TX.

Hayes, S. C., Barnes-Holmes, D., & Roche, B. (Eds.). (2001). *Relational frame theory: A post-Skinnerian account of human language and cognition*. New York: Plenum.

Hayes, S. C., & Berens, N. M. (2004). Why relational frame theory alters the relationship between basic and applied behavioral psychology. *International Journal of Psychology and Psychological Therapy, 4,* 341–353.

Hayes, S. C., Bissett, R., Roget, N., Padilla, M., Kohlenberg, B. S., Fisher, G., et al. (2004). The impact of acceptance and commitment training and multicultural training on the stigmatizing attitudes and professional burnout of substance abuse counselors. *Behavior Therapy, 35*, 821–835.

Hayes, S. C., Brownstein, A. J., Haas, J. R., & Greenway, D. E. (1986). Instructions, multiple schedules, and extinction: Distinguishing rule-governed from schedule-controlled behavior. *Journal of the Experimental Analysis of Behavior, 46*, 137–147.

Hayes, S. C., & Feldman, G. (2004). Clarifying the construct of mindfulness in the context of emotion regulation and the process of change in therapy. *Clinical Psychology: Science and Practice, 11*(3), 255–262.

Hayes, S. C., Fox, E., Gifford, E. V., Wilson, K. G., Barnes-Holmes, D., & Healy, O. (2001). Derived relational responding as learned behavior. In S. C. Hayes, D. Barnes-Holmes, & B. Roche (Eds.), *Relational frame theory: A post-Skinnerian account of human language and cognition* (pp. 21–50). New York: Plenum.

Hayes, S. C., & Hayes, L. J. (1989). The verbal action of the listener as a basis for rule-governance. In S. C. Hayes (Ed.), *Rule-governed behavior: Cognition, contingencies, and instructional control* (pp. 153–190). New York: Plenum.

Hayes, S. C., Hayes, L. J., & Reese, H. W. (1988). Finding the philosophical core: A review of Stephen C. Pepper's *World hypotheses: A study in evidence. Journal of the Experimental Analysis of Behavior, 50*, 97–111.

Hayes, S. C., Luoma, J. B., Bond, F. W., Masuda, A., & Lillis, J. (2006). Acceptance and commitment therapy: Model, processes, and outcomes. *Behavior Research and Therapy, 44*, 1–25.

Hayes, S. C., Masuda, A., Bissett, R., Luoma, J., & Guerrero, L. F. (2004). DBT, FAP, and ACT: How empirically oriented are the new behavior therapy technologies? *Behavior Therapy, 35*, 35–54.

Hayes, S. C., Nelson, R. O., & Jarrett, R. B. (1987). The treatment utility of assessment: A functional approach to evaluating assessment quality. *American Psychologist, 42*(11), 963–974.

Hayes, S. C., & Shenk, C. (2004). Operationalizing mindfulness without unnecessary attachments. *Clinical Psychology: Science and Practice, 11*, 249–254.

Hayes, S. C., & Smith, S. (2005). *Get out of your mind and into your life: The new acceptance and commitment therapy.* Oakland, CA: New Harbinger.

Hayes, S. C., Strosahl, K. D., Bunting, K., Twohig, M., & Wilson, K. (2004). What is acceptance and commitment therapy? In S. C. Hayes & K. D. Strosahl (Eds.), *A practical guide to acceptance and commitment therapy* (pp. 3–29). New York: Springer.

Hayes, S. C., Strosahl, K., & Wilson, K. G. (1999). *Acceptance and commitment therapy: An experiential approach to behavior change.* New York: Guilford.

Hayes, S. C., Strosahl, K. D., Wilson, K. G., Bissett, R. T., Pistorello, J., Toarmino, D., et al. (2004). Measuring experiential avoidance: A preliminary test of a working model. *The Psychological Record, 54,* 553–578.

Hayes, S. C., Wilson, K. G., Gifford, E. V., Follette, V. M., & Strosahl, K. (1996). Emotional avoidance and behavioral disorders: A functional dimensional approach to diagnosis and treatment. *Journal of Consulting and Clinical Psychology, 64,* 1152–1168.

Hayes, S. C., Zettle, R. D., & Rosenfarb, I. (1989). Rule-following. In S. C. Hayes (Ed.), *Rule-governed behavior: Cognition, contingencies, and instructional control* (pp. 191–220). New York: Plenum.

Haynes, S. N., & O'Brien W. O. (2000). *Principles of behavioral assessment: A functional approach to psychological assessment.* New York: Plenum/Kluwer.

Haynes, S. N., & Williams, A. E. (2003). Case formulation and design of behavioral treatment programs: Matching treatment mechanisms to causal variables for behavior problems. *European Journal of Psychological Assessment, 19*(3), 164–174.

Hersen, M., & Porzelius, L. K. (2002). *Diagnosis, conceptualization, and treatment planning for adults.* Mahwah, NJ: Erlbaum.

Hollon, S. D., & Kendall, P. C. (1980). Cognitive self-statements in depression: Development of an automatic thoughts questionnaire. *Cognitive Therapy and Research, 4,* 383–395.

Iwata, B. A., Dorsey, M. F., Slifer, K. J., Bauman, K. E., & Richman, G. S. (1994). Toward a functional analysis of self-injury. *Journal of Applied Behavior Analysis, 27,* 197–209.

Jacobson, E. (1929). *Progressive relaxation.* Chicago: University of Chicago Press.

Jacobson, N. S., & Christensen, A. (1996). Acceptance and change in couple therapy: A therapist's guide to transforming relationships. New York: W. W. Norton.

Jacobson, N. S., Dobson, K. S., Truax, P., Addis, M., Koerner, K., Gollan, J., et al. (1996). A component analysis of cognitive behavioral treatment for depression. *Journal of Consulting and Clinical Psychology, 64,* 295–304.

Jacobson, N. S., Wilson, L., & Tupper, C. (1988). The clinical significance of treatment gains resulting from exposure-based interventions for agoraphobia: A reanalysis of outcome data. *Behavior Therapy, 19,* 539–552.

Jones, M. C. (1924). A laboratory study of fear: The case of Peter. *Pedagogical Seminary, 31,* 308–315.

Jung, C. G., Baynes, H. G., & Baynes, C. F. (1928). *Contributions to analytical psychology.* London: Routledge & Kegan Paul.

Kanfer, E. H., & Grimm, L. G. (1977). Behavior analysis: Selecting target behaviors in the interview. *Behavior Modification, 1,* 7–28.

Kantor, J. R. (1959). *Interbehavioral psychology: A sample of scientific science construction.* Bloomington, IN: Principia.

Kantor, J. R. (1963). *The scientific evolution of psychology.* Chicago: Principia.

Kashdan, T. B., Barrios, V., Forsyth, J. P., & Steger, M. F. (2006). Experiential avoidance as a generalized psychological vulnerability: Comparisons with coping and emotion regulation strategies. *Behavior Research and Therapy, 9,* 1301–1320.

Kashdan, T. B., & Breen, W. E. (2007). Materialism and diminished well-being: Experiential avoidance as a mediating mechanism. *Journal of Social and Clinical Psychology, 26*(5), 521–539.

Kastak, C. R., & Schusterman, R. J. (2002). Sea lions and equivalence: Expanding classes by exclusion. *Journal of the Experimental Analysis of Behavior, 78*(3), 449–465.

Kastak, D., & Schusterman, R. J. (1994). Transfer of visual identity matching-to-sample in two California sea lions (*Zalophus californianus*). *Animal Learning and Behavior, 73,* 427–435.

Kazdin, A. E. (2001). *Behavior modification in applied settings.* Belmont, CA: Wadsworth/ Thompson Learning Publishers.

Kazdin, A. E., & Wilson, G. T. (1978). Criteria for evaluating psychotherapy. *Archives of General Psychiatry, 35*(4), 407–416.

Keller, F. S. & Schoenfield, W. N. (1950). *Principles of psychology: A systematic text in the science of behavior.* New York: Appleton-Century-Crofts.

Kingdon, D., & Turkington, D. (1994). *Cognitive-behavioral therapy of schizophrenia.* Hove, UK: Erlbaum.

Koerner, K., & Linehan, M. M. (1997). Case formulation in dialectical behavior therapy for borderline personality disorder. In T. Eells (Ed.), *Handbook of psychotherapy case formulation* (pp. 340–367). New York: Guilford.

Kohlenberg, B. S. (2000). Emotion and the relationship in psychotherapy: A behavior analytic perspective. In M. J. Dougher (Ed.), *Clinical behavior analysis.* Reno, NV: Context Press.

Kohlenberg, R. J., Kanter, J., Bolling, M., Parker, C., &. Tsai, M. (2002). Enhancing cognitive therapy for depression with functional analytic psychotherapy: Treatment guidelines and empirical findings. *Cognitive and Behavioral Practice, 9,* 213–229.

Kohlenberg, R. J., & Tsai, M. (1991). *Functional analytic psychotherapy: Creating intense and curative therapeutic relationships.* New York: Plenum.

Kupfer, D. J., First, M. B., & Reiger, D. A. (2002). Introduction. In D. J. Kupfer, M. B. First, & D. A. Reiger (Eds.), *A research agenda for the DSM-V* (pp. xv–xxiii). Washington, DC: American Psychiatric Association.

Kuyken, W. (2006). Evidence-based case formulation: Is the emperor clothed? In N. Tarrier (Ed.), *Case formulation in cognitive-behavioural therapy: The treatment of challenging and complex cases.* New York: Routledge/Taylor & Francis Group.

Lazarus, A. A. (1972). *Behavior therapy and beyond.* New York: McGraw-Hill.

Lazarus, A. A. (1973). *Multimodal behavior therapy.* New York: Springer.

Lazarus, A. A. (1984). On the primacy of cognition. *American Psychologist, 39,* 124–129.

Lewinsohn, P. M., Hoberman, H. M., Teri, L., & Hautzinger, M. (1985). An integrated theory of depression. In S. Reiss & R. Bootzin (Eds.), *Theoretical issues in behavior therapy* (pp. 331–359). New York: Academic Press.

Lewinsohn, P. M., Munoz, R., Youngren, M. A., & Zeiss, A. (1986). *Control your depression.* Englewood Cliffs, NJ: Prentice Hall.

Lewinsohn, P. M., Youngren, M. A., & Grosscup, S. J. (1979). Reinforcement and depression. In R. A. Dupue (Ed.), *The psychobiology of depressive disorders: Implications for the effects of stress* (pp. 291–316). New York: Academic Press.

Lindsley, O. R. (1956). Operant conditioning methods applied to research in chronic schizophrenia. *Psychiatric Research Reports, 5,* 118–139.

Lindsley, O. R. (1963). Free-operant conditioning and psychotherapy. In J. H. Masserman (Ed.), *Current psychiatric therapies: Vol. 3* (pp. 47–56). New York: Grune and Stratton.

Lindsley, O. R. (1968, March). Training parents and teachers to precisely manage children's behavior. Address presented at the C. S. Mott Foundation Children's Health Center, Flint, MI.

Linehan, M. M. (1993). *Cognitive behavioral treatment of borderline personality disorder.* New York: Guilford.

Longmore, R. J., & M. Worrell. (2007). Do we need to challenge thoughts in cognitive behavior therapy? *Clinical Psychology Review, 27,* 173-187

Luborsky, L., & Crits-Christoph, P. (1998). *Understanding transference: The core conflictual relationship theme method* (2nd ed.). Washington, DC: APA Books.

Luoma, J. B., Hayes, S. C., & Walser, R. D. (2007). *Learning ACT: An acceptance and commitment therapy skills-training manual for therapists.* Oakland, CA: New Harbinger.

Machiavelli, N. (1984). *The prince.* Translated by D. Donno. New York: Bantam Classics. (Original work written in 1513 and published in 1532)

Marlatt, G. A. (2002). Buddhist philosophy and the treatment of addictive behavior. *Cognitive & Behavioral Practice, 9,* 44–49.

Marlatt, G. A., & Gordon, J. R. (Eds.). (1985). *Relapse Prevention: Maintenance strategies in the treatment of addictive behaviors.* New York: Guilford.

Martell, C. R., Addis, M. E., & Jacobson, N. S. (2001). Depression in context: Strategies for guided action. New York: W. W. Norton.

McCracken, L. M. (1998). Learning to live with the pain: Acceptance of pain predicts adjustment in persons with chronic pain. *Pain, 74*, 21–27.

McCracken, L. M., & Eccleston, C. (2006). A comparison of the relative utility of coping and acceptance-based measures in a sample of chronic pain sufferers. *European Journal of Pain, 10*(1), 23–29.

McCracken, L. M., Vowles, K. E., & Eccleston, C. (2004). Acceptance of chronic pain: Component analysis and revised assessment method. *Pain, 107*, 159–166.

Menzies, R. G., & Clarke, J. C. (1995). The etiology of phobias: A nonassociative account. *Clinical Psychology Review, 15*, 23–48.

Merriam-Webster. (2003). *Merriam-Webster's Collegiate Dictionary* (11th ed.). Springfield, MA: Author.

Meyer, V., & Turkat, I. D. (1979). Behavior analysis of clinical cases. *Journal of Psychopathology and Behavioral Assessment, 1*(4), 259–270.

Michael, J. (1993). Establishing operations. *The Behavior Analyst, 16*, 191–206

Miller, W. R., & Rollnick, S. (2002). *Motivational interviewing: Preparing people for change.* New York: Guilford.

Miltenberger, R. G. (2001). *Behavior modification: Principles and procedures.* Belmont, CA: Wadsworth.

Mineka, S., & Zinbarg, R. (1996). Conditioning and ethnological models of anxiety disorders: Stress-in-dynamic-context anxiety models. In D. Hope (Ed.), *Nebraska symposium on motivation* (pp. 135–210). Lincoln, NE: University of Nebraska Press.

Moran, D. J., & Tai, W. (2001). Reducing biases in clinical judgment with single subject design methodology. *The Behavior Analyst Today, 2*(3), 196–203.

Mowrer, O. H. (1950). *Learning theory and personality dynamics.* New York: Ronald Press.

Nathan, P. E,, & Gorman, J. M. (2002). *A guide to treatments that work* (2nd ed.). New York: Oxford University Press.

Paclawskyj, T. R., Matson, J. L., Rush, K. S., Smalls, Y., & Vollmer, T. R. (2000). Questions About Behavioral Function (QABF): A behavioral checklist for functional assessment of aberrant behavior. *Research in Developmental Disabilities, 21*, 223–229.

Paul, G. L. (1969). Behavior modification research: Design and tactics. In C. M. Franks (Ed.), *Behavior therapy: Appraisal and status* (pp. 29–62). New York: McGraw Hill.

Pavlov, I. P. (1927). *Conditioned reflexes.* New York: Liveright.

Pepper, S. C. (1942). *World hypotheses: A study in evidence.* Berkeley, CA: University of California Press.

Persons, J. B. (1989). *Cognitive therapy in practice: A case formulation approach.* New York: W. W. Norton.

Persons, J. B. (1991). Psychotherapy outcome studies do not accurately represent current models of psychotherapy: A proposed remedy. *American Psychologist, 46*(2), 99–106.

Porzelius, L. K. (2002). Overview. In M. Hersen & L. K. Porzelius (Eds.), *Diagnosis, conceptualization, and treatment planning for adults* (pp. 3–12). Mahwah, NJ: Erlbaum.

Price-Bonham, S., & Addison, S. (1978). Families and mentally retarded children: Emphasis on the father. *Family Coordinator, 27*(3), 221–230.

Rincover, A., & Devany, J. (1982). The application of sensory extinction procedures to self-injury. *Analysis & Intervention in Developmental Disabilities, 2,* 67–81.

Rogers, C. (1951). *Client-centered therapy.* Boston: Houghton Mifflin.

Rogers, C. (1961). *On becoming a person.* Boston: Houghton Mifflin.

Rothbaum, B. O. (1992). The behavioral treatment of trichotillomania. *Behavioral Psychotherapy, 20,* 85–90.

Salzinger, K. (1975). Behavior theory models of abnormal behavior. In M. L. Kietman, S. Sutton, & J. Zubin (Eds.), *Experimental approaches to psychopathology* (pp. 213–244). New York: Academic Press.

Sandoz, E. K., & Wilson, K. G. (2006). *Body Image Acceptance Questionnaire: Embracing the "normative discontent."* Unpublished manuscript, University of Mississippi at Oxford.

Schulte, D., Kunzel, R., Pepping, G., & Schulte-Bahrenberg, T. (1992). Tailor-made versus standardized therapy of phobic patients. *Advances in Behavior Research and Therapy, 14,* 67–92.

Segal, Z. V., Williams, J. M. G., & Teasdale, J. D. (2002). *Mindfulness-based cognitive therapy for depression: A new approach to preventing relapse.* New York: Guilford.

Shafran, R., Thordarson, D. S., & Rachman, S. (1996). Thought-action fusion in obsessive compulsive disorder. *Journal of Anxiety Disorders, 10,* 379–391.

Shimoff, E., Catania, A. C., & Matthews, B. A. (1981). Uninstructed human responding: Sensitivity of low-rate performance to schedule contingencies. *Journal of the Experimental Analysis of Behavior, 36,* 207–220.

Skinner, B. F. (1953). *Science and human behavior.* New York: The Free Press.

Skinner, B. F. (1969). *Contingencies of reinforcement: A theoretical analysis.* New York: Appleton-Century-Crofts.

Skinner, B. F. (1974). *About behaviorism.* New York: Random House.

Skinner, B. F., Solomon, H., & Lindsley, O. R. (1954). A new method for the experimental analysis of the behavior of psychotic patients. *Journal of Nervous and Mental Disease, 120,* 403–406.

Smari, J., & Holmsteinssen, H. E. (2001). Intrusive thoughts, responsibility attitudes, thought-action fusion, and chronic thought suppression in relation to obsessive-compulsive symptoms. *Behavioral and Cognitive Psychotherapy, 29*(1), 13–20.

Smith, N. W. (2001). *Current systems in psychology: History, theory, research, and applications.* Belmont, CA: Wadsworth/Thompson Learning Publishers.

Sperry, L., Gudeman, J. E., Blackwell, B., & Faulkner, L. R. (1992). *Psychiatric case formulations.* Washington, DC: American Psychiatric Press.

Spiegler, M. D., & Guevremont, D. C. (2003). *Contemporary behavior therapy* (4th ed.). Belmont, CA: Thomson Higher Education.

Steketee, G. S. (1993). *Treatment of obsessive compulsive disorder: Treatment manuals for practitioners.* New York: Guilford.

Strosahl, K. D., Hayes, S. C., Wilson, K. G., & Gifford, E. V. (2004). An ACT primer: Core therapy processes, intervention strategies, and therapist competencies. In S. C. Hayes & K. D. Strosahl (Eds.). *A practical guide to acceptance and commitment therapy* (pp. 31–58). New York: Springer.

Sturmey, P. (1996). *Functional analysis in clinical psychology.* New York: John Wiley.

Task Force on Promotion and Dissemination of Psychological Procedures. (1995). Training in and dissemination of empirically validated psychological treatments. *The Clinical Psychologist, 48*(1), 3–23.

Turkat, I. D. (1985). *Behavioral case formulation.* New York: Springer.

Tversky, A., & Kahneman, D. (1974). Judgment under uncertainty: Heuristics and biases. *Science, 185,* 1124–1131.

Twohig, M. P., Hayes, S. C., & Masuda, A. (2006). Increasing willingness to experience obsessions: Acceptance and commitment therapy as a treatment for obsessive-compulsive disorder. *Behavior Therapy, 37*(1), 3–13.

Twohig, M. P., & Woods, D. W. (2004). A preliminary investigation of acceptance and commitment therapy and habit reversal as a treatment for trichotillomania. *Behavior Therapy, 35*(4), 803–820.

Urasenke Foundation. (n.d.). *Chanoyu, the art of tea.* Retrieved November 23, 2007, from www.urasenkeseattle.org/page 22.

Walen, S., DiGiuseppe, R., & Dryden, W. A. (1992). *A practitioner's guide to rational emotive therapy.* New York: Oxford University Press.

Watson, J. B., & Rayner, R. (1920). Conditioned emotional reactions. *Journal of Experimental Psychology, 3*(1), 1–14.

Weerasekera, P. (1996). *Multiperspective case formulation: A step towards treatment integration.* Malabar, FL: Krieger Publishing Company.

Wegner, D. M., Schneider, D. J., Carter, S. R., & White, T. L. (1987). Paradoxical effects of thought suppression. *Journal of Personality and Social Psychology, 53*(1), 5–13.

Wegner, D. M., & Zanakos, S. (1994). Chronic thought suppression. *Journal of Personality, 62*(4), 615–641.

Wenzlaff, R. M., Wegner, D. M., & Klein, S. B. (1991). The role of thought suppression in the bonding of thought and mood. *Journal of Personality and Social Psychology, 60*(4), 500–508.

Wilson, K. G. (2006a). *Valued Living Questionnaire working manual.* Unpublished manuscript. Available on www.contextualpsychology.org/clinical-resources.

Wilson, K. G. (2006b). *Creating a home: Who are we, what do we want to be?* Symposium presented at the meeting of the Association for Contextual Behavioral Sciences World Congress II, London, England.

Wilson, K. G. & Byrd, M. R. (2004). ACT for substance abuse and dependence. In S. C. Hayes & K. D. Strosahl (Eds.), *A practical guide to acceptance and commitment therapy* (pp. 153–184). New York: Springer.

Wilson, K. G., & Groom, J. (2002). The Valued Living Questionnaire. Available from K. G. Wilson at the Department of Psychology, University of Mississippi, Oxford, MS.

Wilson, K. G., Hayes, S. C., Gregg, J., & Zettle, R. D. (2001). Psychopathology and psychotherapy. In S. C. Hayes, D. Barnes-Holmes, & B. Roche (Eds.), *Relational frame theory: A post-Skinnerian account of human language and cognition* (pp. 221–238). New York: Plenum.

Wolpe, J. (1958). *Psychotherapy by reciprocal inhibition.* Stanford, CA: Stanford University Press.

Wright, J. H., & Davis, D. (1994). The therapeutic relationship in cognitive-behavioral therapy: Patient perceptions and therapist responses. *Cognitive and Behavioral Practice, 1,* 25–45.

Wulfert, E., Greenway, D. E., Farkas, P., Hayes, S. C., & Dougher, M. J. (1994). Correlation between a personality test for rigidity and rule-governed insensitivity to operant contingencies. *Journal of Applied Behavior Analysis, 27,* 659–671.

Yates, A. J. (1970). *Behavior therapy.* New York: John Wiley.

Zettle, R. D., & Rains, J. C. (1989). Group cognitive and contextual therapies in treatment of depression. *Journal of Clinical Psychology, 45,* 438–445.

Patricia A. Bach, Ph.D., received her doctorate from the University of Nevada in 2000. She is assistant professor of psychology at the Illinois Institute of Technology, where she does ACT and RFT research and trains students of clinical psychology. She practices ACT at the MidAmerican Psychological Institute and trains ACT therapists.

Daniel J. Moran, Ph.D., BCBA, received his doctorate from Hofstra University in 1998. He began his training in acceptance and commitment therapy in 1994 and founded the MidAmerican Psychological Institute in Joliet, IL in 2003. He is the director of the Family Counseling Center, a division of Trinity Services, where he trains future clinicians and practices clinical behavior analysis.

Foreword writer **Steven C. Hayes, Ph.D.,** is University of Nevada Foundation Professor of Psychology at the University of Nevada, Reno. He has authored several books on ACT, including *Get Out of Your Mind and Into Your Life* and *Learning ACT.*

Index

experiential avoidance, 6, 45, 95-97; case study on, 243-244; context pertaining to, 245-246; similarity among clinical problems, 251-252; unwillingness and, 242-243; values and, 248-249. *See also* avoidance

experiential time, 130-131

exposure and ritual prevention (ERP), 155-156

exposure methods, 255

extinction, 23-24

extinction burst, 24

Eye Contact Exercise, 254

Eysenck, H. J., 19

F

FEAR acronym, 113-114, 247, 260

Feeding a Baby Tiger Metaphor, 183-184, 295-296

FEEL approach, 255, 256, 292

feelings. *See* emotions/feelings

first-wave behavior therapy, 20-21

flexibility. *See* psychological flexibility

Fox, Eric, 79

frequency, 56-57

Freud, Sigmund, 82-83

function, definition of, 40

functional analysis, 41-56; antecedents and, 50-54; case studies related to, 46-50, 122-125; consequences and, 42-45; functionally analyzing, 56; in-session behavior and, 122-125; six-step cycle of, 54-55

functional analytic psychotherapy (FAP), 18, 31, 83

functional approach, 40-41

functional contexts, 74

functional contextualism, 33-35, 84

functionally enhanced cognitive therapy (FECT), 31

fusion. *See* cognitive fusion

future, domination by, 110, 111-113

G

gambling, 112

Get Out of Your Mind and Into Your Life (Hayes and Smith), 3

global values, 147

Goals, Actions, Barriers Form, 58

goals: journeys as, 212; outcomes of, 146; values vs., 10, 144

Green Pens Exercise, 209-210

guilty feelings, 256-259

H

Hayes, Steven, 3

"healthy normality" myth, 84

Heavy Computer Bag Exercise, 257

hexaflex model, 7, 94, 127. *See also* inflexahex model of psychopathology

humanistic therapy, 84

I

impulsivity, 101-103

inaction, 101-103

Inflexahex Case-Conceptualization Worksheet, 114-117; case example using, 116-117; samples of, 115, 117, 304

inflexahex model of psychopathology, 94-125; avoidant tracking and, 107; cognitive fusion and, 97-99; conceptualized self and, 99-101; excessive pliance and, 106-107; experiential avoidance and, 95-97; FEAR acronym and, 113-114, 260; inaction, impulsivity, avoidance and, 101-103; in-session behavior and, 122-125; interrelation of domains in, 113; past/future domination and, 109-111; problematic augmenting and, 107; values clarity and, 103-106; weak self-knowledge and, 107-109; worksheets used in, 114-122, 302, 304, 306

inflexible behavior, 94, 154. *See also* psychological inflexibility

in-session behavior, 122-125

insight meditation, 192

intellectualizing, 215

intensity, 57

irrational beliefs, 27

J

Jacobson, Edmund, 20

Jones, Mary Cover, 20

judging: choosing vs., 211; nonacceptance and, 272-273; overcoming habit of, 214

K

Keller, Helen, 242

panic attacks, 181-182

parenting values, 149-150, 204-205, 263

Passengers on the Bus Metaphor, 282-285

past content, domination by, 110-111

pathological gambling, 112

Pavlov, I. P., 20

peer pressure, 106

perseverance, 57

Personal Values Questionnaire (PVQ), 58

perspective taking, 9-10, 135-141; assessment of, 60-61; case conceptualization and, 140-141; conceptualized self and, 136-137; deictic relations and, 135-136; mindfulness and, 196-201; Passengers on the Bus Metaphor and, 284; self as perspective and, 138-140; self as process and, 137-138

persuading clients, 186-187

phlogiston theory, 29

physical functions, 44-45

Physicalizing Exercise, 269-270, 282

pliance, 75-76, 106-107

Polygraph Metaphor, 265

positive punishment, 23

positive reinforcement, 22-23

positive thoughts, 219

Practitioner's Guide to Rational Emotive Therapy, A (Walen, DiGiuseppe, and Dryden), 27

present moment contact. *See* contacting the present moment

problematic augmenting, 107

problematic solutions, 177-180; avoidance, 178; change agendas and, 182-183; clinician mistakes with, 185-187; costs of, 180; reason giving, 178-179; reinforcers and, 179-180; therapist stance and, 185

problem-solving mistake, 186, 262

pseudo-acceptance, 184, 271

psychoanalysis, 82-83

psychological flexibility, 94, 143; commitment and, 154; perspective taking and, 140

psychological inflexibility, 94-125; FEAR acronym and, 113-114; in-session behavior and, 122-125; worksheets for assessing, 114-122. *See also* inflexahex model of psychopathology

psychology, structural approaches to, 39

psychopathology: ACT model of, 94-114; in-session behavior and, 122-125; worksheets for assessing, 114-122

punishment, 23

R

randomized control trial (RCT) research, 35

rational emotive behavior therapy (REBT), 26, 27-28, 31

reason giving, 160-163; "and/but" distinction and, 163; private events and, 161-163; as problematic solution, 178-179; therapist exercise on, 161; unwillingness and, 261

reinforcement: differential, 52-53; negative, 23; positive, 22-23; short-term vs. long-term, 179-180; tangible, 42-43

relata, 72-73

relational contexts, 73-74

relational frame theory (RFT), 34, 63-79; ACT therapists and, 63; applying to ACT, 77-79; arbitrariness and, 67-68; combinatorial entailment and, 69-70; demystifying, 64-72; human behavior and, 63-64; mutual entailment and, 68-69; relational responding and, 65-67; terminology used in, 72-77; transformation of stimulus functions and, 70-72

relational frames, 72-73

relational responding, 65-67; arbitrarily applicable derived, 71-72; conditioned discrimination and, 65-66; derived, 66-67

religion, 196-197

resistance, 186

RFT. *See* relational frame theory

Rogers, Carl, 83, 277

roller-skating girl metaphor, 241, 244-245, 261

rule-governed behavior, 74-77; explanation of, 74-75; importance of, 76-77; types of, 75-76

rules, verbal, 74-75

Russell, David, 130

S

second-wave behavior therapy, 22-31

self: knowledge about, 107-109; three senses of, 136-140

self as content, 9-10, 99. *See also* conceptualized self

self as context, 10, 99, 108, 138-140

self as perspective, 9-10, 108, 138-140; beginning work on, 294; case conceptualization and, 140-141; metaphors related to, 284, 289-291; mindfulness and, 196-201; self-knowledge and, 109. *See also* perspective taking

self as process, 10, 99, 108, 109, 137-138, 196

self-awareness, 137-138, 196
self-blame, 170
self-injurious behavior, 44
self-knowledge, 107-109
sensory reinforcers, 44
setting events, 51
Shakespeare, William, 26
short-term reinforcers, 179-180
Shrinking Room Metaphor, 248
shyness, 285-292
silence, discomfort with, 185-186
Skiing Metaphor, 212
Skinner, B. F., 18
social attention functions, 43-44
Social Values Survey, 58
Socrates, 108
solutions, problematic. *See* problematic solutions
S-O-R approach, 85
spirituality, 196-197
stimulus control, 52-54
structural approach, 38-39
subjective units of distress (SUDS) scale, 57, 255
suffering, model of, 279
Suggestaflex Diagram, 295-297, 308
Suzuki, Shunryu, 222
symptoms, normalizing, 84-85

T

Take Off Your Glasses Exercise, 235
Taking Your Mind for a Walk Exercise, 234-235
tangible reinforcement, 42-43
"Thank Your Mind For That" Exercise, 236-237
therapist exercises: on acceptance, 274; on controlling feelings, 176; on creative hopelessness, 176, 182-183; on fusion and mental polarity, 168; on mindfulness, 195; on overcoming the habit of judging, 214; on reason giving, 161; on unworkable change agendas, 182-183. *See also* exercises (specific)
therapist stance, 185; acceptance and, 272-273; defusion and, 230, 237; values and, 213, 215; willingness and, 252, 263
third-wave behavior therapy, 31-32, 33-36
Thought-Action Fusion (TAF) Scale, 59
thoughts: defusion and, 228-229; fusion to, 219-220, 228; mindfulness of, 228; techniques for stopping, 30
time, 129-134; experiential, 130-131; verbal, 131-132

tracking, 75
transformation of stimulus functions, 70-72
transposition, 65-66
trivial matters, 105
truth criteria, 33
Tug-of-War with a Monster Metaphor, 184

U

unattached embracing, 190
unwillingness: avoidance and, 242-243; case conceptualization and, 247; case study related to, 243-244; language and, 246-252. *See also* willingness
unworkable change agendas, 182-183

V

valued living, 35, 58
Valued Living Questionnaire (VLQ), 58
Valued Living Questionnaire Working Manual (Wilson), 58
values, 10-11, 143-152, 203-215; action related to, 151; assessment of, 58; aversive contingencies and, 150-151; beginning work on, 292-293; behavior guided by, 148, 207-210; case conceptualization and, 156-158; case studies on, 149-150, 151-152, 213; choices based on, 210-211; clarifying, 103-106, 144-149; client exercise on, 209-210; cognitive fusion and, 220-221; committed action and, 153; definition of, 145, 204; desires and, 146; disabled clients and, 104; ethics and, 213; exploring, 204-207; global, 147; goals vs., 10, 144; guiding work on, 204-207; identifying, 103-104; judgments vs., 211; life consequences and, 145-146; metaphors related to, 212, 283, 286-287; motivation and, 212, 280; origin of term, 149; personal nature of, 215; reason for working on, 203; starting ACT treatment with, 279-281; stimulating discussion of, 148-149; therapist exercise on, 214; therapist stance on, 213, 215; "traps" for therapists, 214-215; unrecognized, 104; verbally construed, 147-148; willingness and, 253-254
Values Assessment Rating Form, 58
Values Bull's-Eye, 58
Values Narrative Form, 58

verbal behavior: defusion and, 233-237; depression and, 247-248; therapist stance on, 171; willingness and, 249, 252-253

verbal rules, 75-76

verbal time, 131-132

vitality focus, 212

W

Watson, John B., 20

What Are the Numbers? Exercise, 224

White Bear Suppression Inventory (WBSI), 59

willingness, 8, 153-154, 241-263; case conceptualization and, 247, 260-261; case studies on, 253-254, 256-259; client exercises on, 248, 254; committed action and, 153-154, 254-255; explanation of, 244-245; metaphors related to, 241, 244-245, 248, 259, 261, 286-287; therapist stance on, 252, 263; values and, 253-254; verbal behavior and, 249, 252-253. *See also* acceptance

Wolpe, Joseph, 20

words, use of, 171

work values, 206-207

workaholism, 180

worksheets: ABC Functional Analysis, 118-119, 302; Event Log, 119-122, 306; Inflexahex Case-Conceptualization, 114-117, 304

worrying, 178

Y

Yates, A. J., 19

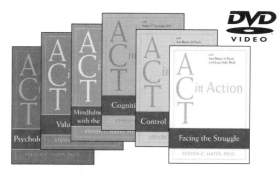